THE SOURCES OF ISLAMIC LAW
Islamic Theories of Abrogation

for Moira

THE SOURCES OF ISLAMIC LAW

Islamic theories of abrogation

JOHN BURTON

EDINBURGH UNIVERSITY PRESS

Edinburgh University Press
22 George Square, Edinburgh

Set in Lasercomp Baskerville
and printed in Great Britain by
The Alden Press, London and Oxford

British Library Cataloguing
in Publication Data
Burton, John
The sources of Islamic law: Islamic theories of
abrogation.
1. Islamic law, history
I. Title
340.5909

ISBN 0 7486 0108 2

Transliteration: the *Encylopedia of Islam* sytem is used

CONTENTS

Foreword		vii
Introduction	The sources of Islamic Law and the origins of the concept of *naskh*	1
Chapter 1.	The sources of Islamic Law	9
1.	The Ḳur'ān	9
2.	The *Sunna*	10
3.	The Islamic sciences	11
4.	*uṣūl al-Fiḳh*	14
Chapter 2.	The theories of *naskh*	18
1.	The general theory	18
2.	The general theory and the special theory	21
3.	Opposition to the *Sunna* source	22
4.	The application of the general theory	25
Chapter 3.	The special theories of *naskh*	32
1.	The general and special theories	32
2.	The science of *naskh*	37
3.	*Naskh* in the *Sunna*	39
4.	The 'modes' of *naskh*	41
Chapter 4.	The first mode of *naskh*	43
1.	*naskh al-ḥukm wa-' l-tilāwa*	43
2.	Reported loss of Ḳur'ān material	49
3.	Dating of the 'loss' of revealed matter	53
4.	Ḳur'ān and *muṣḥaf*	53
Chapter 5.	The second mode of *naskh*	56
1.	*Naskh al-ḥukm dūna 'l-tilāwa*	56
2.i.	The 'original' *'idda*	57
2.ii.	Subay'a bt. al-Ḥārith	63
3.	Leaving the matrimonial home	65
4.	Furay'a	67
5.	The widow's legal entitlements	67
6.	The clash between the widow's rights and the interests of her fellow-heirs	70
7.	Analysis	73

Chapter 6.	The alleged Ḳur'ānic basis of *naskh*	81
1.	Ṭabarī's comment on Ḳ.16:101	82
2.	Ṭabarī's discussion of Ḳ.2:106[a]	86
3.	The second occurrence of the root *naskh* : Ḳ.22:52	107
4.	Ṭabarī's comment on the *aw nunsi-hā* clause	108
5.	Ṭabarī's discussion of Ḳ.2:106[b]	110
6.	Ḳ.2:106 in the post-Ṭabarī exegesis	114
Chapter 7.	The third mode of *naskh: naskh al-tilāwa dūna 'l-ḥukm*	122
1.	The penalty for fornication in the view of the *fuḳahā'*	127
2.	Shāfi'ī's discussion on the stoning penalty	136
3.	The third mode of *naskh* in the period after Shāfi'ī	158
Chapter 8.	The Ḳur'ān's doctrine on *naskh*	165
1.	The exegetes' discussion of the change of *ḳibla*	173
2.	The Ḳur'ān's discussion of the change of *ḳibla*	179
Chapter 9.	Internal *naskh* affecting the Ḳur'ān texts	184
1.	The Night Prayer	186
2.	The offering payable in advance of a private audience	189
3.	The three 'modes' of *naskh*	198
4.	The definitions of *naskh*	202
5.	Conclusion	205
	Postscript	210
	Notes and References	214
	Bibliography	222
	Glossary	225
	Index of Subjects	228
	Index of Proper names	231
	Index of Ḳur'ān verses	233

FOREWORD

The Prophet Muḥammad died in the year AH 11/AD 632. With the sole exception of the Holy Ḳur'ān, the oldest surviving monuments of Islamic literature date, however, only from the second half of the second century *hidjrī*, about one hundred and fifty years later. This is the gap between the Ḳur'ān and the first expression known to us of what we might call 'Islamic consciousness'. Among the earliest writings of the Muslims, we find either exegeses of the Ḳur'ān or the records of the extra-Ḳur'ānic Tradition, the *Ḥadīth*, and some of the first compilations of what is loosely termed 'Islamic Law', for example, the *Muwaṭṭa'*, a digest of the legal opinions of the scholars of Madīna, the Prophet's town, as reviewed and commented on by Mālik b. Anas, [d. AH179/AD795]. Mālik's book contains references to relevant Ḳur'ān texts but more frequently his discussions set out the texts of numerous reports conveying the opinions of a large number of individuals ranging from his own contemporaries backwards through the generations to that of the Prophet and his associates.

Contemporary with Mālik was Sībawayhi of Baṣra whose remarkable book, which might be thought to do for Arabic language studies what Mālik's book does for Islamic 'legal' studies, also makes frequent reference to relevant Ḳur'ān texts. Citing his teachers and other authorities, Sībawayhi quotes Ḳur'ān verses alongside the verses of the Arab poets to illustrate the Arabic usage he is engaged in describing, just as Mālik, citing his teachers and other authorities, quotes the Ḳur'ān verses alongside the exegeses and opinions attributed to notable Muslim personalities to illustrate the Islamic usage he is describing, the *sunna*, or 'practice and conduct of the Muslims'.

We have information on other outstanding scholars engaged in linguistic studies in the second great Iraqi centre at Kūfa. From surviving works and from reports on their studies, we note that the Kufan scholars differed somewhat from Sībawayhi in approach and method. Kūfa was also a seat of Islamic learning and from their writings we note that the Kufans differed in both approach and method from Mālik and his Arabian colleagues. We possess, for example, the copy of Mālik's *Muwaṭṭa'* made and annotated by his Kufan pupil, Muḥammad b. al-Ḥasan al-Shaybānī, who died about ten years after Mālik. That, together with Muḥammad's own prolific writings, and those of his fellow-pupil, Ya'ḳūb b. Ibrāhīm, better known as the Ḳāḍī Abū Yūsuf, are instructive for the views of the Iraqi masters, especially Abū Ḥanīfa [d. AH141/AD758].

A second pupil of Mālik's, and an equally prolific writer on 'legal' themes was the Makkan Muḥammad b. Idrīs al-Shāifi'ī [d. AH 204 AD 819] whose career was one long tireless debate with Mālik's other pupils, with the Iraqis and with representatives of a wide range of contemporary Muslim opinion. His work is recorded in his numerous writings which are regarded as among the most outstanding expositions of Islamic thinking on legal themes, especially legal theory.

We are thus well supplied with documents from the second half of the second Islamic century onwards, and, once begun, the supply of documents rapidly multiplies. The interval between the Prophet and Ḳur'ān in the first decades of Islam and the second half of the following century is, however, not well documented and we can thus rely only upon the speculations of modern research, in so far as those are borne out by fragmentary hints in the original Arabic sources. For example, the principle of 'abrogation' if not the vocabulary of the later fully-developed theories, is already implied in certain of Mālik's discussions. Thus, in his review of the question of whether the Muslim traveller should observe or may postpone the obligation to fast during the month of Ramaḍān, which involves him in a comparison of conflicting opinions reported from many prominent Muslims of the past, including contradictory reports as to the practice of the Prophet himself, Mālik states that his teacher Zuhrī had told him that the Muslims had adopted as standard the latest of all the Prophet's reported actions.[1] The matter is important for the establishment of the *sunna* on this particular question, while, in another chapter, Mālik himself actually states that of the two relevant Ḳur'ān rulings, one had replaced the other.[2] Elsewhere, Mālik rejects the notion that a ruling remains valid despite the reported withdrawal of the wording of the supposed Ḳur'ān 'verse' said to have originally imposed the ruling in question.[3] These are very important matters, the investigation of which must throw additional much-needed light on the movement of Islamic thinking in the interval since the Prophet's day. From the few examples cited here, the Muslims have clearly moved already far beyond the Ḳur'ān. One wishes to know how this might have occurred. In the three questions with which Mālik was concerned, the Ḳur'ān texts lay at the very heart of his discussions, and the manner in which they were severally treated suggests the centrality of the Ḳur'ān in the intellectual activity of the Muslims. The intervening century-and-a-half had, in other words, been an age of the exegesis of the Ḳur'ān. From the minutest analysis of the revealed texts had flowed a stream of *ḥadīths* and views which were then taken by the Muslims as starting-point for the construction of their 'Law'.

The Islamic theories of *al-nāsikh wa-'l-mansūkh* make an exciting study, in terms of the questions raised. As may have already been surmised, these include the view the Muslims formed of the history of the Ḳur'ān texts since the death of the Prophet; the relations between some parts of the Ḳur'ān and other parts, and between some parts of the *Sunna* and other parts–more crucially, the relations between *Sunna* and Ḳur'ān as sources for Islamic 'practice' and 'Law'.

Western scholars have hitherto shown an incomprehensible indifference to the Muslim discussions on *naskh*. In fact, the present study is the first attempt by a Western investigator to open up the entire subject of *naskh* in detail, despite our having been familiar with a number of native works on the subject for over a century. In so far as any notice has been taken of the theories in the West, such references as are to be found show our Western authors to have been singularly uncritical, not to say downright incurious. Two out of many references are here selected to represent their attitudes. The two passages chosen are not untypical:

> More difficult to account for is Muḥammad's view of the naskh, the abrogation of one, and its replacement by another, verse. It has been suggested that the naskh echoes the New Testament idea of the abrogation of the Old Testament Law [Eph. 2:15; Col. 2:14] but the Koranic conception seems somewhat more mechanical. Muslim scholars have given a great deal of attention to the subject, but have never put the problem on the proper metaphysical level by discussing the possibility of change in a pre-existent text. The Jews are said to consider the naskh mere caprice. Acutally, however, it is due to God's taking into account the element of change in making long-term stipulations. In this, His motivation is taisir (or takhfif) the lightening of man's burden. But, at the same time, the abrogation of individual verses has to be seen in parallel with the abrogation of revealed codes by later prophets. In this sense, Islam abrogates all previous codes of which it is the perfection. . .[4]

This doctrine is based on verses of the Ḳur'ān: 2:100; 16:103; 22:51.

> What is referred to in the last verse is supposed to have been completely removed, so as not to occur in the Ḳur'ān. The doctrine has been voluminously discussed in Islam, not from the point of view of literary criticism, but from that of Law, it being important for Islam to decide what ordinances of the Ḳur'ān were abrogated and what remained valid. In some respects, the doctrine was extended on the one hand to include the abrogation of laws of the Pagan Arabs or of the Jews or Christians through the revelation of the Ḳur'ān and on the other, to admit the possibility of an ordinance of the Ḳur'ān being abrogated by the Sunna. Ash-Shāfi'ī, however, laid it down that when this happened, [5]there must be something in the Ḳur'ān to confirm the Sunna. Others held that the proper sense of naskh was that one verse of the Ḳur'ān abrogated another and that, in regard to

this, we must not follow the opinions of exegetes or the founders of legal schools, but have the authority of a direct statement of the Prophet or of one of the Companions, though it might be possible to infer naskh from plain contradiction of two verses, combined with a knowledge of their dates.

Other restrictions of the doctrine were introduced: it applies only to commands, not to narratives or promises or threats; alterations of practice, such as the commendation of patience in Meccah and fighting in Medinah, are not properly included under abrogation, but are rather instances of postponement of promulgation of the full law of Islam because of unsuitable circumstances. There are other cases in which, though a different law is laid down, it remains allowable to act according to the earlier one. Al-Suyuti in his *Itqān*, adopting these restrictions, reduces the number of cases of abrogation to twenty of which he gives a list. One should not perhaps expect the result of such legal discussion to confirm results of literary analysis, though, in a few instances, it does. What interests us is that Islam does recognise that deliverances were sometimes replaced by others. Further, the fact that these abrogated deliverances have been retained in the Ḳur'ān as it has come down to us affords a strong presumption that no attempt was made to adapt it to any preconceived ideas. The retention of the recitation with the abrogation of the ordinance is a difficulty for Islam. Suyuti gives two grounds: a) the abrogated verses were the Word of Allah which it was meritorious to recite; b) abrogation was generally directed to making things easier, and the earlier ordinance was retained as a reminder of God's mercy[6]

This study will show the inadequacy of these minimal responses to the voluminous Islamic discussions on *naskh* in the extensive literature devoted to the subject.

Too many questions have been floated for the reader to be prepared to pass on quickly to the next topic without having some of his curiosity satisfied. What are the texts–rather, what are the contexts of these verses from which *naskh* is said to have been derived: Ḳ.2:100; Ḳ.22:51; and what is it that is referred to in this last verse which has been 'completely removed' from the Ḳur'ān texts? What is the connection between the theories of *naskh* and the 'Law'? Have any Ḳur'ānic regulations been dismissed by the Muslims as 'no longer valid', and on what grounds have they been so described? What was thought to have been the relation between Ḳur'ān and *Sunna*, if the Muslims could allege the abrogation of the one by the other? Are there indeed contradictions between Ḳur'ān verses? How do we learn the dates of the revelation of the verses? It is not enough for the historian to point out what the Muslims have said on these topics, and then fall silent. The reader wishes to know why the Muslims have these conclusions. One would imagine that the abandonment of regulations, which they believed had been formally revealed by God to His Prophet, must have been based on very solid evidence, so great is the Muslim reverence for the texts of their revelations. In out study, answers will be sought for all these questions which can be summarised by the following question: what happened in the interval between the death of Muḥammad and the appearance of the earliest Islamic literary records? Finally, if we are to investigate the role played by the Law in the evolution of these ideas of *naskh*, it would be well to begin by looking first into the background of that Law, considering its supposed sources and how they were thought to relate to each other.

Grünebaum begged the question of whether Muḥammad had even heard of *naskh*, as defined, while Bell generalised, speaking of 'Islam' when, in fact, the discussions were between individuals, some of whom denied the occurrence of *naskh*. Those who accepted that it had occurred, differed widely on 'the mechanics' of *naskh*, and, indeed, on almost every aspect of *naskh*.

INTRODUCTION

THE SOURCES OF ISLAMIC LAW AND THE ORIGINS OF THE CONCEPT OF *NASKH*

In what follows it will become evident that there are, in fact, several Islamic theories of *naskh*. Each arose independently in response to a particular stimulus and they originated in different phases of Islamic scholarship. The first stimulus was the texts of the Ḳur'ān itself, or rather, their exegesis. The first response was thus wholly exegetical in origin. Muslims thought they detected contradictions in their basic source, the Holy Ḳur'ān.

Contradictions in the Ḳur'ān

Some thought that: '. . . and the angels hymn the praises of God and pray that He will forgive those on earth',[1] conflicted with: '. . . and the angels around the Throne hymn the praises of God and pray that He will forgive those who believe'.[2]

Clearly, the thinking was that the second verse replaced the first which had been couched in too general a wording. Similarly, '. . . and whoever believes in God and the Last Day and does good works will have his reward with God',[3] was held by the majority to have been set aside by 'Those who seek their religion elsewhere than in Islam, that will not be accepted.'[4] Belief in Islam, it was thought, was the first prerequisite for salvation. In: 'God and those who curse will curse those who conceal the clear signs and the guidance that We have revealed, after We have made it clear to men in the Book – except those who repent and make amends',[5] the exception was thought to have modified an earlier severity.

A great number of verses counselled the Prophet to show becoming patience in the face of the mockery and insults of the unbelievers, for instance: Ḳ.2:109; Ḳ.6:106; Ḳ.10:109; Ḳ.15:85; Ḳ.29:46. These and many other verses were thought to have been swept away by Ḳ.9:5, the so-called 'sword-verse': 'So kill the *mushriks* wherever you find them', a verse said to have superseded no fewer than one hundred and twenty-four revelations.[6] 'Do not contend with the Scriptuaries other than by the fairest words', was taken to have been cancelled by Ḳ.9:29: 'Fight those of the People of the Book who do not believe in God and the Last Day and do not forbid what God and His Prophet forbid, nor render true judgment [or, nor follow the true religion] until, in humiliation, they extend their hands to pay the *djizya*.'

Ḳ.9:31 denounced these People of the Book as *mushriks*. Ḳ.9:29 thus shows that even the 'sword-verse' is restricted in its application. Ḳ.2:256: 'There is [to be] no compulsion in religion', while seen to have been abrogated in respect of infidels by Ḳ.9:5, was now thought to refer to the People of the Book who are not to be converted by force, but reduced to the status of tributaries.

So some of the oldest exegetes included indiscrimately under *naskh* all and every verse where they noted a degree of contradiction, however slight, such as Ḳ.2:160's exceptive clause, or the difference between 'those on earth' and 'those on earth who believe'. Others restricted the appeal to *naskh* exclusively to verses involving command or prohibition.[7] That was a refinement of exegetical technique caused by the idea that two conflicting affirmative statements could not both be true. A statement is either true or false. Yet scruple realised that, as every single statement emanating from God, the fount of all trust, must be accepted as true, divine statements of fact must all be true and hence excluded from the discussions on *naskh*. This was made possible by the distinction between 'general' statements and 'specific' statements. Ḳ.42's 'those on earth' had acquired a higher degree of precision in Ḳ.40's 'those who believe'. The two verses can therefore be read, the one in the light of the other. In the same way, Ḳ.2:160 is the continuation of Ḳ.2:159 and so the two verses should be read as a unit. This insistence that *naskh* is a function of conflict between verses occurring in separate contexts served to eliminate the exceptive clause from the *naskh* theories.[8]

Naturally, the condition that *naskh* affects only verses occurring in separate contexts led to the further condition that *naskh* is a function of the passage of time: the later supersedes the earlier pronouncement, but only if both verses involve commands, i.e. imperatives or prohibitives. Some had included under 'imperatives' statements which imply commands: Ḳ.24:3, for example: 'The fornicator shall wed only the fornicatress, or the *mushrik*; the fornicatress shall wed only the fornicator or the *mushrik*', could be added to the class of 'imperatives', as implying a prohibition. The verse in any event ends: 'that is forbidden to believers'. A more satisfactory example is provided by Ḳ.12:47: 'You will sow for seven years as usual, but what you harvest, leave in the ear', i.e. 'Sow' and 'keep it for sowing, not eating.'[9]

Non-imperative verses occurring in separate contexts and exhibiting some degree of non-correspondence, were thus eventually removed from *naskh* theorising and treated as embodying an enhanced degree of specification. Their function was to supply *bayān* of the type known as *takhṣīṣ*; some verses are general [*ʿāmm*] others are particular, specific [*khāṣṣ*]. They are also known respectively as *djumla* and *mufassar*. Other terms used are *muṭlaḳ*, 'unqualified'; *muḳayyad*, 'qualified'.

The label *naskh* thus came to be restricted to conflict between verses involving commands. The Creator and Sovereign Lord of the Universe shares His absolute power with none. To test men's obedience, God may order them to do whatsoever He chooses, or to desist from whatsoever He wills. He may command what was never previously required [*mubāḥ*] or forbid what was previously unregulated [*muṭlaḳ*]; equally, He may prohibit what He Himself had actually commanded, or command what He Himself had previously prohibited. Nor need He consult in what He commands or prohibits other than His own sovereign divine will. Nor may men question anything that God requires of them. They must only identify what God has commanded or forbidden and act immediately to demonstrate their creaturely status and humble obedience. To do this, they must identify the *nāsikh* and the *mansūkh*, in order to recognise which of the divine commands or prohibitions they are required to observe in the hope of pleasing the Godhead and winning entry to His paradise; to avoid His displeasure and the catastrophe of being doomed to Hell.

Contradictions in the *Sunna*

Any student of the *Sunna* is aware of the extent to which *sunna* contradicts *sunna*. Within this body of the documents of the Tradition of the community, conflict is so rife that scholars such as Goldziher have been led to doubt that here one is dealing with a single, unitary body of information.[10] What, however, concerns us here is the recognition by the Muslims of the array of contradictions visible to them in their Tradition and the means they adopted to tackle the immense problems this caused. Once more, the instrument they used was *naskh*: the later supersedes the earlier pronouncement, to the extent that they conflict. In a well-known report, Muḥammad is declared to have stated: 'I previously forbade you to visit graves – now I declare that you may visit them.' He is also reported as saying: 'I previously forbade you to preserve the flesh of sacrificial offerings for more than three days – I now declare that you may preserve their flesh and store it for as long as you see fit.' A third report has Muḥammad rescinding his earlier ban on the use of containers made of specific types of materials for the storage of liquids. 'The container renders liquid neither permitted nor forbidden – providing the Muslim consumes no alcohol.'

Like the above series of Ḳur'ān verses, these reports are found in handbooks on *naskh*.[11] Obviously, originally separate *ḥadīths* had reflected incompatible views on the matters dealt with. What we see is the end-product. The conflicting views had been harmonised under the aegis of the concept of *naskh*, and the resultant combinations showing the reconciliation can now be used to illustrate the *fact* of *naskh* as a phenomenon affecting the *Sunna*, so alleviating the anxiety felt by the non-specialist confronted by apparent conflict within the *Sunna* source.

Thus, disquiet at the thought that there were conflicting statements in each of his primary sources spurred the scholar to discover a way of removing embarrassment and problem at one and the same time. The concept of *naskh* was the Muslim's ingenious response to the stimulus of embarrassment.

Contradiction between Ḳur'ān and *Sunna* sources

As mentioned earlier, according to the Muslim, the Law had been constructed from two primary sources. The claims that contradictions occur in each of the Ḳur'ān and *Sunna* sources having been dealt with separately, it must now be considered whether it was thought that there could be contradictions between the Ḳur'ān and the *Sunna*. Certainly, rulings occur in the Law which conform with Ḳur'ān statements, but contradict *Sunna* statements. Other rulings conform with *Sunna* statements, but contradict Ḳur'ān statements. This might have been expected to cause a major embarrassment for the Muslims, but again the majority complacently took the view that in such instances either the Ḳur'ān had superseded the *Sunna* or been replaced by it. For example in Ḳ.4:15–16, the exegetes found the ruling that certain fornicators are to be locked up for life. The Prophet, however, is credited with having introduced the ruling that is found in the Law where the death penalty is provided for adultery. That was therefore taken as one clear instance of the *naskh* of the Ḳur'ān by the *Sunna*. In addition, the Law provides for fornication the penalty of one hundred strokes of the lash. Such a penalty is mentioned in Ḳ.24:2. That, therefore, was taken as one clear instance of the *naskh* of the Ḳur'ān by the Ḳur'ān.[12] Ḳ.60:11: 'If any of your wives rejoin the unbelievers, repay their believing husbands the dowries which they laid out', follows the ruling that if believing females should join the Muslims at Madina, abandoning their unbelieving husbands, by making the *hidjra* to Muḥammad, the Muslims were to examine these women and, if satisfied that they were genuine in their belief, they were not to return them to the unbelievers. The most the Muslims may do is to repay to the unbelieving husbands the dowries that they had laid out. This Ḳur'ān ruling was thought to contravene the terms of the Treaty of Ḥudaybiya by which Muḥammad had undertaken to return all persons who joined him without the consent to Ḳuraysh. Thus it is cited as a clear instance of *naskh* of the *Sunna* by the Ḳur'ān.

It must be said, however, that the number of instances in which the Ḳur'ān had superseded the *Sunna* that can be mustered is minimal, compared with the number of instances of the alleged *naskh* of the Ḳur'ān by the *Sunna* which are cited.

Readily acknowledged by the oldest exegetes, the twin principles of *naskh* of Ḳur'ān by *Sunna* and *naskh* of *Sunna* by Ḳur'ān met determined opposition. One argument was that if the *Sunna* had *naskh*ed the Ḳur'ān, the unbelievers might have argued that Muḥammad was saying or doing the opposite of what he alleged was being revealed to him by God; if the Ḳur'ān had *naskh*ed the *Sunna*, they could have taunted Muḥammad by pointing out that God was belying the man who claimed to be His Prophet. Either way, Muḥammad's credibility would have suffered.[13] But, with the weight of Tradition behind them, and in view of 'the clear instances' that could be adduced, the two principles could not be dislodged from the developing theory. Their continued presence in the theory of *naskh* was to act as yet a third stimulus which would provoke yet other scholars to a third response, with consequences for the shape of the final theories of *naskh*. Both controversy and the passage of time produced ever more refined principles. Later theorists could, in an internal Muslim debate, appeal to the notion that, like the Ḳur'ān, the *Sunna* had also been revealed to Muḥammad, and thus, *naskh* was merely the replacing of one element of revelation by another. The *naskh* of the Ḳur'ān by the *Sunna*, it would be alleged, was no different from the *naskh* of the Ḳur'ān by the Ḳur'ān; the *naskh* of the *Sunna* by the Ḳur'ān was no different from the *naskh* of the *Sunna* by the *Sunna* – *naskh* is merely the replacement of revelation by revelation.[14] God having insisted that true faith consisted in belief both in Himself and in His Prophet, the Muslim must adhere to the *Sunna*, as he adhered to the Ḳur'ān. The sole significant distinction between the two sources is that, whereas both the rulings and the wordings of the Ḳur'ān are of divine composition, the rulings of the *Sunna* are of divine origin, but its wording is of human composition. That is why only Ḳur'ān wordings may be recited in the ritual prayers. It was alleged, on both sides of this internal debate, that the Ḳur'ān had taken the lead in the formulation of these opposing views. The argument that the *Sunna* had been revealed was based on Ḳ.53:2–3: 'Muḥammad does not speak from whim; this is really divine inspiration', cited usually with appropriate emphasis on the first sentence. The opposite view, that the *Sunna* had not *naskh*ed the Ḳur'ān appealed to Ḳ.10:15: 'Say: " It is not for me to alter it on my own initiative; I merely follow what is being revealed to me." ' Knowing in advance the stance that would be adopted by the unbelievers in the event that He decided to alter some of His own rulings, God revealed Ḳ.16:101: 'When We replace one *āya* by another, they say, "You're just making this up." ' God also said,[15] 'Whatsoever *āya* We *naskh*, or cause to be forgotten, We shall bring one better than it, or similar to it.' These verses could be used to establish, not merely the *fact* of the *naskh* of the Ḳur'ān by the Ḳur'ān, but, by close focus upon the precise wording, to make the case that only an *āya* replaces an *āya*; that only God replaces His *āya*s.

Both sides in the debate as to whether the *Sunna* had or had not *naskh*ed the Ḳur'ān could make common appeal to Ḳ.59:7: 'Whatsoever the Prophet gives you, accept it; whatsoever he denies you, accept his denial with good grace.' Those opposed to the principle of the *naskh* of the Ḳur'ān by the *Sunna* alleged that this meant: 'Whatsoever the Prophet gives you [in the Ḳur'ān] accept it.' Proponents of the principle argue that, on the contrary, it means: 'Whatsoever the Prophet gives you [that is not in the Ḳur'ān, i.e. in the *Sunna*] accept it.'[16]

Here, one clearly sees the Ḳur'ān being appealed to as prop to this theory or that. Both interpretations ignore the context in which the verse (and indeed, the other verses cited) occur. Ḳ.59, in fact, refers to neither *Sunna* nor Ḳur'ān, but to Muḥammad's distribution of properties accruing to him from his enemies, while both Ḳ.16 and Ḳ.2 employ the ambiguous Ḳur'ānic term *āya* – and not every exegete conceded that the word meant 'a verse of the Ḳur'ān'.[17] In short, exegesis lies behind this theory or that.

Alone of the major scholars, al-Shāfi'ī broke ranks by vehemently denying the two principles that Ḳur'ān had ever *naskhed Sunna*, or *Sunna* Ḳur'ān.[18] Turning to the Ḳur'ān for his support, he insisted on underlining God's deliberate use of 'We' in Ḳ.16 and in Ḳ.2. His procedure was thus, equally exegetical. From these verses Shāfi'ī derived the propositions:

i. The *naskh*, or replacement of an *āya* is an exclusively divine prerogative.

ii. An *āya* can be replaced solely by another *āya*. God has told us that He it is Who replaces His verses, and He spoke only of replacing His own verses. Thus, only Ḳur'ān *naskh*s Ḳur'ān, and Ḳur'ān *naskh*s only Ḳur'ān.

iii. Ḳur'ān *naskh*s only Ḳur'ān; *Sunna naskh*s only *Sunna*. Ḳur'ān does not *naskh Sunna*; *Sunna* does not *naskh* Ḳur'ān.

Shāfi'ī sought next to base on these propositions an analogy, exploiting the terms of Ḳ.2:106: 'superior'; 'similar'. As no statement propounded by another human being, however elevated, may be deemed similar, let alone superior to a statement propounded by a prophet, nothing, save only the *Sunna* of Muḥammad has ever *naskh*ed the *Sunna* of Muḥammad.[19]

The weakness of his analogy was hidden from Shāfi'ī himself. It had originated in his refusal to accept the view of his contemporaries that many legal rulings had been derived from the opinions reported from the Prophet's Companions, or even from scholars of a later generation, the Successors. Where, in connection with the same legal questions, different legal rulings purporting to come down from the Prophet were known to him, Shāfiʿī insisted on rejecting the hitherto accepted rulings, adhering only to those reported as having been Muḥammad's. We shall see, however, that often this did not involve disturbance of the Law itself, but only of its documentation. If that documentation involved reference to the Ḳur'ān, then Shāfiʿī was prepared to extend his analogy to include even propositions revealed by God Himself. So great was his solicitude for the *Sunna* of the Prophet and his determination to avoid opening any door that might conceal danger for the acceptance of the *Sunna* or threaten any element of the *Sunna*, that Shāfiʿī became blinkered to the direction in which his scholarly procedures were carrying him.

We have heard that the death penalty for adultery allegedly introduced by Muḥammad still formed part of the Islamic Law. Shāfiʿī's contemporaries continued to argue, as their teachers had argued, that that is but one instance of the *naskh* of the Ḳur'ān by the *Sunna*. But Shāfiʿī had closed off that avenue. He made a vain attempt to insist that the death penalty, introduced in the *Sunna*, had superseded a corporal punishment previously introduced in the *Sunna*, and so was an instance of the *naskh* of the *Sunna* by the *Sunna*, not of the *naskh* of the Ḳur'ān by the *Sunna*. But the stubborn fact remained obvious to everyone with eyes to see: that earlier punishment had been established by the Ḳur'ān, in Ḳ.24:2.

On an unrelated second question, the definition of the minimum number of breast-feedings that establishes a life-long barrier to the marriage of the Muslim male with any females to whom he is related by milk,[20] the *imāms* had had at their disposal a large volume of *ḥadīths* from the past. Here, his own insistence on ascertaining the *Sunna* of the Prophet led Shāfiʿī to acknowledge a report from ʿĀ'isha on the 'revelation' of a relevant Ḳur'ān ruling. Given his views on what could and what could not *naskh* the rulings of the Ḳur'ān, Shāfiʿī could not do other than bow to this information, (although it came not *from* the Prophet, but from his widow *about* the Prophet.) A second stubborn fact remained visible: that this relevant Ḳur'ān ruling is nowhere to be found in our texts of the Ḳur'ān.[21] Here, then is a further potential source of acute embarrassment, a stimulus which provoked a response that has had momentous consequences for the further shaping of the theories of *naskh*. Accepting the ʿĀ'isha report, Shāfiʿī was driven to accept that there may be verses *of* the Ḳur'ān which are no longer *in* the Ḳur'ān. Even if not now *in* the Ḳur'ān, such verses *of* the Ḳur'ān may supersede verses *of* and still *in* the Ḳur'ān.[22] Succeeding generations of Muslims, devoted followers and defenders of Shāfiʿī's *madhhab*, or system of ideas, and members of other, rival *madhāhib* alike, would, in discussing *naskh*, soberly adduce reported instances of *naskh* of the verses of the surviving Ḳur'ān by verses of the 'original' Ḳur'ān. This was a result of Shāfiʿī's intervention in these discussions on *naskh* and shows how the inter-*madhhab* debates on sources proceeded with a kind of dialectic, with each *madhhab* having to take account of views developed in other *madh āhib*. This accounts for the incorporation into the literature of the other *madh āhib* of a type of *naskh* required to be posited only in the Shāfiʿī *madhhab*.

We have noted the extent to which the elements of all the theorising were based on exegesis. In the following pages, we enquire into the degree to which not merely the theories of *naskh*, but the Law itself and its documentation in the *Ḥadith* or *Sunna*, was similarly exegetically based.

One

THE SOURCES OF ISLAMIC LAW

1. The Ḳur'ān

In the Muslim view, the religio-legal system of Islam is grounded in the revelations made to the Prophet. Muḥammad having himself begun the process of collecting the revelations into a written record, this source was available for analysis from an early date. Into this volume have been assembled the texts of the individual revelations brought down by the angel from God directly to Muḥammad throughout the course of his Prophetic career [Ḳ.2:97]. The book thus constituted contains, in the Muslim view, not one single word contributed by Muḥammad himself, nor, *a fortiori* by any other human. The Ḳur'ān is, in strict literal fact, the Book of God. The contents of the book composed by God Himself and divulged phrase by phrase to His human amanuensis who arranged to make it available to men by having it recorded, represent the final and fullest revelation to Man of His Divine Will by the Creator and Master of the Universe.

> Muḥammad was God's choice as 'seal of the prophets' and recipient of the fullest message.[1]

The religion inculcated in the Book of God, Islam, is that religion in which God Himself has directly instructed His creatures and by which alone He desires them to know Him and serve Him [Ḳ.5:3]. The regulations it conveys in the private, ritual, civil, penal or commercial spheres are the blueprint of the constitution, on whose basis at God's direct command and under His personal day-to-day supervision, there was once historically constructed between AD 613–32 the ideal human society most pleasing to its divine legislator.

To the Muslim, Islam, in both its citizen-to-citizen and its cosmic creature-to-Creator relationships, represents a perfection *once achieved* in the ordering and governance of human affairs that can be recovered whenever men acknowledge that the sole source of all authority, religious and secular, is vested in the Will of God eternally operative throughout the universe which He created and which He continues to sustain from moment to moment. For *Sunnī* Islam, (as opposed to the *Mu'tazilī* doctrine that Good and Evil can be at least partly apprehended by unaided human reason) Good is conformity with the divine will; Evil is ignorance of, heedlessness towards – at worst, defiance of the revealed Will of God. Since, in His own Book,

God has made clear to all His holy Will, no man henceforth will have the excuse of ignorance.[2]

During the course of its serial revelation the Book was known to Muḥammad and his contemporaries as the Ḳur'ān; the completed revelation, now collected into volume-form, was known to their successors as the *muṣḥaf*.

2. The *Sunna*

Post-Muḥammadan Islam made two very important claims. First, throughout the twenty-three years of Muḥammad's mission there had arisen in the ordinary day-to-day affairs of the community problems of individual or of corporate conduct on which the Faithful had consulted their Prophet. Certain of these difficulties, it is asserted, had been resolved by the *ad hoc* revelation of a divine ruling on the matter. The texts of these heavenly replies have survived to this day in their original wording in the *muṣḥaf*.[3]

Secondly, similar difficulties had also been settled by the Prophet acting either upon the basis of his inspired judgment, or even on his own human initiative. It might well be that the problems did not arise in the Prophet's immediate circle and so the decision had fallen to the responsibility of Muḥammad's appointed local agent acting on the basis of what he knew of the Prophet's policies, with the intent to consult Muḥammad when next he returned to Madīna. The Prophet had then endorsed, or not, his agent's actions.[4] Perhaps questions did not cause anxiety until death had already removed the Prophet from his people. The requisite solution would have been sought from those who had been close to the Prophet in life – one of his widows, or one of his most faithful adherents best acquainted with Muḥammad's daily behaviour and best placed to describe how he had acted in similar circumstances.

It was also asserted that any queries as to the correct reading or interpretation of the texts of the divine revelations had been satisfactorily resolved in the same way.

From the records of all these questions and replies there had grown both during and since the Prophet's day, alongside the Book of God, a parallel documentation of the demeanour and practice of Muḥammad and his associates, whether in their observance and performance of the rituals required of Man by God, or in the conduct of daily secular affairs and relations with fellow members of the community of God, or, in the privacy of the home with their immediate household.

There thus exist, in the Muslim view, *two* primary sources for our knowledge of the evolution of Islam which define all men's requirements in every particular: the direct revelation, or *al-waḥy al-matlū*, preserved in the records of the communications from God to

Muḥammad, intended to form the texts of the Ḳur'ān, brought together and published in the *muṣḥaf*; and the indirect revelation, *al-waḥy ghair al-matlū* (literally, the inspiration not intended to be solemnly recited in the ritual prayers) which is preserved in the records of the words and actions of the Prophet and of his Companions. The contents of these records, or *Ḥadīth*, are known as the *Sunna*. The collection and publication of the *Ḥadīth* was, however, a somewhat slower process completed only some two centuries after the time when the *muṣḥaf* was thought to have been first collected and promulgated.

3. The Islamic sciences

All men were summoned by the Prophet to participate in the construction of God's kingdom, here on earth. To do so, they must identify and analyse the contents of the twin *waḥy* of the Ḳur'ān and the *Sunna* in which will be found all the materials needful for the fulfilment of their divinely imposed task. In the two sources, the complete statement of the Will of God has been made available.

> No problem will confront a member of the community of God to which an indication cannot be found in the Book of God, pointing the way to the solution.[5]

To win the glittering prizes promised by God and His Prophet is for a man but a question of choice. He simply has to give ear and respond, for Islam is presented as a bargain offered to the passer-by. The first step is mere exercise of will, of deciding whether to accept the proffered transaction[6] to enquire what is demanded in the way of general discipline then give or withhold one's assent. 'Do this, and paradise will be yours; refuse, and an eternity of torments awaits.' Following the initial act of volition, all else is purposive action directed at faithful fulfilment of the norms of behaviour set out in the dual revelation. Reward will surely follow, both in this world, in the establishment of the perfect, God-designed, God-directed society, and, in the Hereafter, in its continuation in an eternity of felicity. To acquit one's human side of this bargain, the basic requisite is knowledge of the contents of the twin revelations of Ḳur'ān and *Sunna*. Such are the presumptions of Muslim thinking and they explain why the characteristic activities of the Muslims were described by their practitioners as 'sciences' [*'ulūm*] and why the various sciences, as these developed in the generations following the Age of Revelation, were viewed as ultimately related aspects of a general act of exegesis.

> Knowledge is of various grades. The first is knowledge of the Book and the *Sunna* – if the individual report be authentic . . . No account is taken of anything else when Book and *Sunna* are available.[7]

Clearly, the source of the Islamic revelation is one – the Word

> of God. The word of the Prophet is neither decisive nor binding *per se*. It informs us on God's behalf that He has decided so-and-so; the imposition is God's alone. The Muslim consensus indicates that the source is the *Sunna*, and the *Sunna* points to a divine decision. But, if we consider our knowledge of any decision, we find that, for this, we are dependent upon the Prophet, since we do not hear the voice of God nor that of Gabriel. We are aware of the Book of God solely by means of the communication conveyed by the Prophet. In that sense, as far as we are concerned, the source is the Prophet.[8]

The function of the scientists, *'ulamā'*, *fuḳahā'*, was conceived to have been one of derivation: *istinbāṭ*, *istikhrādj*, that is, the review in their entirety of the documents of the twin revelations and the extraction from their texts of a clear statement of the ideal behaviour revealed to men and required of men. To the sum of the prescriptions/proscriptions resulting from their labours was given the name *sharī'a*, the path to be followed, the truly Muslim 'way of life' which the commands, prohibitions, exhortations and recommendations contained in the documents had been shown to embody. The study itself was called *Fiḳh* – 'understanding', while the processes of derivation and definition were prolonged and belated – how prolonged and belated is shown by the fact that the great names of Islamic *Fiḳh* span, as we have seen, the hundred years from the mid-second to the mid-third centuries of the Islamic era. The century-and-a-half gap, which we have also noticed, between the Age of Revelation and the oldest surviving monuments of the *Fiḳh* is bridged by the formula that the *fuḳahā'* merely made explicit what was always implicit in Ḳur'ān and *Sunna*. The verification of this last assertion was the function of a secondary science, the science of the sources of the *Fiḳh*, whose earliest systematisation was one of the achievements credited to the great second century scholar Shāfi'ī. Merely human premisses are thus held to have been excluded from participation in the processes which had resulted in the formulation of the Islamic *Fiḳh*.

> Nothing is imposed by human reason. Only the commands and the prohibitions of the divine Lawgiver impose obligations upon men.[9]

Having been appropriated by the Muslims, the term *Sunna* became gradually narrowed down in Islamic usage. Originally, this Arabic term bore reference to all that tribal tradition transmitted of the approved manners and customs of the forebears to serve as the unquestioned basis and sanction of the conduct of succeeding generations. Since the Islamic entity which had created the new '*Sunna* of the Muslims' constituted a much greater and a more heterogeneous population scattered over a far wider territorial extent than any pre-Islamic tribe, or indeed, than the compact, although considerably mixed community presided over by Muḥammad at Madīna, the close-knit social unity and similarity of outlook which the institution of adherence to the *Sunna* of the ancestors both bespeaks and fosters, could not possibly have been achieved. The outstanding psychological feature exhibited by the men engaged in laying the foundations of second-century *Fiḳh* within and without the Arabian peninsula, was their chauvinism, their loyalty to the ways and views of their respective local communities. Mālik's (or rather, the Mālikīs') preference for the contemporary and immediately past practice of a single city is typical.[10] The same might be said of the Makkans, Kufans, Basrans – indeed, of all local scholarly groupings.

Modern research shows that, in fact, the *Fiḳh* had first been regionally organised. It was to become a matter of scandal in pious circles that the several local schools of *Fiḳh* showed considerable disagreement and variety of view. There arose the Tradition movement, begun as a conscious Islamic opposition to these differing groups of *fuḳahā'* whom it now accused of inadequate reference to 'the legacy of Muḥammad'. Shāfi'ī was to become the most prominent mouthpiece of these Traditionists and so prove the fiercest critic and opponent of the local schools of *Fiḳh*.

Schacht, for example, has shown the different starting-points and the differing techniques which had led to the ever-widening gulf opening up between the findings of the various local statements of the *Fiḳh*. His detailed studies have rendered historically indefensible the classical Islamic formula on the sources of the *Fiḳh* from which we began above.[11]

The slogan of the Tradition movement was the demand for strict documentation of the *Sunna* – i.e. of the *Fiḳh*, and, once the significance of the challenge was perceived, the Arabian and Iraqi scholars responded by culling from (or adding to) their respective local literatures materials which to them appeared best fitted to supply the documentary pedigree of the *usus* and *cultus* approved by the Muslims of their respective regions. The crux was attribution. The practice of attributing the current *Fiḳh* doctrines to the immediate ancestors, at first informal, yet indicative of a demand for such attribution, became, when challenged, more formal and as the challenge acquired greater precision, the attribution was carried beyond the fathers to their ancestors, to Successors, to Companions, and finally, to the Prophet.[12] Parallel with a backward growth of attribution, went a growing sophistication of technique as the debate widened into a general inter-school polemic. In Mālik's *Muwaṭṭa'*, for example, the demand for documentation was only sporadically satisfied, which argues that the demand was recent and not yet regularised. As locally-held views came to be represented as views of the Companions, even of the Prophet, the frequent undisguisable contradictions became even more obvious. Ways of resolving such difficulties had to be devised.

The clearest evidence of the next phase of development is afforded by the writings of Shāfiʿī who seized every opportunity to criticize his contemporaries' failure to furnish clearly defined Islamic criteria for many of their legal conclusions:

> Only the Book and the *Sunna* provide binding knowledge and it is incumbent upon every Muslim to obey them implicitly.[13]

Single-mindedly, Shāfiʿī foreshortened the historical perspective by insisting that scholars restrict their consideration to statements produced during the twenty-three years of the Prophet's public activity. That is, for Shāfiʿī, consistency could be achieved solely by defining *Sunna* as exclusive reference to the words and actions of Muḥammad alone. He thus laboured to impose a rigorous, formal distinction between 'the *Sunna* of the Prophet' and the non-authoritative '*Sunna* of the Muslims' – more especially, as the two so often clashed. One source of contradiction between *ḥadīth*s was removed by a rule to be applied whenever reports from Companions were at odds with reports from the Prophet:

> A *ḥadīth* from the Prophet is self-validating, requiring confirmation from no other quarter. It is neither reinforced nor weakened by a report from any other source. Should it be reported that one of the Companions acted otherwise, it is incumbent upon people to follow the report from the Prophet, ignoring all other reports. It is possible that one of his oldest associates, well-versed in the Prophet's ways, may yet have been unaware of some element of his practice known to another.[14]

That disposes neatly of conflict between Companion-reports and Prophet-reports. Shāfiʿī's activities represent no less than a radical change of direction in the development of the Islamic source-theory. The change, of which he was both conscious and boastful, was dictated by a novel outlook, a completely fresh way of expressing the uniqueness of the Prophet-figure. The change had been necessitated by the confusions in the contemporary *Fiḳh*, and inconsistencies in accounting for its findings, the result, in Shāfiʿī's view, of the failure by the Muslims to produce a coherent theory of sources. He saw that the route to consistency and coherence lay in recalling the Muslims to the simple idea that Islam had resulted from an act of divine revelation. Where his contemporaries and their precedessors had engaged in defining Islam as a social and historical phenomenon, Shāfiʿī sought to define a revealed Law.

> When the Prophet died, God's impositions ceased abruptly. They will be neither added to nor subtracted from throughout all subsequent Time. The 'practice' is meaningless.'[15]

4. UṢŪL AL-FIḲH (I)

It must be emphasised that this radical change of tone was occurring in the late second century. As a formal discipline, the subscience of *uṣūl al-Fiḳh* did not exist until Shāfiʿī laid down for the first time, the basic definitions and rules. Similar principles and rules, it is asserted, had governed the deductions of the pre-Shāfiʿī scholars. He is therefore not seen as having 'invented' the rules of the *uṣūl*, any more than Aristotle 'invented' the rules of logic, but rather, as having extracted and codified them.[16] By the time Shāfiʿī appeared, much had already been derived. On the basis of the rules he now drew up, he found in the techniques and methods of his contemporaries and their predecessors much to criticise. His *Risāla* was a polemic work by a leader of the Tradition party, and his opponents, who clearly were not prepared to jettison the results of several previous generations of scholars, adopted the new tools of the *uṣūl*, as they had previously adapted their argumentation to accommodate the *ḥadith*, using them to justify and so preserve intact their main *Fiḳh* teachings.

Mālik had described the *Fiḳh* (both actual and ideal[17]) thought to have been the outcome of Madīna's historical links back to the perfect society that had been constructed in the city in the days of the Prophet. That society had not ceased to function on Muḥammad's death, but had continued to operate and to evolve daily along lines determined by its particular identity. Shāfiʿī, on the contrary, was concerned for the implications, for his own and for all succeeding generations of believers, of the irruption of the voice of God at a known date into human affairs. Muḥammad, or rather, Muḥammad's Madīna, was, for Mālik, the ultimate putative historical *terminus ad quem*; for Shāfiʿī, Muḥammad, or rather, the Prophet-figure, is the one, necessary, universal *terminus a quo*. Mālik looked vaguely, but only sporadically backwards; Shāfiʿī gazed forward and to him, the classical Muslim view of the *sharīʿa* as purportedly derived by the *fuḳahā'* from the twin revelations of the Book of God and the *Sunna* of the Prophet of God is most certainly applicable – for the very good reason that it mainly derives from his ideas. It is doubtful whether it has consistent relevance for any earlier Islamic figure.

Shāfiʿī's principal achievement was the reduction of the vague term *Sunna*[18] until it invariably meant only the *Sunna* of the Prophet. The expression was, however, merely a catchword, signifying those doctrines of the *Fiḳh* to which he was prepared to assent. In quite another direction, his more lasting and perhaps most significant contribution to the Islamic sciences was the imposition of a formal theoretical distinction – although, paradoxically, this was far from the effect he intended – between 'the *Sunna* of the Prophet' and the Ḳur'ān, especially where the two fundamental sources appeared to clash.

Appearing at a relatively late stage in the history of the processes of derivation, Shāfi'ī was not free to initiate his own programme of derivation by returning direct to Ḳur'ān and *Sunna*. His activity cannot therefore be viewed as one of construction. Rather, it was confined to correction and refinement through polemic. Even more, Shāfi'ī was concerned primarily with documentation. Much of the *Fiḳh* had already been derived and accorded widespread acceptance. *For that very reason*, it commended itself to his approval. Conclusions such as, for example, the number of the daily ritual prayers, their form, content and timing; the manner and timing of the Fast; the timing and minimum rites of the Ḥadjdj; the amounts of *zakāt* due on various items and when payable; and the penalties for certain felonies, he acknowledged and accepted since they had been transmitted 'from the many to the many'.[19] But on many matters of practical detail where disagreement was still not merely possible, but prevalent, Shāfi'ī set out to review the bases from which both contemporary and earlier *fuḳahā'* had apparently derived their several opinions and the methods by which they had reached their conclusions. To his investigations he applied an incisive critique which he had perfected on the basis of his own simple, yet novel theoretical starting-point: that Islam was a divine revelation made to one, single specific individual – the Prophet. Conclusions which before his time had received general assent, he likewise reviewed and *justified*. In this sense, his method was both retrospective and normative. More strikingly, however, it was verificative and self-consciously Islamic. The function of *uṣūl al-Fiḳh* was thus, in Shāfi'ī's hands, two-fold: to tidy up such loose ends of detail as were yet determinable by the individual scholar; and for these, and for the broad lines of the *Fiḳh*, as it had developed in the century and a half before his birth, to provide the justification of an exclusively Islamic documentation.

The actual history, therefore, of the second century Islamic legal sciences is ultimately reducible to the record of the shifts in men's attitudes on one major methodological question: that of the relative status qua source to be accorded to the Book of God on the one hand, and on the other, to whatever passes at the given moment for the *Sunna*.

The significance of Shāfi'ī to our understanding of these matters is that to him chiefly Islam is indebted for the elevation of the second of its alleged sources to revealed status. This principle enabled him to ignore the many contradictions in the reports transmitted as coming from the Successors and Companions. It also enabled him to resolve the problems occasioned by the frequent clashes between such reports, and between many reports now being attributed to the Prophet. Only the latter were henceforward to be considered, and if reports from the Prophet continued to show contradiction, the means was also at hand by which this problem too could be solved. Contradictions had also been alleged even between the verses of the Book of God. The same means could be extended to solve this problem as well.

UṢŪL AL-FIḲH (2)

The successors of the *fuḳahā'*, the *uṣūlīs*, confronted a highly confused situation further complicated by the range of their own 'explanations' of the obvious differences between the conclusions arrived at by their several *imāms*, and now preserved and cherished in the several *madhāhib*. The primary business of the *uṣūl* was to maintain by verifying the *Fiḳh* of the *madhhab*. The *uṣūlīs* had attempted to achieve this aim by identifying the precise source from which the founders of the *madhhab* could be presumed to have derived the *Fiḳh* of the *madhhab*. At first, the various individual rulings had had to be attributed to outstanding personalities known to have flourished in recent past generations: the Companions, or their Successors, or the successors of these, who had actively contributed to the islamisation of the separate local communities. Views differed from locality to locality and were explained as the natural differences between the views of those notabilities. However, that position was doomed once the call for uniformity of practice, and more importantly, the demand for uniformity of attribution, was raised. An obvious unifying personality was the Prophet. There being but one God, Who had revealed but one Book to one man, there should be but one set of *Fiḳh* regulations to be called Islam and to be universally espoused. The regions should now either jettison much of the theoretical work of the last century and a half, or bow to the inevitable by modifying its documentation for, once made, the demand that the *Fiḳh* be attributed to the one figure guaranteed to provide both certainty and unity could not be withstood. There is simply no cogent counter-argument. None would dare challenge a *Fiḳh* attributed to the Prophet. But neither could a Muslim reject his entire cultural past. However, he might still challenge the attribution to the Prophet of any one of the several regional systems of the *Fiḳh* to the exclusion of his own. He might, that is, challenge the claim of any rival system of *Fiḳh* to possess a stronger organic link with the Prophet, now that the general insistence on demonstrating descent from the Prophet had made rivals and competitors of previously complementary and mutually tolerant streams. The field on which the scholars would now wage their intellectual competition would be that of attribution. Attribution is *isnād*; *isnād* implies chronology and chronology is the very essence of *naskh*.

Two

THE THEORIES OF *NASKH*

1. The general theory

We have seen that the *Fiḳh* was organised on a regional basis and that each local school had generated its own school of *uṣūl*. The techniques employed in an almost incessant inter-school polemic were subject to changes in fashion and one methodological development whose first appearance cannot as yet be precisely dated is that referred to by the technical term *naskh*. That it had been introduced by some unknown *uṣūlī* is probable, given the careful choice of name, and the fact that this word occurs in the Ḳur'ān underlines the allegation of divine warrant for the reality of the thing named.

The first point that must be made clear is that this term *naskh* refers not to one, but to several quite unrelated 'phenomena' which were gradually brought together under the one rubric, owing to a series of decisions taken in the course of the development of what was to prove a spectacularly 'successful' theory. The phenomena accommodated under the cover of this single comprehensive term were not originally phenomena at all, but merely assumptions which, proving attractive and useful as problem-solvers, were increasingly called upon in a science devoted to the retrospective legitimation of the Islamic history of the various local *Fiḳh* doctrines. The powerful attractions of the theory lay in its extreme simplicity.

By *naskh*, the *uṣūlī*s understood in the most general terms a revelatory process by which certain divine decisions, enacted at a given date, had been overtaken and superseded by other divine decisions enacted at a later date. The idea had been current, not only before the elaboration of the Islamic sciences, but before even the foundation of Islam itself.[1] The idea is certainly referred to in the Ḳur'ān. The term *naskh* has, therefore, when used without further qualification, the meaning of supersession, but in the quite strict sense that it is God alone Whose divine prerogative it is to *naskh*, that is, either withdraw or repeal one of His divine decisions embodied in one of His divine revelations by providing a further revelation embodying a quite different decision on the same topic. The impression is therefore gained that from the outset, the basic meaning of the term *naskh* is 'replacement'. Whether this 'replacement' would be seen as restricted exclusively to the texts of the revealed Ḳur'ān, depended upon how widely the individual scholar was prepared to interpret the notion of 'revelation'. By Shāfiʿī's time, the question had become crucial.

It must also be appreciated that there was not necessarily to be found in the source documents in all instances a formal explicit divine announcement of *naskh*. The fact alone of the 'simultaneous existence' of two divine enactments on one and the same topic was held to provide sufficient warrant for the inference that *naskh* had occurred, and thus that only one of the two rulings was intended to be acted upon.

> It is quite unacceptable to say of any part of the Ḳur'ān that it has either been replaced by so-and-so, or has replaced so-and-so, in the absence of complete certainty. Such a declaration would concern what God intends, which cannot be ascertained other than by an explicit Ḳur'ān statement, or by a 'sound' *ḥadīth* from the Prophet (which is a revelation) or by an indubitable consensus reported from his Companions, reporting in turn from the Prophet that such has occurred, or by unavoidable intellectual compulsion – by which is meant that it is absolutely certain that one of the two texts is later than the other and that it is quite impossible to implement the two texts jointly. We are then made aware that God has nullified the earlier of His revelations by the revelation of the later.[2]

There being, however, no single verse in the Ḳur'ān which unequivocally points to the *naskh* of any other verse, nor any irreproachable *ḥadīth* from the Prophet which identifies any one verse as having either undergone or effected *naskh*, we are left with only what is here called 'unavoidable intellectual compulsion' (*ḍarūra*), i.e. inference. In brief, *naskh* was the outcome of exegesis applied to the sources by those concerned to extract from the texts the practical regulations making up the *Fiḳh*. The elements required to be identified in any one alleged instance of *naskh* are three:

i. the divine origin of both injunctions;

ii. conflict between two enactments such that it is 'quite impossible to implement the two texts jointly';

iii. knowledge of the relative dates of both revelations.

Within the body of the revelations – (for some, both Ḳur'ān and *Sunna*) – there are, it is alleged, statements occurring in one context dealing with a particular topic which appear to be at variance with other statements occurring in other contexts, but treating of precisely the same topic. Sometimes these parallel statements are so seriously divergent as to be incapable of reconciliation. It is quite impossible to act on both statements simultaneously. According to the general theory of *naskh*, the founders of the several regional systems of the *Fiḳh*, acting on evidence at their disposal had, in all such cases, selected only one of the conflicting revealed statements to be identified as the sole basis of valid Islamic practice and had consciously ignored the alternative text entirely. But different evidence had been at the disposal of the several *imāms* who had, therefore, naturally selected different sources from which to derive the individual theses of the *Fiḳh*.

The general theory of *naskh* was thus admirably adapted to serve the regional *uṣūlīs* in their task of justifying the selection made by the founders of their respective *madhāhib* and of 'tracing the errors' committed by the founders of rival *madhāhib*. The theory also rendered unnecessary any assumption that 'real conflict' can exist between revealed sources. Any replaced enactment had been valid from the time of its first revelation to the time of the revelation of the successive regulation. Each of the two regulations, the *nāsikh* and the *mansūkh* was true and valid for its own period.[3]

We have seen that the general theory of *naskh* stated that the *imām* of the *madhhab* had given preference, in every instance of *naskh*, to that divine ruling which he had ascertained to have been the later of two (or more) in date of revelation:[4]

> The ruling which is later replaces the earlier if it materially differs from it. Conflict and contradiction between the Ḳur'ān source and the *Sunna* source is inconceivable, those being the marks of fallibility and thus impossible to be posited of God. The 'conflict' arises solely on account of our ignorance of the relative dates which makes it impossible for us to distinguish the *nāsikh* from the *mansūkh*. Given knowledge of the relative dates, however, opposition between the two sources vanishes, for the later is the *nāsikh* of the earlier. Our primary task is thus to determine the dating without knowledge of which conflict will persist – although only so far as we are concerned. Conflict cannot obtain between divine utterances.[5]

This theoretical necessity to determine the relative dates of various utterances explains the cultivation by the Muslims of the historical and the biographical sciences. That should give us ample warning against taking too trusting an attitude to any assertion on dating, whether that takes the form of the *isnād* (attribution) of any *ḥadīth*, or the 'circumstances in which any particular Ḳur'ān verse was revealed', its *sabab*.

The Muslims stress that the Prophet's mission extended over some twenty-odd years. The *naskh* theory is thus rooted in a concept of the gradual development of the revelation(s). The theory does not, on that account, hint even remotely at mutability of the Divine Will, much less of the Divine Knowledge. These discussions on *naskh* were thus not attended with any potentially embarrassing metaphysical or theological implications. The entire processes of history, and hence the entire sweep of revelation history were present to the divine consciousness in a single moment. Before even the universe, and with it, Time began, God had foreknown the precise instant at which the successive revelations, and the minutest detail within each of those revelations, would come into and pass out of vigour. All was both known and willed in advance. Objections to the theory of *naskh* based on theological considerations such as 'the changing of the divine mind' or 'the growth of the divine knowledge' when used as counter-arguments, since all were agreed that both were absurd, were rare and easily dealt with. God had known before imposing any obligation the precise duration He intended that obligation to have, the precise date on which the intended replacement regulation would be revealed, and the precise duration of its replacement, *ad infinitum*. As God's knowledge is eternal, for Him, time is irrelevant. Time affects only men and it is only men who would suppose that when some divine regulation is revealed it is intended to endure. However, when a regulation is revealed, we are required to believe that it is intended to endure unless it is replaced later. When its replacement is revealed, men are obliged to revise their former belief. Knowledge of the relative dates of the divine enactments is thus crucial in the derivation of the *Fiḳh* from the accumulated masses of information locked up in both the Ḳur'ān and the *Sunna*.

2. The general theory and the special theory

Before proceeding, it may be convenient now to distinguish two aspects of the methodological principle of *naskh* which we may conveniently refer to as, respectively:

(a) the general theory of *naskh*; and

(b) the special theories of *naskh*.

The definition and practical application of 'the general theory' have been neatly summarised by Abū ʿAbdullāh:

> This branch of Islamic science is an indispensable adjunct to *idjtihād*, since the main prop of *idjtihād* is knowledge of what has been handed down to us, an integral part of which is knowledge of the *nāsikh* and the *mansūkh*.
>
> The handling of Tradition reports is easy and it is not difficult to assume the burden of that charge. The difficulty lies in the techniques of extracting legal principles from the body of the documents. Part of the art of this type of investigation . . . is the determination of the later and the earlier situation.[6]

The twin keys to the knowledge of the divine revelation 'in its final form' are thus: knowledge of the documents that have been handed down, the Tradition; and the evidence enabling us to discriminate between the documents which describe the earlier, and those which describe the later situation. This means that one's knowledge that the principle of *naskh* has been in operation throughout revelation history, and the knowledge of its precise location within the Islamic revelation is both derived from and guaranteed by knowledge of the Tradition. By 'Tradition' is meant both the Ḳur'ān and the *Sunna* which have been handed down by the Muslims.

Zuhrī, who is credited with a book on *naskh*, it credited with the following dictum as well: 'He who does not know the *nāsikh* and the *mansūkh* will make errors in his religion.'[7]

In setting out the 'conditions' by which *naskh* is recognised, another scholar stresses the relative dates of the documents: 'One of the conditions is knowledge of which is the later, since the *nāsikh* must be later than the *mansūkh*. This knowledge of the relative dating of the two documents can be derived solely from the Tradition.'[8]

Western scholars have hitherto confined their attention to only one aspect of the general principle of *naskh* – the alleged operation of *naskh* on the texts of the Ḳur'ān.[9] There is, however, in the extensive Islamic literature on *naskh*, and in the *uṣūl* literature, no warrant for this restriction which has, in fact, led to a failure to grasp that it is in the very unity of the undifferentiated Tradition that the solution of many otherwise intractable problems created for the Muslims by the apparent conflict between certain of their source documents is to be found.

3. Opposition to the *Sunna* source

Attempts by certain Muslim groups about the time of Shāfiʿī to impose a clear formal distinction between the Ḳur'ān and the extra Ḳur'ānic component of the Islamic Tradition are discernible, and it was chiefly to refute these efforts that Shāfiʿī composed his *Risāla*. A study of these processes offers valuable clues to the successive steps by which the Muslim discussions had advanced. The evidence shows that these groups had adopted a fundamentalist stand and distrusting the criteria which were said to guarantee the authenticity of the *Sunna*, refused to accept as binding any statement not found in the Ḳur'ān. There were fine gradations of opinion on the matter and the range of views held is illustrated by Shāfiʿī's reports. One group of scholars had been inclined to argue that, as a prophet, Muḥammad had been given legislative *carte blanche*; for them, the *Sunna* was a body of material independent of the Ḳur'ān, self-subsisting and equally sovereign with the Book – especially on matters on which the Ḳur'ān was silent.[10] A second group refused to accept any *sunna* on any matter not adumbrated in the Ḳur'ān [*lahā aṣl fi-'l-Ḳur'ān*]. The only *ḥadīth*s this group would countenance were, obviously, *tafsīr*-reports. A third, more rigorous opinion, rejected out of hand all *sunna*s on matters not explicitly mentioned in the Ḳur'ān [*laisa fīhi naṣṣ kitāb*]. From this we see that Ḳur'ān and *Sunna* were competing sources. The first group are recognisably '*ahl al-Ḥadīth*' while the last group might, with justice, be termed '*ahl al-Ḳur'ān*', vigilant against any attempt to introduce from whatever quarter additions to the provisions of the revealed Book of God. Diversity of opinion of the sort alluded to here by Shāfi'ī lies at the very point of emergence of the theories of *naskh*.

One attempt to resist demands for reliance upon the *Sunna* is documented in the following: the Prophet was reported to have said, 'Let me find none of you reclining on his couch who, when confronted with a prohibition or a permission from me says, "I do not know – we will follow only what we find in the Book of God."'[11]

Abū Naḍra said,

> We were exchanging *ḥadīth*s at 'Imrān's when one man said, 'Enough of this, bring us the Book of God.' 'Imrān exclaimed, 'Fool! do you find the ritual prayer set out in detail in the Book of God? or the Fast? On such matters the Ḳur'ān legislates in a general way and it is the *Sunna* which clarifies the details.'[12]

The *ḥadīth*s, the second of which depends upon and expands and elucidates the first, are typical of the propaganda of *ahl al-Ḥadīth* who wore down and broke the resistance of the schools of *Fiḳh* against a rising flood of *ḥadīth*s purportedly reflecting the opinions of the Prophet's generation. Reports had been circulated with the express aim of countering certain of the *Fiḳh* doctrines, thus affecting the outcome of further, incomplete discussions.[13] The Traditionists are here seen to attack those who would reject a *sunna* on the plea of the sufficiency of the Ḳur'ān revelation. Pro-*ḥadīth* propaganda was thus evidently aimed not merely at so-called *ra'y*, (*opinio*), but had, as its second target, those who thought that the Ḳur'ān should be the sole binding source. The first report pre-supposes the assumptions of the later Traditionists: that the production of a decision purporting to be traced from the Prophet would automatically determine the outcome of discussion. It further purports to document this principle by placing it in the mouth of the Prophet. This report, in brief, encapsulates an *uṣūlī* viewpoint and thus derives from a secondary stage of development. The opposition views alluded to in these edited 'discussions' would seek to distinguish the Ḳur'ānic from the non-Ḳur'ānic components of the Tradition; they would, in fine, attempt to counter extra-Ḳur'ānic evidence with Kur'ānic evidence in the formulation of Islamic rulings. The reports are thus counter to, and hence later than the explicit doctrine of *ahl-al-Ḥadīth*, but finally they failed, owing to the inadequacy of the Ḳur'ān's legal content. That failure, in turn, ensured the inevitable success of the main thesis of the Traditionists who, borrowing the techniques of their opponents, embarrassed them by quoting the Ḳur'ān back at them in support of the claims of the *Sunna*. This type of discussion, as we shall see, owes a great debt to the work of Shāfi'ī.

The Prophet said,

> I have been given the Ḳur'ān and along with it, its like. [the

> *Sunna*] At any moment now, a man seated on his couch will say: 'Keep to the Ḳur'ān; whatever you find to be declared lawful there, declare that to be lawful; whatever you find there to be declared unlawful, declare that to be unlawful.'[14]

This should be considered with the following: The Messenger of God said,

> It won't be long before a man, sitting on his couch will be informed of one of my *ḥadīth*s and will retort, 'There is between us and you the Book of God; what we find to be declared lawful there, that we shall deem to be lawful; what we find to be declared unlawful there, that we shall deem to be unlawful', – yet what the Prophet has declared to be unlawful is like what God has declared to be unlawful.[15]

The intervention of the Traditionists is even more unmistakable in: 'Let me hear of none of you installed in his couch saying, when informed of a *ḥadīth* from me: "Recite a Ḳur'ān!" – whatever good doctrine is enunciated, I, Muḥammad, originated it.'[16]

The tell-tale use of the work 'like', *mithl*, in the reports alerts one to the use made by *ahl-al-Ḥadīth* of the Ḳur'ānic vocabulary to support their thesis. In this instance, the reference is to Ḳ.2:106: *mā nansakh min āya aw nansa-hā na'ti bi-khairin min-hā aw mithli-hā*, i.e. the very text from which the technical term *naskh* had been borrowed, for the dispute recorded in the above *ḥadīth* concerns the very delicate question of the status of *Sunna* relative to Ḳur'ān source. This is borne out by yet another argument that ushers us into the very midst of a typical methodological discussion:

> The Prophet prohibited certain things during the Kuaybar campaign, saying, 'There will soon come a time when a man, installed in his couch, and informed of a *ḥadīth* from me will say, "There is the Book of God between us and you. What we find to be declared unlawful there, we shall deem to be unlawful; what we find to be declared lawful there, we shall deem to be lawful." ' But what the Prophet prohibited is like what God has prohibited.[17]

All the 'things' referred to here as having been prohibited by the *Sunna*, are, in fact, covered by Ḳur'ān statements, while the things listed are either additional to or in conflict with the relevant Ḳur'ān rulings. The *sunna*s were allegedly later, Kuaybar having been conquered in the year AH 7. The solicitude for dating *sunna*s, exemplified in the *ḥadīth*, should enable us to assign it to a discussion on *naskh* theory. We shall meet with numerous instances of the careful and deliberate dating of *ḥadīth*s, or discussions on their *isnāds* – which is precisely the same thing. The 'unsuccessful' viewpoint in respect of the dating of *ḥadīth*s is illustrated in: 'He shall be the *imām* who best recites the Book of God and whose knowledge of the Book reaches furthest back in time. If two men be equal in respect of knowledge of the Book of God, he shall be *imām* whose *hidjra* was earlier than the other's.'[18]

This view was dislodged by the *naskh* doctrine, probably during Shāfiʿī's lifetime, for he shows himself uncharacteristically undecided in one specific case of *isnād*-comparison.[19]

The *ḥadīth*s considered above were not concerned solely with distinguishing the Ḳur'ānic from the extra-Ḳur'ānic component of the Tradition. They referred to differing attitudes on the question of the relative priority to be accorded to each component, in the event that they appeared to clash. The situation envisaged is characteristic of mid-second-century concerns. The first *ḥadīth* dates from before Shāfiʿī's time. It occurs, and with the same *isnād*, in his *Risāla*, on page 15. The second concentrates on the functional role for the *uṣūlī* of the alleged statements or actions of the Prophet on matters on which the Ḳur'ān had already provided specific statements. These would be cases in which there were both Ḳur'ān verses and *sunna*s, so what is here represented is an even more advanced, since more detailed discussion on an important point of methodological principle. As formulated, the *ḥadīth* would be later than the time of Shāfiʿī, since it betrays an acquaintance with his *uṣūl* views, while the examples it exploits had been cited by him.[20]

The anti-*Sunna* position failed completely and in the light of the view that was to prevail, the study of all aspects of *naskh* must take account of two sets of documents underlying the *Fiḳh*: Ḳur'ān and extra-Ḳur'ānic *Sunna* – within a context of prolonged dispute as to their relative status. The victory of the Traditionists made the theory of *naskh* inevitable.

4. The application of the general theory

By appeal to the general theory of *naskh*, it is thought, the legal and exegetical specialists had been able to pick and choose their several ways through labyrinths of conflicting source materials, all of which, in the Muslim view, had come down from the first generation. That they had managed to select as relevant to their supposed task of deriving the *sharīʿa* certain elements, as opposed to others, amid the vast undifferentiated corpus of materials accumulated since the time of the Prophet, without exposing themselves to charges of arbitrariness [*ra'y*] was thought to have been in no small measure due to the sanction of the general theory of *naskh* which all alike had employed. That the individual *fuḳahā'* had, nevertheless arrived at differing conclusions, although all working from the same sources, was similarly explicable, in the Muslim view at least in part, in terms of the differences between the special theories of *naskh* which, it was assumed, the *fuḳahā'* had devised for the working of the raw materials which they extracted from their sources. Differences are apparent, not only between adherents of rival *madhāhib*, but even between scholars working in one and the same *madhhab*:

> Here, the Mālikīs are not unanimous. Abū al-Faradj and other Mālikīs thought that the *Sunna* had superseded the Ḳur'ān, whereas, on the same question, Mālik himself has found the Ḳur'ān to be the *nāsikh*.[21]
>
> There was disagreement on the principle among the Shāfi'īs, for some of them thought that the *Sunna* could supersede the Ḳur'ān – although they had not found an attested instance in which this had actually occurred.[22]

By the practical application of the general theory of *naskh* is meant that, if within the mass of the source documents the *faḳīh* was faced with two apparently conflicting statements on one and the same point of legal or ritual regulation, his first concern would have been to determine the total meaning of each. Skilful application of exegetical techniques can remove many an apparent difficulty:

> The occurrence of *naskh* in the Ḳur'ān would be contrary to the expectation aroused by its revelation. Wherever exegesis can circumvent the assumption of *naskh*, resort to exegesis is obligatory – and what verse of the Ḳur'ān is not susceptible of exegesis?[23]

If satisfied, however, that even exegesis will not solve his difficulty, since the two statements really do treat of precisely the same aspect of a single obligation, the scholar must pursue his endeavours to achieve an interpretation which will permit of the reconciliation, and thus of the application of both regulations. For, since each comes from God, neither is lightly to be set aside.[24] Where any degree of reconciliation is feasible, however slight, the principle of *naskh* may not be invoked.[25] This attitude was enshrined in the tag: *al-djam' yamna' al-naskh* – reconciliation rules out appeal to *naskh*.

Should reconciliation prove, however, beyond the wit of scholarship, because the two statements were irreconcilable to the point of mutual exclusion in all respects, rendering their simultaneous implementation inconceivable, the scholar's responsibility moves on to minute enquiry into the circumstances in which each of the parallel, but incompatible enactments had been enunciated, to establish their relative dates. Shāfi'ī provides an example of close scrutiny of incompatible source materials for this very purpose of relative dating.[26] This last demand that the dates he examined generated yet another science, *asbāb al-nuzūl*, 'one of whose merits, in that it distinguishes the Madinan from the Makkan revelations, is the knowledge thus provided as to which is the later, and thus the *nāsikh*.'[27]

Applying all these aspects of the theory, the *fuḳahā'*, it is alleged, had been bound, under the principle of *naskh*, to pronounce in favour of the *ḥukm* of one of any two conflicting revelations, the later or *nāsikh*, and to abandon the earlier, or *mansūkh*, on the grounds that it had been shown to have been overtaken and superseded.[28]

It is perfectly clear that this entire structure of theory was merely an exegetical tool of incomparable utility to later generations of scholars aware of the differences between the individual theses of the rival *madhāhib* to which they severally belonged. Their varying *Fiḳh* views, inherited from earlier ages, had allegedly been arrived at by consideration of different sources of differing date.

Shāfiʿī illustrates the application of the general theory in its simplest form: Ḳ.8:65 reads:

> Oh Prophet! incite the believers to war. If there be of you twenty patient believers, they will overcome two hundred; if there be of you one hundred, they will overcome one thousand of the unbelievers.

Immediately following this verse 66 reads, however,

> Now God has alleviated your burden, knowing that there is weakness in you. If there should be of you one hundred, they will overcome two hundred; if there should be of you one thousand, they will overcome two thousand . . .

Shāfiʿī comments:

> Then God made it clear in His Book that He had relieved the Muslims of the obligation to fight the unbelievers in the ratio of one against ten, and had imposed upon them the obligation to fight one against two. ibn ʿAbbās said, 'When the first verse was revealed, it was enjoined that twenty should not flee from two hundred. *Subsequently*, God revealed the second verse by which it was enjoined that one hundred should not flee from two hundred.' The matter, [concludes Shāfiʿī] is, if God please, as ibn ʿAbbās has said, and as God has made explicit in the verse itself *which requires no exegesis*.[29]

Shāfiʿī employs here as his apparatus not merely the two allegedly conflicting Ḳur'ān statements, but also their exegesis embodied in the *tafsīr-ḥadīth* attributed to ibn ʿAbbās, whose information he accepts without question, although the verse, according to him, '*requires no exegesis*'.

The Ẓāhirī scholar, ibn Ḥazm, a fierce opponent of the above conclusion, maintains,

> Some have alleged that this verse [v. 66] superseded v. 65. That is wrong, since
>
> i. this view is not unanimously held by the scholars,
>
> ii. there is no indication of *naskh*.
>
> The verses concern the obligation to wage war on the unbelievers. When the forces of Islam meet the forces of unbelief, it is not permissible for any Muslim to turn his back upon the entire unbelieving population of the world. Is there any mention in the verses of fleeing? The second verse merely announces *in advance* future victory conditional upon patience and promises divine assistance to the steadfast.[30]

It was not open to either of the two masters to read the verses in the light of Muḥammad's campaign to incite his followers to secure their political position by resort to violence against their opponents, and to circumvent their natural reluctance to fight, based upon a prudent assessment of their own relative numerical inferiority, reinforced, in many cases, by ties of blood or political connection. Nor need we treat Shāfiʿī's use of the verses as seriously as ibn Ḥazm. For Shāfiʿī, the verses supported no specific *Fiḳh* doctrine, although they formed part of the highly elaborate apparatus he had built up to establish 'the fact of *naskh*' as a 'phenomenon' affecting the texts of the Ḳur'ān. That ibn Ḥazm did not feel the need to see this as an instance of *naskh* in the Ḳur'ān underlines that the conflict lies not between two verses of the Book of God, but between two exegeses of a Ḳur'ānic passage.

In the same vein, Shāfiʿī adduces the following examples to establish the 'reality' of *naskh* in the *Sunna*:

> The Prophet mounted a horse and was thrown, grazing his right side. He performed the ritual prayers seated and we prayed behind him, also seated. After the prayer, he turned round and said, 'The *imām* has been appointed that the lead might be taken from him. When he prays standing, stand; when he prostrates, prostrate; when he raises his head, raise yours, and when he says, "May God hearken to him who praises Him," respond: "Our Lord art Thou, and to Thee be praise." When the *imām* prays seated, sit.'
>
> The Prophet came out during his illness and went over to Abū Bakr who was standing leading the people in the prayer. Abū Bakr moved back, but the Prophet signalled that he should continue. Muḥammad sat at Abū Bakr's side. Abū Bakr followed the Prophet's lead, while the people followed Abū Bakr's prayer.
>
> This particular prayer [comments Shāfiʿī] was performed by the Prophet during his final illness, seated. The men behind him prayed standing. This is an indication that his command to the Muslims, at the time when he fell off his horse preceded the illness which led to his death. His praying seated during his final illness, while the people behind him prayed standing, is therefore the *nāsikh* of the regulation that men should sit in conformity with the sitting of the *imām*.[31]

The *ḥadīth*s exploited here, amount to nothing more than a discussion of the role of the prayer-leader in very general, catechism-like terms. Shāfiʿī's teacher, Mālik, had insisted that the *imām* had been appointed to give the lead at prayer. The congregation ought to imitate his actions and not act differently from him.[32] Only Shāfiʿī sees in the second narrative evidence for *naskh*. But that this instance of *naskh* was, nevertheless inferential, is clear from a second Shāfiʿī comment: 'But that the first command was *mansūkh* the people behind the Prophet in the second narrative would have sat'. He rejects the Mālikī suggestion that, on the second occasion, Abū Bakr was the people's *imām*, characterising their *ḥadīth* to this effect as *mursal* – and, besides, he can amass more *ḥadīth*s than they can.[33]

Shāfi'ī would have us understand that the examples of *naskh* illustrated above are perfectly straightforward. Of the first instance, he had alleged that exegesis was quite unnecessary, (i.e. an ancient *tafsīr* has already become a historical 'fact' – it is *Sunna*). Clearly the subject matter in the two Ḳur'ān verses was one and the same: In the *djihād*, the number of unbelievers against whom the Muslim is required to stand fast – in v. 65, ten; in v. 66, two.

In the second series of examples, concerning the relation between the actions of the *imām* and of those following his lead at prayer, the people were told that if the *imām* prays seated, owing to some indisposition, they should pray seated; in the second, the *imām* was seated, owing to some indisposition, yet the people prayed standing. Ten and two are mutually exclusive; sitting and standing are mutually exclusive. In each of the two sets, there is held to be evidence of disparity of date. In the Ḳur'ān instance, that was held to have been stated by God Himself: '*Now* God has alleviated your burden', while 'alleviation' means 'change'. In the second instance, the second narrative refers to the Prophet's final illness – at any rate, we learn from further evidence that Abū Bakr's beginning the prayer as *imām* had occurred on that occasion.

Thus, in both instances alike, no difficulty is thought to face the scholar. The texts treat of a common topic. The rulings are in conflict and cannot be simultaneously acted upon. The conflicting texts are of different date. One thus pronounces in favour of the later of the texts which is the *nāsikh* of the earlier, the *mansūkh*. The word 'Now' of Ḳ.8:66 might, with Shāfi'ī, be alleged to convey the notion: 'Now, as opposed to what went before'. It might equally, with ibn Ḥazm, be alleged to convey the opposite: 'Now, as opposed to what will come in the future.' Shāfi'ī, however, seized upon the work 'alleviated' in the same verse, for by his day, that had already become a quasi-technical term denoting '*naskh*', or rather, the rationalisation of '*naskh*'. He himself uses it on occasion as a synonym for *naskh*.[34]

> 'God used to reveal impositions to His Prophet, one after another, imposing what had not previously been imposed, and also alleviating what had previously been imposed.'[35]

Shāfi'ī further overlooked the wider theological implication of the conclusion he had reached on the meaning of the work 'Now'. For, if the verse were alleged – with ibn 'Abbās – to alleviate a prior regulation, it might be read as suggesting that God has now realised what He had failed to realise when He imposed the v. 65 regulation – the current weakness of the Muslims. His 'subsequent' revelation would imply development of the divine knowledge, which the theologians are unanimous is not merely, by definition, a theological and a logical absurdity, but frank unbelief.[36]

Our conclusion may then be justified: only a mind bent upon finding documentary evidence for *the fact of naskh* operating upon the Ḳur'ān texts in question, and informed of the technical vocabulary of the Islamic *naskh* theories would have construed the Ḳ.8 passage in the way in which Shāfi'ī did. The choice of examples in this particular instance may be thought uncharacteristically inept, yet they had been carefully selected as affording 'the clearest evidence' for the operation of *naskh* upon the Ḳur'ān and *Sunna* sources. Like his contemporaries Shāfi'ī had inherited a *Fiḳh* (and the underlying *tafsīr*) which invited just such a conclusion as he had drawn. Thus, for the scholars of the literary age, by 'sources' is meant not simply the crude texts of Ḳur'ān and *Sunna*. Their *Fiḳh* and the interpretations of the texts which they had inherited from their predecessors cannot be left out of our account as we analyse their approaches to the Ḳur'ān and *Sunna* documents. The *naskh* theorising had been born from men's recognition of the gaps between the Ḳur'ān, the *Sunna* and the *Fiḳh*, and their observation of conflicts between all three and within the documents of each of the three. Their aim had been merely to bridge the gaps.

What is instructive about the examples used by Shāfi'ī to demonstrate instances of *naskh* is that, in each of the two sets he adduces, his theoretical position led him to import into his reading of the texts a non-existent element of conflict. One of the clichés of Shāfi'ī's technical reasoning is the argument that, but for the indications furnished by the *Sunna*, the *fuḳahā'* would, in many cases, have applied the rulings *that we find in the Ḳur'ān*![37] Analysis of some of those cases will show that the *Fiḳh* had established conclusions irreconcilable with the regulations set out in the Ḳur'ān. Shāfi'ī was thus, no more free to question the *Fiḳh* than he was to question either the *Sunna* or the *Tafsīr*. Wherever and by whomever it is made, any allegation of conflict of sources must satisfy us from this point forward. As the scholars insist, such 'conflict of sources' is invariably illusory. For them, it merely points to *naskh*. We should rather be aware of conflict of exegesis, dating back to the original reading of the sources, especially of the Ḳur'ān, while, for our purposes, as opposed to those of the Muslim scholars, the sources will be deemed to be two, the Ḳur'ān and the *Sunna*. The *Fiḳh* we propose to regard as a secondary source, as opposed to the Muslim *uṣūlī* for whom, as we see, it ranked with Ḳur'ān and *Sunna*. All that will then remain to be analysed will be conflict of *Fiḳh*, to be confidently identified as the source of the entire structure of *naskh* theorising.

A modern Muslim opponent of the alleged operation of *naskh*, at least as this is alleged to affect the Ḳur'ān source, asks some very pertinent questions:

That there is *naskh* in the Ḳur'ān is not an article of Muslim faith. It was merely a technique employed by the exegetes of the first century. When one of them was faced with a problem in his understanding of certain verses, imagining that they were in conflict, he would grasp this principle to remove his difficulty. But a Companion's interpretation of a Ḳur'ān verse is not binding. If it were, the majority would not have, on occasion, disagreed with ibn ʿAbbās, the most learned of the exegetes of his generation, nor would certain of the Companions have rejected the principle of *naskh*. Ubayy, for example, did not accept it and refused to abandon anything he had heard from the Prophet. The Ḳur'ān nowhere announced that verse so-and-so is *nāsikh*, or that verse such-and-such is *mansūkh*. The scholars did not possess an undeniable indication that one verse is earlier or later than any other verse, in all the detailed questions they discussed. They merely asserted without proof that one verse was later than another. We do not even know why, in their estimation, some verses are *nāsikh* rather than *mansūkh*, nor how it is possible to distinguish the verse which is the sole valid source for obligatory action from the verse whole ruling has been abandoned, given the absence of any such declaration in the Book itself; even more surprising is the absence of a single agreed *ḥadīth* from the Prophet which might be taken to be a certain documentary proof that verse so-and-so is the *nāsikh* of verse so-and-so. They were not even agreed on the number of verses supposedly *mansūkh*, and were prepared to abandon the insistence upon *naskh* when they came to realise that the verses they were discussing were not in actual conflict.[38]

Three

THE SPECIAL THEORIES OF *NASKH*

1. The general and special theories

In view of the significance of Shāfiʿī in the history of the *Fiḳh* and in view especially of the earliness of his dates, we noted that he was the first scholar to attempt to systematise the range of techniques and methods to be employed in the derivation of the *Fiḳh* rulings from the documents of the revelation – and since he was also the author of the earliest attempt to regularise appeals to the principle of *naskh*, his ideas in this particular regard have a strong claim to our attention. For Shāfiʿī, *naskh* is an integral aspect of the divine revelatory activity, motivated by a divine desire to alleviate the burdens He had placed upon men.[1] God, in fact, had announced in the Ḳur'ān that He proposed to employ *naskh*. In a series of revelations, He had explained that the regulations of the Ḳur'ān would be replaced only by other Ḳur'ān regulations, and never by the *Sunna* whose role was restricted to the elucidation of the details of the application of the Ḳur'ān's very generally worded statements. Ḳ.10:15 shows that when the unbelievers, not caring for the revelations Muḥammad was bringing them, asked him to bring a different Ḳur'ān, or to change the Ḳur'ān, Muḥammad replied: 'It is not for me to change it on my own initiative. I utter only what is revealed to me and fear the punishment of a dreadful day, if I should disobey my Master.' Muḥammad would have disclaimed any authority to alter any of the divine regulations on his own initiative, for here God had asserted through the medium of His Prophet that the *Sunna* lacked the status to alter any of the Ḳur'ān's provisions. That was exclusively a divine prerogative.

> God erases what He wills and endorses what He wills. With Him is the master copy of all the revelations. [Ḳ.13:39]

Some scholars had interpreted this verse in the sense that God here grants licence to His Prophet to institute regulations under divine guidance on matters not the object of a specific Ḳur'ān revelation. Others held the verse to mean that God erases such regulations as He wills and endorses such regulations as He wills, seeing in the verse, therefore, a divine reference to *naskh*. Shāfiʿī considers this the more likely interpretation and finds its 'confirmation' in Ḳ.2:106: *mā nansakh min āya aw nansa-hā na'ti bi-khairin min-hā aw mithli-hā*. Here again God announces that only the Ḳur'ān can *naskh* (replace) the Ḳur'ān, a motif repeated in Ḳ.16:101: *wa idhā baddalnā āya makāna āya* – 'When *We* substitute one verse for another.'

Shāfi'ī's argument can be summarised as follows:

> In the same way, nothing can *naskh* (replace) the *Sunna* of the Prophet save only another *Sunna* of the Prophet. Thus, were God to reveal to His Prophet something at variance with a *sunna* which Muḥammad had already instituted, Muḥammad would immediately introduce a fresh *sunna* on the lines of what God had now revealed, in order to demonstrate to people that it was this second *sunna* of his which replaced (*naskh*) his earlier, differing *sunna*. Indeed, this principle is itself mentioned in the *Sunna* of the Prophet. Since only Ḳur'ān replaces Ḳur'ān, the Ḳur'ān having no peer (*mithl*) other than the Ḳur'ān, one might ask what evidence there is for the view that in the same way only the *Sunna* may replace (*naskh*) the *Sunna*. The evidence Shāfi'ī insists, is that there are only two primary sources, adherence to which God has formally imposed upon all men: the Ḳur'ān and the *Sunna*. Now, as amidst all the *Ḥadīth* materials in circulation the *Sunna* of the Prophet has no peer (*mithl*) save only another *sunna* of the Prophet, it follows that nothing can *naskh* a *sunna* of the Prophet, save only another *sunna* of the Prophet. The *Ḥadīth* is secondary and subordinate to the *Sunna*.
>
> Furthermore, in any case of the *naskh* of the *Sunna*, Shāfi'ī insists that a replacement *sunna* is invariably transmitted in the form of a *ḥadīth* from the Prophet. As adherence to the *Sunna* of the Prophet has been decreed by God, every replacement *sunna* must have been preserved and handed down. Otherwise, the *sunna* of the Prophet could soon be considerably reduced by mere presumption of *naskh*. On the contrary, *naskh* must always be demonstrated by the production of the alleged replacement *sunna* – for no obligation is ever abandoned without another being promulgated in its place. This may be illustrated by the case of the *ḳibla*: When the Jerusalem *ḳibla* was abandoned [*nusikhat*] the Makkan *ḳibla* was instituted. This need for a replacement regulation applies to every single instance of *naskh* in both the Ḳur'ān and the *Sunna*. Were a *sunna* to be replaced, for example, by a Ḳur'ān revelation, a fresh *sunna* would accompany this revelation, in order to demonstrate that the Prophet's later *sunna* had superseded his earlier *sunna* – so that men should be left in no doubt that only like had superseded like [*mithl*]. To admit, in even only one instance, that the Ḳur'ān had repealed a *sunna* instituted by the Prophet, without a second *sunna*, the replacement of the earlier *sunna* being preserved and transmitted, would enable some to argue the possibility that the relevant *sunna*

> predated the relevant Ḳur'ān verse dealing with the same issue, and that only this Ḳur'ān verse should therefore be considered; or, in certain other instances, where the *Sunna* does not verbally coincide with the Ḳur'ān regulation, it could be alleged that the divine ruling has superseded the *Sunna* ruling. Presumptions of the kind would lead to the abandonment of the *Sunna*, particularly where there happen to be statements in both the Ḳur'ān and the *Sunna*. But the *Sunna* can never be at variance with the Ḳur'ān, since the Prophet ever spoke only in God's name. Wherever a *Sunna* wording does not coincide verbally with the corresponding Ḳur'ān wording, or is more fully worded than the relevant verse, it must be remembered that the Ḳur'ān texts are couched in very general terms which it is the function of the *Sunna* to expand and elucidate, to make God's meaning absolutely clear.

This disquisition should be compared with the following: 'The meaning of *naskh* is: God abandoned an obligation He had earlier imposed.'[2]

The interchangeability of the two definitions of *naskh*: 'abandonment' and 'replacement' will occupy us more fully below.

Shāfi'ī's selection of instances of *naskh* for the analysis which we considered above represented something more than merely the application of the general theory of *naskh*. It will be observed that, in each of those two sets, not only were the two allegedly conflicting texts thought to refer to precisely the same aspect of the same topic, but, in each instance, the pair of texts was derived from a single source. In the first, both texts were statements found in the Ḳur'ān; in the second, both came from the *Sunna*. In other words, his examples represented one of the special theories of *naskh*, namely the theory that the principle of *naskh* applies within the confines of a single source without reference to the documents of the other, or, in its more usual formulation, on occasion the Ḳur'ān supersedes the Ḳur'ān – and only the Ḳur'ān. Similarly, on occasion the *Sunna* supersedes the *Sunna* – but only the *Sunna* can do so. We should note the emphasis: The Ḳur'ān supersedes only the Ḳur'ān, but only the *Sunna* supersedes the *Sunna*.

We have seen that by '*Sunna*', Shāfi'ī understands only the *Sunna* of the Prophet which he set rigorously apart from reports reaching us from all other human beings, the *Ḥadīth*. We shall see hereafter that he sets the *Sunna* of the Prophet rigorously apart also from information reaching us in the Book of God. No information *from whatever quarter* may overrule a report coming from the Prophet. We saw that some of his contemporaries attempted to emphasise the primary role of the Ḳur'ān. Shāfi'ī could not dispute that – no Muslim could – but Shāfi'ī was quick to perceive the anti-*Sunna* motive which lurked beneath it. If pressed, this principle would threaten any *Ḥadīth* which chanced to be more fully worded than the corresponding Ḳur'ān statement, as he also realised. He took it as axiomatic that Ḳur'ān and *Sunna* could never be at variance – for him, both came from God as aspects of the divine revelation. Since 'true conflict' between the two sources can never occur, one must always seek to reconcile Ḳur'ān and *Sunna* by taking both into account in seeking to derive from their joint consideration the full measure of the divine intent. But *naskh* affects only one Ḳur'ān verse considered with another verse, or one *sunna* considered with another *sunna*, and it applies in no other sense. Apparent contradiction between one Ḳur'ān statement and one *sunna* lay quite outside Shāfi'ī's theory of *naskh*, being dealt with in a special theory of exegesis, the theory of *takhṣīṣ* to be examined more fully below.

Two stages in the development of the discussions on *naskh* are discernible: that Ḳur'ān and *Sunna* are each separately susceptible of *naskh*. Shāfi'ī was not concerned in his *Risāla* to establish this broad principle. The general theory of *naskh* had originated before his time – how long before, it is not yet possible to suggest with certainty, since his is the earliest systematic discussion of the subject that has come to light. Shāfi'ī was clearly able to take much for granted, while his introduction of Ḳur'ānic 'proofs' was perfunctory, and, in any event, directed at the establishment of his special viewpoint. He appears to have been the first to develop this view in a series of consistent and quite unambiguous propositions and it has since been linked especially to his name.

Shāfi'ī's special theory of *naskh* provides, therefore, one useful starting-point for our investigation. By nature a negative statement, it implies reaction against a positive view, itself the expression of an earlier, somewhat looser treatment of the source documents, the Ḳur'ān and the *Sunna*, especially the latter, since he lays great emphasis upon the role and function of the Prophet whose utterances cannot be jeopardised by reports as to the views of any of his contemporaries. Muḥammad was a unique figure whose *ḥadīth*s have no peer among the utterances of ordinary mortals. Thus, neither the Ḳur'ān, nor reports from the Companions can supersede any statement emanating from the Prophet.

Whereas there is the appearance, at least in the available sources, of a tolerable consensus on the general theory of *naskh*, there has never been unanimity among the Muslims at the level of the special theories of *naskh*. In his work on *naskh*, Naḥḥās (d. AH 338/AD 949) could already list five different views:[3]

i. Both Ḳur'ān and *Sunna* supersede Ḳur'ān. This view he ascribes to the Kufans, i.e. the Ḥanafiyya.

ii. Ḳur'ān supersedes Ḳur'ān; *Sunna* may not supersede Ḳur'ān. He ascribes this view to Shāfi'ī and 'some who follow him'.

iii. *Sunna* supersedes both *Sunna* and Ḳur'ān.

iv. *Sunna* supersedes *Sunna*; Ḳur'ān does not supersede *Sunna*.

v. An intermediate view, apparently a cautious refusal to adopt the restrictions of a consistent theory: 'Utterances clash and the one should not be judged in the light of the other.' Presumably the relative status of Ḳur'ān and *Sunna* is to be reviewed *de novo* in every instance arising of conflict between the two sources.

The differences highlighted here reflect the methods attributed by the *uṣūlīs* to the *fuḳahā'* in judging of the relative merits of Ḳur'ān and *Sunna* statements on one and the same topic. The differences are fundamental and go far to account, in the eyes of the Muslims, for the far-reaching differences between the *madhāhib* on the details of the *Fiḳh*.

Compared to the volume of literature devoted to the discussion of these special theories of *naskh*, relatively little space, and consequently, relatively little fresh thinking was devoted to the evaluation of the general theory. One might be tempted from this to suppose not merely that the formulation of the general theory had preceded that of the special theories, as it is alleged to be logically prior,[4] but also that the general theory commanded widespread acquiescence throughout the course of the discussions on sources. The discussions had occurred far in advance of the literary treatment of *naskh* in which the documented disputes over the special theories merely underline the absence in the surviving literature of sharp divisions over the general theory.

We noted a cleavage as to the relevance of the *Sunna* on topics not mentioned in the Ḳur'ān;[5] and another on the relevance of the *Sunna* on topics already mentioned in the Ḳur'ān. There had been some who considered that where the Ḳur'ān did make a statement, that sufficed. The triumph of the general thesis of *ahl al-ḥadith* had put an end to such disputes, but only to give rise to another, more acute split on the relative status of *Sunna* and Ḳur'ān source where both had a statement to offer on one and the same topic. What is abundantly clear from the demeanour and arguments of Shāfi'ī is that his major polemic effort was directed against the view that, where the Ḳur'ān did offer a statement, the ruling of the Ḳur'ān must necessarily prevail. His special theory of *naskh* had developed from his conscious opposition to the view that a relevant Ḳur'ān made a relevant *sunna* redundant. He saw that that opinion was reactionary for, since the *Sunna* had been largely the creation of those whose task it had been to furnish the Islamic documentation of those elements of the *Fiḳh* not adumbrated in the Ḳur'ān, any appeal back to the Ḳur'ān threatened the *Fiḳh*. To preserve the *Fiḳh*, Shāfi'ī felt impelled to separate the *Sunna* source from the Ḳur'ān source, treating the *Sunna* where it agreed with the *Fiḳh* as invariably the later of the two source statements.[6] He then defended his view on the basis of considerations which he worked up into a special theory, not of *naskh*, but of *takhṣīṣ*, using as his evidence certain Ḳur'ān statements the import of which both he and all later Islamic scholars tended to distort. Properly understood, those verses serve for the construction of a theory of *naskh* – but a theory of *naskh* which bears very little resemblance to the theory of *naskh* historically elaborated by Muslim scholarship.

The actual function of the general theory of *naskh* in the hands of the scholars was, in fact, to vindicate the 'proven' instances of *naskh* which they individually alleged. If *naskh* were not possible, it would not have occurred.[7]

The function of the special theories of *naskh* was partly to document one *Fiḳh* doctrine in its competition with other views, but mainly it served to guarantee the preservation of the *Fiḳh* in general in the face of criticism voiced by men moved perhaps by the great contemporary debate on the nature of the Ḳur'ān to look again more closely at the actual contents of the Ḳur'ān, that is, to compare the *Fiḳh* with the *muṣḥaf*.

The common impulse which produced both the general and the special theories of *naskh* was recognition of serious conflict between the *Fiḳh* and its putative sources. That was further complicated by recognition of serious differences between the regulations conveyed in the Book of God and those conveyed in the *Sunna*, although both purported to come down from the Prophet. The scholars, we have asserted, were here struggling to reconcile three sources: *Fiḳh*, Ḳur'ān, *Sunna*.

2. The science of *NASKH*

There is an extensive Islamic literature on *naskh* and, at the forefront of most books devoted to this science, a sense of the crucial nature of this particular branch of learning is inculcated by the use of a series of *ḥadīth*s which purport to establish the high antiquity, and hence in the eyes of Tradition-minded Muslims, the high respectability of the science of *naskh* by projecting its cultivation back into the generation of the Prophet's oldest and most determined supporters.

Abū ʿAbdullāh informs us that the reports under this heading are very numerous from which he quotes only a small selection 'to show the solicitude evinced by the Companions for the science of *naskh*, both in its Ḳur'ānic and in its *Sunna* manifestations – which are *but a single concern*.'[8]

For Hibatullāh, the starting-point of the science of *naskh* is 'adherence to what has been handed down from our Islamic past.'[9] The principle commonly enunciated in these introductory exhortations is that none may occupy judicial or religious office in the community who is not equipped with this indispensable knowledge and who is thus incapable of distinguishing *nāsikh* from *mansūkh*. The commonest versions of the *ḥadīth*s feature ʿAlī and relate his expressed dissatisfaction with the performance of *ḳāḍī* (or a *Ḳāṣṣ* – the difference amounting to a single dot in the manuscript). Thus, Abū ʿAbdul Raḥmān al-Sulamī reports that ʿAlī passed a *ḳāḍī* and asked, "Can you distinguish *nāsikh* from *mansūkh*?" The man replying that he did not know the difference, ʿAlī advised the man that he had endangered not only his own soul, but the souls of his listeners.'[10]

Naḥḥās devoted an entire introductory chapter of his work to these traditions, interestingly entitled: 'Stimulating the desire to acquaint oneself with knowledge of *nāsikh* and *mansūkh*'.[11] That might appear to suggest continuing resistance to the general theory, best overcome by exhortations to imitate the practice of the pious forebears. Other versions of the story feature, instead of ʿAlī an ʿAbdullāh – literally any believer, but variously identified as either ibn ʿAbbās or ibn ʿUmar.[12] Concern for the science of *naskh* had thus been expressed by several of the greatest 'authorities' of the past. The reports were designed to give an impression of the unanimity of the Companions who had endorsed the authenticity of the *naskh* principle. But we hear of a breach in the unanimity: ibn ʿAbbās states that ʿUmar said,

> The Ḳur'ān expert among us is Ubayy; the legal expert among us is ʿAlī. We have abandoned certain elements in Ubayy's legal doctrine for he maintains that he will never abandon anything he heard direct from the Prophet, yet God says: *mā nansakh min āya aw nansa-hā na'ti bi-khair min-hā aw mithli-hā*.[13]

The concern shown here is evidently with the Ḳur'ān source. In a doublet to the above, ʿUmar's words refer rather to the Ḳur'ān document: 'We have abandoned certain elements in Ubayy's text for he maintains that he will never abandon anything he heard direct from the Prophet.'[14]

Companions were brought in in this way to endorse the various theories, for the specific purpose of providing validation from the mouths of men believed to have known the Prophet's mind best. Generally speaking it would be immaterial which Companion features in a *ḥadīth*, his role being merely to represent his generation and, by extension, the Prophet. Hence the above reference to an ʿAbdullāh. The defection of Ubayy might therefore be thought an unfortunate breach of the allegedly 'unanimous' Companion endorsement of *naskh*. But the theory of *naskh* had many facets, all of which the Muslims tried to cover with *ḥadīths*. One series was designed, as we have just seen, to deal with the Ḳur'ān as both source and document, for like ourselves, the scholars hoped to have their cake and eat it. Part of the theory of *naskh* had been exploited to resolve and rationalise problems in the literary history of the Ḳur'ān using the same materials that had been exploited in the *Fiḳh* history of the Ḳur'ān. The theory therefore had a role to play also in discussion of the *extent* of the surviving Ḳur'ān texts when the Muslims tried to account for the collection of the texts into the *muṣḥaf*, additional to its role in their discussion of the *content* of the Ḳur'ān and its relevance to the history of the *Fiḳh*. However seemingly unfortunate, therefore, this defection of Ubayy for the alleged Companion-consensus on *naskh*, it was the price that must be paid for the inestimable advantage that his defection would yield elsewhere.[15]

The sayings of the Companions could be adduced by the *uṣūlīs* in support of their proposition that capacity to distinguish the *nāsikh* from the *mansūkh* was no mere desirable academic accomplishment, but an indispensable requisite for salvation as furnishing the sole key to aknowledge of which of the divine requirements can with certainty be identified with the *final* expression of the divine will, and which we may confidently regard as having been abandoned. Thus, to know only the Ḳur'ān will not suffice. This attitude is explicit in Hibatullāh's comment that the man 'Alī rebuked had set himself up as an authority to instruct the people, only to confuse divine commands with divine prohibitions and matters legally indifferent with matters legally prescribed.[16] The wording, which is Ṭabarī's, has been frequently borrowed. The discussions on *naskh* were conducted under the aegis of the certainty that Islam was a divine revelation. It was thus crucial to reach correct conclusions on all matters of Law.

A second *ḥadīth*-series, used in the same interest as the above, features Ḥudhayfa who, on being approached for a *fatwā*, replied, 'Three classes of persons deliver *fatwā*s: he who knows *nāsikh* from *mansūkh*.' They asked, 'Who knows that' He replied, 'Umar; – and a sultan who has no choice but to hand down decisions, and thirdly, an officious pedant.'[17] Ḥudhayfa declined to pronounce a *fatwā*. Naḥḥās has:[18] '. . . a man who knows the *mansūkh* of the Ḳur'ān.' In Hibatullāh's version,[19] the categories are four: an *amīr*; his deputy; he who knows *nāsikh* and *mansūkh*, and a brainless officious pedant.

In making their decisions, the civil authorities may incur the wrath of the scholars, but do at least have the excuse of office. Any other, not having such excuse, who undertakes to make public pronouncements on 'the Law for the Muslims', without expert knowledge of the theories of *naskh*, runs the risk of endangering, not merely his own immortal soul, but those of his followers. *Fiḳh* is a very grave matter, now that Law [*Sunna*] has become commandment [*farḍ*]. 'It was woeful ignorance of the science of *naskh* displayed by the exegetes of his day that induced Hibatullāh to compose his book on the *nāsikh* and the *mansūkh* of the Ḳur'ān.'[20]

Aḥmad b. Ḥanbal and Isḥāḳ b. Ibrāhīm al-Ḥanẓalī both said:[21] 'He who does not know the 'sound' from the 'unsound' *ḥadīth* or cannot tell the *nāsikh* from the *mansūkh* is no scholar.'

3. *NASKH* IN THE *SUNNA*

The *uṣūlīs* were able to give the appearance of justifying the application of *naskh* to the Ḳur'ān by reference to statements made in the Ḳur'ān. No generally accepted statements can be adduced from the *Sunna* to vindicate the application of the theory to the *Sunna* texts. It is therefore implied that that is based on the analogy of the Ḳur'ān.

> The *ḥadīth* of the Prophet is like the Ḳur'ān – one part supersedes another. Part of the *ḥadīth* of the Prophet used to replace another part, just as part of the Ḳur'ān used to replace another part.
>
> ʿUrwa declared, 'I testify that my father told me that the Prophet would make a statement, then subsequently replace it with another statement, just as the Ḳur'ān, in certain places, supersedes other parts.'[22]

An unsuccessful attempt was made to project a like statement back to the Prophet: a man reports from his father that ibn ʿUmar reported the Prophet's words, 'Some of my *ḥadīth*s supersede others.'

But the *isnād* is not regarded as credit-worthy by the *Ḥadīth* specialists. Djaʿbarī accepted the report, although it is a *maḳṭūʿ* of ibn ʿUmar's only. Ignoring the specialists' reservations on the *isnād*, he therefore draws from the report a statement on the *naskh* of the *Sunna* which, for him, carries the Prophet's authority, notwithstanding this weakness of the lower part of the *isnād*. He thus alleged both divine sanction for the application of *naskh* to the Ḳur'ān, based on Ḳ.2:106; and Prophetic sanction for its application to the *Sunna*.[23] Shāfiʿī had done as much, but unhappily, neglected to quote the relevant *ḥadīth*.[24] Thus, not only were certain Ḳur'ān verses seen as rendering certain other verses redundant; certain *sunna*s were also seen as rendering certain other *sunna*s redundant.

The mere existence of the above reports suggests the novelty of the argument they represent. It would not, in fact be advanced until reference to *ḥadīth*s from the Prophet became a regular feature of the documentation of the *Fiḳh*, replacing the tendency to adduce the *ḥadīth*s from the Companions. That development had removed one ready means of harmonising *ḥadīth* conflict by insisting on giving the preference in all cases in which *ḥadīth*s from Companions conflicted with *ḥadīth*s from the Prophet, to those reported from the Prophet. When, more and more the *ḥadīth*s are being attributed to the Prophet but continue to clash, appeal to a principle of *naskh* becomes inescapable. This reference of the *ḥadīth*s to the Prophet did not become the general practice until after Shāfiʿī's time – largely owing to his tireless campaigns – and his works show the considerable advance that had already been made in the application of the theory of *naskh* to the *Sunna* of the Prophet in case of conflict.

Having once accepted that *naskh* was a device resorted to, on occasion, by the divine author in His direct revelations, the Muslims found it as easy to accept that He might resort to it also, on occasion, in His indirect revelation. Here is yet another instance of appeal to the

Ḳur'ān to substantiate a thesis of the Traditionists. The effect intended was to guard against the rejection of all the *ḥadīths* on the excuse that far too many of them were mutually contradictory and that their use might court the risk of error. We know that to have been the view of some of the *Mu'tazila* who went further: *ḥadīths* not only contradicted each other, some of them were even at variance with the rulings of the Ḳur'ān.[25]

As with Shāfi'ī, appeal to the general theory of *naskh* arises in the case of Hamadhānī's *ḥadīths* not prior to, or in anticipation of, but rather, in defence of and so posterior to the appeal to the special theories of *naskh*.

4. The 'modes' of *NASKH*

If, as for the most part Western scholars still think, *naskh* had only one connotation, that of 'supersession', then only this one kind of *naskh* would be found to be discussed in the Islamic literature on *naskh*. That would be the alleged replacement of one Ḳur'ānic ruling by another in instances in which both Ḳur'ānic wordings are still to be found in the *muṣḥaf*. But this is only one 'mode', known in the jargon of the *uṣūlīs* as: *naskh al-ḥukm dūna 'l-tilāwa*. This formula makes sense only if translated: the suppression of an earlier ruling without, however, the suppression of the earlier wording. That is, it cannot be translated: the supersession of an earlier ruling without, however, the supersession of the earlier wording. The whole point of the theory lies in the allegation that the earlier verse has, indeed, been superseded.

This has to be stressed to bring out the confusion that can attend the unwary reader. One must remain alert to the extreme subtlety and complexity of these Muslim discussions.

In fact, three 'modes' are discussed in the literature.[26] In addition to the above formula, one meets also:

naskh al-ḥukm wa-'l-tilāwa: the suppression of both a Ḳur'ān wording and the ruling it conveyed.

naskh al-tilāwa dūna 'l-ḥukm: the suppression of a Ḳur'ān wording, but not of the ruling it conveyed.

This presentation of the three-fold modality of *naskh* may suggest merely the development of an originally simple idea at the hands of scholars with a marked penchant for theoretical tidiness and 'a horror of the "unexplored avenue"' and it has, in fact, been described as just that.[27] On the contrary, we shall find on investigating the evidence presented by the literature, that it is this three-sided structure of the theory which will most easily come apart, revealing an artificial theoretical construction built from materials derived from a number of disciplines, not originally connected save in one respect only: apparent conflict between the three sources of *Fiḳh*, Ḳur'ān and *Sunna*. Further, it should also be noted that the three-fold modality of *naskh* has never been unanimously conceded.[28]

We propose to pursue the stages leading up to the development of this admirably articulated theory, tracing the arguments for and against each of its three elements and uncovering the bases on which they were severally thought to rest, until finally we identify the successive phases of accretion by which the three 'modes' were slowly – and inevitably – brought together under the unifying rubric of *naskh*. We will attempt to suggest the reasons for the adoption of the term *naskh* itself to express the technical senses which the word has been made to bear and in which it united originally quite independent academic theorems.

THE FIRST 'MODE' of *NAS<u>KH</u>*

1. *NAS<u>KH</u> AL-ḤUKM WA-'L-TILĀWA*

The first of the three 'modes' of *nas<u>kh</u>* – the suppression of both a Ḳur'ān wording and the ruling it conveyed – alleges the loss of some part of the documents of the direct revelation, the Ḳur'ān. If materials which had once formed part of the documents of the divine revelation have been irrecoverably lost, neither the wording nor the ruling surviving, there would presumably be no reliable means of our knowing that they had been lost, or indeed, that they had ever existed. Quite apart from the use in the rubric of the term '*tilāwa*', this first mode of *nas<u>kh</u>* can refer only to the operation of *nas<u>kh</u>* upon the Ḳur'ān texts. Admittedly, neither '*tilāwa*' nor the root *ḳ r'* was, according to the scholars, restricted exclusively to references to the Ḳur'ān, although it is patent that this argument, wherever used, is always tendentious.[1]

But, had both the words and the ruling of a *ḥadīth* been suppressed, the *ḥadīth* would quite simply have been non-existent. *Ḥadīth*s either exist or not; they are either accepted or not. Where a *ḥadīth* text survives, yet the *sunna* it embodies is not accorded general recognition, this is usually rationalised as indicating some dissatisfaction with the *isnād*. The extreme instance of critical reserve towards a *ḥadīth* is the attitude adopted by most to the *<u>kh</u>abar al-wāḥid* (although the precise meaning of the term is not always clear to the scholars). However, to attract any attention in the literature, a *ḥadīth* must, at the very least, exist. No *ḥadīth* therefore satisfies the conditions of the first mode of *nas<u>kh</u>* which must, therefore, refer exclusively to the Ḳur'ān.

Various criteria of 'soundness' were applied to the *Ḥadīth* reports which were classified according to their 'spread' – the number and the quality of their transmitters. On the contrary, a transmitted document was either flatly admitted to be a Ḳur'ān or it was not. There are no degrees of 'Ḳur'ān-ness'. The test of a Ḳur'ān must, one therefore can assert with full confidence, be its inclusion in the *muṣḥaf* – unless both its wording and its ruling have been 'suppressed'. The first mode of *nas<u>kh</u>* thus made its first appearance in the course of the discussions on the extent of the surviving Ḳur'ān. Allegations would be made that a particular set of words, not now present in the *muṣḥaf*, had once stood in the Ḳur'ān, or, at least had once actually been revealed to the Prophet. They had then, for some reason, either been omitted from the corpus of revealed texts later collected into the *muṣḥaf*, or somehow lost or mislaid before the texts were finally brought together. The presence in the theory of this first mode of *naskh* underlines the Muslim belief that the *muṣḥaf* is incomplete relative to the body of divine revelations historically communicated to the Prophet. A belief in the incompleteness of the *muṣḥaf* is easy to explain: it stemmed from the Ḳur'ān, or rather, since one must always be careful in the choice of expressions, it can be traced to the interpretation of statements in the Ḳur'ān which appear to suggest the possibility of the Prophet's forgetting parts of the revelation, or rather, of his being caused to forget certain (unspecified) portions of the revelation. For example, Ḳ.87:6–7 reads:

> We shall teach you to recite it and you will never forget it – except what God wills. *sanuḳri'uka fa-lā tansā illā mā shā'a 'llāhu . . .*

From this wording, some Muslims concluded that Muḥammad would assuredly forget certain portions of the Ḳur'ān, for whatever God wills will inevitably occur. Their consolation lay in their noting that Muḥammad would not forget the Ḳur'ān from mere carelessness nor from mere human frailty. The Ḳur'ān, they thought, very clearly states that the final form of the revelation will be determined by its divine author. Muḥammad's humanity had not frustrated the divine plans.[2] The *muṣḥaf* is incomplete, in the sense that not everything that was once revealed to Muḥammad is to be found today in our *muṣḥaf*. The Ḳur'ān, however, is complete, in the sense that everything that God intends us to find in the *muṣḥaf* we shall find there, for whatever God intended to include, He made sure to preserve:

> We it is Who have revealed the Reminder, and We shall certainly preserve it. [Ḳ.15:9]

This positive statement was *thought* to be reinforced by the implied negative of Ḳ.17:86:

> If We wish to We can easily take away what We have revealed to you

although, exegesis being what it is, some argued that Ḳ.17:86 is an implied positive, linked to Ḳ.87.

The Muslim view that the *muṣḥaf* is incomplete was not, however, arrived at without the most determined experimentation as the scholars engaged in hammering out a means of expressing a wide range of accepted 'facts' and beliefs which had first to be reconciled with the notion of the *muṣḥaf*'s incompleteness, for since this was alleged to be derived from the Ḳur'ān itself, it could not be challenged. It was therefore argued, from Ḳ.87, that Muḥammad had forgotten parts of the Ḳur'ān. That was, however, only one interpretation far from being universally conceded in the early period.[3]

In the *Ḥadīth* literature, two distinct orders of phenomenon are reported which are dependent upon the two distinctly opposed attitudes to the interpretation of Ḳ.87. These are, respectively, the removal of revealed matter from the Prophet and his Companions by the simple natural failure of the human memory; and loss of revealed matter occasioned by the miraculous intervention of the divine author Himself.

> The Prophet had instructed [*aḳra'*] ʿAbdullāh b. Masʿūd in the recitation of a revelation which ʿAbdullāh both got by heart and recorded in his personal *muṣḥaf*. At night, ʿAbdullāh found that he could not recall the passage which he had wished to incorporate into his prayers. In the morning he therefore consulted his notes – only to find the page blank! He informed the Prophet of this and Muḥammad replied, 'That passage was withdrawn last night.'[4]

ʿĀ'isha reports:

> The Prophet heart a man recite in the mosque and said, 'God have mercy on that fellow! He has reminded me of such-and-such a verse from *sūra* so-and-so.'[5]

In a parallel version, an addition states that the Prophet said,

> 'I had dropped them [*asḳaṭṭuhunna*] from *sūra* so-and-so.'

Considerable effort and ingenuity have been expended in the commentaries to avoid any suggestion that the Prophet and the Companions had been capable of forgetting the revelations. Forgetting Ḳur'ān was now regarded as highly reprehensible. The Prophet is alleged to have said, 'No man learns the Ḳur'ān then forgets it, except in punishment of some grievous sin, for God says in His Book, "Whatever misfortune befalls you it is in requital for what your hands have earned." '[6] The sins of his community were paraded before him and Muḥammad thought none more heinous than forgetting Ḳur'ān.

Failing to understand how one could forget the Ḳur'ān, the later Muslims put that down to neglect of religious duty. Given the doctrine of the sinlessness of prophets, already emerging in Shāfiʿī's day,[7] the fate of *ḥadīths* such as those cited by Bukhārī, was harmonisation.

> It is possible that a thing is forbidden or regarded as indifferent, depending upon the circumstances. Where forgetting the Ḳur'ān results from pre-occupation with other religious duties, such as holy war, a man may say, 'I have forgotten verse so-and-so.' His forgetting was not caused by neglect. This is how any such utterances reported from the Prophet should be viewed. It is only those whose forgetting resulted from pre-occupations of a secular nature who may not use this expression.[8]

Ḥadīths to the effect that the Prophet not only could forget, but had admitted forgetting parts of the Ḳur'ān, having entered into the

Sunna, were never quite overcome by the doctrine of the sinlessness of the Prophet Muḥammad. *Ḥadīths* deploring the forgetting of the Ḳur'ān were part of the early campaign against neglect of the sacred texts. *Ḥadīths* reporting Muḥammad's forgetting the Ḳur'ān were part of the campaign in support of one of the *tafsīrs* of Ḳ.87. That much is clear from Bukhārī's incorporating Ḳ.87 into the wording of his chapter-heading, while the manner in which the verse is there used enables ibn Ḥadjar to conclude that this showed that Bukhārī was himself among those who understood that Muḥammad would never forget any of the revelations made to him – except those which God willed him to forget, i.e. that Muḥammad did forget parts of the Ḳur'ān.

The opposing exegesis inclined, on the contrary, to regard Ḳ.87:6–7, not as a negative, but as a prohibitive: 'Do not forget, except what God wills.' As this makes less logical sense, work was done to establish that, in Arabic, the root *n s y* has meanings other than 'forgetting'. One alternative meaning is 'abandoning'. The exceptive clause, 'except what God wills' also attracted much discussion and Farrā' took the view that it is not an exceptive, but merely a pious formula analogous to 'if God wills' [*in shā'a 'llāh*]. Nothing has been excepted and nothing needs to be added to: 'You will not forget.' Nothing of the Ḳur'ān was ever forgotten by Muḥammad.[9]

Both Ḥasan and Ḳatāda explained the particle '*illā*': 'except what God wills to withdraw from public recitation – in which event, Muḥammad will be divinely caused to forget the wording.' This is to make of: *naskh al-ḥukm wa-'l-tilāwa*: *naskh al-tilāwa li-adjli naskh al-ḥukm* – Muḥammad would be caused to forget the wording so that the ruling could be suppressed.

ibn ʿAbbās was credited with the interpretation: except what God wills to cause Muḥammad to forget so that he might then establish a *sunna*. 'I forget – or I am caused to forget – in order to introduce a *sunna*.'[10] This might mean that the Ḳur'ān which might be withdrawn by divine decree could have been replaced by a *sunna* on the same topic, *naskh al-Ḳur'ān bi-'l-Sunna*; or Muḥammad had laid down the precedent of what one should do, in the event that one was forgetful – at prayer, for example, the remedies for which were naturally traced to the *Sunna*, or 'practice' of the Prophet.[11]

Finally, to get away altogether from this troublesome concept of the Prophet's forgetting revelation, yet another meaning was suggested for the Arabic root *n s y*: 'to leave'. Ḳ.87 could now be explained as meaning: 'You, Muḥammad, will not leave off basing your practice on the Ḳur'ān source – except where God wills to *naskh* the Ḳur'ān, in which case alone will you leave off basing your actions on its rulings.'

To the proponents of Muḥammad's forgetting the Ḳur'ān, this is *naskh al-ḥukm wa-'l-tilāwa*. To the outright opponents of the idea that Muḥammad could ever have forgotten anything of the Ḳur'ān, it is, however, *naskh al-ḥukm dūna 'l-tilāwa*.[12]

The 'Ā'isha *ḥadīth* cited earlier, comes in a variant:

> The Prophet heard a man recite a *sūra* by night and said, 'God have mercy upon him! he has reminded me of verse so-and-so which I had been caused to forget from *sūra* such-and-such.'[13]

The commentator rightly regards *unsītuhā* as the *tafsīr* of *asḳaṭṭuhunna*, cited above. 'Presumably, his expression, "I had dropped them from *sūra* such-and-such," means, "I had *accidentally* dropped them."'[14]

ibn Ḥadjar goes so far as to imply that as 'I had dropped them' may perhaps have sounded rather strong for certain ears, it had had to be toned down. It was then further modified to bring it into line with theological perceptions by removing any suggestion that the Prophet had attributed the act of forgetting to himself, it being God alone Who is the true agent in human actions which He alone creates – hence the causative passive of: *unsītuhā*. What ibn Ḥadjar suspects of *asḳaṭṭuhunna* is true equally of *nasītu*. The need 'to tone it down' provided the occasion for the reading: *unsītuhā*.

The commentators proceeded to classify the Prophet's admissions that he had forgotten Ḳur'ān into distinct categories:

i. The type of (human) forgetting where, however, he quickly recalls what he had forgotten by reason of human frailty. Muḥammad had allegedly said, 'I am human and forget as you forget,' (and, when I do forget, then remind me).

ii. Forgetting resulting from God's withdrawing from Muḥammad's memory materials whose public recital God purposed to suppress. This was said to be the force of the exceptive of Ḳ.87.

The classifications represent the old exegeses of Ḳ.87. The first insisted on distinguishing 'forgetting' from *naskh*, arguing that Muḥammad's 'lapses' had been merely temporary. The other rationalised Muḥammad's forgetting as one of the modes of *naskh*. As, given the first construction, Muḥammad soon calls to mind what he had forgotten, his forgetting may be ignored. Further, we have the divine reassurance delivered in Ḳ.15:9. No part of the Ḳur'ān has been lost. The second construction attributed the Prophet's forgetting of the Ḳur'ān to divine action, seen by its proponents to have been foreshadowed in Ḳ.2:106 '*mā nansakh min āya aw nansa-hā*' (more commonly read *aw nunsi-hā*). 'Whatever verse We *naskh* or cause you to forget . . .'

That there were those who insisted on distinguishing Muḥammad's forgetting from *naskh* is guaranteed by the report that

> the Prophet omitted a verse while praying.[15] Completing the prayer, he asked, 'Is Ubayy in the mosque?' Ubayy spoke up. 'Why didn't you prompt me" asked Muḥammad. 'I thought the

verse had been suppressed,' answered Ubayy. 'It wasn't suppressed,' insisted Muḥammad, 'I merely forgot it for the moment.'

Thaʿlabī painstakingly commented on this *ḥadīth*:

> It is possible to hold that the Prophet forgot that which God, not willing to endorse its inclusion in the *muṣḥaf*, wills him to forget. But ordinary human forgetting is an affliction from which the Prophet was protected until he had effected the communication to others of what had been revealed to him. Equally, after effecting its communication, he was divinely protected from forgetting, except where one of the Companions had got by heart what had been communicated.[16]

This is not a discussion of 'memory', but of the integrity of the Ḳur'ān revelations. That the divine revelations are divinely protected is driven home by a comment of Ḳasṭallānī's:[17] in the Yunīnī recension of the ʿĀ'isha report, the text reads: 'God has reminded me of verse so-and-so . . .' The word 'God' would appear, in addition, to have been penned in red ink. If only God causes Muḥammad to forget the Ḳur'ān, then, presumably, it is only proper that God should remind him.

The ʿĀ'isha *ḥadīth* could never, in any case, be used to establish the suppression of that part of the Ḳur'ān which the Prophet is alleged to have forgotten – since he was immediately reminded of it. We have seen that some preferred to separate forgetting [Ḳ.87] from *naskh* [Ḳ.2], i.e. there was a residual exegetical dispute as to whether the two contexts were even connected. The attempt to argue that they were not and that each verse treated of a discrete phenomenon was doomed to fail owing to the fortuitous circumstance that Ḳ.2 and Ḳ.87 shared the same vocabularly, each using the root *n s y* – more, Ḳ.2:106 associated the two roots *n s y* and *n s kh*. Ubayy who represents the effort to keep Ḳ.87 separate from Ḳ.2 must be presumed to have accepted the principle of *naskh* on this occasion, since here, his information was endorsed by the Prophet [cf. p. 38].

That there was the intimate connection we allege between discussions on Muḥammad's memory and discussions on the phenomenon of *naskh*, is confirmed by our finding both the topic of joint discussion before the end of the second century. This occurs in the *tafsīr* of Ḳ.2:106, the verse which apparently had long served as Ḳur'ānic 'proof' of the reality of the phenomenon:

> *mā nansakh min āya aw nunsi-hā*: the majority of the Reciters regard this '*nunsi*' as derived from *n s y*, meaning 'to forget'. Indeed, ʿAbdullāh recited it: *mā nunsika*, while Sālim read: *nunsika-hā*. Both are readings which reinforce the 'forgetting' interpretation. *Naskh* means: acting on the basis of an *āya* until another *āya* is revealed to form the 'basis of the practice', the first *āya* being then abandoned.

Here, *n s y* has one of two aspects:

1. to leave undisturbed: i.e., not *naskh*ing it, as in Ḳ.9:67: *nasū 'llāha fa-nasiya-hum* – they ignored God so He has ignored them.
2. to forget, as in Ḳ.18:24: 'Call to mind your Maker when you forget.'[18]

The two 'aspects' of the root *n s y* yield two meanings: 1. forgetting, i.e. suppression of wording and ruling. 2. overlooking, i.e. suppression of the ruling, and not of the wording, which is 'left undisturbed' to survive in the *muṣḥaf*.

In support of the 'forgetting' exegesis, Farrā' reproduces the *ḥadīth* of the Prophet's hearing the man recite in the mosque. His version reads' 'God have mercy on that fellow *for his having reminded me* of verses which I had been caused to forget.'

That exegesis was already exerting pressure on the reading of the Ḳur'ān texts is instanced by the two alleged ancient 'readings' adduced by Farrā' which preclude meanings other than 'forgetting'. Farrā' found additional 'evidence' in the *ḥadīth* for the 'forgetting' *tafsīr*. But that *ḥadīth* could not originally have had any connection with the scholarly theorising on *naskh*, since the suggestion that it had been possible for the Prophet to forget verses, and then be reminded of them, might be exploited in a dispute as to the exegesis of Ḳ.87. It does nothing, however, to confirm Muḥammad's forgetting *irrecoverably* any revealed matter, so that it could not be collected into the *muṣḥaf*, which is the very essence of *naskh al-tilāwa wa-'l-ḥukm*.

'Confirmation' of this mode of *naskh* is finally provided from the Ḳur'ān itself, once Ḳ.2:106 had been suitably amended by the affixing of the personal objective suffix to 'clarify' the meaning of: *mā nansakh min āya aw nunsi-hā*. Reading: *nunsika/nunsika-hā* refers the verse instantly to the Prophet and links Ḳ.2:106 indissolubly to Ḳ.87, or Ḳ.87 to Ḳ.2:106.

2. Reported loss of Ḳur'ān material

It is clear that there was an ancient pre-literary *tafsīr* which both exerted pressure on the reading of the Ḳur'ān texts and provided fertile soil for the cultivation of *ḥadīth*-reports. ibn ʿUmar reports:

> Two men recited a *sūra* [unspecified] which the Prophet had taught them to recite [*aḳra'*] and which they had been in the habit of reciting. One night, they stood up to pray, but could not recall a syllable. Next morning, they repaired first thing to the Prophet and informed him of what had happened. He replied, 'That *sūra* is part of what has been withdrawn [*nusikha*] – so pay no further heed to it.'[19]

We met above the representative *ḥadīth* showing the extreme development of the notion that certain passages of the Ḳur'ān had been not merely 'mislaid' or otherwise 'lost', but deliberately removed by miraculous intervention not only from the memories of the Muslims, but even from their written sources. Immediate and spectacular divine intervention is the subject of numerous reports. As revealed material was 'lost' by miraculous action, the prodigious memories of the Arabs become irrelevant for the preservation of the revelations. These losses had occurred following communication by the Prophet and equally striking was his admonition that the Muslims dismiss the removed material from their minds. Both wording and ruling had ceased to be of any account.

Anas reports, 'In the lifetime of the Prophet we used to recite a *sūra* as long as Ḳ.9, but all I now recall of it is one single verse.'[20] This report would represent the loss of a hundred and twenty-eight 'verses' at a stroke. As for Ḳ.9 itself, Ḥudhayfa stated, 'You don't recite a quarter of the *sūra*.'[21] That disposes of another three hundred verses.

Even more striking is ibn 'Umar's warning:[22] 'Let none of you say, "I have the whole Ḳur'ān." How does he know what the whole Ḳur'ān is? Much of the Ḳur'ān has vanished [*dhahaba*]. Rather let him say, "I have what is extant." '

We even know the 'wording' of 'lost' Ḳur'ān verses:

> Ubayy asked Zirr, 'How many verses do you reckon in Ḳ.33? Zirr replied, 'Seventy-two or three.' Ubayy declared, 'It used to be as long as Ḳ.2, and we used to recite in Ḳ.33 the stoning-verse.' Zirr asked what the stoning-verse was, and Ubayy 'recited': 'If the shaykh and shaykha fornicate, stone them outright, as an exemplary punishment from God. God is mighty, wise.'[23]

There are today two hundred and eighty-six verses in Ḳ.2, so we would appear to have lost a further two hundred and thirteen verses from Ḳ.33.

Umāma b. Sahl's aunt said, 'The Prophet instructed us [*aḳra'*] to recite the stoning-verse: "the *shaykh* and the *shaykha* stone them outright, in requital of the pleasure they took." '[24]

Abū Wāḳid said,

> It was the Prophet's custom when revelation came upon him to instruct us [*aḳra'*] in some of what had been revealed to him. I came to him once and he said, 'God says: "We sent down property for the upkeep of prayer and the giving of *zakāt*. Were ibn Ādam to possess one *wādī*, he would earnestly desire a second. Were he to have it, he would desire a third – nothing fills the maw of ibn Ādam but dust. But God forgives him who repents." '[25]

Ubayy said,

> The Prophet said to me, 'God commands me to teach you the Ḳur'ān [*aḳra'*].' Muḥammad recited: 'The ingrates of the people of the Book and the *mushrik*s . . .' The verse continues, '. . . were

ibn Ādam to ask for and receive a *wādī* of property, we would ask for a second, on receiving which, he would ask for a third. Nothing fills the maw of ibn Ādam but dust. But God relents to him who repents. The true religion in God's sight is the *Ḥanīfiyya* – not Judaism nor Christianity. Whoso does good, it will not go unthanked.'[26]

Abū Mūsā reports the revelation of a *sūra* similar to Ḳ.9. It was later 'retracted' [*rufiʿat*] but he could still recall one passage:

'God will assist this religion with folk who have no share in the Hereafter. Were ibn Ādam to possess two *wādī*s of property, he would hanker after a third. Nothing will fill the maw of ibn Ādam but dust. God relents to him who repents.'[27]

In the *Djawāb* of *al Bādjī*, we read the following:

al-Bazzār relates a *ḥadīth* from Burayda who stated: 'I heard the Prophet recite "ibn Ādam" at prayer.' The men named in the *isnād* are trust-worthy. The verse was part of *sūrat Yūsuf*.

Aḥmad relates an ibn ʿAbbās *ḥadīth*, in the course of which he says, 'Were ibn Ādam to have two *wādī*s of property, he would desire a third. Nothing will fill the maw of ibn Ādam but dust. God relents to him who repents.' ʿUmar asked, 'What is this?' and ibn ʿAbbās replied, 'Ubayy taught me to recite this [*aḳra'*].' ʿUmar took ibn ʿAbbās along to confront Ubayy to whom ʿUmar said, 'We don't say this.' Ubayy assured ʿUmar that the Prophet had taught him to recite it, [*aḳra'*]. ʿUmar asked, 'Shall I write it into the *muṣḥaf*?' Ubayy said, 'Yes.'[28]

The incident was said to have occurred before the copying of the so-called "ʿUthmān *muṣḥaf*s' on the basis of which 'the practice was established'. Ubayy has been represented both as refusing 'to abandon anything he had heard direct from the Prophet' and as the most enthusiastic to collect 'all the Ḳur'ān'. ʿUmar said, 'Ubayy is more persistent than any of us in reciting what has been "retracted"'.[29]

Bukhārī, however, also reports Ubayy himself as saying: 'We used to imagine that "ibn Ādam" was part of the Ḳur'ān until Ḳ.102 was revealed.'[30]

This means that, despite what was said above about the Prophet's having 'recited' 'ibn Ādam' at prayer – the hallmark of a Ḳur'ānic revelation – and that the 'verse' had formed part of the 'original' Ḳ.12, it had never, in fact, been part of the Ḳur'ān text nor revealed to the Prophet as such. It had been only part of the exegesis of Ḳ.102.

The different statements recorded here show once more that there were two sides to the argument over the possibility that Ḳur'ān material has been lost.

Abū Mūsā reports,

We used to recite a *sūra* which we likened to one of the '*musabbiḥāt*' but we have forgotten it [or, we have been caused to forget it]. However, I remember from it the following: 'Ye who believe! do not say that which you will not do lest there be written a testimony about your necks and you be asked about it on the Day of Judgment.'[31]

ʿUmar said, 'We used to recite, "Do not deny your fathers, that would be ingratitude on your part."' He then asked Zaid b. Thābit if that were not the case, and Zaid confirmed what ʿUmar had said.[32]

ʿUmar asked ʿAbdul Raḥmān b. ʿAwf, 'Don't you find among what was revealed, "Strive, as you strove at the first"? for we cannot now find it.' ʿAbdul Raḥmān replied, 'That is among those parts of the Ḳur'ān which have fallen out.' [*usḳiṭat fī mā usḳiṭa min al-Ḳur'ān*][33]

Maslama b. Khālid asked, 'Tell me of the two *āya*s of the *Ḳur'ān* which were not included in the *muṣḥaf*.' They could not, although Abū 'l-Kunūd Saʿd b. Mālik was among those questioned. Maslama resumed,

Those who have believed and have left their tribes and striven in the cause of God with their wealth and their lives, hear now the glad tidings! Ye it is who have succeeded. And those who sheltered them and assisted them and strove in their defence against those who have incurred the wrath of God – soul cannot divine what joys have been treasured up for them for what they did.[34]

Anas is reported in both *Ṣaḥīḥ*s to have stated,

There was revealed concerning those slain at Bi'r Maʿūna a Ḳur'ān which we recited until it was retracted [*rufiʿa*]. 'Inform our tribe on our behalf that we have met out Lord Who has been well satisfied with us and has satisfied our wants.'[35]

In his *Nāsikh wa mansūkh*, al-Ḥusain b. al-Manārī states:[36]

Among those parts of the Ḳur'ān whose records have been retracted [*rufiʿa*] yet whose remembrance has not been retracted, are to be reckoned the two *sūra*s of supplication in the *witr*, known as *sūrat al Khalʿ* and *sūrat al-Ḥafd*.

This statement rationalises reports that the two '*Sūra*s', not found in our *muṣḥaf*, the so-called *muṣḥaf* of ʿUthmān, had been recorded in 'the codex of Ubayy'.[27]

That certain of the *Sunnī* scholars reserved their position on this *naskh al-ḥukm wa-'l-tilāwa*, or 'omissions from the Ḳur'ān', is shown by Makkī's remark.[38]

It is conceivable that God retract the entire Ḳur'ān by removing it from the memories of His creatures and withdrawing its regulations without replacement. There are many reports to this effect from the Prophet while it is further indicated by Ḳ.17:86: 'If We wish to, We can remove what We have revealed to you.' Something of the sort occurred, judging by what has been reported about Ḳ.33. But the knowledge of this kind of thing derives exclusively from *ḥadīth* reports, and God knows best whether it is 'sound'.

3. DATING THE 'LOSS' OF REVEALED MATTER

'Ā'isha stated, 'Ḳ.33 was recited in the lifetime of the Prophet as consisting of two hundred verses. When 'Uthmān copied out the *muṣḥaf*, we could not produce more than the *sūra* now contains' [i.e. the present 73 verses].[39]

Ḥumaida reports,

> In his eightieth year, my father recited to me the following verses from the 'codex of 'Ā'isha': 'God and His angels bless the Prophet! Ye who believe! bless him also and give him a pure greeting and greet also those who pray in the foremost ranks. She added, 'That was before [*ḳabla*][40] 'Uthmān changed the *muṣḥaf*s.[41]

'Uthmān, usually credited with having 'copied' [*n s kh*] the *muṣḥaf*, is here accused of having 'changed' it [*ghayyara*].

The celebrated *ḥadīth* in which 'Ā'isha placed the 'loss' of certain 'Ḳur'ān materials' into the period following the death of the prophet was to cause the scholars untold difficulties.[42] Perhaps the least impressive of the attempts to rehabilitate her report is the following:

> We were too occupied with the preparations in the Prophet's sick-room to give any thought to the safe-keeping of the sheets on which the revelations had been written out, and while we were tending our patient, a household animal got in from the yard and gobbled up some of the sheets which were kept below the bedding.[43]
>
> Those who would account for all events here below in terms of divine agency could see in this most unfortunate mishap nothing incongruous with the divine promise, having revealed the Reminder, to preserve it. Here, indeed, was the working of the divine purpose. Others, perceiving a contradiction, subjected 'Ā'isha's report to prodigies of *ta'wīl*, with the conscious objective of removing the loss of these verses into the period before the Prophet's death. In either event, their removal, as an aspect of the divine revelatory procedures had been determined by God and had occurred under effective divine control. Having determined that these 'verses' would not appear in the final draft of His Book, God had arranged for their removal. The revelation was never, at any time, at the mercy of accidental forces.

4. ḲUR'ĀN AND *MUṢḤAF*

A delegation waited upon ibn 'Abbās, cousin and supporter of 'Alī. They next called upon Muḥammad b. al-Ḥanafiyya, son of 'Alī and himself a figurehead in the Shī'a's claims on behalf of the Holy Family. To the question of whether Muḥammad 'had left anything', each of these notables had replied in his turn that the Prophet had not left 'more than is between the two covers', i.e. of the *muṣḥaf*. ibn Ḥadjar comments:[44] 'Muḥammad did not exclude from the *muṣḥaf* any part of the Ḳur'ān which ought to be publicly recited at prayer.' He thus read the report as denying the existence outwith the *muṣḥaf* of Ḳur'ān materials which ought properly to be included. There is, however, Ḳur'ān matter which quite properly has been excluded from the *muṣḥaf*, since only what may be publicly recited at prayer should be included in the texts. His interpretation of the *ḥadīth* is 'confirmed' by the reports which mention Ḳur'ān materials revealed but subsequently 'retracted'. Some 'verses' had been retracted only in respect of their wording with no effect for the validity of the rulings in the *Fiḳh*. One instance of this category of 'verse' would be the *Fiḳh*'s stoning penalty for adultery, derived from the 'stoning-verse', once revealed to the Prophet but, according to 'Umar, retracted in respect of its wording alone.

Other verses had been retracted in respect of both their wording and their ruling. Examples in this category would be the Anas *ḥadīth* on the verse revealed about the Bi'r Ma'ūna martyrs. There is also Ubayy's remark on the original length of Ḳ.33 and Ḥudhayfa's on the length of Ḳ.9. These are all 'sound' *ḥadīth* reports. Two classes of revealed matter have been thus omitted from the *muṣḥaf*:

i. The 'stoning-verse': *naskh al-tilāwa dūna 'l-ḥukm*; and

ii. The other reports: *naskh al-tilāwa wa-'l-ḥukm*.

The Ḳāḍī Abū Bakr has stated:

> The entirety of the revealed Ḳur'ān which God commanded to be recorded in writing and which He did not suppress and whose wording He did not withdraw following its revelation to the Prophet is this which is between the two covers of the 'Uthmān *muṣḥaf*.[45]

Only revealed matter unaffected by two modes of *naskh*: *naskh al-ḥukm wa-'l-tilāwa*, and *naskh al-tilāwa dūna 'l-ḥukm* has been included in our *muṣḥaf*, which in consequence, contains only instances of *naskh al-ḥukm dūna 'l-tilāwa*.

It has been held

> likely that the Prophet did not himself collect the Ḳur'ān on account of his expectation that withdrawal would affect certain of its regulations, or certain of the wording. Once the Prophet died and the revelation ceased, God 'inspired' the Companions to the task of collecting what God had promised to preserve.[46]

The effort to argue that a prophet could not be conceived to be capable of forgetting any of the revelations made to him by God proved a failure in the face of the exegesis of Ḳ.87: *sa-nuḳri'uka fa-lā tansā – illā mā shā'a 'llāh*. The exegesis of the verse generated a mass of *tafsīr-ḥadīth*s which, being *ḥadīth*s, i.e. *Sunna*, consolidated the 'fact' that the Prophet had forgotten parts of the Ḳur'ān revelation – for such has been 'soundly' reported. The effort to keep Muḥammad's 'forgetting' of the Ḳur'ān separate from the phenomenon of *naskh* was likewise doomed to failure, given the fortuitous fact that Ḳ.2:106, the basis of the entire *naskh* theorising, associated the two roots *n s kh* and *n s y* in a single sentence: *mā nansakh min āya aw nansa-hā* [*aw nunsi-hā*]. Ḳ.2:106's juxtaposition of the two roots facilitated the accommodation of Muḥammad's 'forgetting' of the Ḳur'ān under the *naskh* rubric as a mode of *naskh*: *naskh al-ḥuhm wa-'l-tilāwa*, and, as *naskh* is an exclusively divine prerogative, the Author being free to do as He wishes with His own book, (and with His own Prophet) Muḥammad's 'forgetting' could be transmuted into Muḥammad's 'being caused to forget' *mā shā'a 'llāh* – thus calming the fears of all those who felt uncomfortable with the idea of a prophet's forgetting revelations.

Five

THE SECOND MODE OF *NASKH*

1. *NASKH AL-ḤUKM DŪNA 'L-TILĀWA*

The *muṣḥaf* contains only instances of this mode of *naskh*. The suppression of an original Ḳur'ān ruling without, however, the suppression of the original wording as well, is the rationalisation worked out by the *uṣūlīs* to explain instances in which they perceived certain Ḳur'ān verses, or certain *sunnas* to be inoperative. Their rulings had not been taken up in the formulation of the *Fiḳh*. Verses and *ḥadīths* alike had been ignored. The wording of the texts embodying those rulings, alleged to have been abandoned, still survives in our records of the Tradition. The *uṣūlīs* set out to explain why the *fuḳahā'* had ignored them. It was because they knew that they had been the subject of *naskh*.

Ḥāzimī points out that this is the 'classic' mode of *naskh*.[1] Of the three modes discussed in the theory, it alone is common to both Ḳur'ān and *Sunna*, which reinforces the suspicion that this mode was undoubtedly the starting-point for all the *naskh* theorising. It is this mode of *naskh*, although only in its Ḳur'ān application which has attracted such attention as Western scholars have hitherto paid to the *naskh* principle. It consists, as we see, of the continued simultaneous presence in the inherited documents of the Tradition of two or more statements on a single topic which the *fuḳahā'* had allegedly noted were in conflict to the point of mutual exclusion. They had therefore selected only one of the documents as the source of the *Fiḳh* regulation, ignoring the other(s).

The 'classic' instance of this 'classic' mode of *naskh* adduced by Ḥāzimī and by countless other Muslim writers to 'prove' *the fact* of *naskh* – more especially, to 'prove' the *fact* of *naskh* in the domain of Ḳur'ānic legislation specifically – concerns the *'idda*, or waiting-period imposed by God upon widows before the expiry of which they may not legally contract a valid second marriage. The topic is allegedly referred to in at least two Ḳur'ān contexts:

> Ḳ.2:240: Those of you who die and leave widows, a bequest to the widows for a twelve-month, without their being turned out of the matrimonial home. K.2:234: Those of you who die and leave widows, such women shall keep themselves in waiting for four months and ten nights.

The ruling of the first verse which concerns the financial provision to be made in favour of the widow conflicts with the *Fiḳh* ruling. Only the ruling of the second verse concerns the *'idda*. The *uṣūlī*s who had inherited an exegesis making both verses refer to the *'idda*, maintained, in the light of this and of the *Fiḳh*, that the rulings embodied in the two verses were hopelessly in conflict to the degree that it is quite impossible to implement both rulings simultaneously. They also maintained that there exists no 'real conflict' between the *Fiḳh* and the Ḳur'ān on this topic, since we have information that the ruling of one of the two verses had been suppressed.

A real difficulty of considerable practical significance had confronted the Muslims who first attempted the definition of *'idda* and its implications. This arose from the incompatibility of the financial and maintenance provisions which might be understood to have been assigned to the widow from the estate of her deceased spouse under the terms of Ḳ.2:240, with the details of the rules to govern inheritances laboriously worked out in the *Fiḳh* on the basis of the Ḳur'ān and *Sunna*. In other words, the verse, and other verses in the Ḳur'ān can be shown to be irreconcilable with the philosophy underlying the inheritance regulations of the *Fiḳh*.

The response of the *fuḳahā'* to this apparent conflict of sources involved two principal expedients. One was to link the financial provisions [*matā'*] introduced in Ḳ.2:240 to the *'idda*, introduced in Ḳ.2:234, and, by assimilating the bequest [*waṣiyya*] mentioned in Ḳ.2:240 to other family bequests laid down in Ḳ.2:180, to appear to be able to give a satisfactory account of the 'evolution' of the principles governing the treatment of widows in Islam. Further, one could exploit the analogy that could allegedly be drawn between the Ḳur'ān's treatment of widows and its treatment of divorced women.

It will be remembered that, for the argument of *naskh* to succeed, it was necessary to establish that the repealed ruling had, as a matter of 'historical fact', been divinely revealed and thus introduced into Muslim 'practice'.

2. i. The 'original' *'idda*

The first stage in a chain of incredibly complex argumentation was to establish that the *'idda* had 'originally' been observed for twelve months, the period mentioned in Ḳ.2:240. It could then be shown that this onerous burden had been 'alleviated' and the argument advanced that, in that event, the financial provision revealed in the widow's favour had been rescinded.

> The majority of the *'ulamā'* consider that Ḳ.2:234 superseded Ḳ.2:240, on the grounds that for a brief period, when a Muslim died and left his widow *pregnant*, he would make a bequest in her favour to accommodate her and finance her needs for twelve

> months, on condition that she did not remove herself from the matrimonial home, nor re-marry. This situation was subsequently altered by the imposition of a reduced *ʿidda* of four months and ten nights (Ḳ.2:234] *and* by the revelation of the inheritance regulations [Ḳ.4].[2]

The exegetical character of this statement is unmistakable. Ḳ.2:240 speaks of widows, without regard to whether or not they chance to be pregnant. The unwarranted interpolation of this qualification was, however, necessary to prepare the ground for a further assertion of *naskh*. The two Ḳ.2 verses occur in an environment of references to various aspects of marriage: the avoidance of sexual contact with menstruant women [v.222]; the regulation of the *īlā'* institution, with its *ʿidda* for *the husband* of four months [v.226]; the *ʿidda* of *divorced* women [v.228]; general definitions [vv.229–32]; regulations on breast-feeding [v.233]; the *ʿidda* of the widow [v.234]; proposals of re-marriage to widows [v.235]; the compositions [*matāʿ*] payable to *divorced* women [vv.236–7]; the compositions [*matāʿ*] payable to widows [v.240]; the maintenance payable to *divorced* women [v.241].

It comes as no surprise that a connection was early formed between the topics treated of in vv.234/240 which affect only widows, and further regulations established in Ḳ.65 which, however, affect only *divorced* women. It is from Ḳ.65 that the qualification of pregnancy, just noted, derives.

ibn ʿAbbās is reported to have commented that Ḳ.2:240

> refers to the practice of requiring the widow to observe an *ʿidda* of a whole year, her needs being provided for out of the deceased spouse's capital. Ḳ.2:234 was revealed *later*, imposing an *ʿidda* of four months and ten nights on every widow who was *not pregnant*. *Later* still, the inheritances verses were revealed. God detailed the individual shares, including the widow's. Following this last revelation, the widow's title to maintenance and to a bequest in her favour by the deceased husband 'lapsed'.[3]

The reference to Ḳ.65 is again unmistakable.

Those from whom it is reported that the ruling of Ḳ.2:240 had been abandoned included ʿUthmān while the connection between *naskh* and the so-called ʿUthmān *muṣḥaf* is emphasised by an unsuccessful protest raised against the whole theory of *naskh al-ḥukm dūna 'l-tilāwa*:

> ʿAbdullāh b. al-Zubayr is said to have confronted ʿUthmān demanding to know why the caliph had included the wording of Ḳ.2:240 in the *muṣḥaf*, when he knew it to have been superseded. ʿUthmān replied that he would on no account alter any part of the Ḳur'ān from the place which he knew it to occupy in the text.[4]

Even if its ruling has been suppressed, the wording, having been revealed, is quite properly to be recorded as forming part of the Ḳur'ān text.

One senses here the perfectly sensible objection that the presence of the wording in the transmitted text of the Ḳur'ān raises doubts about the supposed suppression of its revealed ruling. Would not the wording have been similarly abandoned? The dispute was both logical and semantic and the form the *ḥadīth* takes varies with the purpose which it serves. It re-appears in a version which voices an equal concern over the anomaly that a *nāsikh* comes before a *mansūkh*, although, by definition, the *nāsikh* ought to be later. Once more, 'Uthmān replies that he would on no account interfere with the order of the verses in their *sūras*.[5] This was intended to suggest that the present order of the verses was also revealed, that it had not been the work of the Companions. Following settlement of the theoretical principle that in *naskh*, the later supersedes the earlier, it had had to be pointed out that the sequence of the verses in our *muṣḥaf* bears no relation to the chronological order in which they had been revealed. Thus, the protest that in the inherited texts Ḳ.2:234 precedes v.240 was neutralised. 'Uthmān had set down the Ḳur'ān in the order in which he had heard it from the Prophet, without regard to the fact that he knew that a particular verse had been superseded. The wording of the verse had certainly not been suppressed.

The arbitrary nature of assertions on *naskh* is shown by the claims made by other scholars that no *naskh* has occurred here. An 'original' *'idda* of four months and ten nights has merely been increased by seven months and twenty nights to make the complete year.[6] This flies in the very face of the *Fiḳh* doctrine and whilst Ṭabarī might appear to favour this view, he predicates it, not of the *'idda*, but of the accommodation and financial provisions.[7] The reverse view was also held: there is here no *naskh*. The 'original' *'idda* of twelve months has merely been reduced by seven months and twenty nights. That was held to be analogous to the reduction of the ritual prayer granted to travellers who are permitted to curtail the number of *rak'as*. This view was then documented on the basis of a *ḥadīth* transparently only an exegesis of Ḳ.4:101 and is dismissed by Naḥḥās as palpably erroneous.[8]

> If the Ḳ.2 regulation had clearly stated that, providing she did not leave the matrimonial home [here, the concept of *'idda* has merged with that of *matā'*] although, if she did choose to leave, she was not to be prevented, the widow should observe a twelve months' *'idda*, and that regulation was then abolished on the imposition of a four months and ten nights' *'idda* during the course of which she might not go out [here, Ḳ2 has been confused with Ḳ.65] that is indisputably an instance of the alteration of a regulation – i.e. *naskh*.

ibn al-Arabī commits a similar confusion:[9] 'It was stated in Ḳ.2:240 that the widow might either elect to remain in the matrimonial home or leave it. Her liberty of choice was suppressed on the revelation of Ḳ.2:234.

The alleged restriction was based, however, not on the Ḳur'ān, but on a *tafsīr*. According to Naḥḥās, the travel-prayer has nothing to do with the *'idda*.[10]

> It is reliably reported from 'Ā'isha that ritual prayer had originally been imposed as consisting of only two *rak'a*s. The number had subsequently been increased only for the non-traveller. For travellers, the 'original' number, two, remained the obligation. This view, held by a number of scholars, had been challenged on the grounds that, notwithstanding this statement of hers, 'Ā'isha had never abbreviated the ritual prayer. It is said that, even when travelling, she had always completed four *rak'a*s [i.e. there was a counter-*ḥadith*]. The *fuḳahā'* replied, on the basis of *ta'wīl*, that there was no inconsistency: Her reported statement as to the original institution of the *ṣalāt* is attested but, as the Mother of the Faithful, 'Ā'isha was always among her children, wherever within Islam she might alight. Always and everywhere 'at home' she could never be a 'traveller'! Her statement about the abbreviation of the prayer could never apply to her own behaviour [the *ḥadith* conflict is harmonised].

The discussion on the abbreviation of the prayer failed to supply an analogy for a decision on the length of the *'idda*.

What finally settled the *naskh* of Ḳ.2:240 was a *ḥadith* reported as from Zainab bint abī Salama:

> I visited the Prophet's widow, Umm Ḥabība when her father, Abū Sufyān died. She called for some perfume containing some cosmetic matter and smeared, first a slavegirl then herself, saying, 'I don't really need the perfume, but I heard the Prophet say, "It is not fitting for a woman who believes in God and the Last Day to mourn a dead man for more than three nights – save only her husband. She should mourn him for four months and ten nights." '

Naḥḥās mentions three *ḥadith*s, but gives only two.[11] Shāfi'ī adduces all three[12] and his and Naḥḥas' second is identical with the above, except that, for Umm Ḥabība, it features a second widow of the Prophet, Zaynab bt. Djaḥsh, on the occasion of the death, not of her father, but of her brother, 'Abdullāh. The Prophet's words are made the more solemn by being delivered from the pulpit, a common device in the *Ḥadith*, reinforcing verification by widening the 'spread' of hearers.

The first Zaynab also reports her own mother, yet another widow of the Prophet, Umm Salama, as saying:

> A woman came to the Prophet, saying, 'My daughter has just been widowed. Her eyes are troubling her, may I treat them with kohl?' The Prophet said she might not, repeating his prohibition once or twice and adding, 'It is now only four months and ten

nights! In the Djāhiliyya, one of you women would cast a handful of dung only on the anniversary of the husband's death.'

Abū ʿUbayd reports Zaynab's *ḥadīth*s featuring three widows of the Prophet:[13] Umm Ḥabība, Umm Salama and Zaynab bint Djaḥsh. Ṭabarī adds to this growing list of Prophet-widows the names of Ḥafṣa and ʿĀ'isha[14] both of whom are also mentioned by Shāfiʿī.[15] That makes a grand total of five widows of the Prophet. In the documentation of this topic, there appears to be a clear determination to attach a *Fiḳh* doctrine on widows to a widow of the Prophet, who would be doubly qualified. Shāfiʿī inserted his *ḥadīth*s, not in his chapter on the *ʿidda*, but in that on mourning. The tendency to confound mourning with *ʿidda* is doctrinised by Shāfiʿī's insistence that 'all who are required to observe the *ʿidda* of widowhood are required likewise to observe mourning.'[16]

The *ḥadīth*s have little to do with the topic under discussion here, but represent the attempt to introduce into the *Fiḳh* the notion that mourning is an additional requirement on the widow – an idea which Ḥasan Baṣrī denounced as groundless.[17] Because, however, they conveniently mention two periods, one of twelve months and the other of four months and ten nights, they were exploited to identify mourning with *ʿidda*, to convey the impression that the *ʿidda* had once been verifiably observed for a whole year. To qualify as a *mansūkh*, a regulation must be shown to have been 'practised'. The reference to the Djāhiliyya is another commonplace of the *Ḥadīth*, calculated to give the impression that, by extension, a regulation persisted into the 'early days of Islam'. ibn al-ʿArabī seized this point:[18] 'The widow's *ʿidda* in early Islam, as it had been in the Djāhiliyya, was for twelve months'.

The Ḳur'ān's mention of the twelve months was unhelpful as to dating, as was also the position the verse occupied in the text. The *ḥadīth*s were therefore introduced to supply this deficiency by 'demonstrating' that the 'original' *ʿidda* had been reduced by none other than God Himself, as His Prophet here explains, to only four months and ten nights. Thus and only thus is the claim that the ruling of Ḳ.2:240 had been suppressed sustained. Naḥḥās observed that this one *ḥadīth* is 'full of *Fiḳh*'[19] and from it he deduced no fewer than eight *Fiḳh* propositions, of which two only are of immediate interest: that mourning is obligatory; and that the Prophet's words: 'It is now only four months and ten nights,' – a reference, he insists, to the *Fiḳh* view on the *ʿidda* of the widow who chances *not* to be pregnant – exclude the pregnant widow from this divine imposition.

Thus far, we have seen: the concept of the *ʿidda* being confounded with that of the *matāʿ*; widowhood confounded with divorce; mourning confounded with the observance of the obligatory *ʿidda*. It would, therefore, be helpful before proceeding, to clarify the recurring confusion between the pregnant and the non-pregnant widows. Neither Ḳ.2:234 nor Ḳ.2:240 makes the slightest reference to pregnancy. The two verses may therefore be regarded as bearing upon all widows. They have been held, as we see, to be general in wording only, and particular in their ruling, i.e. bearing only upon the non-pregnant widow specifically. If this view were justified, the *ʿidda* of the pregnant widow would be discoverable elsewhere. Only the Muslims' insistence on treating these two Ḳ.2 verses as if they shared a common topic led to this confusion.

The general view was that, although apparently restricted to the pregnant divorcée, Ḳ.65:4 applies generally to all pregnant women required to observe an *ʿidda* for whatever cause. Indeed, noting that Ḳ.2:234 established an *ʿidda* of precise length, the scholars asserted that, if originally intended to apply to all widows, that regulation had been superseded by the ruling of Ḳ.65:4, in the case of the pregnant widow. Ḳ.2:234, it follows, is now the ruling governing non-pregnant widows. 'If it be objected that Ḳ.65:4 applies restrictively to divorced women, we hold that this connection with the pregnant divorcée does not hurt its general application to all pregnant women required to observe an *ʿidda*.'[20] On the analogy of that of the divorced, the *ʿidda* of the pregnant widow is held to be determined by childbirth. This one slender thread of connection between the exegeses of Ḳur'ān verses, each mentioning an *ʿidda*, once formed, soon permeated the entire discussion of the manifold implications of widowhood which is thereby rendered intolerably complex.

> If the widow be pregnant, her *ʿidda* is determined by childbirth, in the view of ʿUmar and ibn Masʿūd. ʿAlī held that the widow should observe the longer of the two periods, Ḳ.65:4 or Ḳ.2:234. This was because the words 'and those who are pregnant' of Ḳ.65:4 impose the period of the entire pregnancy, whereas Ḳ.2:234 imposes only the four months and ten nights. ʿAlī would have argued that the sources ought to be jointly observed. If the widow were to give birth before the expiry of the four months and ten nights, ʿAlī would not consider that she was free to re-marry. For him, her *ʿidda* is the longer of the two periods. One should preserve the letter of the Ḳur'ān. However, it is 'soundly' reported from [ʿAbdullāh] b. ʿUmar and [ʿAbdullāh] b. Masʿūd that K.65 is '*ḳāḍiya ʿalā*' Ḳ.2. ʿUmar's view was that if the widow gave birth while her husband lay yet unburied, she had fulfilled her *ʿidda*.[21]

Once more, the point of dispute was settled by appeal to *ḥadīth*s: ibn Masʿūd said, 'I challenge any man who cares to engage in mutual oath-making to deny that "the shorter sūrat al-nisā'" [K.65] was revealed later than Ḳ.2:234.'[22]

2.ii. Subay'a bint al-Ḥārith

The 'proof' of 'Abdullāh's contention and 'Umar's supposed view is a *ḥadīth*.

> Subay'a gave birth nine days after the death of her husband. Asking whether she was now free to re-marry, she was told that she was not, so she consulted the Prophet who told her that 'the Book had expired';[23] she was free to marry if she wished to.

Naḥḥās attributes the view that Ḳ.65 superseded Ḳ.2:234 to: 'The majority of the Companions, successors and *fuḳahā'*, including: 'Umar, ibn 'Umar, ibn Mas'ūd, Abū Mas'ūd, Sa'īd b. al-Musayyab, Zuhrī, Mālik, Awzā'ī, Thawrī, *aṣḥāb al-ra'y* and Shāfi'ī.'

The contrary view, that the *'idda* of the pregnant widow is the longer of the two periods, he attributed to 'Alī and to ibn 'Abbās. When 'Alī accused the younger Companion Abū Mas'ūd of 'lack of knowledge', he had retorted with the Subay'a *ḥadīth* which 'Alī averred he had never heard. Asked to give a *fatwā* on this very topic, ibn 'Abbās and Abū Salama had differed. ibn 'Abbās declared 'Her *'idda* is the longer of the two periods,' whereas Abū Salama had stated, 'When she gives birth, she is free to re-marry,' in which view he was supported by Abū Hurayra. ibn 'Abbās' freedman was sent to consult the Prophet's widow, Umm Salama. She sent him back with the *ḥadīth* about Subay'a.

Here, the view of the younger Companion, ibn 'Abbās, fails. For Naḥḥās, when, on any disputed question, the view of the Prophet reaches one, the view of no other man is of any account, not least when, as here, *there is a text in the Ḳur'ān.*

The scholars are unanimous that if, at the completion of the four months and ten nights' *'idda*, the widow remains pregnant, she is not free to re-marry. Pregnancy must therefore be the primary consideration. Thus, the tendency of the Subay'a *ḥadīth* was to propound the view that adherence to Ḳ.65 has precedence over adherence to Ḳ.2:234.

> The ibn 'Abbās view that the pregnant widow should observe the longer of the two periods, being designed to secure observance of both verses, would have been unexceptionable, but for the Subay'a *ḥadīth*.[24]
>
> ibn al-'Arabī goes further: Even if the Subay'a *ḥadīth* were not 'sound', the ibn 'Abbās view could not be held. Pregnancy is dealt with at Ḳ.65:4 not Ḳ.2:234. With the childbirth, the object for which the *'idda* was instituted is achieved. What, in that case, would be the object of waiting the remaining months? If the widow completed the Ḳ.2:234 *'idda* and remained pregnant, no scholar would say that she was free to re-marry. The Subay'a *ḥadīth* removed all anxiety by topping every whim and *ra'y*.[25]

By their application of this (non-Ḳur'ānic) distinction between pregnant and non-pregnant widows, the scholars improved upon the Ḳur'ān's silence, sowing the seed of the idea of the conditional nature of Ḳ.2:234, allegedly the *nāsikh* of Ḳ.2:240.

The ʿAlī-ibn ʿAbbās opinion, on the contrary, represented the argument that widows are not divorced women, that Ḳ.2:234 is unconnected with Ḳ.65:4.

> What muddled ʿAlī was that childbirth makes it plain that the womb is unoccupied. In *tarabbuṣ* [Ḳ.2:234] the condition of the womb is not the consideration since, in widowhood, minors and quite elderly ladies are held to be under the same *ʿidda* obligation as women of child-bearing capacity, as opposed to their position in the matter of the *ʿidda* of divorce.[26]

But the ʿAlī 'opinion' represents an unbending conviction that the minimum *ʿidda* for the widow is that set out in Ḳ.2:234, sc. four months and ten nights. The opposing opinion is less logical and can be summarised as follows:

> the *ʿidda* had allegedly been instituted to determine that the womb was unoccupied when the widow came to seek re-marriage. The condition is manifestly satisfied by childbirth, and in the case of the pregnant widow no further consideration was applied. Childbirth was held to terminate her obligation to observe an *ʿidda*, imposed by Ḳ.2:234. Why then, insist upon observation of the four months and ten nights' *ʿidda* by minors and elderly ladies whose pregnancy was unlikely? Why, indeed, insist upon the Ḳ.2:234 *ʿidda*, in the case of the widow of the unconsummated union?
>
> ʿAlī's alleged view was that *tarabbuṣ* and pregnancy were mutually independent, neither affecting the other. That was a *ḳiyās*, embedded in the reflection that *tarabbuṣ* was imposed upon women whose pregnancy was inconceivable.

Sarakhsī returned to the problem from the linguistic angle:

> Consummated or not, the institution is known as 'marriage' the participating woman as 'wife'. Ḳ.2:234 specifies 'wives', a term which embraces females in their minority and elderly dams beyond child-bearing age, virgins and non-virgins alike. The *ʿidda* is a legal claim residing in the institution of marriage and arising from its dissolution.[27]

Passages of the sort convey a sense of the influence of the wording of the Ḳur'ān upon the Muslim mind, especially in those cases where the earliest exegesis had created no problems. Minors and quite elderly ladies are thus required to observe the *ʿidda* of widowhood, although the Muslims could not explain why. It was enough that both Ḳur'ān and *Fiḳh* imposed it. The problem of the *Fiḳh*'s doctrine on the bequest by the dead husband to his widow must therefore be pursued amid the discussions of other aspects of widowhood.

3. Leaving the matrimonial home

Some, we saw, argued that Ḳ.2:234 and Ḳ.2:240 were mutually independent, so that the rulings of both continued to be valid. In Naḥḥās' view, that opinion was nonsense.[28] It was based on a *Fiḳh* argument that the widow might not spend a night away from the matrimonial home. Were that view 'sound', he argues, widows would linger under that ban for twelve months. In any case, there is no reported *idjmāʿ* on this question of the widow's having to keep to her house. The first generation of the Muslims and those who succeeded them were divided on this question. Those who insisted that widows must stay in their homes included: ʿUmar, ʿUthmān, Umm Salama, ibn Masʿūd and ibn ʿUmar. They were followed in this view by 'the majority'.

Mālik held that widows might pay social calls after the night prayer, but, on no account might they spend the night elsewhere than in the matrimonial home. The same view is reported from Layth, Thawrī, Abū Ḥanīfa and Shāfiʿī. Shaybānī maintained that neither the widow nor the absolutely divorced women might in any circumstances leave the matrimonial home.

Sarakhsī, however, distinguishes between the widow and the divorced woman in this respect:[29]

> No woman, either absolutely divorced, or under a single pronouncement of divorce, whether final or revocable, may leave the matrimonial home by either day or night until the expiry of the *ʿidda*, for God says, 'They shall not go out.'[30]

Similarly, according to ibn al-ʿArabī,

> There is no possibility of the widow's removing from the matrimonial home. That was the view of the scholars, except for ibn ʿAbbās, ʿAṭā' and Thawrī, all of whom were under the misapprehension that Ḳ.2:240 had not been repealed.[31]

The last remark refers to Ḳ.2:240's 'they shall not be evicted – *ghayr ikhrādj*', and provides further evidence of the confusion of the Ḳ.2 vocabularly with that of Ḳ.65:1. ibn al-ʿArabī glosses the term *khurūdj* as: *khurūdj intiḳāl*, i.e. 'moving house.' On *khurudj al-ʿibāda*, he says:

> ibn ʿAbbās and Aṭā' both held that widows might perform the Ḥadjdj and the *ʿumra*. Both ʿUmar and his son took the opposite view and ʿUmar used to intercept women in *ʿidda* who intended to make the pilgrimage, sending them home.

Reporting the same, Sarakhsī specifies *ʿidda* of widowhood.[32]

We are here once more faced with a confusion of Ḳur'ān statements. Revealed to regulate the affairs of widows, Ḳ.2:240 uses the expression *ghayr ikhrādj* – widows are not to be evicted from the matrimonial home, although they may leave if they freely choose to do so. Ḳ.65:1 uses the expression: 'You shall not evict them, not are they to be turned out, unless they commit some grave sin.' Traditionally, however, this is read: 'You shall not evict them, nor shall they go out, unless they commit some grave sin,' a reading of doubtful intelligibility. What here concerns us, however, is the transfer of this regulation from the divorced to the widowed. ibn al-ʿArabī ended his discussion by simply asserting that 'the widow's liberty to move or not to move had been abolished by the imposition of *tarabbuṣ* in Ḳ.2:234.' That explains his assertion that ibn ʿAbbās and others had been under the misapprehension that Ḳ.2:240 had not been repealed.

Those who held that the widow might go out, even for the Ḥadjdj, included ʿAlī. That is attested as his view by his having, on the assassination of ʿUmar, removed the victim's widow, his daughter Umm Kulthum, from ʿUmar's to his own house, before she had completed her *ʿidda*.[33] Sarakhsī reports this of ʿAlī and an identical report about ʿĀ'isha and her sister, also called Umm Kulthum, whom ʿĀ'isha removed on the occasion of the death of her husband, Ṭalḥa b. ʿUbaydullāh.[34] The ʿAlī opinion is also attributed to ibn ʿAbbās who argued that God had imposed upon the widow the obligation to observe the *ʿidda*, without stipulating where she should observe it.[35] In his view, she could observe it wherever she chose. That, however, is a view carrying financial implications. Thawrī reports ibn ʿAbbās as having said, 'Neither the widowed nor the divorced woman is required to remain in her house, and neither is entitled to maintenance.'[36]

This 'required to remain in the matrimonial home' acquired a shift in meaning. Ṭaḥāwī states:[37] 'The widow, pregnant or not, is entitled to neither accommodation nor maintenance.'

Sarakhsī's distinction between the divorced and the widowed derives explicitly from the same question:[38]

> The women who lost their husbands complained to ibn Masʿūd and he exceptionally granted them permission to exchange visits in daytime, provided they did not spend the night time away from the matrimonial home.

Shāfiʿī uses the same *ḥadīth*, but *from the Prophet*!

> The women widowed at Uḥud complained of loneliness and isolation and the Prophet permitted them to exchange visits by day, provided they returned to their homes by nightfall.[39]

Sarakhsī sees as the principle involved here the fact that there is no financial entitlement in widowhood. Widows may, thus, have to go out to earn their livelihood. The divorced, who must be maintained, have no such need.[40]

In addition to ʿAlī and ibn ʿAbbās, ʿĀ'isha and Djābir are credited with the view that the widow need not remain in the matrimonial home. That makes four Companions advocating this view, but, says Naḥḥās, the Ḳur'ān is against them! The word '*tarabbuṣ*' means: they must shut themselves away.[41] That is, the *tafsīr* is against them.

Ṭabarī held the word to mean: 'they must shut themselves away for the entire period of the *'idda*, refraining from re-marriage, the use of perfumes, cosmetics and pretty clothes. They must, in addition, desist from removing from the matrimonial home.'[42] The alleged 'Alī opinion derived by exegesis from Ḳ.2:240: *in kharadjna* – 'if they should choose to go out,' placed in opposition to *ghayr ikhrādj*, 'but they shall not be turned out.' The man's heirs may not evict his widow from his house during the Ḳ.2:240 twelvemonth, [*matā'an ilā al-ḥawli*]. The 'majority opinion' derived from equating *khurūdj* with *ikhrādj*. The majority also read Ḳ.65:1: 'Do not turn them out of their homes, nor may they choose to go out.'

4. Furay'a

Furay'a's husband was killed when he overtook his runaway slaves, leaving her without shelter and with no funds. She asked the Prophet's permission to return to her people. Having at first granted her permission, the Prophet later withdrew it telling her to remain in her house 'until the book shall have expired.'[43] The story provided ibn al-'Arabī with conclusive evidence that 'the widow's liberty to remove had been suppressed.' which inclined him to suggest that, on that account, she was probably entitled to accommodation.

Naḥḥas saw in it evidence against ibn 'Abbās.[44] The widow may not go out, but is required to remain in her home, while, noting that the Prophet did not scold her for coming out to consult him, Sarakhsī concludes that the widow may not be absent overnight from her home. He considers that she may not travel for any purpose during the *'idda*.[45]

5. The widow's legal entitlements

Those who sought to resist the view that Ḳ.65 superseded Ḳ.2:240 were finally overwhelmed by accumulation of *ḥadīth*s. Fascinating as they are, the discussions were wholly academic departing, as they did to a greater or lesser extent, from the wording of the Ḳur'ān on which they affect to be based. The arguments were directed at the ulterior question of the widow's entitlements. Apart from the Prophetic statement we considered above the sole authority for the assertion that there had ever been a twelve months' *'idda* in Islam, and that there had been any restriction on the widow's freedom of movement, occurs in an isolated *tafsīr-ḥadīth* attributed to ibn 'Abbās: commenting upon Ḳ.2:240, he is alleged to have declared:

> When a man died, leaving a widow, she observed her *'idda* in the matrimonial home, her expenses being met from his capital. *Subsequently*, God revealed Ḳ.2:234, introducing what is now the widow's *'idda* – unless she be pregnant, in which case, her *'idda* terminates with the pregnancy.[46] Then, in Ḳ.4:12, God specified

> the widow's share in her husband's goods, and so abandoned both the bequest from the husband and the maintenance.

The allegation is that the Ḳ.2:234 *ʿidda* concerns only the non-pregnant widow. The pregnant widow's *ʿidda* is dealt with at Ḳ.65:4. Ṭabarī and Naḥḥās share the same *isnād* for this report.[47] A century earlier than both, Abū ʿUbayd used the same *ḥadīth*, with the same *isnād*.[48] Of the three versions, Naḥḥas' report alone lacks the words: 'in the matrimonial home', while the position of the words: 'unless she be pregnant' betrays their exegetical origin. We should note too, the unsupported assertions that Ḳ.2:234 was revealed later than Ḳ.2:240, and that Ḳ.4 was revealed after both. We may note also that Ḳatāda took the line that Ḳ.2:234 which instituted the widow's *ʿidda* superseded the accommodation and financial rights granted her for twelve months in Ḳ.2:240, although, in the same breath, he declares that these rights had been superseded by the Ḳ.4 inheritance regulations.[49] He does not, however, actually state that there had ever been a twelve months' *ʿidda*. The twelve months' arrangement had had two aspects:

> throughout that period, maintenance was payable to the widow from the estate of her dead husband, providing she did not voluntarily remove herself from the matrimonial home in which the deceased husband's heirs were obliged to accommodate her. No particular *ʿidda* is mentioned.

Even at this stage, had the *ʿidda* been one of four months and ten nights, the regulations are reconcilable with ease: the widow might not re-marry for four months and ten nights. Indeed, at this point, Naḥḥās' version reads: as long as she did not move out to re-marry.[50]

> On the lapse of the four months and ten nights, if she wished to avail herself of it, the accommodation and maintenance must continue to be made available to her up to a term of twelve months from the date of the husband's death. Should the widow, however, at the expiry of the four months and ten nights' *ʿidda*, choose to move out of the matrimonial home, to spend the remainder of the twelve months in alternative accommodation, nothing in the Ḳur'ān would hinder her. No blame would attach to her, nor to the husband's heirs – providing they had had no hand in her removal.

Her rights to maintenance had, it is, however, alleged, been regularised (i.e. terminated) by the Ḳur'ān's having allotted her a specific share in the inheritance from the deceased husband's estate. In the Naḥḥās version there is still no allegation that there had ever been a twelve months' *ʿidda*. To that extent, the Ḳatāda report differs from that of ibn ʿAbbās. What appears to have allegedly been superseded by Ḳ.4's inheritance regulations, was the widow's right to expect maintenance [*matāʿ*] for the full twelve months. What seems to have been superseded by the four months and ten nights' *ʿidda*, was the prohibition of the heirs' evicting her during the full twelve months. As to whether there was an obligation upon the heirs to continue to provide the accommodation for the four months and ten nights, two views circulated: neither maintenance nor accommodation need be provided; no maintenance, but only accommodation must be provided. Shāfiʿī, for example, was somewhat hesitant on the question of her accommodation:

> Since her accommodation is mentioned in the same verse as her maintenance, it is possible that the accommodation, like the maintenance, had been repealed, both for the twelve months and for the four months and ten nights. The maintenance for both periods has certainly been replaced. Now, it is possible that the obligation to provide the accommodation had been reduced from the twelve months to the shorter period and that the widow is thus included among those women for whom accommodation must be provided, as they observe their *ʿidda*. As to divorced women, God says, 'do not evict them, nor shall they go out.' He thus imposed an obligation to provide their accommodation. Like the divorced, the widowed are also required to observe an *ʿidda*. It may well be that they are, therefore, entitled to their accommodation. If this is no longer the case, it could be that the obligation to provide the accommodation had been contingent upon the longer *ʿidda*. What I recall from the *ʿulamā'* is that the widow is entitled to the accommodation, but not to any maintenance.[51]

Rabīʿ appears to have expressed the view that Ḳ.2:240 applied before the revelation of the Ḳ.4 inheritance verses.[52] '"Originally" the widow was entitled to both accommodation and maintenance for a whole year, if she chose to avail herself of it. This arrangement was, however, repealed on the revelation of Ḳ.4, laying down the widow's specific entitlement. The *ʿidda* was laid down in Ḳ.2:234.' This differs from Ḳatāda's exegesis only to the extent that he gave the impression that the twelve month arrangement had been repealed on the revelation of the shorter period. Suddī's *tafsīr* is clearer:

> When Ḳ.2:240 was revealed, a man would make a bequest in favour of his widow, to provide her accommodation and her maintenance for a whole year. Her *ʿidda* was four months and ten nights. If she left his house on the completion of this four months and ten nights' *ʿidda*, her right to maintenance lapsed. This is the meaning of God's words: *in kharadjna*. That was before the revelation of Ḳ.4 which specified the inheritance share due to the widow, and that replaced the maintenance provision. Following the revelation of Ḳ.4, the widow had the right to neither accommodation nor maintenance.[53]

No attempt is made here to argue that the *ʿidda* had ever been for twelve months. In consequence, *ḥadīth*s which make that point fall under immediate suspicion as appearing to support only an interpretation, and that not the most obvious interpretation of the verses. More interesting is that Suddī made no effort to assert that Ḳ.2:234 had replaced Ḳ.2:240. The *nāsikh* would appear, for him, to be Ḳ.4. Here is a clue which makes it certain that the widow's rights, as recognised by the *Fiḳh*, had not originated from the direct reading of this Ḳ.2 passage, an unobstructed reading of which indicates that the two verses, v.234 and v.240 treat independently of quite unrelated topics.

Ḳ.2:234 established the *'idda* of widowhood. The verse is followed immediately by 'Enter into no firm undertaking to re-marry, until the book shall have expired,' a phrase which the *ḥadīth*s had not hesitated to appropriate.

Ḳ.2:240 required the dead husband's heirs to provide one year's accommodation and maintenance in favour of the widow as a right to which she was entitled. God expressly forbade the heirs to evict the widow from her home, as He forbade the husband in Ḳ.65:1 to evict the divorced wife from her home.

Ṭabarī realised that the widow's 'remaining in the home' and her mourning the dead husband had never been an obligation imposed upon her.[54] It had been something which God had declared lawful for her to do, if she chose. On the other hand, if she freely chose to leave the matrimonial home no blame attached to her or to the man's heirs in respect of her lawful conduct.

There being no topic in common linking these two verses, there can be no conflict between them. There can therefore be no *naskh*.

6. The clash between the widow's rights and the interest of her fellow-heirs

A problem had, however, arisen from the obvious clash of material interest between the widow and the husband's heirs. Hers would appear to be a dual entitlement: under Ḳ.2:240, [*matā'*] and under Ḳ.4 [*mīrāth*]. *Ḥadīth*s introduced to sustain the assertion that the accommodation and financial privileges of the widow had been contingent upon the 'original' *'idda* of twelve months, served to give a degree of plausibility to the argument, based by some on appeal to Ḳ.2:234, that the 'longer' *'idda* had been set aside. Ḳ.2:234 which mentions the 'shorter' *'idda*, was now silent on the accommodation and maintenance provisions. It could thus be argued that these too had been set aside.

> Ḳ.2:240 imposed four rulings: the twelve months' *'idda*, later reduced to four months and ten nights; the maintenance and accommodation rights, later replaced by the inheritance rights; God had originally granted these rights to the widow as a

> bequest, as He had granted the bequests to the parents and near of kin [Ḳ.2:180.] All these family bequests were replaced by the Ḳ.4 inheritance regulations. There was also mourning, *indicated by the verse*! and endorsed in the Sunna. Fourthly, the widow's right to remove, the prohibition of which was endorsed.[55]

Additional *tafsīr-ḥadīth*s about 'remaining in the home' had obscured the issue, for it could be and was argued that, if that were an obligation, then perhaps provision ought to be made for its fulfilment. There thus emerged a reserve explanation of the *Fiḳh*'s treatment of widows: Ḳ.2:240 had spoken of the widow's rights as a bequest, *waṣiyya*. This bequest by the dying husband was, as we see, assimilated to other family bequests spoken of at Ḳ.2:180 and like them, declared to have been replaced once and for all by Ḳ.4: 'I know of no-one who expresses a view other than that the financial provision for the widow, whether for the year or for the shorter period, has been repealed.'[56] But, to support their views, the scholars were forced to look *outside the Ḳur'ān*. Mālik's position had been that Ḳ.4 had superseded Ḳ.2:180's bequests to parents and nearest kin. Some of his followers had based this ruling upon an alleged instance of the *naskh* of the Ḳur'ān by the *Sunna*.[57] But, on this very topic, the word *mansūkha* makes its one and only appearance in the *Muwaṭṭa'*.[58] Mālik's pupil, Shāfi'ī linked the two bequest verses, Ḳ.2:180 and Ḳ.2:240, declaring that given the Ḳ.4 verses regulating inheritances, in addition, the Ḳur'ān has become on these questions 'ambiguous':

> The verses are capable of being read so as to confirm the obligation to make bequests in favour of the parents, nearest kin and spouses *over and above* the inheritance provision. In effect, they would benefit twice. The verses could be read so as to show that the inheritance rights had superseded the right to benefit by bequest. This ambiguity had forced the scholars to seek further indications in the Ḳur'ān, *which they failed to find* and so were forced to turn to the *Sunna* where, whatever they accept as coming from the Prophet, they accept as coming from God, since God had imposed upon Muslims the obligation of obedience to His Prophet.[59]

In the *Sunna*, Shāfi'ī found a formally unsatisfactory *ḥadīth* which, however, was 'widespread', to the effect that the Prophet had said in the Year of the Conquest of Makka, 'There is to be no bequest to any heir.' He accepts this *ḥadīth* 'on account of the general recognition it has been given, and also on account of the general unanimity of the scholars on the doctrine which it conveys.' He concluded therefore that Ḳ.4 superseded the bequest verses. Ḳ.2:180 mentions, however, persons who, although related to the decedent, would not expect to inherit. Employed in support of the *Fiḳh* doctrine, the *ḥadīth* used by Shāfi'ī, as worded, *lā waṣiyya li-wāri*th, did not extend to the disqualification of such relatives, mentioned along with the parents. The exegetes inclined to the view that these kin, if not automatically entitled under the Ḳ.4 terms to inherit, might continue to benefit in terms of Ḳ.2:180. The *Fiḳh* scholars found justification for this interpretation in a second *ḥadīth* which conveniently conveyed the Prophet's endorsement. They therefore deduced, since the *ḥadīth* extended the right to unrelated persons to benefit by bequest that *a fortiori*, related persons 'retained' this right, especially as there is, in addition to the *ḥadīth, a Ḳur'ānic reference to that right*! For the purposes of narrow documentation, the *uṣūlīs* would continue for generations to debate whether this 'attested instance of *naskh*' had been effected by Ḳur'ān or by the *Sunna*. But for the purposes of the *Fiḳh*, unanimity reigned that the obligation to make bequests in favour of parents and spouses had unquestionably been set aside by the revelation of the inheritance regulations. The legal criterion upon which this conclusion rests is quite unambiguous: inheritance bars from bequest.

The Ḥanafī, like the Mālikī *uṣūlīs*, continued to argue that both Ḳ.2:180 and Ḳ.2:240 had been superseded by the *Sunna*. Embarrassed by the technically unsophisticated argument of his predecessors, Sarakhsī improved upon it by demonstrating that the Ḳur'ān had indicated the withdrawal of the *obligation* to provide for the parents by means of bequest; the *Sunna*, in its turn, had indicated the withdrawal of the *legitimacy* of doing so. In the course of a somewhat lengthy disquisition, he incidentally adduced a developed wording of the *ḥadīth* upon which Shāfi'ī had relied:[60] 'God has appointed to everyone with a valid claim his legal due – there is to be no bequest to any heir.' This wording precisely reflects the *uṣūlī*'s attitude on the delicate problem of the status of the *Sunna* relative to the Ḳur'ān, adopted in the period after Shāfi'ī. The words 'God has appointed' point to Ḳ.4's inheritance regulations. An even later date than that alleged by Shāfi'ī has been assigned to this Prophetic dictum by others.[61]

Shāfi'ī, interested in all aspects of *naskh*, had a particular facility for dating his source-materials but, by placing this dictum two years earlier in his timetable, perhaps demonstrated that the really important thing was the dating, rather than the precise date. Shāfi'ī also preserved 'and from more than one specialist in Ḳur'ānic science, the assertion that Ḳ.2:240 had been revealed simultaneously with Ḳ.2:180.'

The scholars here referred to also held that the Ḳ.2:240 bequest covering the widow's needs for a year 'had been suppressed.'[62] God had declared her, instead, to be entitled to a specific share in the inheritance.

> He had imposed upon the widow the four months and ten nights' *'idda* during which time she might not go out, even voluntarily, and before the expiry of which she is not free to re-marry. It is

the *Sunna* which indicates this obligation to remain within the matrimonial home 'until the Book shall have expired' – unless she be pregnant, in which case, her *'idda* terminates with the childbirth, be this late or soon. [Here, Ḳ.65:4 supersedes Ḳ.2:234].

That the bequest of one year's maintenance had been set aside by the Ḳ.4 inheritance regulations is something which to Shāfi'ī's knowledge, 'is neither disputed not challenged.' The doctrine of the majority *thus coincides with the Sunna*. The verificatory aspect of Shāfi'ī's work is thus made clear.

7. Analysis

A mind unburdened by the need to establish *the fact* of *naskh*, has no difficulty in reading Ḳ.2:180, Ḳ.2:240, Ḳ.2:234 and Ḳ.4 and Ḳ.65 and appreciating that all these contexts treat quite independently of their respective topics without any need ever to be juxtaposed. The scholar's constant habit of referring back and forth between Ḳ.2 and Ḳ.65, on the plea that both contexts speak of 'women required to observe an *'idda*', would have been equally unnecessary if his predecessors had kept in view the essential circumstantial distinction between the widowed and the divorced, for each of whom the Ḳur'ān had legislated separately. But the ancient exegetes had needed every assistance they could have in the task of interpreting the Ḳur'ān texts, and one of the commonest devices was the comparison of verses which shared a common vocabularly or dealt with a common theme. Shāfi'ī himself had failed to resolve the problem of the widow's accommodation rights. It is clear that to transfer the obligation to remain in the matrimonial home – if there be any such obligation – from the divorced to the widowed, is to transfer from the husband of the divorced the obligation to provide that accommodation. But, as Shāfi'ī ruefully reflected, the husband of the widow is dead, an essential distinction between him and the divorcing husband which raises important fundamental property rights issues.

It was perhaps natural that the distinction between the *'idda* of the pregnant widow and that of the non-pregnant widow should arise, especially after all widows, pregnant and otherwise, had been denied their God-given right to a year's *financial support and accommodation*. The Ḳur'ān makes no reference to pregnancy in connection with its legislation on widow's entitlements, but the possibility of pregnancy may well underlie the generosity of the Ḳ.2:240 provisions which would allow for any normal pregnancy, including full-term posthumous pregnancies. Once made, however, that distinction was exploited to reinforce the alleged connection between Ḳ.2 and Ḳ.65. The Muslim exegete, observing that the right to remove, mentioned in Ḳ.2:240 and unrestricted by any minimum or maximum time limit was 'no longer' referred to in Ḳ.2:234, and assuming, on the basis of mere assertion, that Ḳ.2:234 had been revealed later than Ḳ.2:240, concluded *e silentio* that that right, since now unmentioned had been withdrawn. This forged yet another link to Ḳ.65, which was being read: 'and they shall not go out.'

Reading the whole Ḳ.2 section on marriage and related questions on the assumption that it was revealed as a unit – until the contrary is established – in which v.234 defined the minimum period that must elapse before the widow may re-marry; and v.240 set out the financial and other arrangements to be made in her favour, it is clear that she retained, since she had never lost her right to remove if she wished. The view that she had lost that right was the residue of the argument that v.234 had been revealed later than and had superseded v.240. The assertion that the *ʿidda* had been reduced from an 'original' length of twelve months was part of the same argument and could be sustained only by recourse to extra-Ḳur'ānic material. That argument was secondary and supplementary to the assertion that the bequest in her favour had been suppressed. This Ḳ.2:234 *ʿidda* is, according to Shafiʿī, one of many Ḳur'ān provisions which suffer from a regrettable 'ambiguity':[63]

> it is capable of being read as imposed generally upon all widows, free and slave, pregnant and non-pregnant. It is also capable of being read as imposed only upon free, as opposed to slave widows, or upon non-pregnant, as opposed to pregnant widows.

Apparently only the *Sunna*, i.e. the Subayʿa *ḥadīth*, can guide to the certain knowledge that the reference is restricted to non-pregnant widows. In respect of the pregnant woman required to observe an *ʿidda*, the dissolution of marriage with the consequent liability to observe *ʿidda*, arise equally and impose identical obligations, whether the dissolution is occasioned by the husband's divorce, or by his death.

Shāfiʿī knows a *ḥadīth* to the effect that ibn ʿUmar, giving a decision that a pregnant widow was free to re-marry on giving birth, was gratified on being informed that his father, ʿUmar, had taken the view that if the widow were to give birth while the deceased husband lay unburied, she was free to re-marry. He knows a parallel *ḥadīth* from [ʿAbdullāh] b. Masʿūd to the same effect. Pregnant or not, the widow, being entitled to benefit by inheritance, has the right to nothing further. This severe opinion Shāfiʿī holds good, even if the widow, being *mushrika* or slave, is entitled to no inheritance whatever.

The systematic doctrine underlying these conclusions is that a man's property rights die with him. Cross-reference to the regulations of divorce [Ḳ.65] had not caused this harsh attitude to the widow. Ḳ.65:6 insists 'if they are pregnant, maintain divorced women until they have given birth.' The references from Ḳ.2 to Ḳ.65 are thus arbitrary, selective and artificial.

It is possible that in the matter of his obligation to provide the accommodation, the husband of the divorced woman alone is addressed and that there the analogy ceases, since this husband retains full rights in his property. Possibly such an obligation does not extend to the husband of the widow, since once he dies, his rights in property pass to others. The accommodation of the widow thus lies in the discretion of the dead husband's heirs.

But that is precisely where Ḳ.2:240 says it does not lie.

Shāfiʿī realises that what derives from the Furayʿa *ḥadīth* is the conclusion that, if the house in which the widow is lodged is rented, the rent is to be paid from the dead husband's estate, as it would be paid by the divorcing husband whether or not he owned the property. But, the discussion on widows is less clear. Two views are tenable:

that what applies to the divorced, applies in precisely the same terms to the widowed. Those who took this view asserted that the Prophet's words to Furayʿa indicate the widow's entitlement to her accommodation, the cost being met out of the deceased husband's estate. The house in which she is lodged may neither be cast into the divisible property to be shared by the heirs, nor sold, until her *ʿidda* is completed. The second view is that her accommodation lies in the discretion of the heirs, who are now the owners of the property. If they do not choose to accommodate the widow, her husband, now dead, has certainly no rights in the property and cannot assign the house to his widow. She will, in this case, have no right to the accommodation, as she has no right to any financial support either.

Those who advocate this view apply *ta'wīl* to the Prophet's words, re-interpreting them to mean: 'Remain in your house – [so long as you are not turned out if it belongs to another]'. Furayʿa had explained that her husband had not owned the house.

If the widow owned the house, or if the husband's kin owned it and did not turn her out, she had no right to leave it until she had completed her *ʿidda*.

This may have been Shāfiʿī's final conclusion, since, pregnant or not, the widow receives no financial support and, as the husband's property rights die with him, the property is not his to dispose of.[64] It passes beyond him to his estate which has now become the joint property of all his heirs.

The doctrine that neither maintenance nor accommodation need be provided, even when the widow is pregnant, is traced to ibn ʿAbbās, ibn al-Zubayr, Djābir, Ḥasan Baṣrī, ibn al-Musayyab, ʿAṭā' and, among the *fuḳahā'*, to Mālik, Abū Ḥanīfa, Zufar, Abū Yūsuf, Shaybānī, and Shāfiʿī.

The contrary view on maintenance only is traced to: ʿAlī, ibn

Mas'ūd, ibn 'Umar, Shurayḥ, Djallās b. 'Amr, Sha'bī, Nakha'ī, Ayyūb, Ḥammād, Thawrī and Abū 'Ubayd, all of whom said that her maintenance should be provided out of the undivided estate. Ḳabīṣa thought it should come out of the share due to the child she was carrying.[65]

Ḳ.2:240 reads, as we have seen: 'Those of you who die leaving widows, a bequest to the widows, as a provision [*matā'*] for a twelve-month. They are not to be turned out, although, if they voluntarily opt to leave, you will incur no blame in respect of what they lawfully do . . .''

Ṭabarī was familiar with the concept that a man's property rights die with him, but considered that irrelevant to the discussion of the bequest which God had here granted direct to the widow. He is also familiar with two 'readings' of 'bequest'. An accusative reading tending to imply that the validity of the bequest depends upon the husband's act, he prefers the nominative reading which emphasises the obligatory, one might almost say, automatic character of the bequest.[66] The reading dispute was clearly the product of an ancient *tafsīr* argument that, prior to the revelation of Ḳ.2:234, the right of the widow to remain in the matrimonial home had been her legal due irrespective of whether the husband had made a bequest in her favour or not. The clear absurdity of supposing that a man can act after death – the implication, it was thought, of the accusative reading – induces the assertion that a *waṣiyya* is essentially an *inter vivos* arrangement by which a man arranges for the posthumous disposal of his property. It is merely intended to be given effect after his death. Thus, God Himself has granted the widow her right to a full year's accommodation following her husband's death. This must be regarded as a right conferred directly upon the widow, without reference to the husband who has ceased to exist. Further, were the right dependent upon the husband's act, and he failed to act, it would be lawful for the man's heirs to evict his widow – but God has expressly forbidden that. In support of these views, Ṭabarī can adduce *ḥadīth*s from: Ḳatāda, Rabī', ibn 'Abbās, Ḍaḥḥāk and ibn Zayd.

Those holding that the bequest depends upon the husband's act, include, however, Ḳatāda in addition to Suddī. But it is the Ḳatāda *ḥadīth* which brings out the juxtaposition of Ḳ.2:240 with Ḳ.2:180 most clearly:

> A man would make a bequest in favour of his wife and whoever else he pleased. That was repealed on the revelation of the Ḳ.4 inheritance regulations. The faculty of benefiting by bequest was thereupon restricted to those of his nearest kin who were not entitled to inherit anything.[67]

God had granted direct to the widow her accommodation and financial provision for twelve months and forbidden the man's heirs from interfering with her enjoyment of any of these rights. He declared the widow herself, however, free to abdicate her claim. The financial provision was later set aside, while the accommodation rights were reduced by seven months and twenty nights. The hollowness of this, his final conclusion is borne out by Ṭabarī's overlooking the fact that the four months and ten nights' *'idda* was not the widow's entitlement, but an obligation she was not at liberty to neglect. He does not consider the twelve months to have ever been an associated obligation imposed upon her. Hence, even on Ṭabarī's own *uṣūl*, the twelve months could never be said to have been subject to *naskh*, since he himself had defined *naskh* in his (now unhappily lost) *K. al-Bayān 'an uṣūl al-Aḥkām*, as: 'affecting the Ḳur'ān and the *Sunna* although there can be no *nāsikh* other than such as replaces an already valid, divinely imposed obligation.'[68] In this technical statement, Ṭabarī has incidentally thrown light on the impulse to show that 'the original *'idda*' had, indeed, been historically one of twelve months. Ḳ.2:234 and Ḳ.2:240 are not in conflict. Indeed, they do not treat a common topic. No acceptable evidence of a disparity of revelation date has anywhere been adduced. The two verses are perfectly capable of simultaneous implementation. Even Shāfi'ī conceded that Ḳ.2:240 need not be seen to be in conflict with Ḳ.4's inheritance regulations. His task as *uṣūlī* had, of course, been to verify an already existing *Fiḳh* doctrine elaborated before he was ever born. Ḳ.2:234 imposes the minimum period that must elapse before the widow may be permitted to contemplate re-marriage. Ḳ.2:240 declares her entitlement to both financial provision and accommodation from the dead husband's estate up to a maximum period of twelve months. This was a legal right she was to enjoy whether or not she was pregnant. It was thus not at all conditional upon her being pregnant, yet generous enough to include all normal pregnancies, even full-term posthumous pregnancies.

The undeniable rights of the widow had been tampered with in the post-Muḥammadan period, as the Ḳur'ān's regulations were being extracted and codified. In the age of the exegesis, unwarranted connection between the Ḳur'ān's provisions for widows with those made for divorced women and with those made in favour of related persons other than spouses had been made. All bequests to related persons who are also entitled to inherit had been suppressed, to avoid setting up two categories of heirs: those who would benefit both before and after the division of the heritable estate, including widows, parents and certain of the nearest kin; and single beneficiaries who would benefit only on the division of the estate – the other heirs. No mention is made in the discussions of the fact that, in the very Ḳ.4 verses on inheritances, regularly appealed to as having superseded the bequest verses, there occurs a four-times repeated refrain to the effect that the estate is to be divided only after the deduction of the deceased's debts and any bequests that he may have made.[69] These references were subsumed into the presumption that they concerned bequests to quite unrelated, or to non-inheriting related persons. Metaphysical and legal arguments to the effect that dead men are incompetent to act legally were exploited. However, a bequest is not a posthumous, but an *inter vivos* act maturing only after death. The systematic arguments were, in any case, incomplete, for logically they should have invalidated all classes of bequests, not merely selected classes of bequests that chanced to clash with the legal maxim: 'there is to be no bequest in favour of any heir.' Some tried to evade the maxim and the legal arguments on the counter-argument that the widow's rights were not dependent upon any act of the decedent but had been conferred direct by God without reference to the husband who had owned the property in his lifetime. Differing attitudes on this question had generated, they had not originated in, different 'readings'. One variant doctrine had appealed beyond the consonantal outline of the transmitted Ḳur'ān text to a 'variant reading' attributed to ʿUthmān's contemporary ʿAbdullāh b. Masʿūd, while, by varying the vowelling, a second 'reading' appealed to the text of the ʿUthmān *muṣḥaf* itself. Application of the principle that dead men are incompetent to act did not exclude their acting validly in favour of non-inheriting kin, nor indeed, of quite unrelated persons. This exposes the origin of the entire argument-structure in a legal principle: that no individual may benefit twice from one and the same estate. Not from the Ḳur'ān texts, but from an extra-Ḳur'ānic abstract legal maxim incompatible with the Ḳur'ān, all other arguments, whether in the form of *tafsīr-ḥadīth*s, or of *Sunna-ḥadīth*s, were amassed to proceed inexorably to a pre-determined conclusion. Indeed, it is interesting to observe that this legal maxim in the course of prolonged disputes, and especially in the context of the methodological debate as to the source of the *Fiḳh*, (expressed in the debate as to whether the *Sunna* had or had not ever superseded the regulations of the Ḳur'ān) developed a modified wording that incorporated expressions adapting it for use in those circles which argued that only the Ḳur'ān superseded the Ḳur'ān. It thus passed from being a simple *Sunna-ḥadīth* to take on the appearance of a *tafsīr-ḥadīth*, more correctly, an *uṣūl-ḥadīth*. '*God has granted* to all who have a valid claim their legal due; there will therefore be no bequest in favour of any heir.' The Prophet was thus made to testify that the bequests to parents, to widows and to nearest kin who are also heirs had been suppressed by God, not by the *Sunna*, but by the Ḳ.4 inheritance regulations. This developed form of the wording was probably later than Shāfiʿī's time, for, in its absence, he was at much greater pains than he need have been, had he known it in this form which so exactly conforms to his methodological principles on the relative status of Ḳur'ān and *Sunna* qua source in matters in which *naskh* is alleged. Both Makkī[70] and Sarakhsī[71] use the modified form to establish that this is an undeniable instance of the *naskh* of the Ḳur'ān by the Ḳur'ān.

The inconsistencies in the various appeals to *tafsīr*, with persons holding opposing views, nonetheless appealing to the same verses, or remaining silent on inconvenient verses – a procedure facilitated by, perhaps even fostering the selectivity and atomism of the exegesis – and the unnecessary complications imported into the discussions by the regular confounding of regulations governing divorce with those governing widowhood; the appeal to uncontrollable *Ḥadīth* materials, on the frank admission that the scholars had failed to discover 'indications' favourable to the *Fiḳh* doctrine in the Ḳur'ān itself, all point to a conclusion that the impulse to declare one verse superseded by another not evidently in conflict with it, came from outside the Ḳur'ān.

The Ḳur'ānic bequests to parents, nearest kin and widows had come into conflict with the *Fiḳh* doctrine on inheritances. When urged in their favour, the Ḳur'ān verses which unequivocally imposed those bequests, became the casualties of the clash.

The exclusion of the pregnant widow by appeal to the analogy of Ḳ.65:4 was one useful device for sowing the seed of the idea that *naskh* had affected Ḳ.2:234. That was next extended to the relation alleged between Ḳ.2:234 and Ḳ.2:240 specifically. Those represented in appeals to the authority of ʿAlī and ibn ʿAbbās, in support of their idea that the *ʿidda* of the pregnant widow was the later of the two terminations, that of the *ʿidda* itself, or that of her pregnancy, had engaged in a hopeless rearguard action to preserve at least a semblance of adherence to the texts of the Ḳur'ān. They were, however, overwhelmed by appeal, first to the authority of ibn ʿUmar, verified by projection from son to father, or to father's contemporary (also called ʿAbdullāh) ibn Masʿūd, until finally sealed by attribution to the Prophet himself. It had also been the Prophet who had allegedly declared, by appeal to the authority of God Himself, that the 'original *ʿidda*' had, indeed, been one of twelve months, later reduced to four months and ten nights. Exclusion of the pregnant widow from the regulation established in Ḳ.2:234 was the express function of the Subayʿa *ḥadīth*.

Reduction of Ḳ.2:240 to the Ḳ.2:234 period was the express function of the *ḥadīth*s of the Prophet's widows, Umm Salama *et aliae*.

The connecting of Ḳ.2:234 with Ḳ.65:1 was the express function of the Furayʿa *ḥadīth* which completes the grand circle cementing Ḳ.65:1's 'They shall not go out' to Ḳ.2:240's 'but, if they do go out.'

'Shown' to have been modified in one respect, Ḳ.2:240 could with a measure of plausibility, be shown to have been modified in further respects. Thus, the *'idda* of the widow was assimilated to the *'idda*s of other women 'required to observe an *'idda*.' The bequest to the widow was similarly assimilated to bequests to other relations. These exercises in exegesis represent a belated effort to adjust the Ḳur'ān texts to a *Fiḳh* doctrine which is fundamentally incompatible with the Ḳur'ān because it is initially formulated on the basis of something other than the Ḳur'ān wording. Its source had been that Ḳur'ān wording passed through the prism of early exegesis. Two stages in that ancient exegesis have been noted: the twelve month period for the whole duration of which the widow would have been entitled to her accommodation and financial provision had first been reduced, consequent upon the reduction of the 'original' *'idda* from twelve to four months and ten nights. Significant to our conclusion was Ṭabarī's general recognition that the explicit Ḳur'ānic obligation placed upon the husband's heirs to support the widow for any period had been removed on the revelation of the Ḳ.4 inheritance regulations. Ḳ.2:240 thus had two abrogands: Ḳ.2:234 and Ḳ.4:11–12.

Ḥāzimī had cited the Ḳ.2:240/Ḳ.2:234 case, as have also many of the writers on the *nāsikh* and the *mansūkh* as the 'classic' instance of the 'classic' mode of *naskh* – *naskh al-ḥukm dūna 'l-tilāwa*. But this 'classic' instance of the alleged *naskh* of the Ḳur'ān by the Ḳur'ān has failed to survive our detailed analysis. Serious doubt is therefore cast upon the entire category of *naskh al-ḥukm dūna 'l-tilāwa*, of which this instance is hailed as the least doubted example.

Equally undoubted was the proposition that the Ḳur'ān itself announced the divine employment of *naskh*. We therefore turn next in our enquiry to examine the alleged Ḳur'ānic bases of this proposition.

Six

THE ALLEGED ḲUR'ĀNIC BASIS OF NASKH

Such alleged conflict between Ḳur'ānic verses as we have just considered must surely have proved a source of considerable embarrassment in the first century to the original heirs of this self-contradicting Islamic heritage. That this, however, appears not to have been the case, was partly due to the view that a prophetic mission extending over more than twenty years could naturally have been expected to show signs of development and even some positive changes.

Universally acknowledged as one such admitted change was the alteration of the direction in which one should face for the ritual prayers. That had allegedly been altered some months after the Prophet's arrival at Madīna when the Muslims were bidden to turn towards Makka after having, for some time prayed in the direction, it is said, of Jerusalem. Muslim equanimity on *naskh* was thus principally due to the assertion that such embarrassment as might have been occasioned by the conflicts observable in the Ḳur'ān had already occurred in the lifetime of the Prophet himself and in circumstances which had provided God with the opportunity for a special revelation designed both to relieve Muḥammad of any anxiety and to satisfy Muslims and others as to the source of and the reason for such changes. This special revelation was held to be found in Ḳ.16:101: 'When we substitute one *āya* for another – and God knows best what He is revealing – they say, "Muḥammad, you are just a swindler". Most of them do not know.'

This verse came to be regarded by the commentators as irrefutable and sufficient 'evidence' from God Himself that the replacement of an earlier by a later *āya* was a significant aspect of the processes employed in the divine revelation plan. That this satisfactory resolution of the difficulty had not been achieved without considerable dispute and heart-searching is clear from the divisions in the *Tafsīr* as to the meaning of the verse. Protracted disputes there were which even in our own day have not quite died down. Nowhere in the course of the arguments is it explicitly stated what precisely was the root of the acute disquiet felt by some Muslims, although it is eloquently enough signalled in their unsuccessful attempts to exclude this particular 'evidence', or at least its vocabulary, from the 'proofs' of their *naskh* theories. Clearly some discomfort arose from the implications of the use of the term *tabdīl* [alteration] with its apparent hint at the mutability of the divine will. Perhaps a more satisfactory term ought to be looked for.[1]

Those, and these were the majority, who explicitly equated the Ḳ.16 term *āya* with 'a verse of the Ḳur'ān' and who further equated its term '*baddalnā*' with Ḳ.2's use of the term '*nansakh*', found in Ḳ.16 one of the two Ḳur'ānic props of their entire theory of *naskh*, having, in Ḳ.2:106, found a more appealing name for the principle. In their choice of this term, they have unwittingly supplied the clue that will enable us to pinpoint the source of their own unwavering certainty and at the same time, of the unease felt by their more scrupulous colleagues. The chief appeal of the term '*naskh*' was its 'good Ḳur'ānic pedigree.'[2] Ḳ.16:101 was, therefore, held to establish that *naskh*, as defined by the *uṣūlīs*, was an undoubted 'historical reality'; that, in His revelation, God had attributed *naskh* to Himself as an activity contributory to and integral with the other processes of divine revelation. Moreover, *naskh* was a divine activity the probability of whose occurrence might not be questioned or doubted, given this divine reference to it in the Ḳur'ān. It followed, therefore, that the theory of *naskh* must have been accepted by Muḥammad and the Companions and by each succeeding generation as an article of faith, undisputed and indisputable.

1. Ṭabarī's comment on Ḳ.16:101

Ṭabarī's comment on Ḳ.16:101 is characteristic of this view:

> God says, 'On the contrary, the majority of them do not know;' that means: 'When We *naskh* the ruling embodied in an *āya* of the Ḳur'ān and substitute in its place the ruling embodied in a second āya of the Ḳur'ān – 'and God knows best what He is revealing,' i.e. God knows best what is most beneficial to His creation in such substitutions or changes as He effects in His enactments; 'They say, "You are just a swindler!" ' The *mushriks* would give the lie to God's Prophet, saying to him, 'Muḥammad, you are just a fraud!' but God says, 'On the contrary, the majority of those who say that do not know that what you bring to them – both the *nāsikh* and the *mansūkh* of the Ḳur'ān – is all equally and authentically coming from God. The unbelievers failed to realise the truth of its authenticity.

Far from being a commentary on Ḳ.16:101, this is rather more the rationalisation of the theory of *naskh* 'placed into its historical context.'

The fact of *tabdīl* as an aspect of revelation was clearly, since mentioned in the contemporary Ḳur'ān, an article of the faith of Muḥammed. It must be taken to have been part of the reasoning of the prophet and of his teaching to his fellow-countrymen. Islam would, otherwise, long since have merged into Christianity or into Judaism, to the prophets of which two systems Muḥammed saw himself as heir and successor. But, that Muḥammad's recognition of *tabdīl* implies, as the *uṣūlīs* and exegetes insist, that Muḥammad accepted and approved something resembling their theories of *naskh*, remains to be investigated. The most one can say, at this point, is that it is safe to accord the highest antiquity to a general and as yet informal notion of revelation-by-substitution, evidenced by this very verse as also by Muḥammad's conduct and demeanour.

When Abū ʿAbdullāh says that one benefit of what has been handed down is the knowledge of the *nāsikh* and the *mansūkh*, and hence the capacity to distinguish the later from the earlier situation, thus the knowledge of which of the revealed regulations are still valid for the *Fiḳh*, as opposed to those which have been abandoned, he uses his terms in a narrow *uṣūlī* sense which is to assert, on the basis of mere words, that the *Ḥadīth* is the sole judge of the present validity of the individual revelation. So also the *ḥadīth*s on the *nāsikh* and the *mansūkh* used by the Muslim writers are anachronistic in that they project back into the oldest period both principles and definitions which did not achieve their present formulation until disagreement among the Muslims who attempted the first Islamic statement of the *sharīʿa* highlighted the desirability of rendering one's position on any one of the detailed questions under discussion immune from the charge that it represented nothing more than local custom, worse, merely the result of applying one's own fallible human judgment [*ra'y*] to the issues discussed in the documents of the revelation. It was clear from Naḥḥās' table of differing theoretical views in his day on the relative status of Ḳur'ān source and *Sunna*, [above, p 35] as also from every page of Shāfiʿī's *Risāla*, that these questions were far from being agreed in either the 'practice' or the theory of the Muslims more than two hundred years after Muḥammad and his Companions had been laid in their graves.

The high antiquity of a generalized theory of revelation-by-substitution is doubtless defensible, not only on the grounds of Ḳ.16:101, but from other grounds in the Ḳur'ān, such as the already mentioned change in the *Ḳibla*, to be examined more fully below. As one concrete instance of alteration by substitution, and in an important aspect of the cult, the *Ḳibla* is surer ground for our discussion than the vague and more abstract reference in Ḳ.16:101 with which, however, it shares the inestimable advantage of Ḳur'ānic mention. Moreover, since the *Ḳibla* is discussed in the Ḳur'ān and in a documented discussion contemporary with the event itself, it should afford us more light on Muḥammad's thinking than the academic discussions in the learned literature penned only some two centuries later.

Another consideration in favour of the antiquity of a generalised substitution theory, already hinted at, is that it must presumably have been prior in Muḥammad's thinking at least, and probably also in that of his contemporaries, to the view they took of the relationship, one to another, of the major religious dispensations originated in the historical prophetic cycle in which Muḥammed claimed to participate. Muḥammad's thinking would, of course, have included his own view of himself and the place he occupied in that cycle as the functioning heir to the role played by the prophets of the past in the evolution of the religious-based communities surviving into his own day. Had he, for example, regarded himself as their heir-in-full, he must presumably, it might be argued, have adhered in all main particulars to either the Christian or the Jewish system. Whether Muḥammad's view on this question was conscious and, if articulate, whether it remained consistent, also remains to be discussed. Whether it bore any resemblance to what later came to be known as '*naskh*', is the most important question of all which our study must confront.

What Abū 'Abdullāh and the other writers on *naskh* mean by the term is one or other of the special theories of *naskh* which had evolved by retrospective selection of techniques to document, and thus, legitimise *Fiḳh* doctrines in the discussions and disputes over sources and methods employed by the *fuḳahā'* which were to occupy the scholastic age.

The function of the theories of *naskh*, as their name implies, was to determine, given that *naskh* had occurred, where and when it had occurred. In distinguishing the *nāsikh* from the *mansūkh*, the former was held to be of the highest significance for the legal and theological purposes of the later scholarship, while the latter (if it survives at all) had no legal or theological importance, apart from its mere existence by which, in association with the undoubted suspension of its legal force, doubts that *naskh* had ever occurred could be stilled. To distinguish *nāsikh* from *mansūkh* in this sense, is obviously as a procedure, posterior to recognition of conflict within and between the sources. The definition of *naskh* and the determination of the modes by which it had operated, the extent of that operation, the validity, relative to each other of the major sources, Ḳur'ān, *Sunna*, and *Fiḳh*, the *ḥadīth* reports from Successors and Companions and their several exegeses of the Ḳur'ān, the books and *sunna*s of previous dispensations, the pre-Islamic customs and usages of the territories, Arab and non-Arab, brought under Islamic rule, the fiscal and other administrative arrangements made by successive Muslim administrations, the *idjtihād* of the *fuḳahā'* and the *'ulamā'* – all such questions had first to be settled for the *uṣūl* theory.

In the discussions it was a commonplace assumption, stated or implied, that the special theories of *naskh* – and thus the general theory as well – had all had a Ḳur'ānic origin, chiefly in the two verses commonly adduced as 'proof'-texts in this connection: Ḳ.16:101, already briefly noted, and above all, Ḳ.2:106, to be considered in detail below. Other verses less frequently quoted directly were also pressed into service and so there arose a considerable comment element in the *Ḥadīth*, *Fiḳh* and *Tafsīr* literatures.

In view of this supposed Ḳur'ānic basis, it might be expected that the earliest working out of the general theory would be presented in the exegetical literature. However, the extant overtly exegetical works are already later in the date of their composition than the fundamental products of the *Fiḳh* and *uṣūl* literatures which already exhibit the practical application of the various special theories of *naskh*. Not merely had the special theories predated the general theory whose function, as I have asserted, was to justify the special theories. More interestingly, the exegesis of the Muslims, as we know it, had behind it a protracted period of pre-literary existence. Long before the literary stage of Islamic culture, including the age that produced the first statements of *Fiḳh* and *uṣūl*, before even the production of the oldest *ḥadīth* reports, Islamic exegesis already had behind it a long history. That perhaps has been suggested by the *Ḥadīth* materials we have considered in the foregoing chapters.

On account of the place he occupies in the Islamic *tafsīr*, we turn next to a study of the exegetical treatment of the supposed Ḳur'ānic bases of the *naskh* theorising presented by Ṭabarī [d. AH 310/AD 922] in his *Djāmi'*, the oldest of the surviving major specialist exegetical works. His study will afford us valuable glimpses of the discussion of the different facets of *naskh* among the older exegetes and 'Readers' and their view of the modes of its operation which we can then set beside the conclusions of the practical and theoretical legal sciences for comparison.

By the incorporation of a great quantity of much earlier exegetical material culled from the writings of his predecessors, Ṭabarī stands less at the opening of the detailed consideration of the significance of the several Ḳur'ān passages to the discussions on *naskh*, than somewhat nearer the close of the first theoretical stages. It is less Ṭabarī's own contribution we seek – his dates are too late to lend crucial importance to his contribution to our knowledge of the emergence of the concept of *naskh* and its theoretical development – than the wealth of information from the earlier generations of the Successors and their followers with whose works he was familiar and much of which he preserves in his detailed and lengthy quotations which makes his work valuable. Many of the works of these earlier authors are being gradually brought to light in modern scholarly editions and, where comparison with the original texts becomes possible, Ṭabarī's citations are seen to be accurate, often verbatim. In his capacity of collector and preserver of exegetical materials still in circulation in his day, as handed down from the discussions of the first two centuries on all aspects of the Ḳur'ān text and its exegesis, Ṭabarī provides us with insight into the thinking-processes of the Muslims in their experimental time, as they took their first tentative steps towards what has since become the accepted orthodox formulation. His work presents a wealth of useful information on the detailed dissection of the texts whose consonantal, vocalic, etymological and syntactical features had already long been subjected to minute examination in the several rival regional centres, in an atmosphere still charged with intense and keen divisions on linguistic, legal and theological principles characteristic of a recently opened, lively controversy. In the course of sometimes acrimonious debates, numerous competing factions had hammered out compromises underlying and later reflected in the numerous 'variant readings' ultimately recognised by a less passionate generation as all equally valid and equally revealed by God. These 'readings', each accompanied by its panoply of *ḥadīth* and linguistic 'proofs' are not seen to represent, as the later traditional accounts assume, disinterested scientific attempts by 'academicians' to derive principles from the defective and inefficient primitive script used to record the ancient texts of the *muṣḥaf*, but rather the slogans of warring bodies of competing opinion, by implication differentiated by fundamental oppositions of a philosophical or theological character. Their importance to us is that they parade for our inspection the alternative views which, in their own day, had competed for the palm of recognition as the exclusive standard of Islamic belief.

These old 'readings', considered together with fragments of information dispersed throughout the *Ḥadīth*, *Tafsīr* and *Fiḳh* works, provide us with the documentation of obscure ancient quarrels. For example, of the two foundation-verses on whose basis the scholars have traditionally justified their theories of *naskh*, Ḳ.2:106, no fewer than eleven 'variants' have been recorded, each of which reflects a particular attitude to the manner of God's dealings with men, to the modality of divine revelation, the character and function of prophethood, and the qualities with which God was thought to have endowed His prophets and His prophetic community, Islam, and finally, to the relation thought to subsist between the Book of God and men's 'practice'.

The table of suggested 'readings' adequately illustrates the extent and profundity of the disagreements prevailing between the factions. 'Indeed, it is quite true to say that whatever views Muslims have wanted to project and advocate have taken the form of Ḳur'ān commentaries.'[15] To this, we may now add, 'and of Ḳur'ān "readings".'

Table 1

Ḳ.2:106	*The 'variant readings'*	*Attribution*
1.	mā nansakh min āya aw nunsi-hā	"Uthmān *muṣḥaf*
2.	mā nansakh min āya aw nunsi-ka-hā	Abū Ḥudhayfa[3/14]
3.	mā nunsi-ka min āya aw nansakh-hā	ibn Mas'ūd[4]
4.	mā nansakh min āya aw nansa-hā	ibn 'Abbās[5]
5.	mā nansakh min āya aw tansa-hā	Sa'd b. abī Waqqāṣ[6]
6.	mā nansakh min āya aw tunsa-hā	Sa'īd b. al-Musayyab[7]
7.	mā nansakh min āya aw nansa'-hā	Abū 'Amr[8]
8.	mā nunsikh min āya aw nunsi-hā	'Abdullāh b. 'Āmir[9]
9.	mā nansakh min āya aw nunassi-hā	Ḍaḥḥāk; Abū Radjā'[10]
10.	mā nansakh min āya wa nunsi-hā	'Alī b. abī Ṭālib[11]
11.	mā nansakh min āya aw nunsi'-hā	Anon.[12]
[12.	mā nansakh min āya aw nansu-hā	Anon.[13]]

The twelfth 'reading' properly belongs to an exegetical tradition which equated n s *kh* with t r k, 'to leave undisturbed' in the *muṣḥaf*. It is thus a sub-class of reading No. 4, above. These readings may be classified as under:

a. Hamzated readings:	nansa'	nunsi'	[tansa'	tunsa']
	(The reading tunsi' seems not to be found.)			
b. non-hamzated:	nansa	nunsi nunassi	tansa	tunsa
c. Single suffix:	nansa-hā	nunsi-hā nunsi-ka	tansa-hā	tunsa-hā
d. Double suffix:	nunski-ka-hā			
e. 'variant for nansakh:	nunsikh			

2. Ṭabarī's discussion of Ḳ.2:106[a]

Ṭabarī's discussion falls into three sections:

i. the *mā nansakh* clause; ii. the *aw nunsi-hā* clause; iii. the *na'ti bi-khairin min-hā aw mithli-hā* clause.

The mere presence in the verse of this final clause, and as the apodosis of a condition, ought prima facie to preclude any exegesis based on equating '*naskh*' with 'replacement'.

On turning to the detailed consideration of Ṭabarī's study of the verse, we note from the outset that he came to the verse at a moment when views on the relations between the sources of the *Fiḳh*, the Ḳur'ān and the *Sunna*, and when the conclusions of the legal sciences had reached an advanced stage of complexity. Secondly, we learn from his discussion that certain of the rationalisations embodied in the *naskh* theories were in some danger of breaking down. His discussion reads, in fact, as defensive in tone and apologetic in character. Above all, one is struck by the quite disproportionate brevity of the discussion of the first clause. One might take this as indicating that there had always existed reasonable unanimity on the reading and interpretation of the clause. But such appearances would be misleading, masking the considerable variety of views expressed as to the meaning(s) of the term *naskh* and as to its etymology. The variety merely widens the further we proceed in our consideration of the implications involved in the range of meanings and etymologies proposed. Ṭabarī's analysis assists in relating certain of these suggestions to the perspective of their progressive development. The meaning of *naskh*:

> The meaning of God's expression: *mā nansakh min āya*, is: 'Whatever *regulation derived from a Ḳur'ān verse* We transfer [*nanḳul*] to another regulation such that We replace [*nubaddil*][16] it and alter [*nughayyir*] it . . .' This means that God changes [*yuḥawwil*] the lawful into unlawful and vice-versa; the legally indifferent into proscribed and vice-versa. Such alterations affect, however, only commands and prohibitions, proscriptions or the (initial) absence of legal regulation, the forbidding of actions, or the declaring them to be legally indifferent, [i.e. in imperatives only]. There can be neither *nāsikh* nor *mansūkh* in relation to non-imperative, indicative statements [of fact].

The reading of Ḳ.2:106

Ṭabarī acknowledges only one reading: *mā nansakh min āya* . . . He relates this to the root: *n s kh yansakh naskhan nuskha*. The 'variant' *nunsikh* he rejects as quite simply an error.[17] The origin of the term *naskh* is, he says: *nasakha al-kitāb*, meaning, 'he transferred the book from one exemplar to another.' This is also the meaning of the *naskh* of a *regulation* to another regulation, which means: God's moving it [*taḥwīl*] and transferring it [*naḳl*] (or His utterance regarding it) to another utterance different from the first. Since this is the meaning of the *naskh* of the *āya* [*sic*!] then, once the regulation expressed by the *āya* has been transferred and altered, and the obligation arising out of the *āya* replaced, the duty of the Faithful having been re-directed from what had originally been imposed upon them by the ruling of the original *āya*, it is immaterial whether the wording of the original *āya* is endorsed and left to stand undisturbed in the *muṣḥaf*,[18] or whether all trace of the *āya* is expunged [*muḥiya*][19] erased and forgotten [*nusiya*][20] since, in both events, the *āya* is *mansūkha* and the new regulation which replaces the original regulation, and to which the obligation now imposed upon the Faithful has been transferred, is the *nāsikh*.

This is a very muddled definition of *naskh*. In his role of exegete, Ṭabarī is faced with appalling difficulties in reconciling with the single term *naskh* used in this clause all the multiple strands of the highly complex contemporary theories of *naskh*.

Ṭabarī's Tradition-'proofs'

> Ḥasan's view was the same as ours. Ḥasan commented: 'Your Prophet would be instructed to recite a Ḳur'ān and would subsequently forget it [*uḳri'a ḳur'ān thumma nasiya-hu*].[21] It became of no account. There are also parts of the Ḳur'ān which you still recite which have been *mansūkh* [suppressed/replaced?]

If Ḥasan's view is the same as Ṭabarī's (and he admits that there are 'two events') then Ṭabarī accepts:

i. *naskh al-ḥukm wa-'l-tilāwa*: for Ḥasan, this was clearly derived from Ḳ.87:6–7.

ii. *naskh al-ḥukm dūna 'l-tilāwa*.

His invitation to compare his view with that of Ḥasan underlines the first mode of *naskh* which is not derived from Ṭabarī's etymology of the term. Nor is Ṭabarī's argument that once the regulation has been replaced, it is immaterial whether the original wording be 'expunged, erased or forgotten'. His etymology, *n s kh*, *nuskha*, involves duplication which links, for him, with the co-existence of two Ḳur'ān wordings and two regulations. The principal *locus* of the *naskh* was, for Ṭabarī, necessarily the regulation. That has induced him to interpolate the term regulation [*ḥukm*] into the texts of each of Ḳ.16:101 and Ḳ.2:106, before launching into his interpretation. His chief concern was undoubtedly the survival in the *muṣḥaf* of texts whose regulations were, for the *Fiḳh*, 'inoperative'. The Muslims had regarded certain of the Ḳur'āns verses as 'a dead letter'. But, as for Ḥasan, so also for Ṭabarī, only one *naskh* 'phenomenon' affected the *muṣḥaf*. Conflict of sources had resulted in the retention in the *muṣḥaf* of verses whose rulings had evidently been 'suspended'. The 'second event', the Prophet's [exegetically derived] forgetting of the Ḳur'ān, being devoid of all practical consequence for the *Fiḳh*, can be entirely ignored. The forgotten revelations are as if they had never existed: 'that became of no account'. This, however, is not similar to Ṭabarī's argument that, given *naskh*, (shown by the change of regulation) the *mansūkh* verse has either verbally survived in the *muṣḥaf* or has had its wording 'expunged, erased and forgotten'. This goes beyond Ḥasan's view by adding to the change of the regulation whose wording 'you still recite', cases of the change of the regulation of verses whose wording 'you no longer recite'. For Ṭabarī, himself, there can be no such 'historical' occurrence, since, for him, *naskh* means especially 'change of regulation'. This addition which he has made to what Ḥasan had discussed must be something purely speculative, abstract and theoretical. Although *naskh* means 'replacement', Ṭabarī is here alleging that 'supersession' is a kind of quasi-'suppression'.

Ṭabarī's tafsīr-'proofs'

The scholars have disagreed about: *mā nansakh*: some say it means: Whatever *āya* We withdraw . . . others that it means; Whatever *āya* We replace . . . yet others that it means: Whatever *āya* We record, but replace its ruling . . .

His concern is now to harmonise several independent lines of traditional exegesis. The first of these is the 'replacement' *tafsīr*, attributed to ibn ʿAbbās, but actually a reference to Ḳ.16:101. This would appear to be supported by the reports from the Companions of [ʿAbdullāh] ibn Masʿūd: 'We endorse the wording of the verse, while changing the regulation,' i.e. the 'classic' mode of *naskh*: *naskh al-ḥukm dūna 'l-tilāwa*. Ṭabarī's etymology would stretch only as far as the first clause: 'We endorse the wording of the *āya*.' The second clause derives either from Ḳ.16:101 or from: *na'ti bi-khairin min-hā aw mithli-hā*. Both clauses of the ibn Masʿūd *tafsīr* cannot simultaneously be derived from: *mā nansakh min āya*, since Ṭabarī has insisted that *n s kh* means 'to copy a book'.

The wording of Ḳ.2:106 itself challenges the interpretation Ṭabarī seeks to place upon it: 'Cases of *naskh* where the wording of the original verse survives in the *muṣḥaf* are no different from those cases in which the original wording of the verse disappeared following the change of its regulation.' But no cases have been reported in the literature in which the wording of a Ḳur'ān *āya* disappeared following the alteration of its ruling. Ṭabarī is therefore reacting to the objection: 'if the ruling is, as you say, "inoperative", then why has the wording been permitted to remain in the *muṣḥaf*? Why was not the wording removed?' Ṭabarī's reply is that Ḳur'ān verses whose rulings have been suspended are 'as good as withdrawn'. His problem is now clear, since the harsh reality is that Ḳur'ān verses whose rulings are alleged to have been altered, have not been withdrawn.

The flaws in Ṭabarī's etymology of *naskh* have been noted by other scholars:

> There is in Arabic the usage: *nasakha 'l-kitāb*, but this sense of the root *n s kh* cannot be said to occur in the Ḳur'ān and the scholars have criticised Naḥḥās for supposing that it did. They argue that the *nāsikh* in the Book of God does not reproduce the precise wording of the *mansūkh*. The *nāsikh* cannot be said to be a 'copy' of the *mansūkh*.[22]

The whole point and purpose of the elaboration of the theories of *naskh* had been precisely to account for the occurrence in the *nāsikh* of a wording thought to be seriously at variance with that in the *mansūkh*.

> The view of those who maintain that *naskh* means: turning someone from one rite to another rite is erroneous. The term *naskh* need not imply 'replacement', It can mean simply 'withdrawal'.[23]
>
> *Naskh*, in the Arabic language, has three senses: *nasakha 'l-kitāb*, referring to the transfer of the contents of a book to a second

> exemplar. That in no way *alters* the original. It merely gives rise to a copy identical to the original in wording and meaning. Both copies continue in existence. This sense of the term has no connection with Ḳ.2:106, there being in the Ḳur'ān no verse which is the *nāsikh* of another of which it reproduces both the sense and the wording.[24]

Thaʿlabī makes the point even more explicit:

> The term *naskh* in Arabic has two senses: *naḳl*, as in *nasakha 'l-kitāb min ākhara*; this sense cannot be adduced in the discussion of Ḳ.2, 106. The meaning here, is the second sense: *izāla*, suppression.[25]

But, already long before the birth of Ṭabarī, the first of the great Muslim lexicographers, al-Khalīl [d. c. AH 170/AD 786] had allegedly defined *naskh* in his celebrated *K. al-ʿAin* as:

> izālatuka amran kāna yuʿmalu bihi thumma tansakhu-hu bi-hādithin ghairi-hi: ka-'l-āya fi amrin thumma yukhaffafu fa tansakhu-hu bi-ukhrā . . .
>
> Your suppressing a command which has been acted upon; subsequently you replace it with a new, different command; as, for example, the verse containing a command which is subsequently moderated and you replace the original command by means of a second verse.[26]

Thus, already by the middle of the second century, there had been completed a considerable process of reflection on these matters and certain conclusions had been reached by means of the comparing of a number of Ḳur'ān contexts whose vocabulary can here be detected. Also visible is the influence of the *fuḳahā'*: 'a command which had been acted upon', and the attempts to explain current Islamic 'practice'. *Naskh* had already attracted a number of definitions, two of which are not interchangeable: *suppression* and *supersession*. These are the same *tafsīrs* we met with: 'withdrawal' and 'replacement'. Here, as in the later use of this definition, there is no reference to 'copying'.[27] The emphasis appears to be on the 'practice' rather than on the Book and the *āya* or Ḳur'ān verse is mentioned merely as the incidental vehicle of its ruling, not as the exclusive field of operation of *naskh*. Certainly, in this definition, the term *āya* can refer only to a verse of the Ḳur'ān. The definition already therefore marks a secondary stage in the exegesis. A third element in the definition, *takhfīf*, alleviation, we have already met in Shāfiʿī's vocabulary, where it exhibited a tendency to rationalise rather than define *naskh*. It is an undisguised reference to Ḳ.8:66. Khalīl's is more a gloss than a definition. It is certainly contradictory, since, if *naskh* means *izāla*, i.e. suppression, it cannot simultaneously mean *tabdīl*, or replacement, supersession. Clearly, what is being defined there is no mere lexical item, but a technical term with, already behind it, a lengthy history of use.

For Shāfiʿī, *naskh* was a contrary of *athbata*[28] and synonym of *yamḥū*[29], *azāla*:[30] He uses it as equivalent to *taraka*, i.e., 'to abandon', 'suppress', and that the word really conveyed to him something less than 'to replace' emerges from the dictum: 'No obligation is ever *mansūkh* without another being promulgated in its place.'

Yet, it is interesting to note that Shāfi'ī who at no point in his thesis evinces the least interest in some hypothetical 'proto-Ḳur'ān' from which bits have dropped out, but is concerned solely with what has survived in the *muṣḥaf* and with how that relates to the *Fiḳh*, speaks of the *naskh* of the obligation [*ḥukm*] just as above we noted Ṭabarī's interpolation of the term *ḥukm* into: *mā nansakh min [ḥukmi] āya*.

The *tafsīr-ḥadīth*s adduced in the names of Ḥasan, ibn 'Abbās and ibn Mas'ūd were intended to reinforce acquiescence in a view which had apparently come under attack and which Ṭabarī was concerned to sustain: namely, that the *muṣḥaf* includes 'inoperative' verses. The verses had been ignored in the *Fiḳh* on the plea that their rulings had been seen to be replaced by other rulings. We recall here the story in which the attack on this idea had been projected back to the moment at which 'Uthmān was assembling the revealed materials into the *muṣḥaf*: why, he was asked, had he bothered to record Ḳ.2:240, when he knew its ruling to have been replaced by the ruling of Ḳ.2:234. 'Uthmān had defended his action on the grounds that he knew the wording to have survived 'as part of the Book of God'. In one sense, that verse was *mansūkha*, its ruling had been replaced; in another it was *mansūkha*, to be recorded and copied out in the *muṣḥaf*. The wording was not *mansūkha*, suppressed, abandoned.

Ṭabarī, concerned like Shāfi'ī, with the *Fiḳh*, argued that a verse whose ruling had been replaced is as good as withdrawn. It was 'immaterial' whether its wording survived in the *muṣḥaf* or had also been withdrawn like its ruling. This underlines the continuing tension between two definitions of *naskh*: 'withdrawal' and 'replacement'. In Ṭabarī's time, at the end of a third century, there had been achieved a tolerable consensus in favour of *naskh* as a 'phenomenon' that had been at work on the documents of the Islamic Tradition. There remained, however, resistance to the suggestion that, as far as the Ḳur'ān at any event was concerned, the *muṣḥaf* contained 'inoperative' statements. Some could not conceive of *naskh* as occurring in the Ḳur'ān sphere other than by simple withdrawal of revealed verses. This may be in keeping with our suggestion that one of the roots of the *naskh* theorising had lain in the reactions to the finding of the root *n s y* in both Ḳ.87 and Ḳ.2: 106. *N s y* points to 'forgetting', i.e. 'omission'.

Most could apparently be persuaded, on comparing the *Fiḳh* with its sources in the Ḳur'ān and *Sunna*, that there were indeed instances where the wording of the *nāsikh* and the *mansukh* appeared simultaneously in the documents of the Tradition. Resistance had, however, been expressed to the idea that this could be true of the Ḳur'ān, the Book of God. This could have arisen from the exegesis of certain verses of the Ḳur'ān such as, for example, Ḳ.4:82: 'Were it from other than God, they would find in it many contradictions and conflicts,' perhaps from Ḳ.17:86, or possibly, Ḳ.15:9. Possibly the source of the hesitation lay in the opposing definitions of the term '*naskh*' itself. What has allegedly been suppressed or withdrawn cannot simultaneously survive in the texts. The survival of the wording alone suggests the intended survival of the ruling also.

The *sunna*s which had survived in the literature were such as had either successfully or unsuccessfully challenged some doctrine of the *Fiḳh*. Surviving, but unsuccessful, i.e. 'inoperative' *sunna*s recognised as nonetheless 'sound' in the *isnād*, could be explained as having been superseded by some other element of the Tradition. By definition, there is no such thing as a non-surviving 'inoperative' *ḥadīth*. We have already asserted that *naskh al-ḥukm wa-'l-tilāwa* had never needed to be predicated of any *sunna*, for, alone of the two sources, the Ḳur'ān had to be reckoned with as both source and document. The claim on behalf of the *muṣḥaf* that it is the *mutawātir* record of a revealed book of immediate divine authorship, inimitable alike in its rulings and its wordings, imposed upon the Muslims a need for a degree of delicacy that did not arise in their discussion of the *Sunna* but which must be faced in every attempt to define terminology in vogue in discussions on *naskh*. One *sunna* may, for example, be held to replace another *sunna*, since their author, the prophet, may, like any human, change his mind, or encounter fresh circumstances. In the *Sunna* context, there was no difficulty in defining *naskh* as 'replacement'. Greater circumspection must, however, attend the discussion of *naskh* as it affects the Ḳur'ān. Resistance might be expected to any declaration that the revealed Book of God contained both *nāsikh* and *mansūkh* – supplying evidence of its internal self-contradiction.

Ṭabarī's insinuation that *mansūkh* verses are as good as withdrawn could be countered by the observation that in many instances of *naskh*, the verses have not been withdrawn. Perhaps, it could be insinuated, they have not, as alleged, been *mansūkh*.

The technique adopted by Ṭabarī of distinguishing two types of revealed utterance: imperative and indicative, is aimed at this difficulty. Where *naskh* is defined as *tabdīl*, 'replacement', its operation is confined to imperatives, positive or negative. Where, however, faced in the Tradition with allegations of the *naskh* of statements self-evidently not imperative, the scholar is free to interpret the term as 'simple withdrawal'. The technique is useful for the relief of theological scruples but offered no answer to those who doggedly insisted that *naskh* means only 'withdrawal'.

From Ṭabarī we therefore learn that tension had arisen between two originally independent exegetical traditions: the 'withdrawal' and the 'replacement' schools. Each of the traditions, based originally on opposed views of the Prophet, produced differing exegeses for Ḳ.87, now brought to bear upon their exegeses of Ḳ.2:106. Some had supposed that the verse's use of the two roots *n s kh* and *n s y* indicated that the two were synonymous. That is possibly what lay behind one 'reading' attributed to ʿAlī: '*mā nansakh min āya wa nunsi-hā . . .*'

Both 'withdrawal' and 'replacement' cannot flow from the one term '*nashkh*'. If Ḥasan's reported comment be typical of the pre-Ṭabarī exegesis, it offered views on two quite discrete and separately 'verified' phenomena: the loss of once-revealed matter, justified on the basis of Ḳ.87:6–7; and the co-existence in the Tradition of two (or more) statements (at least one of which figured in today's *muṣḥaf*) dealing in different ways with one and the same topic. That was 'verified' by reference to Ḳ.2:106. In Khalīl's reported gloss on *naskh*, adjustment of the tension was already under way: 'the suppression of a command which had been the basis of the practice *and* its replacement by a second, differing command'. An 'original' ruling is suppressed; the 'original' wording is not suppressed. A fresh wording is revealed whose ruling replaces that of the first wording and both wordings survive.

This and Ṭabarī's exegesis are both of historical significance in that they preserve a clue as to how two originally separate and unconnected phenomena, suppression and supersession, had been brought together in the theoretical synthesis arrived at by the discussions on sources conducted under the aegis of conclusions already reached in their technical discussions by the *uṣūlīs*. Khalīl's gloss refers exclusively to *naskh al-ḥukm dūna 'l-tilāwa*. Ṭabarī's 'removal from the *muṣḥaf*' of the wording of a verse whose ruling has been ascertained to have been replaced, following which, the wording may be erased, expunged or forgotten, is the purely hypothetical basis of the harmony now effected between two unconnected allegations: the substitution of later for earlier rulings [Ḳ.16:101]; the forgetting, resulting in the omission from the *muṣḥaf* of once revealed matter [Ḳ.87:6–7]. Derived from the *tafsīr* of Ḳ.87, the latter was at first a more primitive exegesis which has now been overlaid with a considerable measure of sophistication deriving from the more rigorous view that what had previously been reported in the Tradition to have been 'just forgotten' had not 'just been forgotten'. It had been deliberately removed from His text by the divine author of the Book. The withdrawal had occurred only after the ruling, if any, embodied in the wording, had first been replaced. A consciously planned act of divine revelation, the Ḳur'ān may not be held to have been at any moment during its 'development' exposed to mindless chance. Further, should any body of Muslims persist in the argument that certain verses (such as those alleged by the *Shīʿa* to indicate clearly the divine intent that ʿAlī was to succeed the Prophet) had maliciously been omitted from the *muṣḥaf* by its collector, ʿUthmān, or such as those urged by the Shāfiʿites in support of one of their *Fiḳh* views, and allegedly gobbled up by a domestic beast when the household were pre-occupied with attending to the dying Prophet, it could confidently be asserted that their rulings had incontrovertibly been suppressed.[31] The same argument could also serve in external, as well as in internal polemic, should any non-Muslim be so bold as to seize upon the Muslim admissions that parts of their supposedly revealed book had been 'lost'.

In the purely internal *Sunnī* disputes where the concern, in the course of documenting the *Fiḳh*, was to argue that certain Ḳur'ān rulings had been set aside by replacement rulings, it is the more easily conceivable that *ḥadīth*s 'illustrating' the withdrawal, expunging or forgetting of Ḳur'ānic verses were themselves merely part of the ordnance deployed by those who propounded either a particular exegesis of Ḳ.87, or wished to promote the claims of the *Sunna* rulings. The intention of the latter would be to impart their conviction that the Ḳur'ān, 'incomplete' in the absolute sense, was not fitted to serve as the sole source of the *Fiḳh* regulations.

We have noted a tendency to argue that the Ḳur'ān is 'incomplete' relative to the *Fiḳh* on account of its alleged 'ambiguity'. The ultimate product of ideas of this kind would be the argument that, being 'incomplete' in the historical sense, the *muṣḥaf*, as we possess it, is not fit to serve as the sole source of the Ḳur'ān.

Once acceptance was gained for the notion that certain Ḳur'ān rulings have simply been withdrawn; and for the rationalising notion that certain verses had been withdrawn in order that they might be replaced, assent might also be confidently anticipated in a strictly syllogistical argument, for the notion that certain other verses had been replaced without being withdrawn. That was Ṭabarī's position. But, in that case, ran the objection, why was not the wording of the verses also withdrawn? Because, is the reply, the Ḳur'ān, unlike the *Sunna*, has a dual function. Both its rulings and its wordings have been divinely revealed and, as there is reward for the implementation of the rulings, so also there will be reward for recitation of the wordings. Besides, the survival of a wording following the alleviation of its ruling serves as a permanent reminder of God's Holy solicitude for the Muslims.[32]

All is mere rationalisation designed to meet, step by step, a fading objection to the increased reliance of the *uṣūlī*s on the principles of *naskh*. The regular reply of the scholars was to point to the 'undeniable' conflicts within the body of the triune Tradition of *Fiḳh*, Ḳur'ān and *Sunna*, while stressing the 'unambiguous' words of the Ḳur'ān itself in Ḳ.16:101 and Ḳ.2:106.

The consummation of rationalisation was reached when a scholar was prepared to argue that it is also conceivable that the wording of a Ḳur'ān 'verse' might be withdrawn, without its ruling being replaced. We shall have to consider alleged instances of this 'phenomenon' below.

Ḥasan had appeared to be impressed by the argument from the conflict of sources. He was said to have accepted the '*naskh*' of certain Ḳur'ān rulings by some other unidentified element of the Tradition. The Muslims 'continued to recite the wording'. Ṭabarī discussed two 'phenomena': suppression following 'replacement'; and 'replacement' followed, but only on occasion, by suppression. In this way, by a process of formalisation, the alleged Ḳur'ānic 'losses' had become a mode of *naskh*: *naskh al-ḥukm wa-'l-tilāwa* a formula achieved by a conflation of the exegeses of Ḳ.2:106 and Ḳ.87:6–7, the determining factor being the shared root, *n s y*.

From the observable conflict of sources emerged also: *naskh al-ḥukm dūna 'l-tilāwa*, or *naskh* of the ruling alone, formed on the analogy of the first. The first formula had been the creation of the exegetes; the second was the creation of the *uṣūlīs*. There would emerge the theoretical reflex of Ṭabarī's analogy: that certain Ḳur'ān rulings having been replaced, their wording had become redundant and so might be withdrawn from the texts; whence he had advanced to the argument that certain other Ḳur'ān rulings acknowledged to have been replaced, their wording, although remaining in the *muṣḥaf*, not having been withdrawn, nevertheless had come to be regarded as redundant. The continuing presence in the texts of redundant wording need cause no embarrassment. The *fuḳahā'* had not felt obliged to 'act' on their basis. These wordings were 'quasi-withdrawn'. Thus, mere inclusion in the *muṣḥaf* does not imply 'operativeness'. The mirror image of this proposition would be, was already being urged by, for example, Shāfi'ī's followers: mere exclusion from the *muṣḥaf* does not necessarily imply 'inoperativeness', for that was the inescapable conclusion to be derived from their *imām*'s *Fiḳh*, in the light of his *uṣūl*. He had alleged, as we shall see, the omission of verses from the *muṣḥaf*, the continuing validity of whose rulings was nevertheless insisted upon by the Muslims, as may be seen from the *Fiḳh*.

For Shāfi'ī, and now for Ṭabarī, Ḳur'ān and *muṣḥaf* are not coterminous. For *muṣḥaf* refers to the Ḳur'ān document. But Ḳur'ān refers to the Ḳur'ān source – to all that was revealed to Muḥammad, not all of which, as we see, has survived in the *muṣḥaf*. The distinction implies that, to some, those reports on the Prophet's 'forgetting' revelations refer to some hypothetical proto-Ḳur'ān once revealed to the Prophet. Shafi'ī never once referred to this concept. He had arrived at his conclusions on the basis of the *Fiḳh*, read in the light of his particular *uṣūl*, that is to say, in the light of his special theory of *naskh*. Ṭabarī claims to have reached the same conclusion, but on the basis of his consideration of the implications of the etymology of *naskh*. The term 'Ḳur'ān' if understood to mean 'what is to be recited' [in the ritual prayers] is co-terminous with *muṣḥaf*; if interpreted in the sense of what Muḥammad was bidden to recite to his fellow-countrymen as revelations coming from God, it is not co-terminous with the *muṣḥaf*, since it refers to no known physical object, but to an abstract concept, namely 'all that was ever revealed to the Prophet' relative to which, the *muṣḥaf* which is in our hands must be deemed to be incomplete.

It is inconvenient for the reader that the Muslims, in their discussions on *naskh*, have not consistently observed their own distinction in nomenclature. In addition, both 'Ḳur'ān' and '*muṣḥaf*' are ubiquitously referred to as 'the Book of God'. The theories of *naskh* had been devised to bridge this gap between two aspects of 'revelation': the source and the texts.

The term '*naskh*' occurs twice in the Ḳur'ān, but its discussion has been bedevilled by the insistence of the Muslims on treating the two contexts as circumstantially distinct and unconnected. We have sampled something of the variety of interpretations offered for the term in Ḳ.2:106. Khalīl's gloss had carried echoes of at least three Ḳur'ānic contexts: 'suppression' [Ḳ.22:52]; 'alleviation' [Ḳ.8:66]; 'replacement' [Ḳ.2:106]. Undoubtedly, Khalīl had read the last context in the light of the other two.

We have seen that Shāfi'ī had regarded *naskh* as synonymous with 'suppression' – *izāla*. His thinking had also been influenced by the rationalisation that *naskh* signals 'alleviation', a concept he exploits to explain the 'replacement' of revealed rulings as well as to justify from the Book of God itself, his appeal to the 'occurrences' of *naskh* as allegedly mentioned in Ḳ.8:66; Ḳ16:101; Ḳ.13:39; Ḳ.9:67, and Ḳ.2:106.[33]

The same confusion between 'withdrawal' and 'replacement' is to be seen in the 'evidentiary materials' adduced from the profane language. The various etymologies of *naskh* were collected by Abū 'Abdullāh:[34]

> In the view of the lexicologists, *naskh* has a definable etymology; in the view of the semanticists, it has a definable content, while, in the view of the *uṣūlīs*, *naskh* operates within specific conditions. As to its origin in the language, the root has the sense of the nullification of something *and* the setting up of something else in its place. Abū Ḥātim said the word means: 'The transfer of the honey and the bees from one hive to another.' One instance of this use would be: *nasakha 'l-kitāb*. The word expresses two concepts:
>
> i. coming to an end, ceasing to exist: *in'idām*.

ii. coming to an end, changing locality: *intiḳāl*.
Further, the first of the concepts has two aspects:
ia. supersession: *nasakha 'l-shaibu 'l-shabāba*, grey hair replaced youth.
ib. suppression: *nasakhat al-rīḥu 'l-dīyār*, the wind obliterated the traces.
This aspect is exemplified in the withdrawal of a legal ruling, i.e. its nullification *without* replacement. The *naskh* which means *naḳl*, transfer, derives from *nasakha 'l-kitāb*, which does not mean he terminated the existence of the first book. He merely transferred what was in the first book to the second. A Ḳur'ānic instance of this usage would be K.45:28: *innā kunnā nastansikh mā kuntum ta'malūn* – 'We transfer it by reducing it to writing on records, or from one record to another.'
The generally recognised meaning of *naskh* in relation to the Ḳur'ān is, however, the nullification of the original ruling, while the original wording is recorded. Whether in the *Sunna* or in the Ḳur'ān, both *nāsikh* and *mansūkh* are retained in the texts, save only that the *mansūkh* is no longer acted upon. For example, the *'idda* of the widow was originally one of twelve months [Ḳ.2:240]. That was replaced by a four months and ten nights' *'idda* [Ḳ.2:234]. Both texts are extant in the *muṣḥaf*.

Committed to only one of these etymologies, Ṭabarī had had to bring his exegesis into line with the axioms of the sciences which had already derived the main lines of the *uṣūl*. For consistency, he spoke of the 'transfer of the Faithful from one ruling to another'. The Ḳur'ān spoke of the *naskh* of an *āya*. He next sought to reconcile the two traditional etymologies of the root 'withdrawal' and 'replacement' by finding room for both. Giving main emphasis to the 'replacement' exegesis, he then had to speak of the 'withdrawal' as a possible, but not essential consequence of replacement. Given the replacement of a Ḳur'ān ruling, its wording may be withdrawn, or it may not. That is 'immaterial'.

Shāfi'ī had taken *naskh* to mean 'suppression' necessarily followed by 'replacement'. Logically, if not historically, 'suppression followed by replacement' should bring the same result as 'replacement followed by suppression', providing one is discussing only rulings: Ṭabarī, the exegete, was, however, in addition, discussing the text, and we have seen that in the text of the *muṣḥaf*, many verses appear whose rulings are regarded as 'a dead letter', on the argument that they had been suppressed. Further, the exegete must take account of the accumulated wealth of *tafsīr*-inspired *ḥadīth*s still in circulation.

In defining *naskh* as 'to abandon, *t r k*' Shāfi'ī was less concerned with the wording of the *muṣḥaf*. His business was to justify the *Fiḳh* against the *muṣḥaf*, wherever the two appeared to clash. We have seen the same root *t r k* taken to mean 'to leave something where it is, undisturbed.' This definition has been diverted to the rationalisation of the observable fact that the wording of many are allegedly *mansūkh* Ḳur'ān verse has been left undisturbed where it was in the *muṣḥaf*, despite the alleged abandonment of its ruling.

This was what had provoked a pro-Ḳur'ān counter-argument that whatever had been 'left' in the texts had by that very token, not been abandoned. The argument for the 'replacement' etymology of *naskh* had therefore been developed to counter the propaganda that any verse not suppressed has self-evidently not been abandoned. We have seen just such an attitude work in the *Fiḳh* to produce the views attributed to ʿAlī and ibn ʿAbbās to the effect that the *ʿidda* of the pregnant widow must be 'the longer of the two periods', if all the relevant verses are to be honoured. But, if it be true that this 'replacement' etymology is a counter-etymology, then the older of the two etymologies must be 'withdrawal'. That is in line with the Ḳur'ān's use of the word in Ḳ.22:52, and that such was the case, is borne out by the Khalīl definition and by Shāfiʿī's usage, as well as by Ṭabarī's present problem with the view that verses 'left' in the *muṣḥaf* ought not to have been abandoned in the *Fiḳh*. That objection made it necessary for those using the Ḳur'ān as their 'proof' of *naskh* to distinguish '*āya*' from 'the ruling of the *āya*'. They could then distinguish the *āya*s still present in the *muṣḥaf* whose rulings had been abandoned in the *Fiḳh*. It becomes desirable – indeed, essential – to interpolate the word *ḥukm* into both Ḳ.2:106: *mā nansakh min [ḥukmi]* āya . . . *and Ḳ.16:101: wa idhā baddalnā [ḥukma] āya makāna [ḥukmi] āya* . . .

Here is the procedure which accounts for the awkward wording of the *naskh* formulae and which, at the same time, confirms the suspicion that *naskh* cannot possibly mean 'replace' in: 'Whatever *āya* We X or Y, We shall bring one better than it, or, at least similar to it.'

Nor can *naskh* mean 'replace' in *naskh al-ḥukm wa-'l-tilāwa*, the formalisation, as we saw, of the old 'forgetting' exegesis of Ḳ.87:6–7 and *Ḳ.2:106*. It could never mean 'replace' in: *naskh al-tilāwa duna 'l-ḥukm*, which represents the assertion that a ruling which is still represented by a wording in the *muṣḥaf* had allegedly been replaced by a ruling embodied in a form of words universally admitted *never* to have formed part of the text of the *muṣḥaf*. It might be argued that in the formula representing the 'classic mode' of *naskh*: *naskh al-ḥukm dūna 'l-tilāwa*, one does mean precisely the 'replacement' of the ruling. One could not, however, continue the translation: 'without the replacement of the wording'. Much more satisfactory is the translation: 'the suppression of the (original) ruling without, however, the suppression of the original wording of the verse'. 'Suppression' is thus the only term which can be substituted for *naskh* in each of the three formulae without distorting the meaning of any one.

The distinction between 'wording' and 'ruling' had been forced upon the Muslims especially in their interpretation of Ḳ.2:106: *nat'ti bi-khairin min-hā aw mithli-hā* by pressure from the doctrine of the Ḳur'ān's *i'djāz*. No verse of the Book of God can be thought to be 'superior to' [*khair*] any other verse, the whole being miraculously inimitable and the individual verses individual instances of perfection. Ḳ.2:106 cannot therefore, refer to the Ḳur'ān wording, was the argument. It can refer only to the rulings of the verses. Here is an auxiliary argument in favour of the interpolation of the word *ḥukm* into the wording of *mā nansakh min āya* . . .

This aspect of the interpretation of Ḳ.2:106 is, however, merely another instance of the use of the Ḳur'ān for evidentiary purposes in favour of this or that view based, not directly upon the Ḳur'ān, but again, on the exegesis of Ḳur'ān statements [Ḳ.2:23; Ḳ10:38; Ḳ11:13].

Shāfi'ī, we have said, insulated his discussion of the incidence of *naskh* in the *Sunna* from that of its incidence in the Ḳur'ān. For him, Ḳur'ān rulings replace Ḳur'ān rulings; *Sunna* rulings replace *Sunna* rulings. Nothing can replace a *Sunna* ruling except another *Sunna* ruling. Shāfi'ī does not explicitly say that a Ḳur'ān ruling cannot replace a *Sunna* ruling, although he does argue that a *Sunna* ruling cannot replace a Ḳur'ān ruling. But this is an empty concession, since he was able to extract from the Ḳur'ān itself a rationale that not only preserved the *Sunna* against the Ḳur'ān, but, by references to verses quoted from the Ḳur'ān, gave the *Sunna* the appearance, as *bayān* to the Ḳur'ān, that is, its elucidation, of being consistently posterior to the Ḳur'ān. That makes the *Sunna* indispensable for the understanding and interpretation of the Ḳur'ān which is frequently charged with 'ambiguity'. Besides, the Ḳur'ān lays down only general rules and the *Sunna* makes these specific. The two sources are thus inseparable, mutually interdependent, and from their interplay, one derives the valid *Fiḳh*.

Shāfi'ī, the *uṣūlī*, compares his datum, the *Fiḳh*, with its sources, Ḳur'ān and *Sunna*. Ṭabarī, the exegete, must be concerned with Ḳur'ān as both document and source. By his day, the theoretical role of the *Sunna* had been secured – chiefly through the work of Shāfi'ī. Starting from the *Fiḳh*, Ṭabarī can now afford in cases of apparent conflict between his *Sunna* and Ḳur'ān sources to be more sanguine in the occasional assumption that *naskh* indicates the replacement of a Ḳur'ān ruling by a *Sunna* ruling – even where the original wording is still present in the *muṣḥaf*. The collection of the *Sunna* was now well advanced so, again, unlike Shāfi'ī, should he argue the Ḳur'ān's occasional *naskh* by the *Sunna*,[35] Ṭabarī need not fear reprisals against the *Sunna* from those who would point out its contradiction of the occasional verse. Where the *Fiḳh* points to practice different from that adumbrated in the Ḳur'ān, Ṭabarī can and does conclude that the Ḳur'ān ruling has been abandoned. His certainty cannot be shaken by the consideration that the corresponding Ḳur'ān wording has not been abandoned. The decisive criterion for Ṭabarī, as it had been for Shāfi'ī, is the *Fiḳh*.

Thus, the distinction between the ruling of the Ḳur'ān verse and its wording was essential if the *Sunna* ruling were to prevail over the Ḳur'ān ruling in any given instance of conflict. The wording of the *Sunna*, admittedly of human origin, might not be thought to be either 'superior to' or even 'similar to' the wording of the Ḳur'ān. But the rulings of the *Sunna* could well be, not merely similar to those of the Ḳur'ān, but even superior. This distinction between the wording and its ruling thus neutralised objections to *naskh* based on the *i'djāz* of the Book of God. Similarly, the separation of indicatives from imperatives neutralised any objection based on the concept of the immutable perfection of divine knowledge and the immutability of the divine will. Such objections might always be anticipated when *naskh* was defined as *tabdīl*, 'replacement'. Both imperative and indicative divine statements might be withdrawn. Only divine imperatives might be 'replaced'. This had the effect that the divine Lawgiver must be projected as arbitrary and unpredictable and the divine determinations as unamenable to rational explanation or probing. The Supreme Being imposes or forbids whatever He chooses. Nothing is either good or evil *per se*; God does not command 'the good' and prohibit 'the evil'. What God commands is good and what He forbids is evil. God is under no compulsion to any external moral imperative. Adherence to what He commands will be rewarded; performance of what He forbids will be punished. Both command and prohibition being tests of human obedience, God may *naskh* what He chooses.

In another phase of the discussion, the 'suppression' etymology, also derived from the Ḳur'ān [Ḳ.22:52] and the older of the two etymologies, was exploited in accounting for the history of the Ḳur'ān texts. It explained, for example, the 'disappearance' of the alleged 'variant codices' of the Companions, whose existence may be merely a hypothetical allegation linked perhaps to the 'duplication' etymology favoured by Ṭabarī himself. He informs us, for instance, that when 'Uthmān promulgated his *muṣḥaf*, all other *nusakh* were *mansūkh* – abandoned, suppressed.[36]

We have seen Ubayy, 'Umar and others testify to the loss of certain allegedly revealed matter not included in this *muṣḥaf*. They are elsewhere shown as insisting, however, that the rulings of those 'verses' had not all been abandoned in the *Fiḳh*. Exclusion of 'revelations' from the 'Uthmān *muṣḥaf* was not, therefore a test of the authenticity or inauthenticity of those 'verses'. It merely indicated that, although revealed, Ḳur'ān verses were not understood *on that account alone*, to be destined for inclusion in the *muṣḥaf*. Their exclusion refers in some instances, however, solely to their wording. The *Fiḳh* will show that their rulings have continued to be valid.

This marks a further stage in the growth of the Ḳur'ān-source doctrine. It is, however, a view which would be upheld solely by those who failed to grasp the significance of the distinction being made by others between the ruling and the wording of a text and so could not reconcile themselves to the notion that the non-*mu'djaz Sunna* could ever have superseded the *mu'djaz* Book of God. Clearly, those were scholars who had clung to the 'replacement' etymology of *naskh*.

To account for elements of the *Fiḳh* not mentioned in the *muṣḥaf*, or irreconcilably at variance with what is mentioned in the *muṣḥaf*, these men were driven by their own logic to postulate the existence of a 'Ḳur'ān' outside the *muṣḥaf*. Under the spell of certain *tafsīr-ḥadīth*s, Shāfi'ī had already reached this position on the question of the number of breast-feedings required to establish a lifelong ban on marriage between certain 'milk relations'.[37] The main development of this position which culminated in the addition to our *naskh* formulae of the third mode: *naskh al-tilāwa dūna 'l-ḥukm*, seems to have taken place in the post-Shāfi'ī period, at the hands of those dazzled by his forensic brilliance, but also in consequence of his failure to solve yet another *uṣūl* crux arising out of an observable conflict of sources. In his discussion of Ḳ.4:23, however, Shāfi'ī had undoubtedly pointed the way to this development.

Those on the contrary who could accept with equanimity the notion that the *Sunna* might supersede the Ḳur'ān – and those alone – i.e. those who had adopted the 'replacement' etymology wholeheartedly and, by separating wording from ruling enabling themselves thereby to distinguish between the *mu'djaz* wording and the non-*mu'djaz* rulings of the Ḳur'ān which might be replaced by the non-*mu'djaz* rulings of the *Sunna*, had no need to postulate the existence of a Ḳur'ān distinct from the *muṣḥaf*. Ṭabarī, we see, was of this company.

Explaining the diametrically opposed *uṣūl* stance of two groups of scholars, 'replacement' proclaims that it had become the predominant definition of *naskh*. It is significant in this connection to note the frequency with which etymological disquisitions introduced into the *tafsīr* and *uṣūl* works close with the frank admission that, in any case, the technical vocabulary of the Islamic sciences is independent of the original meanings of words in the Arabic language.[38] The term *naskh* is held to be an Islamic word, a *shar'iyy* term.

Ṭabarī had embarked on the discussion of *naskh* on the basis of linguistic analysis, his task as exegete being to demonstrate that 'both aspects' of the *naskh* phenomenon had been alluded to in the Book of God. But 'both aspects' have not here been demonstrated as arising from the necessary implications of the Arabic root *naskh*. From the outset, as a technical term, *naskh* clearly referrred to 'replacement' and since Ṭabarī insists, although the Ḳur'ān does not, that only imperatives are summarily replaced, *naskh* with that meaning had to be restricted. Indicative statements may not be replaced, for to hold that they might involved theological penalties. His categorical assertion that there can be neither *nāsikh* nor *mansūkh* in relation to indicatives (determined by choice of etymology), and his further assertion that once the ruling conveyed in an *āya* has been replaced, it is 'immaterial' whether the wording of the *āya* remains in the *muṣḥaf* or disappears, far from bringing the two traditional etymologies into a comfortable harmony, merely points up the potential embarrassment which the old 'withdrawal' *tafsīr* represented. It had existed long before Ṭabarī's day and was still in circulation as it featured in a number of 'sound' *ḥadīth*s which guaranteed that it could not be overlooked. It certainly caused him problems in explaining the continued presence in the *muṣḥaf* of supposedly withdrawn or suppressed *āya*s. He attempted therefore to detach the 'withdrawal' exegesis from *naskh*, by applying to it a specialised subordinate role as a merely possible consequence for the earlier of a pair of revealed forms of words. When *naskh* occurs, the earlier wording may be withdrawn, or it may not. Which of the two procedures God decides to adopt in any given instance, is 'immaterial' to us men. In either event, the earlier verse is *mansūkh*. But, if *naskh* means 'replacement' and if indicative statements cannot be replaced, what is to be made of the frequent mention in the Tradition of the *raf'* – or even the *naskh* – of self-evidently indicative statements? These are now to be re-interpreted in the sense of mere 'withdrawal', with no divine intent to replace them. In this assertion, Ṭabarī is surely in breach of his own preferred definition.

A protagonist of the 'replacement' etymology and an advocate of the principle that the *Sunna* had, on occasion, superseded the rulings of the Ḳur'ān, Ṭabarī had no need to postulate the withdrawal of a single word of the Ḳur'ān. He was, of course, under strict obligation to *ḥadīth*s, now hallowed by the Islamic consensus. Accepting information on such withdrawals from the Ḳur'ān, he presumed that they had been revelations of a non-imperative character. He was, however, principally addressing the issue of the alteration of rulings, hence of imperatives, and since he has quite failed to establish that the survival of the wording of the later *āya* is occasionally accompanied by the disappearance of that of the earlier *āya*, within the terms of the necessary implications of the word *naskh*, it follows that any knowledge he displays of such 'disappearances' did not derive from the etymology of *naskh*. It would have been based either upon some unambiguous revelation that such might be expected to happen, or upon mere *ḥadīth* reports alleging that such things have actually happened. In short, Ṭabarī's exegesis of Ḳ.2:106 is not so autonomous as he believes, and would have the reader believe. It shows its dependence upon factors external to and independent of the wording of Ḳ.2:106. If that be thought to be the case, then the claim to find independent Ḳur'ānic support in the verse for the general theory of *naskh* fails. His exegesis is, in fact, circular: the explanation of Ḳ.2:106 depending upon that of Ḳ.16:101 which, in turn, refers back to the *tafsīr* of Ḳ.2:106. Ḳ.16:101 undoubtedly uses the term *tabdīl*; both it and Ḳ.2:106 use the notoriously vague term *āya*. Equating that with 'a verse of the Ḳur'ān', Ṭabarī understands this to refer to regulations, since only regulations can be 'altered'. That his exegesis is circular is placed beyond all doubt by the *ḥadīth*s which, as usual, he amasses in support of his view. From Mudjāhid, he derives the statements: 'Ḳ.16:101 refers to God's revealing an *āya*, withdrawing it and revealing another in its stead.' 'We *naskh* it, replace it, withdraw it and reveal another.'

This use of the term *naskh* looks less like 'replacement' and rather more like 'withdrawal'.

From Ḳatāda, he reproduces: 'Ḳ.16:101 is like Ḳ.2:106: *mā nansakh min āya aw nunsi-hā* . . .'

The significance of the linkage between Ḳ.16:101 and Ḳ.2 is shown by Rāzī:[39]

> In my *Maḥṣūl fī uṣūl al-Fiḳh*, I took the line that the historical occurrence of *naskh* is established by Ḳ.2:106. But, to adduce that verse as one's proof that *naskh* has actually occurred is weak, since the particle *mā* is conditional. One might say, for example: *man djā'aka fa-akrim-hu*. That does not affirm that anyone will come, but merely states that should someone come, it will be necessary to show him honour. Similarly, Ḳ.2:106 does not affirm that *naskh* is an actual occurrence. It merely states that should *naskh* occur, (if it ever does) God will bring that which is better, or similar.
>
> A more satisfactory procedure for establishing that *naskh* does actually occur is to adduce Ḳ.16:101 or Ḳ.13:39.

These observations indicate sufficiently the spirit in which the Ḳur'ān texts are appealed to in *uṣūl* discussions. Rāzī fails to mention that the temporal particle *idhā* of Ḳ.16 does not necessarily imply occurrence; or, more importantly, the general view[40] of the scholars that Ḳ.16 had been revealed at Makka, whereas no instance of *naskh*, in the sense of 'replacement' is reported as occurring before the *hidjra*. The difficulty has not, however, been overlooked. It has been resolved that *idhā*, having a proleptic function, Ḳ.16:101's reference to *naskh* points to the future![41]

Ṭabarī adduces no 'historical' *ḥadīth*s to demonstrate the 'actual occurrence' of *naskh* until he turns, later in his exposition, to the hotly debated question of whether the Prophet might or might not be held to have forgotten any of the divine revelations. The reason for their appearance at that point was his need of 'proof' to counter the denial that such a thing was possible, or had ever happened. The importance of the section is that the old 'withdrawal' exegesis of Ḳ.87 was making difficulties and we now learn how, in the light of the exegesis of Ḳ.2:106, it had finally been formalised. One was, however, hardly prepared to find Ṭabarī in the guise of its champion. It is equally significant to note that in that role, Ṭabarī failed to notice that the old 'withdrawal' *tafsīr* is ultimately incompatible with his 'transfer' exegesis.[42]

The *ḥadīth* information he produces on the ibn Ādam 'verse' and the Bi'r Maʿūna 'verse' considered with other *ḥadīth* reports 'too numerous to cite' leads him to the conclusion that the omission of once-revealed matter from the *muṣḥaf* is too publicly known to be denied. He does not claim that any of the verses mentioned had ever been replaced. He implies that the mode of their withdrawal had been by their being forgotten, which sufficiently explains their absence from the *muṣḥaf*. The interest this passage holds for us is that it emphasises the distinction that had grown up between 'forgetting' and *naskh* and between *naskh* and 'withdrawal'. It thus emphasises the distinction between the linguists' definition of *naskh* and that of the *uṣūlīs*.

> It cannot be considered absurd by anyone equipped with sound intellect [*ʿaḳl*] and valid historical information [*naḳl*] that God should cause His Prophet to forget part of what He had revealed to him . . . The verse adduced by the opponents of this view, Ḳ.17:86, 'If We wish, We can remove what We have revealed to you', does not inform us that God will not remove part of the Ḳur'ān. It merely tells us that He will not remove *all* of it.[43]

Ṭabarī then proceeds to argue that this Ḳ.17 verse announces that God

> removes that part of His revelation which we do not need. Any part of the revelation that has been replaced is unneeded, and may be removed. God also said, [Ḳ.87]: *sa-nuḳri'uka fa-lā tansā – illā mā shā'a 'llāhu* . . . which means that God *will* cause His Prophet to forget that which it pleases Him to have him forget. That which has disappeared [*dhahaba*] from the original revelation is what God here expresses by His use of the exceptive clause – *illā mā shā'a 'llāhu*.

There are thus, for Ṭabarī, two classes of Ḳur'ān 'omission':

i. Bi'r Maʿūna and ibn Ādam – removed, hence 'inessential'.
ii. certain *mansūkh āyas* – inessential, hence removed.

Here, we see the theoretical advance that has been made in the interpretation of Ḳ.87, now formalised in the light of Ḳ.2:106. By treating two types of removed once-revealed matter as separate, Ṭabarī suggests two distinct modes of removal: *naskh al-ḥukm wa-'l-tilāwa*, which provides the base for the analogically derived *naskh al-ḥukm dūna 'l-tilāwa*. For him, the first was either subordinate to and consequential upon the second, the replacement of a Ḳur'ānic ruling; or, additional, a second mode of removing once-revealed matter, independently of the notion of the replacement of rulings, and it was too well documented in the Tradition to be questioned. Some of his opponents would simply call this 'forgetting' and roundly deny its possibility. Ṭabarī failed to fit this type into his system. It lay outside his etymology of *naskh* and its presence in the Tradition ought to have embarrassed him. He would hesitate to call it '*naskh*', since there is no replacement involved; he prefers to regard it as simple *raf'*. He thus treats of three classes of phenomenon: Ḳur'ānic rulings having been replaced, their wording survives; the suppression of Ḳur'ānic wording, following the replacement, i.e. the suppression of the rulings; and removal by withdrawal. The second and third have in common: the removal of some part of the original revelations made to Muḥammad; the mode of removal is forgetting – but forgetting under divine control and in strict accordance with the divine intent to make withdrawal possible by causing the Prophet and the Muslims to forget. His problem with *raf'* is that it derived from the traditions inspired by the exegesis of Ḳ.87 and cannot be accommodated to either Ḳ.16:101 or Ḳ.2:106, his major Ḳur'ānic props. Besides, in *raf'*, only wording is involved. No ruling has been replaced or suppressed. It cannot therefore be accommodated in terms of Ṭabarī's etymology of *naskh*: 'replacement', and to that extent, it eluded his theory of *naskh*.

We must emphasise Ṭabarī's isolation of Ḳ.2:106 from its Ḳ.2 context, and his severe isolation of only this first clause *mā nansakh min āya* from the other clauses of the Ḳ.2:106 conditional sentence. His entire concentration is on the one word: *naskh*. We have seen that he has nothing to say on the third mode of *naskh*: *naskh al-tilāwa dūna 'l-ḥukm* the effect of which, if not the name, was already current among the *uṣūlīs*. Our suggestion was that his own attitude to the sources, Ḳur'ān and *Sunna*, made such a mode unnecessary to his theory of *naskh* since, on occasion, he was prepared to contemplate the *naskh* of a Ḳur'ān ruling by a *Sunna* ruling, as, for example, in the case of his account of the origin of the Islamic penalty of death by stoning for adultery. For this reason, the third mode of *naskh* did not have to find a place in his exegesis of Ḳ.2:106, nor be shown as part of the necessary implications of the 'meaning' of the Arabic root *naskh*.

Ṭabari's reference to the ibn Adam and Bi'r Ma'ūna 'verses' and the use to which he puts them, shows the extent to which his exegesis of Ḳ.2:106 is pre-determined by an earlier layer of exegesis (originally derived from the interpretation of Ḳ.87) but now part of the *Sunna* which the scholar cannot leave out of account in working out the interpretation of Ḳ.2:106.

3. The second Ḳur'ānic occurrence of the root *N S KH*

Ḳ.22:52 We have not sent before you any Messenger or Prophet but that, when he *tamannā*, the Devil cast into his *umnīya* – but God *naskh*s what the Devil casts and then God confirms His *āya*s, *fa-yansakh allāhu mā yulḳī 'l-shayṭān thumma yuḥkim allāh āyātihi*.

The verse sets out, in clear opposition to each other, the action of the Devil and the counter-action of God, thus permitting the exegete little latitude in his interpretation of this term *naskh*, which is perhaps why so much of the effort has fastened instead upon the word *tamannā*. When the verse is adduced as further Ḳur'ān 'proof' for *naskh*, the suggestion is brushed aside:

> Some use this verse to prove the legitimacy of *naskh* as a phenomenon affecting the Ḳur'ān texts. Ḳ.22:52, however, merely indicates God's *naskh* of what the Devil desires to insinuate into the Prophet's recital of the revelations. That does not indicate the *naskh* of what God reveals and imposes. There is here no proof of the legitimacy of the *naskh* of what God considers to be the Truth that He Himself revealed.[44]

With no reference to any other Ḳur'ānic use of the root, Ṭabarī defines *naskh* in Ḳ.22:52 as: 'to remove' [*adhhaba*]; 'to bring to nothing' [*abṭala*] or declare to be such.

> There is no doubt that by *āya*s is meant here the *āya*s of the revelation. We know that the Devil had insinuated into the revelations precisely what God declares that He has *naskh*ed – brought to nought. Then God firmly establishes His own revelations by His *naskh* – by His nullification of the expressions insinuated by the Devil.
>
> The *tafsīr* will be: 'We have not sent before you a Messenger or prophet but that, when he recited the Book of God, or repeated it, or discoursed, or spoke, the Devil insinuated false matter into the Book of God which he was reciting, or repeating, or into his discourse as he spoke. God maintains His revelations by the *naskh* of what the Devil insinuates – God removes what the Devil cast onto the tongue of the prophet, brings it to nothing, and confirms His own *āya*s – God purifies the *āya*s of His own divine Book, ridding it of the vain falsehood which the Devil had insinuated into the speech of his prophet.[45]

That this definition of *naskh* differs so radically from that Ṭabarī offers in his comment on Ḳ.2:106 can be due only to conscious choice on his part. The basis of this difference might perhaps have lain in the realisation that 'what the Devil had insinuated' could, for the monotheist, never constitute a valid ruling or a valid wording. Shāfi'ī had defined *naskh* as: 'God abandoned His earlier imposition which had been true, for its time'.[46] '*taraka farḍa-hu . . . kāna ḥaḳḳan fī waḳti-hī*'.

That could never be applied to the exegesis of Ḳ.22:52. To argue that here, *naskh* means 'transfer' would involve the psychologically unacceptable concept of God and Devil as virtual partners in an act of revelation. The Ḳ.22 phenomenon must thus represent to the Muslim exegete a different order of event from the *naskh* mentioned in Ḳ.2:106. But the word has not changed; the language has not changed. This is still *naskh*! 'But, this is the "linguistic" use of *naskh*, rather than the technical use of the term. As a technical term, *naskh* refers to certain principles accepted in *uṣūl*.'[47]

The *naskh* used by the *uṣūlī* means 'replacement'; the *naskh* used in Ḳ.22:52, means: nullification – suppression. The allegation that the word has two separate connotations, one in Arabic and the other in *uṣūl*, is simply to admit with total candour that the technical term *naskh* which forms the subject-matter of the present investigation cannot be traced to Ḳur'ānic usage – or, at least, not to Ḳ.22:52.

Ṭabarī's appeal to exclusively linguistic considerations in his defining of *naskh* at Ḳ.2:106, is here demolished by a single blow delivered by his own hand. Similarly, we saw Rāzī, although he insists on citing Ḳ.22 in 'proof' of his etymology of *naskh*, cites from preference Ḳ.16:101, Ḳ.13:39 with Ḳ.2:106, when his aim is to establish that 'Islamic *naskh*' has occurred.

4. Ṭabarī's comment on the *aw nunsi-hā* clause

Ṭabarī discusses no fewer than six 'readings' of this clause. That provides further confirmation of the intensity of the earlier debates on the verse and the implications of its interpretation both for the understanding of the 'historical' data of the *Ḥadīth* and for the theological theory.

The Medinese and Kūfans read:[48] *aw nunsi-hā*. This points to one of two possible meanings: i. 'forgetting'.

> Ḳatāda said, 'God used to *naskh* one *āya* by a later *āya*; the Prophet used to recite one or more verses which would subsequently be forgotten and withdrawn.' Ḳatāda used to say, 'God would cause His prophet to forget what He pleased; God would also *naskh* what He pleased.'

Comments of this sort settle the question of the juxtaposition of Ḳ.2:106 with Ḳ.87:6–7.

Mudjāhid reports 'Ubayd b. 'Umayr as saying:

nunsi-hā means: 'We withdraw it from your possession [*raf'*]. 'Forgetting' was also the *tafsīr* of Sa'd b. abī Waqqāṣ who, however, read: *aw tansa-hā*. al-Ḳāsim, hearing Sa'd say: *aw tansa-hā*, informed him that Sa'īd b. al-Musayyab read: *aw tunsa-hā*. Sa'd replied, 'The Ḳur'ān was not revealed to Sa'īd, nor to his family! God says: *sa-nuḳri'uka fa-lā tansā* [Ḳ.87:6–7] and: *udhkur rabba-ka idhā nasīta* [Ḳ.18:24].

The general 'forgetting' *tafsīr* had preceded and determined all these 'readings', parallel Ḳur'ān contexts being appealed to, in support of the suggested 'reading' of Ḳ.2:106. This Sa'd/Sa'īd episode enables us to see more clearly than usual how varying theological considerations had influenced the adoption of this or that pointing and vowelling. *Isnād* critique also operated in Sa'd's questioning the connection of Sa'īd's reading backward to what had actually been revealed. Normally, the variant 'readings' display only the end-result of such quarrels. The detailed documentation leading to the adoption of this or that 'reading' is seldom so clearly presented.

The second of the possible meanings of *aw nunsi-hā* is: ii. 'to abandon', based on *nansa/nunsi* equating with *natruk*, *t r k*. cf. *nasū 'llāha fa-nasiya-hum* [Ḳ.9:67]. 'They abandoned God, and so He abandoned them.'

As God cannot 'forget', whenever applied to the divinity, the root *n s y* must be interpreted as meaning something other than 'forgetting'. Thus, Ḳ.2:106 is to be interpreted: 'Whatever *āya* We *naskh*, i.e. altering its ruling and replacing its injunction, We shall bring something better than what We alter, or at least similar.'

What this interpretation implies is that *aw nunsi-hā* means: 'We leave it – We do not *naskh* it,' i.e. the clause *aw nunsi-hā* can be completely ignored as it adds nothing to the sense of Ḳ.2:106! Associated with this *tafsīr* were ibn 'Abbās: *aw nansa-hā*: 'We leave it – We do not *naskh* it.' Suddī: *aw nunsi-hā*: 'We leave it – We do not *naskh* it.'

The distinction between Form 1 and Form 4 can also be ignored! The interpretation attributed to Suddī generated two daughter-exegeses:

i. 'We do not *naskh* it – We do not replace the wording.'

ii. 'We do not *naskh* it – We do not reveal the wording.' (This is derived from the etymology: *nasakha*, 'to copy' – sc. from the Heavenly original of the revelations.)

i. means 'We do not repeal' and ii. means 'We do not reveal'. Both interpretations represent the flight from the repugnance of attributing 'forgetting' to the Omniscient.

The Heavenly original is once more in view in ibn Zayd's interpretation: *aw nunsi-hā*: 'We expunge it.' [Ḳ.13:39] [*yamḥū 'llāhu mā yashā'u wa-yuthbit – wa-'inda-hu ummu 'l-Kitāb*.] On vocabulary and interpretation grounds, this recalled Ḳ.87.

There is, too, a close affinity between ibn Zayd's *tafsīr* and Ḳ.22:52's use of the root *n s kh* with, however, the contextual environments of Ḳ.2:106, Ḳ.22:52 and Ḳ.13:39 studiously ignored.

5. Ṭabarī's discussion of Ḳ.2:106[b]

A more determined effort to evade the 'forgetting' *tafsīr* altogether is exemplified in the reading: *aw nansa'-hā*, allegedly adopted by certain Companions and Successors.[49] It was then taken up by the 'readers' of Kūfa and Baṣra. This reading, with its interpretation, was promoted by ʿAṭā', ibn abī Nadjīḥ and Mudjāhid, while it is generally ascribed in the literature to ʿAbdullāh b. Kathīr and Abū ʿAmr b. al-ʿAlā'.

A view ascribed to ʿAṭā' [ʿAṭiya(?)][50] has the same ambiguity as that ascribed to Suddī: *aw nansa'-hā* means: 'We defer it – We do not *naskh* it.'

In the literature devoted to the *ḳirā'āt*, we usually do not have to look far for different 'readings' whose exegeses nevertheless coincide. Without a doubt, the interpretation was the prior element, the 'reading' its posterior justification 'from the Ḳur'ān' [*bi-wadjh min al-wudjūh*].

ʿUbayd b. ʿUmayr is reputed to have held that *aw nansa'-hā* means[51] 'We defer it,' which flatly contradicts the earlier report that ʿUbayd was held to have interpreted *aw nunsi-hā* to mean: 'We withdraw it from your possession [*rafʿ*].'

Without a doubt, the attribution was the latest element of all. One man's name has here been borrowed for two quite differing 'readings' arising from two quite differing *tafsīr*s.

For Ṭabarī, *aw nansa'-hā* means:

> Whatsoever verse, having revealed it to you, Muḥammad, We replace – annulling its ruling whilst endorsing its wording – or We defer – endorsing the verse, not altering it but re-affirming it without replacing its ruling – We shall bring another better than, or similar to it.

He prefers 'defer repealing' to 'defer revealing'. For '*naskh*', he prefers '*tabdīl*', replacement, to 'withdrawal'. The *tabdīl* has, however, been imported from his comment on Ḳ.16:101 rather than from that on Ḳ.2:106, while from Ḳ.22:52 he now imports 'annulling' (nullification) of the ruling, although 'endorsing the wording' could never be applied in the interpretation of Ḳ.22. His *tafsīr* envisages only one mode of *naskh*, which points the finger at that mode as the one certain factor in all the ratiocination, i.e. 'annulling the ruling while endorsing the wording,': *naskh al-ḥukm dūna 'l-tilāwa*.

Curiously, not once does Ṭabarī refer to Shāfiʿī's interpretation of the same verse, especially of the reading *aw nansa'* as: 'the deferment of a revelation': *ta'khīr inzāli-hi*.[52] Now, we have also seen that, for

Shāfi'ī, *mā nansakh min āya* meant: 'Whatsoever verse We repeal,' and not 'Whatsoever verse We reveal.' In interpolating the expression *naskha-hā*, [i.e. reveal] immediately after the words *aw nansa'-hā* to reach his final interpretation: 'Whatsoever verse We repeal, or defer [its *naskh*] its revelation,' Shāfi'ī has interpreted this one single term '*naskh*' in two entirely unconnected senses within one and the same Ḳur'ānic sentence.

Although *nasakha 'l-kitāb* was the starting-point of his interpretation, it is an etymology Ṭabarī nowhere further mentions in the course of his *tafsīr* of Ḳ.2:106. Instead, we find him now, not once, but twice defining the term *naskh* as 'nullification' [*abṭala*] the concept he employed in his comment on Ḳ.22. The source of Ṭabarī's 'transfer' definition of *naskh* was not *nasakha 'l-kitāb*, but more probably *naḳala 'l-kitāb*, 'to copy, translate', hence 'transfer'. We may recall Sidjistānī's: 'removing the bees and the honey from one hive to another'. That his own *nasakha 'l-kitāb* etymology did not recur to his mind, once he launched into his exposition, might be inferred from the forthright manner in which he rejects a reading attributed to ibn 'Āmir: *mā nunsikh min āya* – from which, beyond suggesting that it meant: 'Whatsoever *āya* We cause you, Muḥammad, to *naskh* . . .' he apparently derived no useful sense. His reasons for rejecting this reading were its lack of foundation and its failure to conform with the readings of the Tradition.[53]

The reading: *aw tunsa-hā* he lumps with *aw nunsi-hā*. The one being passive and the other causative, the net effect is the same, the efficient agent in either case being God. He rejects *aw tunsa-hā*, and with it, *aw tansa-hā*. Both are *Shādhdh*, departures from the reading-Tradition.[54] He expresses his personal preference for *aw nunsi-hā* – providing it is interpreted in a sense other than 'forgetting'. The equivalent of *natruk-hā*, it means: 'We leave it, We do not *naskh* [alter] it; We leave it undisturbed in the *muṣḥaf*.' Ṭabarī further insists that the two readings: *aw nunsi-hā* and *aw nansa'-hā* [both of which, we suggest, originated in the flight from the reading: *aw nansa-hā*] can be reconciled with ease and, indeed, he proposes to read the meanings of both into one: *aw nunsi-hā*. 'God advises His Prophet that whatever ruling He replaces or alters, or does not replace or alter, He will bring one better than it, or one similar to it.'

He insists that his interpretation is not based on legalistic or theological presumptions, but essentially on purely syntactical factors. The sentence is an *aw* sentence. It thus presents alternatives. Since God begins by stating what He will do in the event of His altering and replacing the ruling of a verse, logically, He should follow that by speaking of what He will do in the event that He does *not* alter nor replace the ruling of a verse. This interpretation, moreover, combines the two concepts of: *nansa'* and *nunsi* on the logical premise that whatsoever is 'left' [*munsā*, *matrūk*] is set aside [*munsa'*] in the very condition it was in at the moment when it was set aside [*matrūk*].[55] He persists in insisting that his interpretation is not inspired by any doctrinaire opposition to the view that God may cause His Prophet to forget some part of what He had *naskh*ed of His revelation. In other words, the formula: *naskh al-ḥukm dūna 'l-tilāwa* is not founded on doctrinaire opposition to *naskh al-ḥukm wa-'l-tilāwa*, which we have seen that Ṭabarī claims to accept. But, we have seen him maintain that, in the event of *naskh*, following the withdrawal of the ruling, the wording may be withdrawn also, or it may not. *Naskh al-ḥukm* does not necessarily imply *naskh al-tilāwa*. Nor need the survival of a Ḳur'ān wording necessarily imply the survival of the Ḳur'ān ruling.

Concentrating on the withdrawal/replacement of Ḳur'ān rulings, Ṭabarī accepts, we have seen, the *naskh* of the Ḳur'ān by the *Sunna*. This explains, in part, his argument that God may alter the ruling, yet leave the wording of a Ḳur'ān verse. For this, he would use the technical term *naskh*. We have also seen him argue that there can be no talk of *naskh* except in relation to some divinely ordained ruling. He was also familiar with the concept of: *naskh al-tilāwa li-adjli naskh al-ḥukm* – withdrawing a wording in order to withdraw its ruling, the interpretation he favoured of Ḳ.87's mention of 'forgetting'. God did not cause the Muslims to forget all of the Ḳur'ān, but He did apparently cause them to forget parts of the Ḳur'ān they no longer needed. Thus, parts of the Ḳur'ān whose rulings had been withdrawn or altered were no longer needed and might be among those portions of the Ḳur'ān spoken of in *ḥadīth*s as 'forgotten'. Verses whose rulings have been withdrawn or altered might all have been forgotten, although some of the wordings have not been withdrawn. They may be regarded, in that event, as quasi-withdrawn. It is precisely these last verses which Ṭabarī's exegesis fails to explain.

In so far, however, as the *Mu'tazila* attacked the *naskh* theories, arguing that, if the ruling be altered, the wording ought to be withdrawn,[56] Ṭabarī's exegesis might be said to be doctrinaire. The tension between the 'withdrawal' and the 'replacement' *tafsīrs* was thus more than merely verbal.

Ṭabarī held and defended the view that, relative to the 'original' revelations, omissions from the *muṣḥaf* had occurred. He sought to document this view not, as others do, from the *aw nunsi-hā* clause, nor yet by appeal solely to *ḥadīth*s. Emphasising, instead, the alleged logical consequences of the 'replacement of the ruling', he was vulnerable to embarrassment in every case of alleged 'replacement' or 'withdrawal' of rulings whose wordings survived in the *muṣḥaf*, and sought to explain them on the analogy of cases where both ruling and wording had been withdrawn together. But his opponent was unconvinced of the effectiveness of the analogy. Ṭabarī might claim that the wording of a verse whose ruling had been withdrawn or replaced was as good as withdrawn. The fact remains that the wording is still present in the *muṣḥaf.* It has not been withdrawn or replaced.

If the idea of 'replacement' derives from Ḳ.2:106, it could not have derived either from the *mā nansakh* clause, nor from the *aw nunsi-hā/ nansa'-hā* clause, both of which Ṭabarī has now examined at exhaustive length. 'Replacement' can surely derive only from the *na'ti bi-khairin min-hā aw mithli-hā* clause which he has not yet so much as mentioned.

We saw that this clause was considered incapable of being construed as a reference to Ḳur'ān wordings. It was generally regarded as referring to Ḳur'ānic rulings, any one of which, unlike the wording, may be considered similar to, or superior to any other. Indeed, the rulings of the *Sunna* might be regarded as similar to, even superior to those of the Ḳur'ān. If an alleviation, and so easier to perform, a ruling can be 'superior' to its predecessor; it will be so in human estimation; if more arduous to perform, it may be superior, in that the anticipated reward might be greater. If of equal difficulty, rulings can be said to be in the same sense similar.[57]

The theologian's doctrine of the Ḳur'ān's inimitability had interfered with the exegete's capacity to find a satisfactory Ḳur'ānic 'proof' of *naskh* in the *uṣūlī* sense of replacement, at least from Ḳ.2:106 and forced him to seek his 'proof' in an inappropriate section of the verse. This exposes his subjection to the technical use of the term *naskh*, as opposed to its 'actual meaning' in the language, and to the lengthy tradition of both *uṣūl* and exegetical discussions that underlay his own investigation of the ramifications of the phenomenon. Tabarī, the exegete, was in thrall to the Tradition. There was, however, this merit in being forced to interpolate the word *ḥukm* into: *mā nansakh min [ḥukmi] āya* – that it showed that the Ḳur'ān itself 'justified' the *uṣūlī* doctrine of those who maintained that the *Sunna* might *naskh* the Ḳur'ān. Materials from the Tradition could then be introduced to 'prove' that that, as a matter of historical fact, had actually happened.

The Shāfi'ī special theory of *naskh* had stated that the *Sunna* could not supersede and had never superseded the Ḳur'ān; and that the Ḳur'ān had never superseded and could not be claimed ever to have superseded the *Sunna*. Shāfi'ī and 'some who followed him' had based this on their exegesis of Ḳ.2:106. Materials from the Tradition were, however, to be used to break down this Shāfi'ī special theory of *naskh*, when even members of the Shāfi'ī *madhhab* adduced 'evidence' of 'actual cases':

> where the Prophet's ruling superseded the Ḳur'ān's ruling, the Prophet was not acting on his own initiative, but was responding to divine inspiration [*waḥy*]. In such cases, the *nāsikh* was not worded in the Ḳur'ān style. Even if we considered Muḥammad

> authorised to repeal a Ḳur'ān ruling by his own personal judgment, the authority to exercise his personal judgment derived from God. God is always the actual agent, acting through the medium of His Prophet. The Ḳur'ān rulings may thus be altered by the Prophet, and not solely by the Ḳur'ān. In all such cases, the *waḥy* is not the Ḳur'ān *waḥy*. Nevertheless, the Word of God is one; the Word of God is both *nāsikh* and *mansūkh*. God does not have two Words which, in some instances, men are bidden to recite at prayer, when it is called Ḳur'ān, but not so bidden at other times, when it is not called Ḳur'ān. God has but one Word which differs in the method of its expression. On occasion, He expresses His word by the Ḳur'ān; on other occasions, in words couched in another style, not recited at prayer, and not called Ḳur'ān, but called *Sunna*. Both kinds of *waḥy* are transmitted by the Prophet. In the event of *naskh*, the agent is God alone Who indicates *naskh* by means of His Prophet, at whose hands, God instructs us of the *naskh* of His Book. This none other than the Prophet is capable of manifesting; none other than God of initiating.[58]

Returning to the appeal to Ḳ.2:106, the earlier Shāfiʿites had emphasised the verb *na'ti* – God alone will 'bring' the *nāsikh*. Once more, the later Shāfiʿī who had broken away from the rigidity of the master's *uṣūl*, could confront and deal with this Ḳur'ānic 'evidence':

> Were God to *naskh* a Ḳur'ān verse by the instrumentality of the *Sunna* of the Prophet, and were He subsequently to bring the second verse, similar to the *mansūkh* verse, in bringing the later verse, He would have made good His unchanging word, although it is not necessary on that account to consider the second verse the actual *nāsikh*. God did not mean to state that He would bring a verse 'superior' to the first. No verse in the Ḳur'ān may be thought of as 'superior' to any other verse. God meant that He would introduce a ruling superior to the earlier ruling, in the sense of its being easier to perform, or, if more difficult to perform, productive of a superior reward in the Hereafter.[59]

6. Ḳ.2:106 IN THE POST-ṬABARĪ EXEGESIS

The ibn ʿĀmir 'reading' *mā nunsikh*, rejected by Ṭabarī as 'unattested in the reading Tradition', was destined to a lengthy career at the hands of linguists and exegetes. It is recorded by Zamakhsharī who explains:[60]

> that, as the *naskh* of an *āya* means its *izāla* [suppression], effected by the substitution of another *āya* in its place [supersession], its *insākh* would mean commanding another that the *āya* be *naskh*ed. God commands Gabriel to declare the *āya mansūkha* by announcing its *naskh* to the Prophet.

The appointment of Gabriel as the agent of *nunsikh* may, perhaps, have been designed to remove the 'forgetting' interpretation even further from God, by ceasing to regard Him as agent.

The explanation of the reading, based on the orthodox image of the mechanism of revelation – the descent of Gabriel to instruct the Prophet in the correct recitation of the revelations and the correct performance of the rituals – seems not to have commended itself, on this occasion to Ṭabarī, although he himself uses it elsewhere.[61] He defers, however, at Ḳ.2:106, to the strength of the reading-Tradition. Making God the agent of *nunsikh*, Ṭabarī would have read the verse: 'We cause you, Muḥammad, to *naskh* the verse,' while, for him, *naskh* is essentially an exclusively divine prerogative, whether the *nāsikh* is another Ḳur'ān verse, or a *sunna* from the Prophet.

Like Zamakhsharī, Bayḍāwī discusses *aw nunsikh*, explaining: 'We command you, Muḥammad [or Gabriel] to *naskh* the verse.'[62] Bayḍāwī accepts the *naskh* of the Ḳur'ān by the *Sunna* – but so does Ṭabarī. Ṭabarī's whole argument therefore, suggests that Ḳ.2:106 was originally used to 'justify from the Ḳur'ān' the alleged alteration of rulings.

By now, *naskh* has achieved a highly sophisticated definition: 'declaring the termination of the religious obligation to recite the verse, or to apply the ruling embodied in the verse, or the removal of both its recitation and its implementation.'[63]

There is here a detectable move away from the concept of '*tabdīl*' (alteration), probably in response to theological pressure. The concept 'termination' moves into the foreground, and one finds *naskh* interchanged with *intisākh* which emphasises automatic termination. God commands Muḥammad (or Gabriel) to declare a Ḳur'ān wording, or its ruling, or both to have been abandoned.

Alternatively *mā nunsikh* may be estimative, rather than declarative: 'We find the verse is to be *mansūkha*.' However, if the speaker is either God or Gabriel, this effectively means 'We declare that the verse is to be terminated', which is the same as 'We terminate it.' The two readings provide one and the same sense, notwithstanding the difference in vowelling.[64]

But, if '*naskh*' means 'to copy', it cannot be maintained that *n s kh* means the same as *an s kh*. The Form 4 *hamza* imports causation: 'Whatever We cause you, Muḥammad, to copy.' That must refer to the verse's being revealed, thus: 'Whatsoever verse We reveal to you, or cause you to forget, We shall bring another better than it, or similar to it.' The reading *mā nunsikh* can easily be rejected, since the above interpretation implies that the entire Ḳur'ān is *mansūkh* whereas the truth is that only very little of the Ḳur'ān is *mansūkh*.

The entire Ḳur'ān is, of course, *mansūkh*, in the sense that the entire text has been transferred from the Preserved Tablet in Heaven to the earthly *muṣḥaf*.[65] That reflects the usage in which *n s kh* has the force of *n ḳ l*, as in *nasakha 'l-kitāb*. The usage is found in the Ḳur'ān: *innā kunnā nastansikh mā kuntum ta'malūn* [Ḳ.45:29] but *has nothing to do with* the use of the term *naskh* which occurs in Ḳ.2:106.[66]

Zamakhsharī reads: *aw nansa'-hā*, recording *aw nunsi-hā* incidentally, but again, as with Ṭabarī, the meanings he assigns to the two terms are so close as virtually to coincide. The existence of reported 'variant readings' need cause no difficulty to the interpretation: *nasā'u-hā* means: *ta'khīru-hā*. This he explains as physical, rather than temporal: to drive the verse away – *idhhābu-hā lā ilā badal*, which is just a complicated way of saying: 'withdrawal'. The subject being God, this interpretation guarantees all the benefits with none of the embarrassments of the old 'forgetting' exegesis. Forgetting is now under total divine control. *Idhhāb*, being physical, hints at omission from the *muṣḥaf*. *Insā'*, being psychological, refers to the removal of verses from the memories of men who are caused to forget them. Ṭabarī had isolated the same two concepts, but had insisted that the second derived from the principle of 'abandoning', rather than 'forgetting'.[67] It is just another way of saying the same thing. Zamakhsharī states:

> Every *āya* of the Ḳur'ān which God removes, on the grounds that human welfare requires its removal, whether the removal of both the wording and the ruling, or of the one without the other, and whether in favour of a substitute verse or not, He will bring one better than it[68] for Man, in that its practice will be either more productive of heavenly reward, or productive of a similar degree of reward.

Most of the essentials of this *tafsīr* were present already in Ṭabarī's exegesis, where he produced as instances of actual cases of *naskh* that had historically occurred:[69]

i. The exchange of 'similar' rulings, presumably producing 'similar' reward: the substitution of the Makkan *ḳibla* for the Jerusalem *ḳibla*.

ii. The substitution of a more rigorous for an easier regime, productive presumably of an increased heavenly reward: the institution of the month-long Ramaḍān Fast for 'the earlier fast' of only three days.

iii. The substitute ruling might be 'better' for the Muslim in this life as, for example, is the case of the *naskh* of the onerous night vigils that had originally been imposed upon the Faithful by the opening verses of Ḳ.73, but subsequently removed.

Thus, 'better than' may refer either to this life, *'ādjilan*, or to the Hereafter, *adjalan*.

It is interesting to note that Ṭabarī denied that there had been any fast imposed upon the Muslims before the imposition of the Fast of Ramaḍān, when engrossed in his exegesis of the relevant Ḳur'ān passage.[70] His remarks apropos of Ḳ.2:106's *na'ti bi-khairin min-hā aw mithli-hā* therefore bring out more clearly than anything else that might be adduced at this point the extreme atomism of the Islamic exegeses, and the degree to which, in wholly academic discussions, scholars are constantly influenced by each other's arguments and illustrations.

Whether one reads *aw nansa'-hā* or *aw nunsi-hā*, Zamakhsharī, unlike Ṭabarī, appears to derive the 'withdrawal' interpretation from the second clause of Ḳ.2:106. Again, unlike Ṭabarī, he insists that *naskh* means *izāla*, although adding that this is effected by substitution – that *naskh* means: suppression followed by replacement. *Mā nansakh* indicates a *badal*; *nunsi* or *nansa'* indicates lack of a *badal*. The old 'withdrawal' and 'replacement' *tafsīr*s of *naskh* which Ṭabarī had sought to harmonise, are once more separated and 'justified' by appeal to different clauses of Ḳ.2:106. The vocabulary used enables us to perceive the source of their resuscitation in yet another aspect of the discussions on *naskh* and the 'meaning(s)' of the term based, this time, on a specific alleged instance of *naskh* brought forward from the Ḳur'ān in 'evidence' (cf. below Ḳ.58:12–13). *naskh ilā badal*: means withdrawal, followed by replacement. *nansa'* or *nunsi*: means simple withdrawal without replacement, i.e. *naskh lā ilā badal*. What is removed may be either:

i. both wording and ruling: *naskh al-ḥukm wa-'l-tilāwa*.
ii. Ḳur'ān wording alone: *naskh al-tilāwa duna 'l-ḥukm*.
iii. Ḳur'ān ruling alone: *naskh al-ḥukm dūna 'l-tilāwa*.

It is perfectly clear that we have now a conflation in the definition of the term *naskh* of two unrelated concepts: 'withdrawal' and 'replacement'.

Zamakhsharī has quite failed to explain the origin of his 'replacement' concept, and has ignored the relation to the rest of Ḳ.2:106 of the clause: *na'ti bi-khairin min-hā aw mithli-hā*. Similarly, Ṭabarī had ignored this clause and quite failed to explain the origin of his 'withdrawal' concept.

Thus, we find in Zamakhsharī's exegesis all three modes of *naskh*, as they had developed in the classical *uṣūl* theory since the time of Shāfiʿī and Ṭabarī.

For Bayḍāwī, *naskh* meant quite simply: 'removal'.[71] The three modes of *naskh* are somewhat less logically extracted from the single term *naskh* which has now recovered both its aspects: 'withdrawal' and 'replacement'. *Insā'* means: removing verses from men's memories. It appears as a separate phenomenon, reminiscent of Ṭabarī's *rafʿ*. *Nasā'* represented in the Abū ʿAmr – ibn Kathīr 'reading' *aw nansa'-hā* what it conveyed to Shāfiʿī: *ta'khīr inzāli-hi*, the 'deferment of a revelation'. That interpretation had puzzled Ṭūsī who could not see any point in speaking of the 'deferment' of something that men 'know nothing about, have not learned nor heard of, unless indeed it means, "We put off revealing the verse until a future time, revealing instead something else which in the meantime will take its place." '[72] We shall see hereafter that that is precisely what Shāfi'ī had taken it to mean.

Both Zamakhsharī and Bayḍāwī mention a further 'reading': *aw nunassi-hā*, absent in Ṭabarī's list [cf. above, 87, No. 9]. Ṭabarī's silence could be taken to indicate that he had never heard of this reading, although he certainly knew the *musnad* to whom it was attributed.[73] Whether this can safely be taken as evidence that this reading gained currency only between the time of Ṭabarī and of Zamakhsharī, that is between *circa* AH 300/AD 912 and *circa* AH 460/AD 1067, which seems a strong presumption, given Ṭabarī's normal assiduity in amassing 'readings', if only to reject them; or whether it found its way into the *ḳirā'āt* literature from the corresponding *Ḥadīth* discussions,[74] and hence is not strictly a 'reading' as Ṭabarī understood the term; it is more likely that, unless he uncharacteristically ignored it, thinking it 'unfounded in the reading-Tradition', he would have treated it as a variant for *nunsi* which he finally preferred.

The problem of the 'reading' continued to engage the attention of the scholars. Ḳurṭubī[75] ascribed the reading *aw nansa'-hā* to: Abū 'Amr and ibn Kathīr, then asserts that it had been the reading of: 'Umar, ibn 'Abbās, 'Aṭā', Mudjāhid, Ubayy, 'Ubayd, Nakha'ī and ibn Muḥayṣin. For 'Aṭā', 'Ubayd and Mudjāhid, see Ṭabarī [2, 477]. The others do not figure in Ṭabarī's lists, with the exception of ibn 'Abbās who is credited with the meaning, although not the reading of: *aw nansa'-hā*, (*natruk-hā lā nansakh-hā*: *mā nansa*).

Ḳurṭubī states that *nansa'* derives from *ta'khīr* and he mentions the two views discussed by Ṭūsī. A third view, he says, is that *ta'khīr* means: 'We remove it from you, so that you can neither recite it nor recall it.' This is the old 'withdrawal' *tafsīr*, Zamakhsharī's '*idhhāb*'.

Both Abū Ḥātim and Abū 'Ubayd, he says, adopted the reading: *aw nunsi-hā*, taking *nunsi* to mean '*natruk*' as opposed to 'forgetting', a reading and an interpretation that he further ascribes to Suddī and ibn 'Abbās. Abū 'Ubayd is said to have adduced in support of his view of the reading the report of Abū Nu'aym who had checked the reading with the Prophet himself whom he had met in the course of a dream! Muḥammad had expressed his preference for *aw nunsi-hā*.[76]

The usual grammatical objections can be raised against this reading: Form 4 and Form 1 do not carry the same nuance, for, if *nasiya* means 'he abandoned,' *ansā* means 'he ordered another to abandon'; and, on this argument, Zadjdjādj questioned ibn abī Ṭalḥa's report on ibn 'Abbās' *tafsīr*. The reading: *aw nunsi-hā* yields not 'We abandon it,' but, 'We declare it lawful that you abandon it.' 'Alī ibn abī Ṭalḥa had, in fact, reported from ibn 'Abbās: *aw nansa-hā*:

(according to Ṭabarī) and, although, as Goldziher points out, this reading could not pass unchallenged,[77] Ṭabarī reports that ibn ʿAbbās offered the interpretation: 'We leave it – We do not *naskh* it.' Zadjdjādj reports only the words, 'We leave it, *natruk-hā*', as the full substance of ʿAlī's report and he was justified in challenging its accuracy, since in his report of ʿAlī's *ḥadīth*, this was offered as the interpretation of the reading *aw nunsi-hā*. The discussion of many of these *ḥadīth*s is quite bedevilled by uncertainty as to the precise details on how to vowel them. The scholars were thus engaged in the discussion of ʿAlī b. abī Ṭalḥa's qualifications to report from ibn ʿAbbās:

> They say that ʿAlī is trustworthy in respect of his transmission of reports, although some have questioned his reliability, perhaps on account of his Shīʿī leanings. ibn abī Ḥātim quotes from Ḍuḥaym "ʿAlī did not acquire ibn ʿAbbās' *tafsīr* from its author, he cites it indirectly.' From his own father, Abū Ḥātim, he relates a second statement to the like effect. In the *Thiqāt*, ibn Ḥibbān states, "ʿAlī relates from ibn ʿAbbās, but he never actually met him.'

Thus Shaikh Shākir (Ṭabarī, 2, 527, footnote). Suyūṭī was, however, of the contrary opinion.[78]

> A variety of meanings had been assigned to this quite extrinsic term *taraka*: it was said to mean: to leave something alone, undisturbed and in the case of a verse, to leave it unaltered: *naskh al-ḥukm dūna 'l-tilāwa* – that is, to leave the wording in the *muṣḥaf*. It could be said that it means: a. to leave the verse quite unaltered – not to repeal its wording or its ruling; or b. to leave the verse in the Preserved Tablet – that is, not to reveal it at all but to reveal in its place a substitute Ḳur'ān ruling; or not to reveal it for the present, revealing in its stead a substitute interim ruling, until the time came to reveal the verse at last; or c. to leave the verse, that is, to abandon it entirely, to leave off basing one's practice on the verse, abandoning the ruling it embodies while retaining the wording in the *muṣḥaf*. The discussion soon degenerates into a proliferation of more or less justifiable exegetical guesses and the extent to which freedom of 'reading' and of interpretation can be claimed by the scholars, suggests that, for the purposes of deriving (as opposed to verifying) the theories of *naskh*, the Ḳur'ān texts certainly seem to be no longer central. Their function was not to serve as the direct and sole source for their derivation, merely to offer 'evidence' from the Ḳur'ān for the verification of whatever *uṣūl* theory of *naskh* the *Fiḳh* of the various circles called for. Further indication of the quite exceptional confusion clouding all that is said or written about Ḳ.2:106 is furnished by Ḳurṭubī:

The majority of linguists and specialists take the view that *aw nunsi-hā* means: 'We declare it lawful that you abandon it [*taraka*].'[79]

Rāzī asserts the direct contrary:

The majority of scholars interpret the *aw nunsi-hā* reading to mean: 'forgetting' – the opposite of 'remembering'.[80] Forgetting [he continues] in the sense of 'leaving' is figurative usage, and hence secondary. Whatever is forgotten will come, in time, to be abandoned. Now, since being abandoned is one of the concomitant consequences of being forgotten, some of the scholars transfer the effect to the cause. But, in *kalām*, we must base all our discussions upon primary meanings, not upon secondary, derived usage.

Djaṣṣāṣ had an abrupt way with the linguists' definitions:

Some said '*naskh*' means *izāla*; some that it means *ibdāl*; others that it means *naḳl*. The disagreements centre upon what is envisaged as the connotation in Arab usage. But whatever the circumstances of the genesis of the word in Arabic, as a technical term used in the Islamic sciences, it means 'termination'.[81]

The following table, furnished from Rāzī's discussion, illustrates the range of options adopted by exegetes:

Table 2

1. *naskh*: *izāla*, suppression [Ḳ.22:52]. The suppression may refer to the ruling alone: *naskh al-ḥukm dūna 'l-tilāwa.*
aw nunsi-hā then refers to the suppression of both wording and ruling: *naskh al-tilāwa wa-'l-ḥukm. aw nunsi-hā* implying 'We cause the verse to be forgotten' – both wording and ruling are suppressed [Ḳ.87:6–7; Ḳ.2:106].

2. *naskh*: *tabdīl*, 'replacement' [Ḳ.16:101]. *mā nansakh* announces: *tabdīl al-ḥukm*, 'We replace the ruling,' or 'We replace the entire *āya*,' wording and ruling; or, 'We replace the wording only' *tabdīl al-tilāwa.*
aw nunsi-hā then refers to 'We leave the verse unaltered in the *muṣḥaf*,' *natruk-hā lā nubaddil-hā.*
All three modes of *naskh* are derived from the one term *naskh. aw nunsi-hā* then refers to every verse in the *muṣḥaf* unaffected by any of the three modes of *naskh*.

3. *naskh*: *raf'* – 'withdrawal' [Ḳ.87].
aw nansa'-hā then refers to lack of *raf'* – 'We leave the *āya* unaltered and unremoved in the *muṣḥaf*.'

4. *naskh: 'to copy', sc. 'to reveal'. [Ḳ.45:29].*
aw nansa'-hā *then means:* 'We defer the verse, put it right at the back of *umm al-Kitāb*, never to be revealed at all,' or 'We reveal the *āya*, then defer its repeal.' This is the same as 'We leave the verse unaltered in the *muṣḥaf*.'

There are as many *tafsīrs* as there are theories. The role of the Ḳur'ān texts in the discussions is limited only by the extent of the arguments among the scholars.

When all three modes of *naskh* were being derived from the *mā nansakh* clause, Ṭabarsī had to advise against interpreting *aw nunsi-hā/aw nansa'-hā* in the sense that it refers to one of the three modes. That would be tantamount to reading the verse: *mā nansakh min āya aw nansakh-hā!*[82]

Seven

THE THIRD MODE OF *NASKH* – *NASKH AL-TILĀWA DŪNA 'L-ḤUKM*

In the interval between Ṭabarī and Zamakhsharī, the formulation of the general theory of *naskh* as presented by the exegete, had undergone both explicit expansion and a considerable formal refinement. Elements presented in Zamakhsharī's definition of *naskh*, but lacking in Ṭabarī's were of two kinds:

i. the three-fold categorisation of the *naskh*; of the three, Ṭabari had envisaged two as certainly traceable to $Ḳ_2$:106; he had remained silent in the third mode: *naskh al-tilāwa dūna 'l-ḥukm*. ii. the concept of the *badal*: *naskh ilā badal*; *naskh ilā lā badal*. The first represents the 'replacement' definition of *naskh*; the second, the 'withdrawal' definition. Opting for the 'transfer' definition, Ṭabarī had had to attempt to make room within the principle of *naskh al-ḥukm dūna 'l-tilāwa* for some element of withdrawal. He had sought to achieve this by suggesting that in *some* cases of the replacement of a Ḳur'ān ruling, the wording might be withdrawn following the abandonment of the earlier ruling, on the analogy of the withdrawal of other verses containing no regulation. Zamakhsharī, opting for the 'suppression' etymology, had equally to find room in his theory for the 'replacement' that occurs following the suppression of a verse. He formalised the two phenomena under the *naskh* rubric by means of the concept of the *badal*. The *raf'*, or 'simple withdrawal' phenomenon had, as yet, been only partially accommodated within the theory of *naskh*. Zamakhsharī found it documented in the *aw nunsi-hā/nansa'-hā* clause, the source of his *naskh ilā lā badal*. Differences on the 'reading' of the clause no longer caused trouble and the old scruples about the 'forgetting' interpretation had been entirely laid aside. Like Ṭabarī, Zamakhshari failed to take account of the *na'ti bi-khairin min-hā aw mithli-hā* clause.

Bayḍāwī so far 'improved' upon Zamakhsharī's formulation as to derive all three modes of *naskh* from a single clause: *mā nansakh min āya*. From the reading: *aw nunsi-hā*, he derived *raf'*, the removal of relevations from men's memories. From the reading *aw nansa'-hā*, he derived an additional factor: the deferment of a revelation, which had been present in the *uṣūl* vocabulary since at least the time of Shāfi'ī.

Bayḍāwī thus represents the complete accommodation by the *Tafsīr* of all the factors involved in the fully developed *uṣūl* theories, together with the ancient exegesis of Ḳ.87 as a reference to the forgetting of revelations. The tension between the old 'withdrawal' and 'replacement' exegeses has been relieved by the adoption of both and by allotting to each its particular role in revelation-history and in the *naskh* processes, and by assigning to each, at least by the time of Zamakhshari, its own basis in the Ḳur'ān. A means had been found to formalise and so neutralise, at least by the time of Ṭabarī, the old *ḥadīths* about parts of the Ḳur'ān having been forgotten. Now, by the accommodation of the third mode of *naskh*, the *Tafsīr* has brought the Ḳur'ān texts into perfect alignment with certain very important developments in the field of the *uṣūl*.

To understand the origins and historical background to the appearance in the post-Ṭabarī *Tafsīr* of this third mode of *naskh*, it will be helpful if we now turn to consider in some detail the treatment in the *uṣūl* of certain questions which touch immediately the very nerve of the problem of the relative status as source of the Ḳur'ān [*muṣḥaf*] and the *Sunna*.

Whatever may have been the historical source of the *uṣūl* tripartite categorisation of *naskh*, it was not the Ḳur'ān. As soon, however, as we begin to dissect and analyse concrete questions discussed in the legal works, much that hitherto may have seemed obscure becomes at last comprehensible. The gaps in our understanding the course of the evolution of the discussion on *naskh* quickly fill themselves in.

Let us therefore turn and concentrate upon one strategic *Fiḳh* topic whose treatment by the Muslims will answer our remaining questions as to the origin of the third mode of *naskh*, *naskh al-tilāwa dūna 'l-ḥukm*, and suggest how the general and special formulations of the theories of *naskh* had been generated.

Of all the disputed questions in the *Fiḳh*, and especially in the *uṣūl*, none is richer in variety of treatment, or fuller in its appeal to Ḳur'ān and *Sunna* sources, or more acute in tension as to the relative weight that the *fuḳahā'* were alleged to have accorded to each of the sources than that of the penalties for fornication and adultery.

Had the *muṣḥaf* been the source of the penalties, the *locus*, it might be thought must have been Ḳ.4: 15–6.

> Those of your women who commit abomination [*fāḥisha*] seek against them the testimony of four of your number, and, should they swear, detain the women in their quarters until death release them, or until God appoint a procedure for their case [*lahunna*]. Those two of your number who commit a like abomination, punish them, and if they repent and amend, leave them.

Before any penal conclusion could be drawn from these verses, several questions must first be settled. What is meant here by the general term '*fāḥisha*'? Do the two verses refer to the same order of transgression, or do they refer separately to different classes of persons committing different degrees of 'abomination'? Do the verses impose a similar penalty? Does the expression 'or until God appoint a procedure' suggest that what is imposed in v.15 was intended as only a temporary expedient?

The study of the Muslims' answers to these questions can most conveniently begin from Ṭabarī's review of the various and varying interpretations proposed. He comments:

> God means by His words, 'commit abomination' women who engage in *zinā*; and by His words 'of your women' *muḥṣan* females whether they currently have husbands or not. By the words 'or until God appoint a procedure', God means until He provides a means of egress or deliverance from the abomination they committed.[1]

The technical terms *muḥṣan* and *zinā* may, for the present, be taken to mean: 'non-virgin' and 'sexual irregularity'.

Ṭabarī makes it clear that, for him, the expression 'or until God appoint a procedure' indicated that the detention in quarters had been marked from the outset as a temporary measure. He adduces the usual evidence from scholars who had a view 'similar to his'. Thus, he quotes Mudjāhid's comment: 'God commanded that the women be locked up until they died, or until God appointed a way. The 'way' that was to be appointed is a reference to the Islamic penalty.' ibn 'Abbās stated:

> When a woman fornicated, she was confined in a room until she died. Later, God revealed Ḳ.24:2 'The male and female fornicators, flog them both one hundred strokes' – but, if both were *muḥṣan*, both were stoned. That is the way that God appointed for them [*lahumā*].

Here, the final word betrays the origin of this report. This word is dual, common gender. In Ḳ.4:15, which we are discussing, and which this report affects to elucidate, the final word used is *lahunna* – feminine plural. The Ḳur'ān's reference is exclusive to females. The discrepancy was noted, giving rise to a second *ḥadīth* counter to the first, representing a rival view, yet, like the first, attributed to ibn 'Abbās: 'The way appointed for women [*lahunna*] was flogging *and* stoning.'[2]

The traditional *uṣūlī* view was that Ḳ.4:15–16 had been revealed to establish a temporary penalty for fornication. That view was based on one definition of *fāḥisha*. Somewhat illogically, the verse was acknowledged to be an exclusive reference to females, but the equation of *fāḥisha* with *zinā* necessarily implied a dual, and the way was already prepared for the argument of those who insisted on reading both verses together as a reference to male and female partners in an act of illicit intercourse. The substitution of the common gender dual *lahumā* for the Ḳur'ān's feminine plural *lahunna* marks the transition from the *muṣḥaf* text to the *Fiḳh* conclusion by way of the bridge supplied by exegesis. According to Ḳatāda,

> The two verses refer to the situation *before* the revelation of the Islamic penalty. Both partners in the act were punished verbally; only the woman, however, was confined. Later, God appointed the way *lahunna*: the *muḥṣan* were flogged one hundred strokes then stoned; the non-*muḥṣan* were flogged one hundred strokes, then banished for one year.[3]

For Ḳatāda, the position was that the (verbal) violence was offered to both and the locking-up of the woman for life did not represent the penalty, only the practice before the institution of the Islamic penalty. That practice had been based on the Ḳur'ān, but the statement that the way that was to be appointed turned out to be the Islamic penalty shows that the consideration of the Ḳur'ān verses was undertaken retrospectively by people who already knew what the Islamic penalty was, and who understood that it was not derived from this Ḳur'ānic statement. Ḳatāda fails to mention the point, but one is to assume that the 'subsequently revealed' penalty was extended also to the male partner.

Ḍaḥḥāk b. Muzāhim is more specific in his declaration that the penalty, when subsequently revealed, superseded the ruling of Ḳ.4:15–16. This view that the later penalty applied equally to males and females and that it superseded the earlier ruling, implies that v.15 and v.16 are a unit of revelation so that the dual of v.16 refers to both partners in a heterosexual act. Others, impressed by the distinction between the plural feminine of v.15 and the common gender dual of v.16, argued that the two verses were mutually independent. They should be read as references to two classes of *women*. They thought that was confirmed by the differing degrees of severity mentioned in the two verses: locking-up for life, and unspecified violence, conceived, however, as less harsh. They suggested that that indicated that only the first verse refers to the *muḥṣan*, the second only to the non-*muḥṣan*. Ḳ.4:16 refers to fornication; v.15 to adultery. As the Ḳur'ān nowhere makes this distinction, it could be advanced solely on extra-Ḳur'ānic grounds. Mudjāhid was the authority for the opinion that v.15 refers only to women, and is again the authority for the view that v.16 refers solely to males.[4]

Resuming the Ḳatāda *tafsīr*, others considered v.15 as an exclusive reference to females, while v.16 allegedly referred to both males and females, or, as Mudjāhid, in a self-contradictory way allegedly stated, to both *fā'il* and *fā'ila*.[5]

Those who took the dual in v.16 to refer to the male–female partners, divided once more as to whether the reference is general to all illicit conduct, or is restricted to the non-*muḥṣan*, i.e. fornication only. Ṭabarī espoused the latter exegesis: 'the verse deals with the male and female partners in the act of fornication.'

The more grievous sin of adultery he considers, is dealt with in v.15. He might appear to have a point in his favour. Ḳ.4:15 uses *allātī*, the feminine plural, on the face of it, therefore, an exclusive reference to women, while v.16 uses *alladhāni*, which, he argues, being of common gender, includes a second reference to females. That must imply some category of female other than that referred to in the foregoing verse. Ḳ.4:15 spoke of *nisā'ikum*, 'possessed women', thus *muḥṣan*. Ḳ.4:16, he argues, must therefore refer to the non-*muḥṣan*.

In reply to the Mudjāhid argument that v.16 is an exclusive reference to males, Ṭabarī counters with the reflection that, in that event, v.16 ought to have balanced v.15's plural relative by a plural relative referring to males, *alladhīn*. Ḳ.4:15 does not employ a female dual to balance the alleged male dual of v.16. Insisting that the v.16 dual must be of common gender, Ṭabarī completely misses the point of the argument attributed to Mudjāhid.

Mudjāhid did not state that Ḳ.4:16 was a reference to *all* males. He said it was a reference to *two* males. He was not discussing fornication or, indeed, heterosexual, but homosexual acts. This is clear from the report related by ibn Djuraidj:

> Ḳ.4:16 refers to *al-radjulāni al-fā'ilāni*—He [God] does not use circumlocution.

That Mudjāhid's drift wholly eluded Ṭabarī is clear from the argument he develops on the basis of 'Arabic usage':

> When the Arabs wish to express either a threat or a promise in respect of any act, good or bad, they speak of its performers in the plural, or they use the singular with generic sense. They do not employ the dual, unless the act envisaged is such as cannot be performed save by two different individuals. Fornication is such an act which requires two persons of different sex. The dual would thus describe the *fā'il* and the *maf'ūl bi-hi*. The use of the dual to represent an act by two individuals each of whom could perfectly well accomplish the act on his own, or an act the nature of which is such that the two individuals could not associate in its joint performance, would represent a usage unheard of in the Arabic language.[6]

Ṭabarī has further overlooked the possibility that *allātī* may merely be the result of the 'attraction' of the feminine plural, *nisā'ikum*, although there is admittedly nothing in the syntax to prevent the use of the female dual in v.15, if this is what it was intended to convey. In v.15, *allātī* precedes its verb, whereas, in v.16, *alladhāni* precedes its own verb, but follows the verb of v.15. This may afford the presumption, (although it is only a presump-

> tion) that v.15's plural may be merely formal, the notional subjects of both v.15 and v.16 being intended to be dual. Bayḍāwī refers to this, among other possibilities.[7] He may have had in mind the views of Abū Muslim Isfahānī,[8] who regarded Ḳ.4:15 as a reference to female, v.16 to male homosexual behaviour.

In the statements quoted by Ṭabarī from the earlier exegetes, a variety of views was expressed on the question of 'the later situation'. These included assertions that the eventual Islamic penalty was flogging; or flogging followed by stoning; or flogging followed by stoning for certain categories of offenders, with flogging followed by a year's banishment for other offenders. The general opinion was that Ḳ.4:15–16 had been superseded and its ruling had fallen into abeyance. Some though that the *nāsikh* had been Ḳ.24:2; others quite simply identified it as 'the Islamic penalty'.

Ṭabarī concludes that God had replaced the verses by providing a revelation furnishing the penalty for each of the categories referred to in the Ḳ.4 verses. Deciding that v.15 was the harsher of the two 'practices', which indicated that the offence in question was the more heinous, he concluded that the locking-up for life had been directed at the *thayyib*s, i.e. adulterers. The 'lighter' v.16 'practice' had been visited upon non-*thayyib*s for fornication.[9]

Such constructions, however, with their mention of *thayyib*s, and non-*thayyib*s, *muḥṣan* and non-*muḥṣan*, could be arrived at only by reading back into Ḳ.4:15–16 a knowledge of the later *Fiḳh* situation. As Ṭabarī expresses it, this must be so, since the 'way' which God did appoint for the *thayyib*s – death by stoning – is harsher than that He appointed for the non-*thayyib*s, namely one hundred strokes and a year's banishment. God had replaced Ḳ.4:15–16 by the provisions He made for both classes of offenders; for *thayyib*s, He arranged this by means of the stoning penalty awarded to this class of offender in the *Sunna*. For the non-*thayyib*s, God revealed Ḳ.24:2.[10]

> The most correct rendering of the words: 'or until God appoint a procedure' is that the appointed 'way' was, in the case of the *muḥṣan thayyib*, stoning, and of the non-*muḥṣan*, one hundred strokes and a year's banishment. This is indicated by the 'soundness' of the reports that the Prophet had stoned without flogging, and by the unanimity of the Traditional evidence, which, so long as it be unanimous, is incapable of error, absent-mindedness or untruth.[11]

1. The penalty for fornication in the view of the fuḳahā'

In his *Muwaṭṭa'*, Mālik is interested in locating a source for the penalty established in the *Fiḳh*: death by stoning.

> A man came to ʿUmar and reported that he had found another man with his wife. The wife was questioned. ʿUmar's emissary advised the woman that she would not be proceeded against on the strength of her husband's accusation alone. He tried to lead her toward self-exoneration, but she acknowledged the truth of her husband's allegation. ʿUmar had her stoned.

She was stoned on the basis of her unsupported self-condemnation.

> A woman who had given birth in only six months was brought before ʿUthmān who ordered her to be stoned. ʿAlī protested that she had not incurred that penalty since God says, 'The carrying and the weaning shall be thirty months,' [Ḳ.46:15] God also says, 'Mothers shall suckle their infants for two complete years, if one desires to complete the suckling,' [Ḳ.2:233] Thus the carrying can be six months. ʿUthmān sent after her, but she had already been executed.

She was stoned on the basis of a dubious pregnancy.

> When a woman came to the Prophet and confessed that, having fornicated, she was now pregnant, Muḥammad told her to come back when she had given birth. She came and he told her to come back when she had weaned the child. She came and he had her stoned.

She was stoned on the basis of her repeated self-condemnation.

The purpose of these *ḥadīth*s is to inform us that since the time of the Prophet, the Muslims had consistently stoned in cases of adultery. Zuhrī informed Mālik that a man confessed on four separate occasions to the Prophet that he had committed adultery. The Prophet had him stoned.

The man was stoned on the basis of his four-times repeated confession, the equivalent of the testimony of the four witnesses demanded by the Ḳur'ān [Ḳ.24:4; cf. Ḳ.4:15].

> A man had confessed to Abū Bakr, but he told him to keep it quiet, 'as God had kept it quiet.' Dissatisfied, the man went to ʿUmar, and he replied as Abū Bakr had done. Unable to rest, the man confessed to the Prophet. Muḥammad ignored the man three times, and on the fourth, made enquiries. Finding the man sane and married, the Prophet had him stoned.

This man was stoned on the basis of his four-times repeated self-condemnation, since he was a *muḥṣan*.

Stoning, it is alleged, had been applied by ʿUthmān (and acknowledged by ʿAlī) by ʿUmar and by the Prophet to both men and women who, being non-virgin, had engaged in illicit sexual conduct. The stoning penalty is nowhere referred to in the *muṣḥaf*.

> Two men brought a case before the Prophet. One asked him to judge between them 'on the basis of the Book of God'. The other, speaking first, explained: 'My son was hired by this man but

> fornicated with his employer's wife. The man alleging that my son should be stoned, I ransomed the boy with a hundred sheep and a slavegirl. Enquiring of the learned, I later learned that my son had incurred a penalty of one hundred strokes and a year's banishment whereas the employer's wife had incurred the stoning penalty.'
>
> The Prophet, engaging to adjudicate between them on the basis of 'the Book of God', said, 'Your cattle and slavegirl are to be returned to you.' He sentenced the son to one hundred strokes and a year's banishment and ordered the wife to be questioned. As she confessed, he had her stoned.

The whole of the final sentence is found in the *Muwaṭṭa'* to be in indirect speech. In Shāfi'ī's version,[12] it has already been incorporated into the direct speech attributed to the Prophet.

Thus, for the *Fiḳh*, the penalty for adultery is stoning; for fornication, there is the double penalty of flogging and banishment. Both represent the penalty imposed in 'the Book of God' as mediated by the Prophet. All Mālik's *ḥadīth*s are aggregated in a single proposition attributed by ibn 'Abbās to 'Umar: 'Stoning, in "the Book of God" is a rightful claim against any man or woman if *muḥṣan*, when valid proof is laid, or pregnancy ensues, or a confession is volunteered.'

The *ḥadīths* appeared in the *Muwaṭṭa'* in verification of these *Fiḳh* principles. We have stated that Mālik was interested in locating their source:

> 'Abdullāh b. 'Umar reports: 'The Jews came to the Prophet when a man and woman of theirs had committed adultery. The Prophet asked, "What do you find in the Tōra?"[13] They replied, "We humiliate them and they are flogged." 'Abdullāh b. Sallām said, "You are lying! It contains the stoning-verse." They then fetched the Tōra and opened it out, but one of them, putting his hand over the verse, recited only what precedes and what follows it.[14] 'Abdullāh b. Sallām told him to lift his hand and, when he did, there was the stoning-verse! The Jews said, "He's right, Muḥammad, it does contain the stoning-verse." Muḥammad had the two stoned.'

The *ḥadīth* pre-supposes that, if approached by non-Muslims, Muḥammad would not only assume jurisdiction, but would rule in accordance with the law of the litigants. The Jews in the story had allegedly been judged on the basis of the Tōra, 'the Book of God', which was found to contain the stoning-verse. This is a *tafsīr-ḥadīth* designed both to aid in the understanding of the expression 'the Book of God' presented in the story of the employer's wife and to clear up the interpretation of a Ḳ.5 verse. Disagreements had arisen over the exegesis of Ḳ.5:42–9 and the various view-points given expression. They are again, most conveniently assembled by Ṭabarī. Ḳ.5:42

occurs in the course of a divine address to the Prophet on the question precisely of jurisdiction. Certain Jews are spoken of harshly as constantly ready to swallow any calumny concerning Muḥammad's teachings and ready to misrepresent his words.

> If they should come to you, either judge between them or refuse to hear them. If you refuse, they will not harm you, but if you judge, then decide between them equitably.
> But why should they apply to you for judgment, when they have the Tōra in which is God's judgment, and then decline to accept the judgment?
> The Prophets who became Muslim judge the Jews on the basis of the Tōra.
> The rabbis and the priests have judged on the basis of what they have been charged to preserve of the Book of God.

On what basis would Muḥammad have judged the Jews? The Ḳur'ān's 'If they should come to you,' has now become the *ḥadīth*'s 'The Jews did come to the Prophet.' The Muslims were divided on these verses. Some maintained they they had been *mansūkha*; others maintained that that had never occurred. The Prophet had been granted the choice to hear or to refuse; he had retained the choice, and had exercised it.

ʿAṭā', ʿAmr b. Shuʿayb, Ḳatāda, Shaʿbī and Nakhaʿī all argued that the Muslim judge also retained that right of choice. If he did agree to hear these litigants he must, however, render judgment on the basis of what God had revealed.[15] For Shaʿbī, at least, that means that the Muslim judge must render judgment on the basis of the Muslim Law.[16] In cases of theft and homicide specifically, it was argued, there was no alternative course. The Muslim penalty must be applied.

Those who argued for the *naskh* of the verse, maintained that cases brought to the Muslim judge by *dhimmīs* must be heard. The choice of refusing to hear them had been withdrawn.[17] ʿIkrima, Ḥasan, Mudjāhid and Suddī are reported as insisting that the *nāsikh* had been Ḳ.5:49: 'Judge between them on the basis of what God has revealed. Do not follow their fancies, but beware lest they seduce you from part of what God has revealed *to you*...''

ʿUmar II is said to have commanded his governor to give judgment when approached by *ahl al-kitāb*. Zuhrī's view was that on inheritances, *ahl al-kitāb* are to be referred to their co-religionists; but on penal matters, the Muslim judge should decide on the basis of 'the Book of God'. Now, it was Zuhrī who tole Mālik the story of the employer's wife. To Mudjāhid, 'the Book of God' signified *kitābu-nā*.[18] But, in the absence of an *idjmāʿ* on the question, and in the absence of an authenticated statement by the Prophet that one of the two verses had been *mansūkha*, and since there is no conflict between the two verses, Ṭabarī concludes that the Muslim judge retains the right to hear or to refuse to hear cases brought by scripturaries.[19] If, however, he decides to hear, he must render judgment solely on the basis of the Muslim Law, on the basis, that is, of 'the Book of God.'

> When a nobleman fornicated with a low-caste woman, the Jews would stone the female. They would blacken the face of the male and set him up on a camel facing the rear. Similarly when a high-caste female fornicated with a low-caste male, they would stone the man. The Jews brought just such a case to the Prophet and he stoned the woman. He asked the Jews, 'Who is your foremost Tōra scholar?' They indicated so-and-so. Muḥammad sent for him and adjured him by God and by the Tōra which He revealed to Moses on Mt. Sinai to tell what he found in the Tōra on fornicators. The man replied that they stone the low-caste and set the high-caste up on a camel, blacken their faces and point them to its rear. Muḥammad repeated his references to the Tōra which God revealed to Moses. Reluctantly, the Jewish scholar admitted that in the Tōra occurs the verse: *al-shaykh wa-'l-shaykha idhā zanayā fa-rdjumū-humā al-battata.* Muḥammad exclaimed, 'That's it! Take them out and stone them.'[20]

The authority both for Ṭabarī's and for Mālik's *ḥadīth* is ibn 'Umar. The report indicates that by 'the Book of God' is meant the Tōra. Ṭabarī paraphrases Ḳ.5:43:

> Why should the Jews apply to you for judgment, Muḥammad, and be content with your verdict, if you are not a prophet, when they have the Tōra which I revealed to Moses which they affirm to be the truth and assert that it is My Book which I revealed to My Prophet, and that the law which it contains is My Law. They acknowledge all this without cavil. They are further aware that in the Tōra, My verdict on the *muḥṣan* fornicator is death by stoning. Knowing all this, they ignore all of it in defiance of Me and from sheet disobedience.[21]

How should they accept Muḥammad's verdict whose prophethood they deny, having already dared to ignore the verdict of Moses whose prophethood they insist on.

ibn 'Abbās reports: 'At this point, God informed His Prophet Muḥammad of his injunction in the Tōra.'[22] Suddī,[23] Ḥasan,[24] and 'Ikrima[25] explained that this Ḳur'ān verse refers to stoning, while Suddī explained the expression: 'Prophets who became Muslim' as a reference to Muḥammad.[26]

There is a story from Abū Hurayra:

> When Muḥammad first came to Madīna, the Jewish scholars assembled in the synagogue, one of them, being *muḥṣan*, having fornicated with a *muḥṣana* Jewess. They said, 'Take them to Muḥammad and ask him for a ruling. Let him judge them. If he

> treats them according to your practice, you may join him – he will be but a king. But, if he awards them the stoning penalty, beware! He will rob you of what you now enjoy.' When they questioned the Prophet he went and consulted the scholars in their synagogue. The most learned among them were ʿAbdullāh b. Ṣurīya, the one-eyed, Abū Yāsir b. Akhṭab and Wahb b. Yahūdha.

Far from asking the scholars, however, Muḥammad informed them: 'Do you [not] know that in the Tōra God has decreed stoning for the *muḥṣan* who fornicates?'[27]

> In a further version, Muḥammad passed a Jew who had been flogged and had his face blacked. The Prophet importunes the scholars as to 'the real penalty', forcing them in the end to admit that the penalty of the Tōra had had to be abandoned when fornication became so rife among the Jewish upper classes that a lighter man-made penalty had had to be agreed upon. Muḥammad had exclaimed, 'I am the first to revive Your commandment, Lord God, after they had suppressed it.'[28]

'I am the first to revive God's command and His Book and to put it into effect.'[29]

In yet another version, on being approached by the Jews to judge a case of fornication, Muḥammad says, 'I shall judge on the basis of what is in the Tōra.'[30] This exactly parallels Mālik's 'I shall judge on the basis of the Book of God.'

Ṭabarī preserves materials which illustrate an attempt to explain this expression 'the Book of God' as the Tōra which God revealed to Moses.[31] Furthermore, he quotes from the Tōra the actual words of the stoning-'verse': *al-shaykh wa-'l-shaykha idhā zanayā fa-rdjumū-humā al-battata*. Ṭabarī accepts and approves all these statements.

The underlying motive which unites the reports is:

i. to trace the Islamic stoning-penalty to a revealed source, a 'Book of God'.

ii. to counter the alleged objections raised by Jews: Muḥammad is a liar! There is no stoning mentioned in the Tōra, so do not believe him![32]

The measure of Jewish perfidy was laid bare in the Ḳur'ān's denunciation of their *kitmān*, their concealing of the divine revelations, and we have seen one instance in which those references were taken with childish literalness. Ḳ.5:41 accused the Jews of *taḥrīf al-kalim*. Ṭabarī enlarges on this:[33] 'They had altered the *ḥukm* of God. He had revealed in the Tōra *the ruling* that the *muḥṣan* fornicators were to be stoned.' This is the third time Ṭabarī has interpolated the word *ḥukm*. The Jews are here accused of replacing the divine ruling on stoning by one on flogging which was of their own devising!

A second body of *Ḥadīth* material through Ḳatāda makes it clear that an alternative body of *asbāb al-nuzūl* for the Ḳ.5 passage referred none of the verses to sexual misconduct. They were concerned rather, with the question of supposed deviations from the regulations revealed in the Tōra to govern feud law. Like the first, this second ḥadīth strain was based upon an indifferent *tafsīr* setting out, not from Ḳ.5:41, but from Ḳ.5:45 – which at least, is a definite reference to the Tōra regulation of the talion. Competition between these two *tafsīr*s is expressed by ʿUbaydullāh b. ʿAbdullāh b. ʿUtba b. Masʿūd who explicitly accused many of the Muslims of interpreting the verses on the grounds of *asbāb* other than those which historically had occasioned their revelation. The verses concern, in his view, differential rates of blood-wit exacted by elements of the Jewish tribes at Madīna.[34] On this, as on the other, 'the Book of God' can be taken to be a reference to the Tōra. One of Ṭabarī's exegetical *ḥadīth*s combines both *tafsīr*s.[35]

We have noted that the most serious divergence reigned on the question of the meaning of the equally vague expression 'what God has revealed'. Shaʿbī and Ibrāhīm Taymī are credited with the following progression: what God has revealed;[36] the Book of God;[37] the Islamic code.[38] ʿIkrima is credited with the opinion that, like his predecessors in the prophetic office, Muḥammad had judged in accordance with the provisions of the Tōra.[39]

For Ṭabarī, 'the Book of God', in certain contexts and especially that of the stoning penalty is certainly a reference to the Tōra. That was also true of Zuhrī who was prominent in that *ḥadīth* strain that referred to 'the stoning penalty that is in the Tōra.'[40] Zuhrī is credited with the dictum: Ḳ.5:42 was revealed in connection with the stoning penalty.[41]

Thus we find in Ṭabarī's *ḥadīth*s corresponding to Mālik's 'I shall judge in accordance with the Book of God.' 'I shall judge in accordance with the Tōra.'

That the *musnad* is the same in both cases does not relieve one's confusion.

Two versions of the wording of the stoning-'verse' have been volunteered: 'If one of your number fornicates, stone him,'[42] and *al-shaykh wa-'l-shaykha idhā zanayā fa-rdjumū-humā al-battata.*[43]

Mālik, however, also preserves among his *ḥadīth*s one which gives a quite different impression of the meaning of the expression 'the Book of God'.

> ʿUmar returned to Madīna from the Ḥadjdj and addressed the people. 'Men, the precedents have been laid down for you. The obligatory duties have been imposed upon you and you have thus been left in perfect certainty – unless you stray with the people from left to right.' Striking one hand against the other, he declared: 'Beware lest by neglecting it you lose the stoning-

> 'verse'. Some people say, "We do not find two penalties in the Book of God," but the Prophet stoned and we have stoned. By Him in Whose hand is my soul! but that men might say, "'Umar has added something to the Book of God Most High, I would certainly have written it in: *al-shaykhwa-'l-shaykha idhā zanayā fa-rdjumā-humā al-battata* – for we used to recite it.'[44]

This confused document attempts to say two things at once: that stoning is definitely a *sunna* of the Prophet, imitated after him by the *khulafā'*; and that stoning is virtually a Ḳur'ān verse.

That the narrator adds: 'The month had not quite elapsed before 'Umar was killed,' shows a solicitude for the dating of a Companion dictum. As one of 'Umar's latest attested statements, the report suggests the operation of *naskh* theorising. It is not possible to judge whether the wording of the report convinced Mālik that the stoning-'verse' had once properly been part of the Ḳur'ān texts. The use in the *ḥadīth* of the terms *āya* and *ḳara'* make it certain that this was the intent, and the impression is strengthened by 'Umar's supposed admonition that the Muslims should not lose the stoning-'verse' by neglecting to recite it and by his alleged determined over-ruling of the protests of those who objected to the stoning penalty on the grounds that they could not find *two* penalties in 'the Book of God'. 'Umar was minded to write the 'verse' into the *muṣḥaf*, but hesitated lest people should accuse him of 'adding to the Book of God'. From this feature of the *ḥadīth*, we are invited to conclude that the *muṣḥaf* had already been collected some time before, since 'Umar shrank from even appearing to add anything to the texts.

A second version of the 'Umar report[45] explicitly states that the stoning-'verse' had not been part of the Ḳur'ān and that 'Umar knew that it had not. 'Umar said, 'The Prophet stoned, Abū Bakr stoned and I have stoned. But that I am not prepared to add to 'the Book of God', I should have written it into the text, for I fear that there will come people who, not finding it, will not accept it.'

This makes stoning a *sunna*. Here is no disputed allegation that it had once figured in the Ḳur'ān, since it is admitted that it not now in the *muṣḥaf*. The wording of the many reports is equivocal, showing the uncertainties of the Muslims.

'Umar said,

> God sent Muḥammad with the truth and He revealed to him the Book. Part of what was revealed to him[46] was the stoning-'verse'. The Prophet stoned and we stoned after him, and I fear lest with the passage of time, some will say, 'We do not find stoning in "the Book of God"' and thus fall into error by abandoning [*t r k*] an obligation that God revealed.

Bayhaḳī's version of this reads:[47] . . . 'Umar added, 'We recited it and got it by heart', – words normally reserved for references to the revelations.

The authority of the two great experts on Ḳur'ān matters, Ubayy b. Kaʿb and Zayd b. Thābit is employed in the same way:

> The stoning-'verse': *al-shaykh wa-'l-shaykha idhā zanayā fa-rdjumūhumā al-battata* was originally part of the Ḳur'ān text. Ubayy recalled that it had originally been part of the 'longer version' of Ḳ.33 that we no longer possess.
>
> Marwān asked Zayd if they should not add it to the *muṣḥaf*. Zayd thought not, explaining that this had already been suggested in the time of the Prophet. ʿUmar had said, 'I'll solve this for you; I'll go to the Prophet and mention this and that, then when he mentions stoning, I'll say, "Messenger of God, let me write the stoning-'verse'."' ʿUmar did so, but the Prophet replied, 'I cannot let you write it.'[48]

That the objection was to the stoning penalty is clear in: ʿUmar said, 'Some are asking' "What is this stoning? The penalty in 'the Book of God' is flogging." But I say, "The Prophet did stone..."'[49]

Unarguably, 'the Book of God' here, is the *muṣḥaf*: Ḳ.24:2. ʿUmar does not contest this but argues that stoning is the *Sunna* of the Prophet and of his Companions and successors.

Two questions have so far been mooted: Did Muḥammad stone, and if so, on what basis did he do so? Shaybānī asked, 'Did the Prophet ever stone?' and received the answer, 'Yes, he stoned two Jews.'[50] Shaybānī asked ʿAbdullāh b. abī Awfā, 'Did the prophet ever stone?' When ʿAbdullāh replied that he had, Shaybānī asked, 'Was that before or after the revelation of Ḳ.24? ʿAbdullāh replied that he did not know.[51]

That some asked whether Muḥammad had ever stoned shows that this discussion began somewhat late. The point of the question as to when he had stoned is that it had been suggested that perhaps Ḳ.24:2 which has survived textually had superseded the stoning penalty, replacing it with the flogging penalty. Conversely, if the stoning occurred later than the revelation of Ḳ.24, then the stoning penalty had replaced the flogging. There are, however, versions which ask, not whether the stoning had occurred before or after the revelation of Ḳ.24, but before or after the revelation of Ḳ.5.[52] Bukhārī expressed disapproval of these versions. Those who adopted this version have linked stoning, as we already saw, to Ḳ.5, and, accepting that Muḥammad had stoned the Jews, asked on what basis he had done that. But we also saw in the story of the employer's wife (in which there is no mention of Jews) the persistence of the allegation that Muḥammad had stoned. The prophet's words in that story, 'I shall judge betwen you on the basis of the Book of God' caused some problems.[53]

> 'Surely,' it was objected, 'the Prophet never gave any decision except on the basis of the Book of God.' Others questioned the

decision given, since stoning is unmentioned in the Book of God. They therefore re-interpreted the phrase as a reference, not to the Ḳur'ān, but to what God has imposed upon men, including those obligations mediated by the Prophet, i.e. the Sunna. Others responded that the Ḳur'ān is, indeed, what is referred to and that is certainly one's first reaction to the expression. As neither stoning nor banishment is mentioned in the Ḳur'ān, the reference may be to general injunctions to obey the Prophet and accept his decisions as final. In Ḳ.4:15, God said, 'or until God appoint a "way".' The Prophet here explained that the 'way' was the flogging and banishment of the unmarried, and the stoning of the non-virgin. Or, perhaps the expression 'the Book of God' is, indeed a reference to the Ḳur'ān, but to a verse whose wording alone has since been withdrawn: *al-shaykh wa-'l-shaykha idhā zanayā fa'rdjumū-humā*. That was how Bayḍāwī answered this difficulty.[54] However, that verse does not mention banishment. Others argued that 'the Book of God' means the Ḳur'ān, and the reference is to Ḳ.2:188 'Do not consume your wealth among you unjustifiably, then rush with pleas to the judges.' The employer had taken the man's cattle and slavegirl without legal title to them. Deciding on the basis of the Book of God, the Prophet insisted that they be returned to their owner.[55]

In ʿAmr b. Shuʿayb's version, the problems do not arise. There, the Prophet merely says, 'I shall judge between you according to what is right.' This suggests that 'the Book of God' does not refer to the Ḳur'ān, but to God's decisions generally.

A further problem arising from that story concerns the sentence the Prophet passed on the man's son. There being no reference in the *ḥadīth* to the son's status, the scholars have generally presumed that he was unmarried.[56] ʿAmr's version is once more of use. He reports that the father said, 'My son, who is non-*muḥṣan*, was labourer to this man's wife.' Thus, both Bukhārī's and Mālik's versions have been used to establish what both omitted to mention. But ʿAmr's version is formally required to establish the distinction between the two penalties acknowledged in the *Fiḳh*. Three alternative suggestions have so far been proposed for the source of the penalties:

i. that stoning, in particular, had been the *Sunna* of the Prophet;

ii. That stoning is the penalty according to 'the Book of God' may refer to His Tōra, or

iii. it may refer to His Ḳur'ān. In this last event, the stoning-'verse' had had its wording alone suppressed: *naskh al-tilāwa dūna 'l-ḥukm.*

2. Shāfiʿī's discussion on the stoning penalty.

God revealed Ḳ.4:15–16. Later, God replaced both the locking-up and the violence in His Book, saying: 'The female and male fornicators, flog them both one hundred strokes.'[Ḳ.24:2]

It is a cliché of Shāfiʿī's vocabulary that 'the Book of God' is the Ḳur'ān only.

The *Sunna* indicated [i.e. the story of the employer's wife] that the hundred strokes applied solely to those fornicators who, at the material time, had been unmarried. We are further informed by ʿUbāda that the Prophet said, 'Take it from me! take it from me! God has appointed a "way" for them [*lahunna*]: the virgin with the virgin, one hundred strokes and a year's banishment; the non-virgin with the non-virgin, one hundred strokes and death by stoning.'[57]

Later, the *Sunna* indicated that the Ḳur'ān's and ʿUbāda's one hundred strokes had been endorsed in respect of free virgins only, but withdrawn [*mansūkh*] in respect of non-virgins and that stoning alone had been endorsed [the Māʿiz *ḥadīth*][58] for *free* non-virgins. The Prophet said of the man hired by the other, 'The penalty in your son's case is one hundred strokes and a year's banishment.' [The man's wife was stoned, but not flogged.]

The expression 'Take it from me! God has appointed a way' was the first penalty *to be revealed* after Ḳ.4. That *replaced* the Ḳ.4 locking-up and violence. The Prophet stoned Māʿiz but did not flog him and he ordered the man's wife to be stoned [but not flogged]. Here, the *Sunna* indicates *naskh.* In the case of the free non-virgin, flogging was abandoned [*nusikha*] and stoning established as their sole punishment, for what occurs later comes after what occurred earlier. Both the Book of God and the *Sunna* of the Prophet indicate the *exclusion* of the non-free fornicator from these penal provisions, for God says of slavewomen, 'and when they become *muḥṣanāt*, if they should then commit abomination [*fāḥisha*] their penalty shall be half that appointed for the *muḥṣanāt.*' [Ḳ.4:25] The slave-woman's penalty must be flogging, since only flogging is divisible, stoning, a capital penalty, having no definable half.

The Prophet said, 'If one of your slavegirls should fornicate and there is no doubt of her crime, flog her.' He did not say, 'Stone her.'[59] The Muslims are agreed that no slave fornicator is to be stoned.

The last is only a clever debating point. The real issue here, is that the Prophet did not say, 'If she is *muḥṣana*'.

What precluded Shāfiʿī's drawing the conclusion that, if the slave woman's half penalty for fornication is ascertained, then the free woman's whole penalty must be double that, was the, for him, undeniable *ḥadīths* documenting the Prophet's 'practice'. In certain cases, which it is the *mudjtahid*'s business to define, he had allegedly stoned. As *uṣūlī*, Shāfi'ī ought to have decided on the 'facts' available to him, that, on this point, the *Sunna* had unquestionably superseded the Ḳur'ān ruling. We have, however, seen that Shāfi'ī was acutely conscious of the grave consequences for the *Sunna* which must flow from an admission that would have two cutting edges. Expressly to avoid being drawn into any such admission, he laboriously constructed an elaborate apparatus of exegetical techniques which he set out in detail in his *Risāla*. His first and most basic methodological axiom was that real conflict between any two statements emanating from God is inconceivable.[60] Such differences as may appear cannot be satisfactorily resolved except on the basis of a clear understanding of the processes of divine revelation. Understanding depends upon a number of principles which can be summarised in two words: *takhṣīṣ* and *bayān*.

By *takhṣīṣ* is meant[61] that it being a characteristic of the Arabic language in which both Ḳur'ān and *Sunna* are expressed, to employ on occasion terms apparently general without, however, any intention of expressing the full general content of the terms used, it becomes the responsibility of the listener to determine the precise degree of generality implied by the speaker. When, for example, God says, 'He is the Creator of all things, wherefore worship Him Who is responsible for all things,' [Ḳ.6:102]; 'He is Creator of Heaven and earth,' [Ḳ.14:10]; and, 'There is no creature in the earth but depends upon God for its sustenance,' [Ḳ.11:6] all these statements are both apparently and really general in intent. When God said [Ḳ.9:120] 'The people of Madīna and the Arabs around it had no right to absent themselves, nor prefer their own lives above that of the Messenger of God,' that too, is apparently general, yet it refers only to those persons capable of warfare. No person, of course, has the right to put his own life before that of the Prophet, and to that extent, the verse is also general in intent. In Ḳ.49:13, God says, 'We created you from male and female and made you races and tribes that you might recognise one another...'; this is general, and applies to every living creature, before the Prophet, in the Prophet's day and since the time of the Prophet. But the verse continues, 'and know that the noblest among you is the most law-abiding.' This has specific reference, applying only to those who understand law and who can be expected to abide by the law, that is, adult humans, to the exclusion of brute beasts and immature or insane humans.

Bayān is a comprehensive term referring to whatever aids the comprehension of any utterance. However various its modes may appear to the non-Arab, to the Arab, they are all more or less the same thing. There may be several aspects to the *bayān* of the

> obligations God has imposed upon us. Firstly come those cases where God has explicitly stated His command, for example, the obligation to pray, to pay *zakāt*, to perform the Ḥadjdj and to fast and that He has prohibited abominations, overt and covert, in this respect specifically naming *zinā*, wine and the eating of the flesh of animals which die naturally, blood and the flesh of the pig. God also specified the manner of the *wuḍū'*, among other things. Secondly are cases where having imposed an obligation in His Book, God then delegated to His Prophet the task of outlining the details of its performance. These Prophetic instructions are provided in the *Sunna*; for example, the number of daily ritual prayers; the amounts of *zakāt* payable on particular items and when payable. These are known only from the *Sunna*. There are thirdly, cases where the Prophet has laid down a *sunna* on matters *unmentioned in the Book*, but, since God has imposed in the Book the obligation of obedience to His Prophet, whoever accepts these from the prophet, accepts them as from God Himself.[62]

Thus, for Shāfiʿī, the *Sunna* is self-subsistent, sovereign and in principle, Ḳur'ān-indicated.

Although Shāfiʿī here asserts that God specified the manner of the *wuḍū'*, we nevertheless find him resolving certain problems relating to it. Anyone hearing Ḳ.5:6's command to wash face and hands before the ritual prayer might imagine that the minimum number demanded is one, although the verse could mean more than one. There are reports that the Prophet laid down the *sunna* that one wash suffices; other reports state that he performed three washings on occasion. Shāfiʿī determines that the *Sunna* indicates that one is the minimum number of washes required; three washes must, therefore, be supererogatory. *Bayān*, he insists, is necessary owing to what he calls the Ḳur'ān's 'ambiguity', and the obvious clash of *ḥadīth*-reports, none of which may be rejected without adequate grounds. Lacking evidence of *naskh* in the case of the conflicting *ḥadīth*s, he is content to harmonise. But it was the circulation of the conflicting *ḥadīth*s rather than the Ḳur'ān's 'ambiguity' which provoked his theory of *bayān*. The conflicting *ḥadīth*s register conflicting exegeses of the verse. The *Sunna* has also shown us what activities call for *wuḍū'*, while others call for the complete *ghusl*. Further, Ḳ.5:6 could imply that elbows and ankles are included in the obligation to wash. Or they could be excluded, being merely the limits up to which one must wash. Since the Prophet is reported to have declared, 'Woe to the ankles from the Fire!' Shāfiʿī takes that as a warning that the ankles are, indeed, to be washed, and not merely wiped, as others hold. Book and *Sunna* together are the signposts to the Truth. One of the primary functions of this *bayān* is that it serves to indicate *takhṣīṣ*, that is *exclusion*. For example, Ḳ.4:11–12 lays down the proportions that men are required to permit the parents of the deceased to inherit from offspring and the surviving spouse from the husband or wife. These Ḳur'ānic wordings are quite general, yet the Prophet indicated the *exclusion* of certain of the relatives named. The decedent and heir must both be of the same religion, while neither the homicide nor the slave can be admitted to heirship and only the *Sunna* indicates that bequests are restricted to one-third of the decedent's estate.

Part of the Ḳur'ān's alleged ambiguity is shown in the co-existence of 'variant readings'. Thus, in Ḳ.5:6, God specified the washing of the feet, as He specified the washing of the face and hands.[63] But the verse is ambiguous, in that it could state that, in respect of the feet, the obligation cannot be fulfilled except by what fulfils it in respect of the face, which is to be washed, or of the head, which is to be wiped. Further, the verse can be construed as requiring either the washing or the wiping of the feet from some persons to the exclusion of others. That the Prophet wiped his boots and ordered this wiping from those who were already in a complete state of ritual purity when they first put on their boots, resolves our difficulty: the *Sunna* here indicates the inclusion of some only and the exclusion of others from the terms of Ḳ.5:6. (The harmonisation of this *ḥadīth*-conflict, that is to say, *tafsīr*-conflict, was already completed before Shāfi'ī's time.)

In Ḳ.5:38, God ordered the amputation of the hand of the thief. But the Prophet established the *sunna* that there is to be no cutting of hands in the case of those who stole fruit, or the palm-trunk, which indicates that amputation applies only to the stealing of that which is under cover. The Prophet also laid down that there is to be no amputation in the case of the theft of items worth less than a quarter of a *dīnār*. Similarly, in Ḳ.24:2, God imposed the flogging penalty on fornicators who are each to receive one hundred strokes. The Ḳur'ān itself indicates the exclusion of slavegirls from the terms of this verse, since Ḳ.4:25 imposes the slave's penalty. But it was the *Sunna* alone that indicated that the free non-virgin fornicator is excluded from the provisions of Ḳ.24:2, for the Prophet stoned Mā'iz without flogging him.

The power that the *Fiḳh* exercised over the mind of the Muslim scholar could not be more clearly expressed than in Shāfi'ī's words, 'Had we not sought out the indications provided by the *Sunna* and had we decided solely in accordance with the wording of the Ḳur'ān, we should have made none of these exclusions.'[64]

The *bayān-takhṣīṣ* apparatus – merely a device for evading Ḳur'ān-*Fiḳh* conflict – rather underlines than disguises the conflict. Any perplexity arising from the recognition of the conflict is to be minimised by declaring the *Sunna* wherever it is at variance with the Ḳur'ān, its *bayān* or elucidation. We have even seen that the *Sunna* may be the completion of the Ḳur'ān revelation. But Shāfi'ī would argue, this is not to make the *Sunna* the judge of the Ḳur'ān, as some have done, and certainly not its *nāsikh*. For the *Sunna* depends for its validation upon the Ḳur'ān which supplied its credentials and its guarantee. The 'unambiguous' verses of the Ḳur'ān are those which impose the religious obligation of unquestioning obedience to the Prophet. God linked faith in Himself with faith in His Prophet.[65] God stated that complete faith is belief in God and in His prophet.[66] Several Ḳur'ān verses speak of God's granting men the mercy of teaching them the Book and the *Ḥikma*,[67] and Shāfi'ī is not in any doubt that these are all references to the *Sunna* of the Prophet. 'No other exegesis is possible, since of no other source is it possible to claim that it has been imposed upon the Muslims in addition to the Book of God except the *Sunna* of the Prophet.'[68] Ḳ.4:59 imposed upon the Muslims the obligation to refer all questions at issue to God and to his Prophet. The Muslims of generations later than that of the Prophet's can have no access to his decision, however, except through his *Sunna*. These obligations are made quite peremptory by Ḳ.4:65, 80.

Thus, when men accept the Prophet's decisions, they do so in accordance with these divine commands, God having informed them that *Muḥammad's decisions are God's decisions*.[69]

Amassing all these 'unambiguous' verses, Shāfi'ī concludes that whatever Muḥammad has laid down on matters where there is no ruling in the Ḳur'ān, it is by the ruling of the Ḳur'ān that we must accept it. God Himself had verified this, saying to His Prophet, 'You do guide to the right path, the path of God.'[70]

Now, the Prophet has laid down *sunna*s in association with the Book of God, and he has also provided *bayān* on matters not themselves covered by a text in the Book of God. But everything and anything that he has laid down must, by divine command, be followed. God has thus left no loophole through which men can escape the *Sunna*.[71] The Prophet himself has said, 'Let me not find any one of you reclining on his couch and saying when a command from me reaches him, "I do not know. We shall follow what we find in the Book of God."'

The relation between the *Sunna* and the Book of God is two-fold:

i. there is a text in the Book and the Prophet follows it exactly as it is revealed;

ii. the text in the Book is couched in general terms and the Prophet makes clear on God's behalf precisely what God intended by that utterance.

> In both situations, the Prophet is following the Book. No scholar disputes that the *Sunna* falls into three categories, and the scholars are unanimous on two of them. They have just been mentioned. The third category is that of *sunna*s on matters on which there is no text in the Ḳur'ān. This third category is disputed.

> Some scholars argue that, having imposed the obligation of obedience to His Prophet, and knowing that He will direct him to what is pleasing to Him, God assigned to Muḥammad the prerogative to establish these *sunna*s on matters unmentioned in the Book.
>
> Others have argued that the Prophet never laid down a *sunna* on matters other than those mentioned in the Book, for example, the *sunna*s which specified the number of the daily ritual prayers, the manner and the times of their performance, since the general imposition of the prayers was in the Ḳur'ān. The same applies to *sunna*s on commercial matters, since God mentions in His Book the disposal of property, sales, loans, usury and the like. In all such questions, whatever the Prophet declared lawful or unlawful, he was acting, as in the case of the prayers, to provide *bayān* on God's behalf.

We can ignore the first category entirely. *Sunna*s which follow exactly the rulings laid down in the Ḳur'ān are quite supernumerary. What Shāfiʿī does tell us is that the Muslims accept *tafsīr-ḥadīth*s, (his second category). Contention centred therefore only upon his third category: *Sunna*s whose contents are additional to the rulings revealed in the Ḳur'ān. Clearly, one accepts these on one of two conditions: if one prima facie rejects the concept that these *sunnas* can *naskh* the Ḳur'ān, the only remaining course is to accept that, like the Ḳur'ān the *Sunna* too is revealed. Shāfiʿī himself acknowledged as much.

> Part of what is 'cast into Muḥammad's mind' in his *Sunna* – the *Ḥikma* which God mentions. Anything on which a Ḳur'ān revelation comes down is the Book – and both are part of God's favour to men.[72]
>
> Men stand in need of the Prophet and when his *Sunna* provides *bayān* on God's behalf as to the precise meaning that God intended where there is a text, how much more men need him on matters where there is no text.

Schacht's statement that on the inspired nature of the *Sunna* Shāfiʿī showed himself non-commital[73] is shown by this to be inaccurate.

In Shāfiʿī's day, the *Sunna* had not quite prevailed over the Ḳur'ān, although it was well on the way to doing so. Questions had been levelled at many *Fiḳh* doctrines, but providing these could be linked, in however tenuous a fashion, to some text in the Book, a case could be made in their defence. It remained only to recruit into this category such *Fiḳh* doctrines as had no apparent connection with the Ḳur'ān texts, or even those which contradicted Ḳur'ān texts.

Shāfiʿī favoured the argument that alleged conflict between *Sunna* [*Fiḳh*] and Ḳur'ān was only apparent. The *ḥukm* of God and the *ḥukm* of God's Prophet is one and indivisible, both proceeding from the same divine source. The *Risāla* frequently reads like a counter-blast to the slogan: *lā ḥukma illā li-'llāh* cf. *Risāla*, 15: 'Know that Muḥammad's *ḥukm* is God's *ḥukm*.'

We saw previously that for Shāfiʿī, the Ḳur'ān *naskh*s only the Ḳur'ān and the *Sunna* never does. The *Sunna*'s function is merely to follow the Book in the like of that which is textually referred to in the Book, and to elucidate the meanings of texts revealed in the Book in general terms. Since only God originates the divine commands, only God can remove or endorse what He pleases. Similarly nothing can *naskh* the *Sunna* of the Prophet save only another *sunna* of the Prophet. There is no human utterance that can *naskh* the *Sunna* of the Prophet for it has no like except only itself. In its context, this was a subtle device to prevent any appeal from the *Sunna* to the *ḥadīth*s from the Companions and the Successors. It had, however, the side-effect of preventing any appeal from the *Sunna* back to the Ḳur'ān, for we have also seen Shāfiʿī insist that if God were to introduce a new ruling on some matter on which the Prophet had already ruled, the Prophet would hasten to lay down a fresh *sunna* which strictly speaking, according to this argument, must be considered the *nāsikh* of the first *sunna*. We have also heard his declaration that some *mansūkh sunna*s may have failed to survive, but that no *nāsikh sunna*s could be thought to have perished. These are invariably transmitted.

This is to impose upon the Ḳur'ān a subordinate role: the *Sunna* elucidates the Ḳur'ān; the *nāsikh sunna* survives; there is thus never possible – never necessary any need for appeal from the *Sunna* back to the Ḳur'ān.

Were it permitted to say that the Prophet had laid down a *sunna* which God subsequently replaced by a Ḳur'ān revelation without there having been transmitted from the Prophet that *sunna* which properly speaking is the *nāsikh*, it would be possible to hold, for example, concerning those fornicators who are stoned, perhaps Muḥammad stoned them before God revealed Ḳ.24:2.[74]

Undoubtedly, Shāfiʿī showed sound instinct in identifying as a primary source during the lifetime of the Prophet, the *Sunna* of the Prophet. As a Traditionist, however, he has extended this identification to the *Ḥadīth* materials accumulated during the nearly two centuries separating him from Muḥammad's time, and recently pronounced to be the authentic *Sunna* of the Prophet. He also showed an inclination to regard this *Sunna* of the Prophet as divinely inspired. It was in the light of these methodological attitudes that he dealt with the question of the *Fiḳh* penalties for fornication and adultery.

We have considered Shāfiʿī's exposition based upon the documents available to him (above, p. 135–6). We ought now to consider the problems raised in that exposition: He appeared to begin by arguing that the locking-up and the violence [Ḳ.4:15–16] had remained the penalty until superseded by Ḳ.24:2's flogging penalty. In one sense that was essential, given his methods. For he must first locate a penalty from which, according to him, Ḳ.4:25 excluded slave women who are *muḥṣanāt*. As Ḳ.4:25 imposed upon *muḥṣanāt* slave women one-half of an already known penalty – that for *muḥṣanāt* free women – he must locate a divisible penalty. Ḳ.24:2 laid down a penalty of one hundred lashes. Therefore the penalty for *muḥṣanāt* slave women must be fifty strokes.

Crucial to his argument is the ʿUbāda *ḥadīth*: 'the virgin with the virgin, one hundred strokes and a year's banishment; the non-virgin with the non-virgin, one hundred strokes and death by stoning'.

Ḳ.4:15 had ended by saying, 'or until God appoint a "way";' Now, since ʿUbāda begins by saying, 'God has appointed the "way",' Shāfiʿī also argues that this *ḥadīth* must be the first thing that was revealed to Muḥammad since the revelation of Ḳ.4 since by it the locking-up and the violence were *replaced*.[75]

> In the case of the employer's wife and her labourer, the young man was both flogged and banished. The flogging element is therefore endorsed in that penalty. Since we know that the labourer was unmarried, flogging must be the penalty of the free, unmarried fornicator. This elucidates the Ḳ.24:2 verse which must apply solely to the free unmarried offender. Here, the Prophet stoned the employer's wife, but did not flog her. That indicates that, if originally intended to be included in the provisions of Ḳ.24:2, the married offender has been shown by the Prophet's practice to be excluded from that ruling. If they were intended to be included in the provisions of Ḳ.24:2, that verse's flogging element has been *withdrawn*[76] in the case of the married offender. If not originally intended to be included in that verse's provision, married are not the same as unmarried offenders. Ḳ.24:2 thus refers exclusively to free unmarried offenders from the outset. Shāfiʿī thus reads the 'historical' sequence: Ḳ.4:15–16; ʿUbāda; Ḳ.24:2; Ḳ.4:25; Māʿiz, employer's wife.

The ʿUbāda *ḥadith* had dual utility: it distinguished for the first time two categories of fornicators (a matter on which the Ḳur'ān was to remain silent); and, as promised in Ḳ.4:15, it appointed a penalty for each of the categories, in each instance appointing, indeed, a double penalty. ʿUbāda apparently anticipated one part of these dual penalties to be revealed in Ḳ.24:2: the one hundred strokes. Apart from the categorisation of classes of offenders, 'Ubāda imposed in addition to the Ḳur'ānic penalty of flogging, the second element in the punishment of each category: the banishment of the non-*muḥṣan* and the execution of the *muḥṣan*, on both of which also the Ḳur'ān would remain silent. Small wonder that some Muslims protested that they could not find two penalties in the Book of God!

Since the Ḳur'ān cannot *naskh* the *Sunna*, Ḳ.24:2 could not be alleged, by concentrating solely on the flogging element of the two *Fiḳh* penalties, to be *nāsikh* to either the banishment or the stoning.

The suggestion was made that perhaps the Islamic penalty for fornication had been imposed in the Ḳur'ān in an earlier revelation, later moderated [*khuffifa*] by Ḳ.4.77. Shāfi'ī brusquely brushed this suggestion aside by the bald assertion that 'Ubāda had mentioned his *ḥadīth* in a retrospective comment on Ḳ.4, following its *naskh*.

Insisting that 'Ubāda was later than Ḳ.4, and assuming that Ḳ.24 was later than 'Ubāda, Shāfi'ī stressed that the flogging element had been endorsed as part of the punishment of the free unmarried offender. Ḳ.4:25 imposed upon the slave women half the penalty imposed upon free *muḥṣan* women. Shāfi'ī located a divisible penalty applicable to free *muḥṣan* women in Ḳ.24:2. This means that Ḳ.24:2 must have intended the inclusion of free *muḥṣan* women. Insisting that the penalty for free *muḥṣan* adulterers is stoning alone, Shāfi'ī argues that they have therefore been excluded from the provisions of Ḳ.24. The *Sunna* has *naskh*ed the application of Ḳ.24:2 to them.

If, from the outset, Ḳ.24:2 had been intended to apply restrictively to the free non-*muḥṣan* offender, the attempt to locate a penalty one half of which is applicable to slave *muḥṣan* women would be frustrated. Ḳ.24:2 would apply only to free non-*muḥṣan* offenders. The penalty applicable to slave *muḥṣan* women would then be half of that applicable to free non-*muḥṣan* offenders, which is not what Ḳ.4:25 says. Thus, free *muḥṣan* offenders must have been included in the provisions of Ḳ.24:2 from the outset. They have now been excluded by the *Sunna*. The *Sunna* is thus the *nāsikh* of Ḳ.24.

Indeed, on the basis of the Mā'iz and the employer's wife *ḥadīth*, Shāfi'ī did conclude that, in the case of offenders who are stoned, the flogging imposed in both 'Ubāda's *ḥadīth* and Ḳ.24:2 is *mansūkh*. Shāfi'ī flatly asserts that the stoning of the *muḥṣan* occurred later than the revelation of Ḳ.24:2.[78]

It must be emphasised how equivocal is his vocabulary: the 'Ubāda *ḥadīth* is the first thing *to have been revealed* since Ḳ.4:15–16.[79] The 'Ubāda *ḥadīth naskh*ed Ḳ.4:15–16.[80] In the case of the free *muḥṣan*, the one hundred strokes of Ḳ.24:2 were *naskh*ed. Yet, according to Shāfi'ī's technical reasoning, the *Sunna* cannot *naskh* the Ḳur'ān – only the Ḳur'ān can do this. Ḳ.4:15–16 are undoubtedly Ḳur'ān, and the 'Ubāda *ḥadith* is their *nāsikh*. The scholars will now follow one of two routes, depending upon whether they chance to be Shāfi'ī followers or not. In the latter case, if prepared to accept his chronology, the scholar merely continues to repeat the old pre-Shāfi'ī principle that the *Sunna* can and does *naskh* the Ḳur'ān, adducing this instance as one's 'proof'. 'Alī is reported to have said of one such free *muḥṣan* female offender: 'I flogged her on the basis of "the Book of God"; and I stoned her on the basis of the *Sunna* of the Prophet.'[81] This report, however, was circulated by those who favoured the continuance of the dual penalty mentioned by 'Ubāda.

But for those who found Shāfiʿī's technical reasoning both forceful and unassailable, the only route open could have been predicted given the equivocal nature of his language. *Takhṣīṣ*, we have seen, is that form of *bayān* which indicates exclusion. What, however, is unique about the penalties for fornication and adultery is that, over and above the exclusion of the free *muḥṣan* offender from the flogging provision of Ḳ.24:2 which he here argued, he acknowledged that the *Sunna* had established the additional element of stoning. Stoning has no 'basis in the Ḳur'ān'; can the *Sunna*, then, usurp the function of the Ḳur'ān in initiating a penalty on a matter in which there is Ḳur'ānic provision? Shāfiʿī had already established that the *Sunna* never once *naskhed* the Ḳur'ān. Only Ḳur'ān *naskhs* Ḳur'ān, *Sunna* cannot do so. Interestingly, whereas Shāfiʿī draws heavily upon Mālik for his *ḥadīth* materials on this question, as in so many others, the one element he has not borrowed, or at least, has not seen fit to emphasise on this occasion,[82] is the concept Mālik referred to ʿUmar that the stoning-'verse' had once actually been part of the Ḳur'ān revelation texts. Equally interesting is that there is an Mālik's collection not one reference to the ʿUbāda *ḥadīth* on which Shāfiʿī also relied so heavily, but although he does not adduce it, Mālik may conceivably have heard the ʿUbāda *ḥadīth*,for he, in turn, glosses the words shaykh and shaykha of the so-called 'verse' as *thayyib* and *thayyiba*.[83]

The logical outcome of Shāfiʿī's unflagging reiteration of the divine commands to render unquestioning obedience to the Prophet was the emergence of the *Sunna* as an independent source in the documentation of the *Fiḳh*. Shāfiʿī was unable to make the claim on behalf of the *Sunna* in its most extreme form. His entire defence of the role of the *Sunna*, based upon selected Ḳur'ān texts, had been necessitated and conditioned by a historical situation in which the *Sunna* source was being rejected and denied a voice by those who regarded the Ḳur'ān as alone having source status. Reacting in the defence of the *Sunna*, Shāfiʿī stole his opponents' weapon and quoted the Ḳur'ān at them to ensure for the *Sunna* its central role as the second of two revealed sources.

His ingenuity lay in the adoption of the *takhṣīṣ* tool to rehabilitate the impugned *Sunna*. But the methods he used could not be extended to include the penalty additional to Ḳ.24:2's flogging in the face of those who insisted that stoning is nowhere alluded to in the Ḳur'ān, nor in the face of his own studied insistence that *Sunna* cannot *naskh* Ḳur'ān. Nor, indeed, could his method be extended to cover any detail of the *Fiḳh* not having a 'basis in the Ḳur'ān'. It is on these questions, as Schacht points out,[84] that Shāfiʿī's *uṣūl* system breaks down. From the fact of the breakdown despite the effort he expended, we can gauge the strength of the pro-Ḳur'ān argument in his day, which his reasoning had to attempt to match but which it has quite failed to match.

By his skilful deployment of snatches of Ḳur'ān texts, Shāfi'ī rescued the *Sunna* from outright rejection, but he failed to solve the problem of the source of the stoning penalty, because it cannot be solved on the grounds that he himself chose.

It comes, therefore, as no surprise to find that several attempts more explicit than Shāfi'ī's were made to give the 'Ubāda *ḥadīth* the allure of having been a revelation:

> 'Ubāda said, 'Whenever revelation came upon him, the Prophet would be distressed, his face discolouring. One day, revelation coming upon him, he reacted in that way and, when he had recovered, he said, "Take it from me! take it from me! God has now appointed a way for them [*lahunna*]."'[85]

Perhaps this cannot be taken as evidence that the effort here, and in Shāfi'ī's argumentation, was to treat this as undeniably a Ḳur'ān revelation, although it is certainly regarded as a revelation. Shāfi'ī does, however, say:[86] 'The Prophet never imposed any ruling except as the result of *waḥy*; there are two kinds of *waḥy*: recited *waḥy* [*matlū*] and non-recited *waḥy* [*ghayr matlū*] on the basis of which he established his *Sunna*.' Ṭabarānī's version of the 'Ubāda *ḥadīth* mentions that 'when the stoning "verse" was revealed, the Prophet said, "Now God has appointed a way."'[87]

Shāfi'ī's technical arguments, compounded by his equivocal language made it natural to suppose that if stoning superseded flogging, then stoning must at one time have been in the Ḳur'ān. No *uṣūlī* denies that stoning remained the valid *Fiḳh* penalty for adultery. The ruling is nowhere represented by a wording in the Ḳur'ān texts [*muṣḥaf*]. This must, therefore be one instance of the 'historical' occurrence of the third mode of *naskh*: *naskh al-tilāwa dūna 'l-ḥukm*. The *Fiḳh* shows that the ruling has continued to be valid despite the disappearance of the revealed wording.

The irony of Shāfi'ī's intervention in this discussion is that, starting from the *Fiḳh*, he argued that the penalty is stoning *alone*. Conscious that there existed a rival minority view that the penalty is stoning *and* flogging, he expended more time and energy harmonising the two *ḥadīth* strains which separately represented these two opinions, than on the more important task of harmonising the *Ḥadīth*'s mention of stoning with the Ḳur'ān's mention of flogging. For his 'evidence', he was heavily reliant upon the 'Ubāda *ḥadīth* and the Mā'iz and 'the employer's wife' *ḥadīth*s. But these are contradictory, only the latter documenting the *Fiḳh* which he espoused. He used the latter, therefore, to demonstrate the *naskh* of the former. This was an instance of the *naskh* of the *Sunna* by the later *Sunna*, but the complexity of his arguments and the looseness of his language combined to mislead later *uṣūlī*s as to his actual conclusions. As far as Ḳ.24:2 is concerned, he hoped to use the Mā'iz and 'the employer's wife' stories again, to demonstrate the exclusion of the categories of persons stoned without being flogged, i.e. male and female *muḥṣan* offenders, from the provisions of the verse. But once more, the laxity of his language misled others as to his drift.

What may finally have consolidated the idea that the *Fiḳh* penalty had been revealed was his discussion of the question from the angle of jurisdiction.[88] We have learned that some asked, 'Did the Prophet ever stone, and if so, did he do so before the revelation of Ḳ.24?' although we have also seen others ask, 'and if so, did he do so before the revelation of Ḳ.5?' The answer was that Muḥammad had stoned certain Jews.

It was next natural to ask on what basis he had done that. One perfectly sensible answer was that he had done so on the basis of Tōra law. We have 'evidence' that he first asked the Jewish doctors what provision their law made for such cases. Finally, in order to be in no doubt, he had even called for a copy of the Tōra. Satisfied that it laid down a stoning penalty, the Prophet had not hesitated to apply it to Jewish offenders, within the terms of Ḳ.5, 'and if you do give judgment, render judgment on the basis of what God has revealed'.

The next interesting question would be that of how far the Prophet's 'historically attested' conduct towards non-Muslims would constitute *Sunna* for the purposes of the institution of the penalty applicable to Muslims in similar circumstances. That Muḥammad's 'attested' conduct towards Muslims constitutes *Sunna* none in the end would question. But that his conduct towards non-Muslims should be binding on later generations of Muslims was not so readily accepted.

That such conduct constituted *Sunna* in the accepted meaning was a view that encountered resistance, as can be seen from the duplication of *ḥadīth*s to 'attest' the application to Muslims of precisely the same penalty. Parallel to the exegesis of Ḳ.4:15's 'your women' as 'possessed, ergo, married women' – runs a second, more significant assertion that the expression means 'Muslim women'.[89] This is the later interpretation, since it pre-supposes and supplements the other.

In the ʿUbāda, Māʿiz and 'the employer's wife' *ḥadīth*s we witness a series of claims parallel to the series of *ḥadīth*s documenting Muḥammad's stoning of Jews, that he had also stoned Muslims, males as well as females. Only in the case of this latter series of *ḥadīth*s was it found necessary to adduce 'evidence' as to the conduct of Muḥammad's successors, Abū Bakr, 'Umar, 'Uthmān and of 'Alī's alleged opinion.

Stoning, as an 'Islamic penalty' was rejected by some scholars, said to be *Khawāridj* or *Muʿtazilī*, on the grounds that 'We do not find two penalties in the Book of God.' Of the two schools, we know of their reserved attitude on the *Ḥadīth*. The former rejected them for systematic reasons, since they insisted on the principle: *lā ḥukm illā li-'llāhi*.

The latter scorned them for formal reasons, since they doubted the efficacy of the *isnād* safeguard against falsification and since too many *ḥadīth*s contradicted either other *ḥadīth*s, or reason, or, even worse, the Book of God.[90] A means was now at hand to neutralise the objections of both parties and was soon used by the *Sunnī*s. This was quite simply to insist that there are, in fact, (or were) two penalties in the Book of God, flogging and stoning. In association with his *takhṣīṣ* instrument, the Māʿiz and 'employer's wife' *ḥadīth*s might have been more satisfactorily exploited by Shāfiʿī to 'prove' the exclusion of the married fornicator from the provisions of Ḳ.24:2, if he had embraced ʿUmar's remarks on the stoning-'verse' with more enthusiasm. That he did not, shows that his attention was more firmly concentrated upon removing the conflict evident between his two representative *ḥadīth*s, 'Ubāda and Māʿiz, than on the conflict evident between both *ḥadīth*s and the Ḳur'ān verse. He had no reservations about the ʿUmar *ḥadīth*, for he admitted it into his canon. But, as *uṣūlī*, he had had to take account of two further elements in the *Fiḳh* penalties unmentioned not only in the Ḳur'ān as we know it, the *muṣḥaf*, but also in the stoning-'verse' as well. These are the non-Ḳur'ānic distinction between fornication and adultery, that is, between 'virgins' and 'non-virgins'; and, in the case of the former, the extra-Ḳur'ānic penalty of banishment. Shāfiʿī's choice of procedure was amply justified by his objective which was to establish from the *sunna*, not the *naskh* of the Ḳur'ān, but its *bayān* or elucidation. His selection of 'evidence' was doubly unfortunate, for the *ḥadīth* from ʿUbāda presented him with embarrassing problems of *isnād*, and, in addition, even on a superficial reading, it is palpably a fraud. The phrase, 'Now God has appointed a way' is no more than an echo of Ḳ.4:15's 'or until God appoint a way'. But the interpolation of the phrase was essential to establish that the verse on which the 'Ubāda *ḥadīth* is parasitic had indeed been superseded by something other than Ḳ.24:2. Further, Ḳ.4:15 is not universally conceded to be a divine statement about a promised future penalty for the fornicator. It has been realised by some that the verse deals exclusively with females. The same is, of course, true for Ḳ.4:25 and, as is obvious, for ʿUbāda as well. That Ḳ.4:15–16 deals with fornication is mere assertion flowing from one interpretation of the vague negative term *fāḥisha* which, in the Ḳur'ān, has a variety of applications.

The ʿUbāda *ḥadīth* is thus secondary, not merely to consideration of the words of a verse, but to only one of the several possible interpretations of the verse. In exactly the same way, the words, 'Take it from me!' betray their origin in the blatantly partisan *tafsīr* proposed by the *Ḥadīth* party for Ḳ.59:7: 'Whatsoever God grants as spoil from the people of the settlements to His Messenger, is to be enjoyed by the Messenger, the next of kin, the orphaned, the destitute and the warrior, so that it shall not become a thing of contention among the wealthy members of the *umma*. Take whatever the Messenger gives you; what he denies you, desist from demanding.'

Indisputably, the verse concerns the division among the Muslims of the properties of defeated enemies. Nonetheless, one finds this *āya*, regardless of context, basic to Shāfiʿī's ceaseless campaign to fasten upon the Muslims his school's notion of the divine imposition of the religious obligation to render implicit obedience to the Prophet, in the technical Shāfiʿite sense of unquestioning adherence to the *Sunna*. 'God imposed on us the religious obligation of subordinating ourselves to the commands of His Prophet, saying, "Take whatever the Messenger gives you; what he denies you, desist from demanding."'[91]

Nor is there a shortage of irony in the literature. This *āya* which Shāfiʿī is fond of exploiting to establish the legislative faculty of the *Sunna* alongside the Ḳur'ān is also favoured by those who argue that the *sunna* can and does *naskh* the Ḳur'ān:

> Those who hold that the *Sunna* can *naskh* the Ḳur'ān quote: 'He does not speak from fancy' [Ḳ.53:3] and 'Take whatever the Messenger gives you; what he denies you, desist from demanding,' which is general, with no element of the specific. We are therefore obliged to accept the Prophet's word. Those who deny the *naskh* of the Ḳur'ān by the *Sunna* interpret the verse thus: 'Whatever the Prophet brings you of the Book of God, accept it.' The Ḳ.53 verse they say means, 'He does not speak from fancy – this Ḳur'ān which he brings you comes from God. It is not got up by Muḥammad from his own imagination.' As the *Sunna* elucidates the Ḳur'ān, it cannot also be its *nāsikh*.[92]

The artificiality of the ʿUbāda *ḥadīth* is evident from its form, calculated to bridge the gap between Ḳ.4:15 and Ḳ.24:2 on the one hand; while, on the other, it reconciles the 'practice' – the banishment and the stoning of the extra-Ḳur'ānic *Fiḳh* – with the Ḳur'ān's flogging provision. The *ḥadīth* was the *ad hoc* invention of *uṣūl* circles sympathetic to the views of *ahl-al-Ḥadīth*, but who yet, apparently, had to take account of the contents of the Ḳur'ān. The irony is that the stoning penalty may well have had, not merely an Islamic, but even a Ḳur'ānic origin. There is some awkwardness arising from ʿUbāda's bridge-form: it might be argued that it could have been *naskh*ed by Ḳ.4:15–16. Shāfiʿī must therefore insist that the expression: 'Now God has appointed a way,' was to introduce *the first revelation since* Ḳ.4:15. His placing of the Māʿiz and 'the employer's wife' stories later than the revelation of Ḳ.24:2, is again, mere exegete's assertion. Sarakhsī places ʿUbāda earlier than Ḳ.24.[93]

> In the *ḥadīth* the Prophet says, 'Take it from me!' Had the *ḥadīth* followed Ḳ.24, he would have said, 'Take it from God.' [!]

Shāfiʿī further argues that in these two stories, we find the documentation of the Prophet's practice of stoning the *thayyib*, but not flogging him. That is an alleviation. It must, therefore, be later than Ḳ.24:2.[94] The function of 'the employer's wife' tale was to restore the doctrinal situation created originally by the 'Ubāda *ḥadīth*, but now seen to be threatened by being placed too early in the timetable. The two stories had further uses. They vindicated the *Fiḳh* position that stoning is not accompanied by flogging, i.e. they 'prove' the abrogation of the 'Ubāda penalty. 'Ubāda's is a purely verbal statement; these two *ḥadīth*s are reports of actions.[95] This implies that 'Ubāda does not provide evidence that the Prophet actually 'historically' had combined flogging and stoning, or flogging and banishment, whereas the later *ḥadīth*s show the Prophet imposing the dual penalty upon the man's son, who was non-*muḥṣan*, while both this and the Mā'iz story document the assertion that, in the case of the *muḥṣan*, the Prophet had abandoned the flogging element. Their penalty is stoning alone. The reports must, on that account, be later than Ḳ.24:2. The later *naskh*s the earlier, if it differs from it. Both *ḥadīth*s 'confirm' the exegesis of Ḳ.4:15–16, and, more significantly, extend the *Fiḳh* penalties to males! That 'Ubāda had failed to do. Simultaneously, 'the employer's wife' store verifies 'Ubāda in part, and thus supplies the necessary documentation of the Shāfi'ite view that 'Ubāda is in part *mansūkh*. Where stoning is applicable, flogging is abandoned; where flogging is applicable, banishment is added. The Ḳ.24:2 penalty is thus, in some circumstances, endorsed, in others, repealed. These *ḥadīth*s are therefore later than the verse.

No care need be given to the production of evidence to confirm that the Prophet had actually ever combined flogging with stoning, since that view was held only by a dwindling minority of scholars. The majority were certain that the combined penalty had not remained valid in the case of the *muḥṣan*. Further doubt is, however, hereby cast on the 'Ubāda *ḥadīth*. It served merely to link flogging with stoning, so that the link could be immediately broken, leaving stoning alone as the sole penalty in certain circumstances. That the *ḥadīth* of 'the employer's wife' was intended to re-instate the 'Ubāda situation is indicated by Shāfi'ī's presumption that the man's son was '*bikr*'.[96] The Prophet's stoning of the man's wife, and of Mā'iz was later than Ḳ.24:2 and based on 'what the Prophet related as from God'. Stoning was thus based upon a divine communication and, at the close of the second century AH, when the primary concern was still to justify the *Sunna* against those prepared to accept no *ḥadīth*, or, at best, only *tafsīr-ḥadīth*, that is, *ḥadīth*s which had at least a 'basis in the Ḳur'ān', one need not labour the point as to whether here was a ḳur'ānic or a non-ḳur'ānic *waḥy*, or inspiration. The aim was to establish that stoning was an Islamic imposition. In achieving this desired result, the criteria were either a source in the divine book, or a source in the revealed *sunna*. The first criterion was in view in Mālik's report from ʿUmar that stoning had been revealed by God and had once figured in a verse of the Ḳur'ān; and the ibn ʿUmar report that, in fact, there had been a stoning-'verse' in the Tōra. The second criterion lay behind the ʿUbāda, Māʿiz and 'employer's wife' *ḥadīth*s, although we have noted the vacillation as to the category in which to place ʿUbāda's *ḥadīth*. It depended upon the assumptions of the opponent one was addressing.

For Shāfiʿī, the *Sunna* [the *Fiḳh*] was certainly the primary source. It could be further argued, on reflecting that in any case of conflict between Ḳur'ān and *Sunna*, it was invariably the Ḳur'ān [*muṣḥaf*] that had to adjust to the *Sunna*, and never the reverse,[97] that it was historically the prior source of the doctrines which Shāfiʿī espoused. That, however, the *muṣḥaf* had to be seen to be capable of such adjustment, shows that the *muṣḥaf* source could no longer be ignored. In his defence of the *Sunna* against the Ḳur'ān, we see Shāfiʿī respond to a contemporary pressure where the emphasis has shifted from the *Sunna* in the direction of the theoretical primacy of the Ḳur'ān source which must now be shown to underlie the *Fiḳh*. The protests of the *Khawāridj* and the *Muʿtazila* show that this, in turn, had led to a fresh and an acute re-examination of the texts of the *muṣḥaf*.

The expediency of suggesting that the stoning penalty had originated in 'the Book of God', and was not based solely on the *Sunna*, as expressed in Mālik's ʿUmar *ḥadīth*, and again in the prophet's undertaking, 'I shall judge between you on the basis of the Book of God' remains a puzzle. We know that stoning is not mentioned in the *muṣḥaf*. Shāfiʿī evades the issue by arguing that when the Prophet stoned, he was supplying the elucidation of what God had intended in the *muṣḥaf*. At the stage in the development of the *uṣūl* when insistent demands were made that the Ḳur'ān be seen to have been the primary source, the allegation that the Ḳur'ān had been the source of the *Fiḳh*'s stoning penalty ought to have attracted more widespread and vociferous protest. That the claim passed without serious challenge argues that the majority saw that it had merit. So far, the expression 'the Book of God' has been applied to Ḳur'ān, Tōra and the *Sunna*. Further consideration is now required of the starting-point of the whole affair in the exegeses of the Ḳ.5 passages noted earlier:'

> God said, 'If *ahl al-kitāb* come to you, judge between them or ignore them, for they shall not harm you. If you do judge between them, judge *bi-l-ḳisṭ*.' The verse shows that God had granted His Prophet the choice: to judge or not to judge them. This term *ḳisṭ* means: the decision of God which He revealed to His Prophet, the pure and truthful one in His *latest* revelation.[98] God also said, 'and adjudicate between them on the basis of what

> God has revealed. Do not follow their merely human whims. Be on your guard lest they seduce you from part or what God has revealed *to you*.' The verse conveys the same injunction as above – the divine command to judge them according to what God has revealed – to Muḥammad. It is not, however, an absolute command that he must judge between them. The Prophet retained the choice that had been presented to him in the words of the earlier verse.[99]
>
> In the case of two Jews who had fornicated, the Prophet decided that they be stoned. That shows the meaning of the two verses. Whatever member of God's religion adjudicates between *ahl al-kitāb*, the issue must be determined solely on the basis of Muslim law... The Prophet stoned these two Jews. God had commanded Muḥammad to judge on the basis of what had been revealed. He stoned them, the penalty that is inflicted upon the non-virgin Muslim in cases of fornication.
>
> If it be alleged that Ḳ.5:49 *naskh*ed Ḳ.5:42, one replies: *Naskh* is recognised solely on the basis of a report from the Prophet, or from one of his Companions, none of the other Companions dissenting, or on the basis of some matter assented to by the generality of the *fuḳahā'*.[100] Besides, Ḳ.5:49 is capable of being read with *ta'wīl*: 'Judge between them on the basis of what God has revealed – [if you elect to judge them].'...
>
> The Prophet inflicted stoning on non-Muslims that being the *Sunna which he had applied to the Muslims*, and concerning which he had declared, 'I shall judge between you on the basis of the Book of God.'

The significance of the dispute over the *naskh* of Ḳ.5:42 by Ḳ.5:49 lay in the allegation by some that having, at first, been granted the choice between hearing or not hearing the *kitābīs*, Muḥammad had lost that choice. He was required to hear them and to judge them on the basis of what had been revealed. The crux of the entire discussion is 'revealed to whom?' Shāfi'ī would argue 'revealed to Muḥammad' who had applied to Jews the penalty *he had already applied to Muslims*. The assertion is necessary to his argument but is nowhere throughout his writings substantiated. He further assumes, but does not substantiate his presumption, that the Jews whom Muhammad had stoned were not *dhimmīs*.[101] Indeed, Shāfi'ī has not heard that any of the four caliphs had ever judged a case involving *dhimmīs*. The absence of such reports indicates that they had never done so. He knows of no report to the effect that the Prophet had ever judged *dhimmīs* either. He did stone two Jews. However, they were not *dhimmī* but persons subject to Islamic laws who had come seeking his prophetic ruling. *Dhimmīs* are referred to their own confessional courts where they are to be judged in accordance with their own codes. Indeed, if *dhimmīs* refused to repair to their own judges, Shāfi'ī would threaten them with the dissolution of the *dhimma*. If they sought his decision, he would, on Ḳur'ānic grounds, decline to hear them. For the sake of argument, supposing he did decide to hear them, he would accept only Muslim witnesses and warn the litigants that he proposed to apply the Islamic code and no other. The Jews who had come seeking Muḥammad's decision on fornication knew that stoning was the penalty in the Tōra. But they came seeking his prophetic ruling, hoping that it would be something different.[102] God commanded Muḥammad to judge in accordance with what had been revealed *to him* and Muḥammad stoned the two offenders.

Thus, Shāfi'ī was aware that stoning 'is mentioned in the Tōra'. But, for him, that is wholly irrelevant. Stoning was the penalty applied by Muḥammad for adultery. The outcome of the *tafsīr* of the Ḳ.5 passage is, therefore, that stoning is the Islamic penalty, applied by the Prophet, since revealed to the Prophet by God. Mālik's, 'I shall judge between you on the basis of the Book of God' means 'I shall judge between you in accordance with Ḳ.5:42–9'. It is only because Ḳ.5:42–9 refers to what a prophet should do if invited to hear a case involving Jews that it was possible for 'I shall judge between you according to the Book of God' to become transmuted in the exegetical mind into 'I shall judge between you in accordance with the Tōra.' But exegesis is exegesis and it became transmuted in other minds into 'I shall judge between you in accordance with what is in the Ḳur'an.' The 'Umar *ḥadīth* about the stoning-'verse' that had once figured in the Ḳur'ān texts was thus merely the *tafsīr* of a *tafsīr*.

For Shāfi'ī, 'the Book of God' is synonymous with the Ḳur'ān. His inconsistency thus lies in his failure to conclude that, in that case, the stoning penalty must be presumed to have been a Ḳur'ān revelation. Alternatively, since he insists that stoning is the *Sunna* of the Prophet which Muḥammad had inflicted upon Jews because he had already inflicted it upon Muslims, he should have concluded that, in this case, the *Sunna* has been seen to *naskh* the Ḳur'ān.

> The stoning of the two Jews indicates several matters. That it is an obligation to proceed against the *dhimmī* when he fornicates. That is the general view, although the Shāfi'iyya are divided. Neither they, nor Aḥmad, insist upon Islam as a condition of *iḥṣān*.[103] Their view derives confirmation from the explicit statement in certain *ḥadīth*s about these two Jews that they were, in fact, both *muḥṣan*.[104] The Mālikiyya and the main body of the Ḥanafiyya who, however, insist upon Islam as an indispensable constitutent of *iḥṣān*, explain the stoning of the two Jews on the grounds that they were stoned in accordance with the laws of the Tōra.[105] The question of their *iḥṣān* does not arise in that event, if they were not stoned in accordance with the laws of Islam. In

> the Tōra stoning is applied to *muḥṣan* and non-*muḥṣan* alike.[106] They maintain that this event occurred soon after Muḥammad's arrival at Madīna when he was still required to adhere to the laws of the Tōra until its individual enactments should be superseded by specifically Islamic revelations. Thus, the Prophet stoned the Jews on the basis of the Tōra. This was subsequently superseded by the Ḳ.4:15 reference to '*your* women'. Ḳ.4:15 was, in turn, subsequently superseded by the Islamic distinction between *muḥṣan* and non-*muḥṣan*.
>
> Refuting the Ḥanafī view that the Prophet had stoned Jews on the basis of the Tōra, Khaṭṭābī pointed to Ḳ.5: 'Judge them on the basis of what God has revealed.' According to the *ḥadīth*, the Jews had come enquiring what the penalty was, in Muḥammad's view. He disclosed what they had been concealing and proclaimed the penalty of the Tōra. In Muḥammad's view, the Islamic penalty could not have been different, since one may not decide on the basis of any *mansūkh* ruling. Muḥammad had given his ruling, not on the basis of a *mansūkh*, but on that of the *nāsikh*. As for the Abū Hurayra *ḥadīth*, there is an unidentified person in the *isnād*. But, supposing the *ḥadīth* 'sound' and that Muḥammad did say, 'I shall judge between you on the basis of the Tōra,'[107] his aim would merely be to expose the Jews by disclosing the Tōra penalty which they had sought to conceal, and which *coincided with* the Islamic penalty. Within Islam, stoning superseded flogging. No scholar has maintained that stoning was first instituted, then flogging, then stoning again. Stoning has remained the Islamic penalty since it was first instituted. The Prophet did not stone the Jews solely on the basis of the Tōra, but, rather, on the basis of Islamic law with which the Tōra law chances *to coincide*.[108]

Once more, however, this reconstruction interferes with the timetable: if the stoning of Jews occurred on Muḥammad's arrival in Madīna, it would have occurred before the institution of the Islamic penalties; if after that, how many Jews would then remain at Madīna?[109] Further, as stoning is not prescribed in Christian Law, was the stoning of the Tōra thought by the Muslims to have been repealed by its lapse in Christianity? The question was never raised. Some argued:

> That the laws of the dispensations preceding Islam remained laws binding also upon the Muslims, so long as they were attested by indications in the Ḳur'ān, or in 'sound' *ḥadīth*s and so long as the *naskh* of an individual law had not been attested by the legislation of Muḥammad, or of another prophet before Muḥammad.[110]

The legacy that Shāfiʿī has left behind can be summarised thus:

for those who accepted his reiterated *uṣūlī* argument that the *Sunna* could not and had not ever *naskh*ed the Ḳur'ān, as only the Ḳur'ān can do so; that the locking-up and the violence of Ḳ.4:15–16 are *mansūkh*; that Muḥammad ever acted solely in accordance with what was revealed *to him*, and that, in certain cases of fornication, whether the offenders were Jews or Muslims, Muḥammad had stoned; that Ḳ.24:2's flogging penalty was *mansūkh* in the case of those whom Muḥammad stoned; that no Muslim may ever judge non-Muslims in accordance with any code other than the Islamic, the conclusion was inescapable that, therefore, stoning had been revealed. But, as stoning is nowhere referred to in the *muṣḥaf*, whereas the ruling has persisted in the *Fiḳh*, this must be an attested instance of: *naskh al-tilāwa dūna 'l-ḥukm*.

We have now traced two routes by which Muslims came to believe in the existence of a stoning-'verse'. The first, the earlier path to that conclusion, had been purely exegetical. The source of that belief we have located in Ḳ.5:42–9. The second was the technical path blazed by Shāfi'ī, as he endeavoured to make a pattern out of all the materials that he had inherited which would make sense of the inter-relations between the *Fiḳh*, the *Sunna* and the Ḳur'ān. A stoning – 'verse' which had once been revealed to Muḥammad, but which was not taken up into the texts of the *muṣḥaf* was the ultimate result of Shāfi'ī's *uṣūl* principles. Those, however, who owed no allegiance to his *uṣūl* principles were content to argue that Ḳ.24:2's flogging penalty had abrogated Ḳ.4:15–16, while the stoning penalty had abrogated Ḳ.24:2's flogging and was one instance of the *naskh* of the Ḳur'ān by the *Sunna*.[111]

Committed to over-rigid *uṣūl* principles, Shāfi'ī, heir to the *Fiḳh*'s stoning penalty, failed to make his position as to its origin unambiguously clear. Those who followed him, left to draw their own conclusions, reached, as we see, two quite separate and irreconcilable conclusions.

Shāfi'ī showed himself much more positive on another matter which, in the period after him, joined the stoning penalty as a second 'attested instance' of *naskh al-tilāwa dūna 'l-ḥukm*.

Ḳ.4:23b introduced a ban on marriage between persons related by breast-feeding as an addition to the ban on the marriage of persons related by blood introduced in Ḳ.4:23a.

Determined to carry out the divine instructions to the letter and conscious that to err in working out the infinite ramifications of those instructions would be rewarded by an eternity of torment in Hell, the Muslims, as ever, engaged in the minutest enquiries to determine their interpretations of Ḳ.4:23. Attention focused, among many other things, on the attempt to define *the number* of breast-feedings which the

Lord intended should be the minimum required to establish the ban on marriage. The Mālikīs, perceiving that in Ḳ.4:23b, God had used a verb for 'feed', decided that that implied the verbal noun. Hence only one single breast-feeding sufficed to create a lifelong barrier to marriage between the wet-nurse and those whom she took to her breast. Inevitably, many other suggestions were made and there was generated an enormous volume of *tafsīr-ḥadīth*s, to only one strand of which Shāfiʿī was to give ear.

> '*Riḍāʿ*,' he says,[112] 'is a comprehensive term which might well refer to a single breast-feed, or to more than one, up to the complete *riḍāʿ* of two full years, [Ḳ.2:233]. Indeed, it could still apply after the two years. It is therefore incumbent upon scholars to seek an indication as to whether any marriage-ban is established by the minimum that would constitute the *riḍāʿ* or whether some other minimum is intended.'

Scornful of the Mālikī view which he accuses of depending upon mere human guess-work [*ra'y*] he gives his allegiance to a *ḥadīth*, although it comes not from the Prophet, but from his widow ʿA'isha.

> She reported that 'in what was revealed of the Ḳur'ān, ten attested breast-feeds were mentioned as required to estabish the marriage-ban. The ten were replaced by mention of five attested breast-feeds. The Prophet died and the five were still being recited in the Ḳur'ān.'[113] No man ever called upon ʿĀ'isha who had not completed the minimum course of five sucklings.
>
> ʿAbdullāh b. al-Zubayr reports that the Prophet said, 'One suckling does not constitute the ban, nor two, nor does one nor two sucks.'
>
> ʿUrwa b. al-Zubayr reports that the Prophet commanded the wife of Abū Ḥudhayfa to feed her husband's *mawlā*, Sālim, so that he could go on living with them. The Prophet specified five breast-feeds.
>
> Sālim b. ʿAbdullāh reports that he was never able to visit ʿĀ'isha. She had sent him to be suckled by her sister Umm Kulthum who, however, suckled him only three times, then fell sick. Sālim added, 'Thus, I never did complete the course of ten sucklings.'

Nor, adds Shāfiʿī, in the interests of his *Fiḳh* doctrine, had Sālim even completed the course of five sucklings.

Thus, Shāfiʿī adopted the rule that the minimum number of breast-feeds required to establish the Ḳ.4:23b marriage ban is five – from ʿĀ'isha's claim that that was the Ḳur'ān ruling when the Prophet died. Like the Ḳur'ān rulings on theft and adultery, the ruling on the marriage ban had been the subject of *takhṣīṣ*, that is, exclusion: 'We deduce from the *Sunna* that Ḳ.4:23b had been intended, from the outset, to apply to certain persons, as opposed to others, although all are covered by the term *riḍāʿ*.'[114]

He mounts a bitter attack on the Mālikīs, in the course of which he cites a further 'evidence' from Ḥafṣa who had sent

> ʿĀṣim b. ʿAbdullāh b. Saʿd to her sister, Fāṭima, to be suckled ten times, so that he could visit Ḥafṣa. The Mālikīs repeat the ʿĀ'isha *ḥadīth* to the effect that the five sucklings ruling was being recited as part of the Ḳur'ān when the Prophet died; they report the Prophet's advice to Sahla, wife of Abū Ḥudhayfa; they report from two widows of the Prophet, and yet they neglect all this 'evidence' in favour of the opinion of Saʿīd b. al-Musayyab that one single suckling suffices to establish the ban on marriage. They ignore the ʿĀ'isha report and her and Ḥafṣa's statement in favour of Saʿīd's statement which, on other matters they leave aside in favour of their own personal views. They here ignore what comes from the Prophet who had declared that neither one nor even two sucklings sufficed to establish this ban.

At this point, Shāfiʿī is interrupted. His interlocutor asks whether ibn al-Zubayr had heard and preserved *ḥadīth*s direct from the Prophet. Shāfiʿī is certain that he had done, since, on the day the Prophet died, ʿAbdullāh was nine years old.[115]

3. The third mode of naskh in the period after Shāfiʿī

Shāfiʿī's attitude on the question of the *riḍāʿ* is clear. All the relevant materials were Ḳur'ānic. He could thus with ease conclude that there was involved here an instance of *naskh*. An 'earlier' Ḳur'ān statement, the 'ten-sucklings verse', had been replaced by a 'later' Ḳur'ān statement, 'the five-sucklings verse'. The ruling of the latter remained, for Shāfiʿī, the only valid ruling, despite the absence of the wording from the *muṣḥaf*. For both Shāfiʿī and his followers, that was one attested instance of *naskh al-tilāwa dūna 'l-ḥukm*.

Makki noted that this was a most unusual instance of *naskh*.

> It is the Mālikī view that the wording of ʿĀ'isha's 'ten-verse' and the 'five-verse' had both been removed from the *muṣḥaf*. The rulings of both verses had also been abandoned. Here, then, are two attested instances of *naskh al-ḥukm wa-'l-tilāwa*.

This is just his round-about way of telling us that, as the wording which does appear in the *muṣḥaf*, Ḳ.4:23b, adequately accounts for the Mālikī view on the *riḍāʿ*, Mālik had presumably based his view on that wording alone.[116] Having given his allegiance to the ʿĀ'isha *ḥadīth*, Shāfiʿī inevitably had reached a different *Fiḳh* conclusion. We should, however, note how the later Mālikī analyst explained Mālik's position. Accepting the 'five' and the 'ten' 'verses' he *presumes* that Mālik had regarded them both as *mansūkha*. Other analysts, reviewing these differences in *Fiḳh* and *uṣūl* between the two *imām*s, reported correctly that Shāfiʿī had acknowledged the third mode of *naskh*.

Others, unable to reconcile themselves to the notion of the *naskh* of the Ḳur'ān by the *Sunna* were to add as a second instance of the third mode the 'removal' of the wording of the stoning-'verse'.

We hold that there are three types of *naskh*:[117] i. *naskh al-tilāwa dūna 'l-ḥukm*, one instance of which is the stoning-verse, concerning which ʿUmar reported. The *Khawāridj* rejected stoning, since they did not find it in the *muṣḥaf.*

A second instance is the verse on the *riḍāʿ*, according to the followers of Shāfiʿī, on the basis of the ʿĀ'isha *ḥadīth*. Shāfiʿī's view was that the five-verse was *mansūkha* solely as regards its wording; its ruling remained valid. Mālik and *aṣḥāb al-ra'y* maintained that the verse was *mansūkha* in respect of both the wording and the ruling.

There is no dispute about Ḳ.4:15–16. The verses are *mansūkha*. The scholars are, however, divided as to the *nāsikh*. Some, including ibn ʿAbbās and Mudjāhid, held this to have been Ḳ.24:2. Others held that they had been superseded by the ʿUbāda *ḥadīth*. Those who argue thus took the view that the *Sunna* can abrogate the Ḳur'ān. That is a view to be rejected since, were it considered that the *Sunna* might abrogate the Ḳur'ān, the *Sunna*, to do so, must at least be *mutawātira*. The Ḳur'ān may not be superseded by an isolated *ḥadīth* – which the ʿUbāda *ḥadīth* is.

Others held that the 'promised way' was provided in Ḳ.24:2. This is not *naskh*, since the 'way' was already promised and then later provided.

Yet others held that it is a case of *naskh*, effected by means of a Ḳur'ān revelation whose wording was later withdrawn [*rufiʿa*] but whose ruling remained valid. Even the wording of the ʿUbāda *ḥadīth* might be said to indicate this, in the words, 'Now God has appointed. . . ' The implication is that God appointed by means of a revelation whose wording was not instituted for public recital [in the ritual prayers]. This is the view adopted by those who cannot accept that the *Sunna* has ever superseded the Ḳur'ān.

A second instance of the *naskh* of an *āya* concerning the continuing validity of whose ruling there is dispute, is the question of what constitutes *riḍāʿ*. Three opinions have been transmitted from Aḥmad:

i. One suckling suffices. This was the doctrine of Abū Ḥanīfa and of Mālik, both of whom were content with Ḳ.4:23 as source. On that account, they both ignored the ʿĀ'isha *ḥadīth*.

ii. Three sucklings suffice. The Prophet is reported to have said, 'Not one suckling, nor two set up the marriage ban.'

iii. Five sucklings are the minimum, on account of the ʿĀ'isha *ḥadīth*.

Some scholars have interpreted her words 'remained as part of the Ḳur'ān' as a reference to Ḳ.4:23. They hold that were something being recited as part of the Ḳur'ān when the Prophet died, it would have been transmitted to us as the rest of the *muṣḥaf* has been. Had any part of the Kur'ān remained outside what has been transmitted to us, it is conceivable that what has not been transmitted might have been the *nāsikh* of what has – which is patently absurd.[118]

In *naskh*, there are four possible combinations: i. The Ḳur'ān *naskh*s the Kur'ān; ii. the *Sunna naskh*s the *Sunna*; iii. the *Sunna naskh*s the Ḳur'ān, and iv. the Ḳur'ān *naskh*s the *Sunna*.

Shāfiʿī held the last two possibilities to be impossible, on account of Ḳ.2:106. The impossibility of the *naskh* of the Ḳur'ān by the *Sunna* is indicated by the *Sunna*'s inferiority of status, while Ḳ.10:15 states, 'It is not for me to alter it on my own intitiative.' The Prophet said, 'If any *ḥadīth* is reported as coming from me, compare it with the Book of God; if it agrees with it, accept it; if it disagrees with it, reject it.' Were the Book to be superseded by the *Sunna*, some might allege, 'The Prophet is at variance with what he claims to be the Word of his Creator.' Were the Book to supersede the *Sunna*, some might say, 'God is now showing Muḥammad to be a liar, so we will not believe him.' Co-ordination rather, between the Book and the *Sunna* is more fitting.[119]

Shāfiʿī had known the *ḥadīth*, but rejected it on *isnād* grounds.[120] The trend of the *ḥadith* is frankly anti-*ḥadīth* and was one of the stimuli which provoked Shāfiʿī's exegetical inventions of *takhṣīṣ* and *bayān* and the composition of his *Risāla*. We see here a pre-Shāfiʿī *ḥadīth* being given a post-Shāfiʿī interpretation which misrepresents his position. A *ḥadīth* which he rejected is now being read as in conformity with his premise on the inconceivability of disagreement between the two revealed sources of the *Fiḳh*.

Some of our colleagues have argued that the *naskh* of the Ḳur'ān by the *Sunna* is attested in the case of Ḳ.2:180, abrogated by the Prophetic dictum: *lā waṣiyya li-wārith*. Others point to Ḳ.4:15–16, abrogated by the ʿUbāda *ḥadīth*.

This view is quite erroneous: the bequests of Ḳ.2:180 were abrogated by the inheritance verses of Ḳ.4. Besides, the *ḥadīth* states: 'God has granted to every rightful claimant his due share – let there be no *waṣiyya* to any heir.' Further, ʿUmar stated that stoning had been part of the Ḳur'ān. In that case, Ḳ.4:15–16 was abrogated, not by the ʿUbāda report, but by the Ḳur'ān, by the stoning-verse. Originally part of the recited Ḳur'ān, the wording of the verse was subsequently removed from public recital. Its ruling continued to be valid.

> Taftazānī now adds his comments: His observation: 'This was originally part of the recited Ḳur'ān,' means that Ḳ.4:15–16 had been abrogated by the stoning-verse which is *mansūkha al-tilāwa dūna 'l-hukm*, whereas the Ḳ.4 verses are *mansukha al-ḥukm dūna 'l-tilāwa*. Although the stoning-verse is not *mutawātira* – and hence not accepted into the *muṣḥaf* – it is nonetheless considered Kitāb and not *Sunna*. That is why 'Umar feared that he might be accused of adding to the Book.

Ṭabarī had taken the view that, once the replacement of the ruling was ascertained, it was 'immaterial' whether the wording remained in the *muṣḥaf* or whether it was withdrawn from the ken of Man. During Ṭabarī's lifetime, the reflex of this view was already being expressed. The celebrated 'Ā'isha *ḥadīth* accounting for the 'omission' of the wording of the stoning-'verse' *and* the 'ten-suckling verse' had already been circulated in the *Mukhtalif al-Ḥadīth* of ibn Ḳutayba 'AH 213–276/AD 828–889]:

> The stoning-verse and the ten-suckling verse were both revealed. Both were recorded on a sheet which was placed under my bedding for safe-keeping. They were still there at the time the Prophet died, but, as we were pre-occupied in his sick-room, a beast got in from the yard and gobbled up the sheet.

To the unrestrained sarcasm of the *Mu'tazila*, scandalised both at the gross carelessness displayed towards the records of the revelation, but also by a report whose wording, they felt was rebutted by several Ḳur'ān verses, ibn Ḳutayba primly retorted that God employs for His purposes such means as He pleases. Besides, if it is acceptable that a ruling be nullified, while its wording remains to be recited, it is also acceptable that a Ḳur'ān wording be nullified, while its ruling remains valid for the *Fiḳh*.[121] The Prophet did stone, the Muslims stoned after him and stoning was accepted by the *fuḳahā'*.

Shāfi'ī had considered one of his strongest arguments against the *naskh* of the Ḳur'ān by the *Sunna* [and vice-versa] to lie in the wording of Ḳ.2:106: '*We* shall bring one better than it, or at least, similar to it.'

As nothing is either better than or similar to the Ḳur'ān, Shāfi'ī was confident that only the Ḳur'ān can *naskh* the Ḳur'ān, and as nothing is similar to the *sunna* save only the *Sunna*, he was equally confident that the verse indicated that nothing can *naskh* the *Sunna* of the Prophet except only the *Sunna* of the Prophet. ibn Ḳutayba had, however, heard the *ḥadīth*: 'The Prophet said, "I have been given the Book and with it, its like," ' which he interpreted as a reference to the *Sunna* which Gabriel used to bring to the Prophet, as he used to bring him the Ḳur'ān revelations. ibn Ḳutayba was, therefore, sanguine in the assumption that there are *Sunnas* which have abrogated Ḳur'ān verses. Besides, Mālik had cited this 'Ā'isha *ḥadīth*, and in his version, there is no reference to the stoning-'verse'.[122] Mālik's version mentions only the 'ten-suckling' verse. The *isnād* is identical and, in the view of the *ḥadīth* specialists, Mālik is the more accurate transmitter.[123] So also, when Ṭabarī and other exegetes interpolated a reference to the ruling into the words of Ḳ.2:106, they make the ruling of the *Sunna* like the ruling of the Ḳur'ān, or even superior. The one could therefore supersede the other. Comparing ibn Ḳutayba's and Shāfi'ī's exegeses shows how the *tafsīr* of an *āya* can be rebutted by the *tafsīr* of the same *āya*.

ibn Ḳutayba referred Ḳ.59:7 to the *Sunna*: 'Take whatever the Messenger gives you; what he denies you, desist from.' [*wa mā nahā-kum 'an-hu fa-ntahū*] The vocabulary of the verse makes this all the easier, given that the root *n h y* has taken on, for the scholars, the colouring of 'to forbid' and Form 8 of the root that of 'desist from, i.e. avoid,' hence ibn Ḳutayba's comment:

> God knew that the Muslims would accept from His Prophet that which he would communicate to them as the Word of God. But God also knew that He proposed to *naskh* part of His Ḳur'ān by means of His *waḥy* to the Prophet, and that when that occurred, there would well up in some hearts doubt and hesitation. That is why God said to us: 'Take what the Messenger gives you,' i.e. what the Messenger gives you that is not in the Ḳur'ān, or such as abrogates what is in the Ḳur'ān.

ibn Ḳutayba was thus open to two propositions: that the *Sunna* has abrogated the Ḳur'ān; and that the ruling of a 'once-revealed' verse may continue to form a valid *Fiḳh* ruling despite the withdrawal of its wording.

It has to be said that he occupies an intermediate position unique among the scholars. Neither an *uṣūl* nor a *Ḥadīth* specialist, he both allows for the *naskh* of the Ḳur'ān by the *Sunna and* accepts *naskh al-tilāwa dūna 'l-ḥukm*. That may perhaps best be explained by his date, also intermediate, coming as he did between the time of Shāfi'ī and the completion of the main classical collections of the *Ḥadīth*. Sympathetic to *ahl al-Ḥadīth*, he was under obligation to the traditions which commended themselves to the criteria adopted by that grouping, and his acceptance of the stoning-'verse' may be the first signs of the unquestioning acceptance of *ḥadīth*, even by scholars who had no technical reason for accepting them. We have seen that ibn Ḳutayba has accepted the possibility of the *naskh* of the Ḳur'ān by the *Sunna*, and had therefore no impulsion arising from *uṣūl* theory to postulate the existence of the stoning-'verse' and hence no need of *three* modes of *naskh*.

Another celebrated writer on *naskh*, al-Naḥḥās [d. AH 338/AD 949] recognises only two modes of *naskh* and rejects both the stoning-

'verse' and the suckling-'verses'. He is among those who, allowing for the *naskh* of the Ḳur'ān by the *Sunna*, had no need in their theory for the third mode of *naskh* and accused those who did of misinterpreting the relevant *ḥadīth*s.

> 'None,' he says,[124] 'could *naskh*, save only the Prophet who did so on the basis of either the Ḳur'ān, or the non-Ḳur'ānic *waḥy*. As both types of inspiration ceased on the Prophet's death, so also *naskh* ceased.'

On ʿUmar's *ḥadīth* about stoning and stoning-'verse' which he acknowledges is a 'sound' *ḥadīth*, he comments:

> This was not the ruling of the Ḳur'ān which is universally transmitted from generation to generation. It is an ascertained *sunna*, as is shown by ʿUmar's saying, 'But that I should not like it to be said, "ʿUmar has added to the Ḳur'ān" I should have added it.'[125]

Similarly, the following *ḥadīth* has been misinterpreted:

> Mālik reports from ʿAbdullāh b. abī Bakr ʿĀ'isha's report, 'There was revealed in the Ḳur'ān the *āya* "ten attested breast-feedings establish the marriage ban." It was replaced by "five attested breast-feedings establish the marriage ban," which we were still reciting when the Prophet died.' The scholars have much discussed this very problematic report. Among those who ignored it were Mālik himself, (although he is the transmitter, nobody other than Mālik citing it via ʿAbdullāh) Aḥmad and Abū Thawr. Mālik ignored it, basing his view on the wording of Ḳ.4:23 itself. What is problematic in the report is her expression: 'which we were still reciting when the Prophet died.' The specialists point out that the same report has been transmitted by two men more accurate in their transmissions than ʿAbdullāh – al-Qāsim and Yaḥyā b. Saʿīd – and neither of them mentions this sentence. There can be no part of the Ḳur'ān recited after the death of the Prophet which has not been transmitted to us in the *muṣḥaf*. . . . Had part of the Ḳur'ān remained outside what was collected into the *muṣḥaf*, it is possible that what has not been transmitted to us was the *nāsikh* of what has been transmitted and that our practice on the basis of what has been transmitted has all been vain. We seek refuge with God from the very thought, for that is unbelief.[126]

In the matter of the *riḍāʿ*, the older *madhabs*, the Mālikīs and the Ḥanafis, were content not to go beyond exegesis of a verse still present in the *muṣḥaf* [Ḳ.4:23]. On the basis of a *ḥadīth*, Shāfiʿī took an individual line, basing his *Fiḳh* on a 'verse' not present in the *muṣḥaf*. On this question, he therefore deployed his *uṣūl* arguments in defiance of a view older than his and in defence of a novel view which he alone upheld.

On the question of stoning for adultery, all *madhhabs* are unanimous in agreeing on a penalty nowhere referred to in the *muṣḥaf*, indeed, in conflict with the penalty that is mentioned there. The Mālikīs and the Ḥanafīs were sanguine in assuming that this is an instance of the *naskh* of the Ḳur'ān [Ḳ.24:2] by the *Sunna*. Shāfi'ī too accepts the stoning penalty. He, however, breaks ranks, but solely at the level of the discussion of the *uṣūl* of the case. Having denied the possibility that the *Sunna* may *naskh* the Ḳur'ān, his legacy – so equivocal was his language –left men unable to conclude that this was other than the *naskh* of the Ḳur'ān by the Ḳur'ān, and that here therefore was a second instance of a 'verse' revealed, but absent from the *muṣḥaf*, i.e. of *naskh al-tilāwa dūna 'l-ḥukm*. The *uṣūl* disputes, therefore arose not only on *Fiḳh* questions which divided the *madhāhib*, but also on questions on which the *madhāhib* were agreed, providing further opportunities for claims of *naskh* to be made.

Eight

THE ḲUR'ĀN'S DOCTRINE ON *NASKH*.

It is now pertinent to ask what is the Ḳur'ān's view of *naskh*. Here, we must recall the distinction already made between 'external' and 'internal' *naskh*. Up to this point, we have been concerned chiefly with the suppression of a regulation and its replacement by a second regulation within one and the same revealed system. External *naskh* refers to the suppression of a regulation revealed in one dispensation and its replacement by a second regulation revealed in a later dispensation. On this *naskh*, the stand taken by the Ḳur'ān is clear. The various historical systems of religion as revealed to Adam, Noah, Abraham, Moses, Jacob, Ṣāliḥ, Shu'ayb, Christ and finally Muḥammad were alike in two respects. In theological terms, all had agreed on the oneness of God. In social implication, they had agreed that prophethood confers authority. The function of *wa'd* and *wa'īd*, promise or threat, is frankly to compel men's obedience to the rule of the prophet. The *locus classicus* is Ḳ.26:

v.108. Noah said, 'fear God and obey me.'
v.126. Hūd said, 'fear God and obey me.'
v.144. Ṣāliḥ said, 'fear God and obey me.'
v.163. Lot said, 'fear God and obey me.'
v.179. Shu'ayb said, 'fear God and obey me.'
vv.215–6 apply to Muḥammad's contemporaries the lesson to be derived from the history of the prophetic office as to the attitude they should adopt to its holder.

That the office of prophet confers authority implies that the Law to which the individual prophet summons men derives its sanction, in the first place, from his personal tenure of that office rather than from the institution. It follows that there can be periodic variations in the Law. This is the most important single practical doctrine which the Ḳur'ān inculcates. We suggested that had Muḥammad considered himself heir-in-full to the major prophets before him, he might have been expected to proclaim his adherence to either Christianity or Judaism. Had he done so, he would have been a *nabiyy*; but Muḥammad was a *rasūl*. That he attached himself to neither system does not establish that he was content to regard himself as only heir-in-part to his great predecessors in office. What is implied by his final posture of aloofness from both Christians and Jews is the rationalisation he had worked out to explain, partly to his followers, perhaps also partly to himself, the extraordinary fact of his rejection by 'the People of the Book'. Muḥammad and his followers knew that he was a prophet. That the Jews did not acknowledge him as such could not mean that he was not what he claimed to be. It could mean only that they were not what they claimed to be. The Jews steadfastly declined to recognise his pretensions to authority to rule over them and from their refusal two main conclusions flowed: that they were culpably ignoring the texts of their own revealed book in which, Muḥammad asserted, he had been foretold. They were defying the God of Isrā'īl, the God of Moses, the God Who had sent Muḥammad. His consideration of Jewish national history was to bring out that this was far from being an unusual stance on their part. The second grand conclusion was that the Jews were not the offspring alluded to by Abraham in his prayer:[1] 'God tested Abraham with words which he accomplished, God said, "I shall make you a model for men." Abraham prayed, "Do the like to my seed." God replied, "My undertaking does not encompass evildoers."' Abraham had had seed other than the line descended from him through Isrā'īl. These were the Ismā'īl-descended Arabs in whom God's promise to Abraham has now been fulfilled in the calling of Muḥammad to the prophethood. There had been a vast historical breach in the history of prophethood, instanced in the betrayal of God's purposes by post-Mosaic generations who rejected two major prophets – Christ and Muḥammad. This had impelled the latter to circumspection in his dealings with the post-Mosaic systems. This makes it easy to understand why Muḥammad overstepped all recent revelation history to carry his Islam, monotheism (or better, rasūlism), across the ages represented by the major aberrations of Chritianity and Judaism to link it with the pristine source of the unsullied revealed doctrine of Abraham.

That Christianity was error was clear: the Christians had so far departed from the original monotheism revealed by God to Adam, as to declare Christ, the latest in the series of perfect prophets before Muḥammad, the son of God. Unlike the Jews, the Christians had at least accepted Christ, although they had perverted his teachings. The Jews were doubly in error, rejecting both Christ and Muḥammad. Muḥammad, in turn, rejects both as distortions of the Truth. He explains their errors as proceeding from the evil and stubborness of their own hearts. He therefore dissociates the great prophets, Moses and Christ from the perversities of their respective disloyal followers.

Further reflection on prophetic history enabled Muḥammad to perceive the distinction between the eternal and hence essential identity of the theology of the prophets, and the contingent and so alterable character of their social enactments. Christ came to confirm what had preceded him in the Tōra, but also to declare lawful part of what had been declared unlawful.[2] The Ḳur'ān speaks of itself similarly as confirming what preceded it in the Law and testifying to its truth.[3] The Jewish dietary laws are known to have had a definable historical starting-point before which they had not operated.[4] All foods 'were lawful to B. Isrā'īl other than those which Jacob forbade himself, before the Tōra was even revealed'.

That much of the haggling between the Jews and Muḥammad concerned details of the Law is discernible from: 'People of the Book, why do you quarrel with me about Abraham, when neither the Tōra nor the Gospel was revealed until after his generation?'[5]

On basic theological questions, there are, however, matters which are quite immutable: 'What is imposed upon you in religion is what was commanded of Noah which we have now revealed to you, and what was commanded of Abraham, Moses and Christ. We said, "Observe this and do not be divided into various sects." '[6]

The appeal to Muḥammad of Abraham was that there was no contemporary faction identified with him. Abraham had been neither Jew nor Christian. He was outside the sects, a Muslim, certainly not a heathen.[7] The historical contingency of the details of the Law is recognised: We gave Moses the Law after the earlier generations had died out.[8] Only the essential theology is the perennial golden thread uniting the series of the prophets and, as each prophet has individual authority, there is an observable historical mutability in the practical Law. The Jews are referred to as 'those who have been given a part of the Law'.[9] Further, every dispensation founded by a prophet has its foreordained duration. 'Every dispenstion has its duration and when it is completed, they can neither defer nor bring forward.'[10] Every period has its Book.[11] The Jews are one such dispensation to whom God granted a Law, authority and prophecy.[12] God grants authority to whom He pleases.[13]

> Nor should the People of the Book imagine that they have a monopoly of prophecy and authority. That is a favour in God's sole gift and He bestows it on whom He pleases.[14]
>
> God, moreover, grants His prophets authority over whom He pleases.[15] Likewise, He removes authority from whom He pleases.[16]
>
> Those who were granted a part of the Law turn away when summoned to submit themselves to the Law.[17]
>
> God summons them to call to mind His past favours to them and to the Fathers and to fulfil the terms of their Covenant.[18]
>
> They should be the first to proclaim publicly acceptance of what God now reveals in confirmation of what came before in that which they possess. They ought not to be the first to reject it, nor should they wittingly conceal the Truth.[19]

> When God first made the Covenant with Isrā'īl, it was provided that they should proclaim the Law before men and not conceal it, thrusting it out of sight.[20]
>
> In return for the Law and the authority which the prophets had been given, they had undertaken that when there should come hereafter a prophet confirming what they knew, they would proclaim belief in him and assist him. God said to the prophets, 'Do you accept this and enter into the Covenant?' They replied, 'We accept.' God said, 'Swear and We too shall swear.'[21]

The Ḳur'ān proclaims to the Jews of the Ḥidjāz:

> People of the Book. There has now come to you Our prophet to make plain to you much of the Law which you have kept concealed, although much he will also *alleviate*.[22]
>
> The Jews are a people whose fee has been settled; your fee is settled and you will not be asked about what they have been doing.[23]
>
> Will the Jews maintain that Abraham, Ismā'īl, Isḥāḳ, Jacob and the tribes were Jews or Christians? Ask them whether they know best, or God. Who is more evil than he who conceals a matter on which he has exchanged oaths with God? They are a people whose fee has been settled.[24]
>
> Muḥammad is the Messenger of God,[25] the gentile prophet mentioned in the Tōra and the Gospel.[26]
>
> When summoned to accept what God has now revealed, they say, 'We shall accept only what was revealed to us.'[27] Anything beyond that they reject, although Christ had addressed them saying, 'B. Isrā'īl, I am the messenger of God sent to you to confirm what is in your hands in the Tōra, and promising you that there will come after me a Messenger whose name will be Aḥmad – (or, whose name I extol; or, whose name is more praiseworthy).[28]
>
> But the possessors of the Tōra know no more about its contents than would donkeys on whose backs it had been loaded.[29]
>
> Moses, the great Law-giver, had been subjected to intolerable carping at the hands of the Jews.[30]

God's latest prophet, Muḥammad, in being scorned and cross-questioned by these same Jews, far from feeling discredited, is thereby raised in his own estimation, into the same class as Moses, Abraham, Noah and Christ.

> Is it, then the case that every time there comes to them a prophet who brings what is not to their liking they puff themselves up in their pride, either rejecting or even murdering the prophets of the Lord?[31] They invite people to join them and become Christians or Jews, in order to find the truth. But it is the non-sectarian system of Abrahamism that is to be preferred. We believe in God,

in what He now reveals, in what He revealed aforetime to Abraham, to Ismāʿīl, to Isḥāḳ, to Jacob and the tribes, to Moses, to Christ, to the company of the prophets. We do not distinguish one from another.[32]

Judaism and Christianity are the departures and one may circumvent the errors of the schismatics only by returning to the primitive Abrahamism. The true religion in the sight of God is only Islam.[33] He who chooses to follow other than Islam, it will not be accepted of him.[34] God declares that:

He has inspired Muḥammad as He inspired Abraham, Ismāʿīl, Isḥāḳ, Jacob and the tribes, Job, Jonah, Aaron, Solomon and David.[35] God bears witness to that which He has now revealed to Muḥammad, that He has sent it down with His knowledge; the angels in Heaven likewise bear witness.[36] God knows best where He bestows the office of Messenger.[37] God declares that Muḥammad is His Messenger.[38]

Faithful to His part in the Covenant, God Himself overcomes the plots and intrigues of men and proclaims that which the Jews, in breach of their most solemn undertakings, have attempted to keep hidden from Mankind – that Muḥammad is the Prophet the God of Isrā'īl promised the Fathers would be raised in these regions, the Prophet mentioned by name in the Tōra and the Gospel. To Muḥammad, God has now granted, as He earlier granted to Abraham, Jacob, Joseph, Moses and Christ, the mission to convey to God's creation His divine self-revelation, with the authority to proclaim the Law, to declare lawful and unlawful. Both functions of the prophethood are not, however, equally represented in the Ḳur'ān texts, the main burden of which is devoted to ceaseless assertion of the two basic theological tenets: there is only one God Who periodically sends among men His Messengers to summon them to devote their worship exclusively to Him. To reinforce these missions, God has traditionally demanded obedience to His prophets rewarding patient submission both in this world and in the Hereafter while reserving a most dreadful punishment in both lives for those who, rejecting His prophets, defy Him Who sent them. Muḥammad could offer his contemporaries evidence of the terrible chastisement inflicted upon men by the jealousy of the spurned Godhead in the stories of the Deluge, the obliteration of Sodom, the destruction of the proud Egyptians and the sacking of the first and second Temples. An unspecified, but not less fearsome fate awaited those who delayed to accept the claims of Muḥammad and hesitated to submit themselves without question to his will. Characteristic of the Ḳur'ān's devices is this linking of Muḥammad's name with the name of God until, with sufficient repetition, the will of Muḥammad became identified with the will of God and the effect created that to obey the one is to obey the Other; to disobey the one is to disobey the Other.

We sent you as Our witness, both to promise and to warn. That ye might believe in God and in His Messenger, co-operating with Him, venerating and praying to Him, morning and evening. Those who swear allegiance to you [Muḥammad] in reality swear allegiance to God Whose hand is with theirs when they clasp your hand in fealty. Whoso breaks his bond imperils his own soul. Whoso fulfils what he pledges to God, to him He shall give a mighty reward.[39]

Those only are true believers who believe in God and in His Messenger; who, when they engage with him in a joint venture, do not depart without seeking his permission. Those who first seek your permission are they who believe in God and in His Messenger. When they seek your permission to attend to their own affairs, permit whom you please and seek God's pardon for them. Do not treat the Prophet's summons as you would a summons from one of your own number. God is perfectly aware of those who creep out of the assembly. Let those who disobey the prophet's command beware lest trouble befall them, or a grievous punishment.[40]

It is not open to any single believer, male or female, once God and His Messenger have decided some matter, to have any choice in the matter; whosoever disobeys God and His Prophet gives manifest show of having strayed from the Truth.[41]

These and countless similar verses demonstrate the subtle manner in which, by constant association, the will of Muḥammad in temporal, as in spiritual matters, was gradually projected as a manifestation of the divine will of God. Hence Shāfi'ī's justification in his instinctive sense that this identification had shifted the responsibility for unquestioning obedience lying upon the Muslims from the contents of the Ḳur'ān to the contents of the *Sunna*. We can have no quarrel with this interpretation, merely with Shāfi'ī's definition of 'the contents of the *Sunna*'. By that, we would envisage the sum of the legislation introduced by Muḥammand and imposed by him upon the members of the community he was engaged in constructing between the years AD 622–632 and without reference to whether such materials were or were not either at the time or later, recorded and so preserved in documentary form. His credentials affirmed, and his authority to rule established by the Ḳur'ān for those who accepted his pretensions, Muḥammad would have been enabled thereafter to exercise authority without constant reference to the Ḳur'ān, except in unusual circumstances when exceptional resistance induced him to call in the Ḳur'ān to reiterate his God-given right to rule, or to supplement his own outstanding gifts of persuasion and rationalisation. Such periodic crises are evidenced by the Ḳur'ān and concern either matters of the gravest significance to the infant state, or the most private relations between Muḥammad and the members of his own household which might have serious repercussions upon the opinion of a public by no means solidly in sympathy with Muḥammad's aims. It has been pointed out that the Ḳur'ān contains proportionately few legislative enactments.[42] The greater part of Muḥammad's legislative activity would have been exercised outside the Ḳur'ān and on the basis of his own fiat, the legitimation of which had been the first and the chief function of that Book sent down from God in Heaven. In this sense it is proper to assert that the Ḳur'ān justifies the *Sunna*.

Among the crises referred to which were settled only by the intervention of the Ḳur'ān, was that connected with the direction in which one should face for the performance of the ritual prayer. The question has provoked in the literature of the *Fiḳh* and in the *Ḥadīth* collections a considerable body of documentation. Our immediate concern will rather be with the only secure discussion of the issue relevant to our study – the Ḳur'ān's discussion of the problem.

A change in the direction is discussed in Ḳ.2. The bulk of the chapter is occupied with Muḥammad's address to the Jews which varies in tone between appeal and polemic and can be summarised as follows:

> v.40 reminds them of God's past favours, in the light of which they are now summoned to fulfil their ancient Covenant to believe in what is now being revealed, in confirmation of what was revealed to them. They are adjured not to conceal the Truth which is with them and they are reminded of the fate of the Pharaoh who had rejected Moses. When the great Law-giver's back was turned, the Jews themselves had shown their ingratitude by falling down to worship the calf. God had forgiven them this senseless enormity. Unrepentant, they demanded of Moses that they be shown God corporeally. God had forgiven them this grave blasphemy. Yet they continued to treat Moses contumaciously. They had even dared to kill some of the prophets of the Lord. Following the remarkable series of events they had witnessed at Sinai, the Jews persisted in disobedience. Some profaned the Holy Sabbath. Others today demonstrate their rebelliousness in arrogating to themselves the prerogative to pick and choose which of the articles of the Law they are prepared to observe. The Prophet sent by God after Moses they reject. They reject any prophet who does not flatter their whims. They had been hoping to overcome the unbelievers, yet, when the Ḳur'ān came, they rejected it too, from spite and from chagrin that God should reveal to whom He pleased, and not to whom they pleased. When called to accept the Ḳur'ān, they reply that they will accept only what has been revealed to them. Yet even this claim, as the history of their national conduct

brings out, is hollow. Paradise, they assert, is reserved for Jews alone. Their enmity towards Islam shows their enmity for Gabriel, God's great archangel who has been entrusted with its delivery. There could be no clearer evidence of their hostility to God Himself Whose revelations they reject, preferring to cultivate Babylonian magic which they busy themselves to propagate.

Jews and unbelievers alike resent that God should show His favour to the Muslims, but God selects for His blessings whom He pleases, and when He suppresses or consigns one message to oblivion, He, Master of Heaven and Earth, brings in its place one similar to it or superior to it. God is capable of performing whatever He wishes. Or are they determined to emulate the contemporaries of Moses and ask Muḥammad what those had demanded of Moses? Many of the Jews would dearly like to see the believers lapse back into heathenism from mere rancour at the realisation that Muḥammad is speaking the truth. Those who accept Muḥammad and submit are promised their reward. They shall have no cause for regret. Who could offer a greater affront to God than those who prevent His praises from being sung in the temples devoted to His worship and who would seek to bring them into ruin and disuse? They should not dare themselves enter them except in fear and trembling. But these also shall have their just reward, both in this life and in the hereafter. To God belong both East and West and in whatever direction you turn, you will be facing God. They do more than this. They allege that God has adopted offspring. Glory be to Him Who is the possessor of all that is in the heavens and in the earth, Who, when He determines on a thing, has but to say 'Be' and it comes into being. The ignorant ask why God does not speak directly to them, or why does not a sign appear? This is just what those before them said. Our signs we have made clear to those who are sure. We have sent Muḥammad to promise and to warn. Neither the Jews nor the Christians who indulge in mutual recrimination will accept him unless he fall in with them. The sole guidance is that provided by God. Were Muḥammad to follow their imaginings after this revelation which has come to him, none could defend him against God. Those to whom We gave the Book recite it as it ought to be recited. They believe in it. Those who reject it shall be the losers.

These passages are quoted at length in order to counter the atomism of the traditional *tafsīr* and to show the essential unity of the context, which is now confirmed by the repetition at Ḳ.2:122 of the opening address, Ḳ.2:40:

B. Isrā'īl, call to mind My favour which I bestowed upon you.

> Fulfil My Covenant, and I shall fulfil yours. Me alone fear.

The verse continues:

> ...and fear a day when no soul shall avail another aught, nor shall any fee be accepted, nor intercession profit. The God of Abraham tested him and when Abraham accomplished the trial, God said, 'I will make of you a model for men.' Abraham asked, 'And of my seed also.' God replied, 'My covenant does not embrace the evildoers.'

There follows a series of references to Makka, its temple and its alleged connection with the 'Father of the race', Ismā'īl, said with his father to have purified God's Holy dwelling for the performance of prayer and the rites of the pilgrimage. Their joint prayer that Makka be made an asylum to be hereafter the dwelling of their seed from among whom would be raised up a prophet to recite God's *āya*s and instruct them in the Book and the Law and bring them to purity in the faith of the fathers was granted. This was what Abraham commanded of his sons and Isrā'īl of his:

> That they adhere to the religion appointed for them by God Himself. The Muslims will not be asked to account for what the other descendants of the Patriarch have done. They will be guided aright if they follow what God reveals to them, and what He revealed to Abraham, to Ismā'īl, to Jacob and the tribes, to Moses, to Christ and the prophets – making no distinction between them. Will these people dispute of God with the Muslims? Say: 'He is our God and your God. We have our works, you have yours. To Him alone are we devoted. Or will they insist that Abraham, Ismā'īl, Isḥāḳ, Jacob and the tribes were Jews or Christians? Do you know best, or does God? Who is more heinous in actions than he who conceals a testimony from God that is in his possession? God is not unaware of your behaviour.'

They are a nation whose fee has been settled. You shall have what you have earned, nor shall you be questioned as to what they have done. Apparently the era of Christianity and of Judaism is closed. A new age in revelation has opened. The immediate cause of contention was the *ḳibla*. 'Those lacking in self-control will ask, "What has turned them away from the *ḳibla* they have been observing?" Say: "To God belong both East and West. He guides whom He pleases to a valid path."'[43]

1. The exegetes' discussion of the change of ḳibla

The first Muslims to engage in exegesis found the Ḳur'ān a difficult and confusing book, mainly on account of its highly allusive mode of expression. Who, for example, are 'those lacking in self-control'? and what was this 'direction, or *ḳibla*, from which the Muslims have now been turned'?

To ease their task of interpretation, the exegetes adopted a number of techniques, the most prominent of which, verse-comparison, the identification of persons or places left unidentified in the texts [*ta'yīn*], the dating and elucidating the situation which had provoked the original revelation of the individual fragments of the texts [*asbāb*], the 'restoration' of words or phrases 'omitted' in the texts, [*taḳdīr*] and the weaving together of all of these elements into a connected narrative, will become apparent in the following. 'To God belong both East and West so whithersoever you turn, there is the presence of God.' [Ḳ.2:115]

Commenting on this verse, ibn 'Abbās is reported as saying:

> The first regulation of the Ḳur'ān to be repealed was that dealing with the *ḳibla*. When the Prophet moved to Madīna, the majority of whose inhabitants were Jewish, God ordered him to face Jerusalem when performing the ritual prayers. This delighted the Jews, and continued for upward of ten months. But Muḥammad desired to imitate the *ḳibla* of Abraham and, to that end, would engage in private invocations, looking upward toward Heaven. God revealed, 'We see you turning your face to[44] the sky so We shall turn you in a direction which will please you. Therefore turn your face in the direction of the Sacred Mosque and wherever you chance to be turn your faces towards it.' [Ḳ.2:144] At this, the Jews were disquieted and asked, 'What has turned them away from the *ḳibla* they have been observing?' Say, 'To God belong both East and West,' and He said, 'whithersoever you turn, there is the presence of God.'[45]

This *ḥadīth* occurs in Ṭabarī's apparatus to the *Tafsīr* of Ḳ.2:115, but already conflates the wording of that verse with the wording of Ḳ.2:142 and that of Ḳ.2:144. Some scholars maintained that Ḳ.2:115 was revealed before the Islamic *ḳibla* was imposed:

> At prayer, Muḥammad and the Muslims had not faced in any particular direction. God informed them here that they might face any way they pleased. Whatever direction they selected would be God's direction, no direction being devoid of God Who said [Ḳ.58:7] 'He is with them wherever they are.' According to Ḳatāda, Ḳ.2:115 was then replaced on the revelation of the Ka'ba direction.[46]
>
> The Muslims had adopted the Jerusalem *ḳibla* before the Hidjra, and that continued to be their direction of prayer for sixteen months after the Hidjra.

Ḳ.2:115 gave the Muslims free choice of *ḳibla*.

> The Prophet said, 'These people are Jewish and are facing one of God's temples. Let us face it too.' He faced in that direction for sixteen months until he heard that the Jews were saying, 'Muḥammad and his followers did not know what should be their ḳibla until we showed them the way.' Disliking this,

Muḥammad directed his gaze at Heaven and God revealed [Ḳ.2:144] 'We see your turning your face in the sky...'

These exegeses consider that Ḳ.2:115 referred to the *ṣalāt* performed when at home in Madīna. Others, on the contrary, saw the verse as referring to ritual prayer but only when performed in conditions of extreme peril, or in the heat of battle. Apart from such special circumstances, the verse did not refer to formal prayer, but to the supererogatory prayer of the traveller. The direction in which the traveller faced was immaterial. For example, when travelling, ibn ʿUmar would not dismount to perform the prayers, and he would pray facing whatever direction his mount was heading, explaining that that was what the prophet used to do, and referring to Ḳ.2:115. A second recension makes ibn ʿUmar apply his interpretation only to the supererogatory prayer. 'The Prophet,' he says, 'would do this on his return journeys from Makka to Madīna, inclining his head.' [to represent the *rukūʿ* and the *su<u>dj</u>ūd*][47]

A further exegesis refers the verse to the ritual prayer of the traveller.

ʿĀmir b. Rabīʿa relates that, once when travelling by night with the Prophet, the Muslims had been unable to determine the *ḳibla* with precision, owing to dark, overcast conditions. In the morning they had discovered that they had all prayed facing in different directions. When they consulted the Prophet, on account of their scruples, God had revealed Ḳ.2:115 to inform them that each man had prayed validly.[48]

Ibrāhīm Na<u>kh</u>aʿī issued a *fatwā* to this effect. Nor was there any need to repeat a prayer performed in such conditions.[49] Mālik would prefer that the prayer be re-performed, when it became clear that one had not faced the *ḳibla* with precision but only if sufficient of that prayer's 'time-band' remained.[50]

Assigning a different *sabab* to Ḳ.2:115, Ḳatāda suggested that it refers to the death of the Negus of Ethiopia. Although the king had died before he had prayed in the Islamic direction towards Makka, on hearing that he had died, the Prophet had prayed for him. God revealed Ḳ.2:115 and Ḳ.3:199: 'There are scriptuaries who believe in what has been revealed to you and in what was revealed to them, humbly submitting themselves to God,' to justify Muḥammad's act of praying for the soul of a non-Muslim departed.[51]

Mu<u>dj</u>āhid had been credited with the view that Ḳ.2:115 refers to the Islamic *ḳibla*: Wherever a Muslim may be when the time comes for the performance of the ritual prayer, the direction of Makka can always be ascertained.[52] He has also been credited with the view that Ḳ.2:115 refers to private devotions [*duʿā'*] rather than to the formal prayers or *ṣalāt*, for, when God revealed Ḳ.40:60: "If you invoke My name I shall respond," they asked, "In what direction" and He revealed Ḳ.2:115.'[53]

Naḥḥās lists six differing exegeses of Ḳ.2:115;[54] Ḳurṭubī knows ten.[55] According to Ḳatāda and ibn Zayd, the verse is *mansūkha*; it was replaced by the command to face the Kaʿba. Referring Ḳ.2:115 to the Kaʿba, Mudjāhid made it a *nāsikh*. Makkī knows scholars who argue that having first been a *nāsikh*, Ḳ.2:115 later became a *mansūkha*.[56]

> Those who read Ḳ.2:125 as a preterite [*fa-ttakhadhū*] and saw in it a reference to the Kaʿba *ḳibla*, argued that it was replaced by the order to face in the direction of Jerusalem. That order was, in turn, replaced by the order to revert to the Kaʿba direction. Thus, the *mansūkh* finally became the *nāsikh*.

Those who argue that Ḳ.2:115 refers to the exercise of idjtihād in order to ascertain the direction of the Kaʿba in dark, overcast conditions; those who argue that it refers, not to formal, but to informal prayers, either *duʿā'* or *nawāfil*, (the supererogatory prayers of the mounted traveller) and, finally, those who argue that the verse conveys no general ruling, but refers to one specific historical occasion, the death of the Ethiopian king, all considered Ḳ.2:115 *muḥkama*, i.e. neither *nāsikha* nor *mansūkha*. This one discussion shows the range of possibilities open to the first exegetes and demonstrates how one line of possible interpretation invites the conclusion that a verse is *nāsikha*, while other lines of interpretation impose the conclusion that it is *mansūkha* or even *muḥkama*, and so neither *nāsikha* nor *mansūkha*.

A tendency to find a meaning for every single expression in the Ḳur'ān, if wedded to an over-literalness in the interpretation leads, in this manner, to the multiplication of the cases of *naskh*. For Mālik and the Mālikīs, if Ḳ.2:115 was *mansūkha*, then this is a case of *naskh* before the relevant ruling had ever been practised, there being no satisfactory report to the effect that Muḥammad or the Companions had ever performed a formal ritual prayer in whatever direction they pleased, whether settled at Madīna or travelling abroad.[57]

The *rāwī* of ʿĀmir b. Rabīʿa's *ḥadīth* relating Ḳ.2:115 to God's consoling the Muslims by informing them that although, from relying on individual *idjtihād*, they had all prayed in different directions, the prayer of each of them had been accepted as valid is regarded as 'weak indeed' and although we know this *ḥadīth* only in this man's version, 'the majority of the *ʿulamā'* acknowledge the doctrine the *ḥadīth* conveys.' Shāfiʿī insisted that such a prayer be wholly re-performed since, for him, accuracy of *ḳibla* is a condition of the validity of the ritual prayer.[58] Similarly, although they may not accept ibn ʿUmar's account of the *sabab* of Ḳ.2:115, the scholars accept the legitimacy of the statement it contains as to the validity of performing the supererogatory prayers mounted and facing in the direction in which one's mount chances to be heading. It has been adopted into the *Fiḳh*.

Some exegetes attempt to take a broader view of the Ḳur'ānic contexts and one has argued that Ḳ.2:115 points out that as both East and West belong to God, wherever God chooses to order men to face will be the *ḳibla*. No direction has any superiority over any other; the *ḳibla* has thus no intrinsic merit, but is the *ḳibla* simply on account of the fact of God's having imposed it. If God should choose to alter the *ḳibla*, there is no point in men's complaining. Having perfect awareness of what is best for men, God may command whatever He pleases. Perhaps Ḳ.2:115 was revealed to prepare men for a change of *ḳibla*.[59] Alternatively, if a continuation of the previous verse, Ḳ.2:115 may be interpreted as a divine threat uttered against those

> 'who prevent God's name from being mentioned in houses devoted to His worship and who seek to bring them to ruin.' Whithersoever they may flee to avoid God's power they will surely be overtaken.[60] Ḳ.2:115 would, in that event, be 'similar' to Ḳ.55:33 'If you could contrive to penetrate to regions of the Heavens or the Earth, then do so, although you could not do so without authority.'

Or Ḳ.2:115 may be addressed to the Muslims: 'The ruin of the houses devoted to God's worship should not prevent you from worshipping Him wherever you may chance to be in East or West.'[61]

If connected to Ḳ.2:114 and addressed to the Muslims, the *sabab* of Ḳ.2:115 may have been the unbelievers' obstruction of the Muslims' road to Makka in the year of Ḥudaybiya.[62]

In view of the wide range of interpretation possibilities to which Ḳ.2:115 has shown itself to be open, Ṭabarī rejects all suggestions of *naskh*. There can be no *nāsikh* without a *mansūkh*, and no evidence has been adduced which convinces him that Ḳ.2:115 refers to *ṣalāt*. Nor is there any satisfactory evidence that it was revealed after the Prophet and the Muslims had adopted the Jerusalem *ḳibla* to order them to abandon that direction and turn towards Makka. Certain Companions and leading Successors had repudiated that suggestion. We have no information from the prophet himself and the information we do have is contradictory. The *āya* is not *nāsikh*. Similarly, there is no evidence for the view that the verse is *mansūkha*. There can be no *nāsikh* in either Ḳur'ān or *Sunna* save something that countermands some ruling previously instituted as a formal imposition and incapable of being otherwise construed. Nor can there be a *mansūkh* save a formally instituted imposition which is later countermanded. Ḳ.2:115 falls into neither category.[63] The verse is apparently *'āmm*, yet intended to be *khāṣṣ* referring to all the possible circumstances that have been reviewed.

'Āmir b. Rabī'a's mention of their travelling by night with the prophet, being equated with a night patrol suggested that Ḳ.2:115 was later in revelation-date than the alteration of the *ḳibla*, since warfare was imposed later than the introduction of the Makkan *ḳibla*.[64]

According to Ḳatāda, 'they' (which might refer to the Madīnans) were already praying towards the Temple at Jerusalem when the prophet was still in Makka, before the Hidjra. That continued to be their *ḳibla* following Muḥammad's arrival in Madīna for sixteen months until the *ḳibla* was altered.[65]

According to ibn ʿAbbās, Muḥammad, in Makka, prayed towards Jerusalem with the Kaʿba in front of him. That remained his *ḳibla* after he transferred to Madīna for a further sixteen months, until the direction was altered.[66]

One suspects that reports of Muḥammad's already facing Jerusalem when still at Makka were designed to work against the notion that Muḥammad, finding the Jews facing in that direction, adopted their custom and imitated their practice. Both Ḥasan and ʿIkrima had stated that he had deliberately adopted their practice from expedience, hoping to conciliate the Jews and, in winning them over, attract the Arabs also. Thus, the reports that while still at Makka, Muḥammad had prayed in the direction of Jerusalem were designed to break the connection between the prophet's 'practice' and that of the Jews. There is, however, no reference in the Ḳur'ān to Muḥammad's ever facing Jerusalem. That is wholly the product of exegesis, derived from two verses: Ḳ.2:142, 143. The vagueness of the expressions: 'What has turned them away from the direction in which they have been facing?' and 'We appointed the direction that you have hitherto been facing only to test those who would follow the prophet and to distinguish them from those who would turn on their heels,' offered the exegetes a challenge and the knowledge that the majority of the population in and around Madīna were Jewish did the rest.

Those who argue that the Ḳur'ān may *naskh* the *Sunna* exploit this case. The Jerusalem *ḳibla* being nowhere alluded to in the Ḳur'ān, must have been introduced in the *Sunna*, but has been replaced by the Ḳur'ān's imposition of the Makkan *ḳibla*.[67] Others, breaking the connection with the Jews by another means, argued that Muḥammad was required by God to imitate the practice of the prophets before him until informed that a particular practice was superseded by the Islamic ruling. They cited the *ḳibla* as a case in point. The Ḳur'ān had here *naskh*ed the ruling in a previous dispensation. This was thus, a case of 'external *naskh*'.[68] Their opponents, represented by the view attributed to ibn ʿAbbās, seizing upon the Ḳ.2:143 expression '*We* appointed the direction that you have hitherto been facing . . .' argued that this was a clear instance of the *naskh* of the Ḳur'ān by the Ḳur'ān. Or, arguing that Ḳ.2:144 was the *nāsikh* of Ḳ.2:115, others promoted the same technical conclusion.[69] More subtle was the argument from *lugha*:

Ḳ.2:143 does not mean: 'We appointed the direction that you

have hitherto been facing...' it means: 'We appointed the direction which you are now facing' – the verse refers to the Makkan *ḳibla*, since the verb *kāna* in Arabic may have a present tense connotation. This can be shown by comparison with Ḳ.3:110: *kuntum khaira ummatin ukhridjat li-'l-nās*... The verse means: 'You [the Muslims] are the best community...'[70]

There is thus no evidence that God had appointed the Jerusalem *ḳibla*; it had been instituted by Muḥammad, and may therefore be reckoned among his *sunnas*.

From all this, one perceives the depth and intricacy of the discussions and arguments among the Muslims and one can see the extent to which exegesis and *naskh* theorising were mutually interactive.

Whichever is the *ḳibla* referred to in Ḳ.2:143, the verse hints at resistance to its introduction. There may even have been defections from the cause. Both the view that this case represented an instance of the *naskh* of the Ḳur'ān by the Ḳur'ān, and that which views it as an instance of the *naskh* of the *Sunna* by the Ḳur'ān, unite in seeing it as an instance of 'internal *naskh*'. That is to ignore the contextual environment of these passages. Apart from the very lengthy introduction preparing the way for the references to the *ḳibla* – which, as we saw, was addressed to the Jews, and in the course of which this reference to the *ḳibla* was already adumbrated some thirty verses earlier, in Ḳ.2:115, Ḳ.2:144 continues:

> and those who were given the Book know that it is the truth from God and that He is not unaware of what they do. But, if you brought to those who have been given the Book every sign, they would not follow your *ḳibla*, but neither shall you follow their *ḳibla*; nor will they follow each other's *ḳibla*. Were you to follow their fancies after the revelation that has come to you, you would surely do wrong.

Ḳ.2:148 concludes: 'Each has his direction to which he will turn.'

2. The Ḳor'ān's discussion of the change of ḳibla

There is nothing in the entire context to invalidate the traditional Muslim view that, before the institution by the Ḳur'ān of the Makkan *ḳibla*, Muḥammad and his followers had imitated the Jews in facing towards the Temple in Jerusalem. But there is nothing in the context to confirm this either. The Ḳur'ān's expression is too vague and allusive for any cetain conclusion to be derived. According to Shāfi'ī, the first obligation that God imposed upon Muḥammad had been to face in the direction of Jerusalem. So long as that had remained the rule, it was not lawful for anyone to face in any other direction; when God abolished it and instituted the Makkan *ḳibla*, it ceased to be lawful for a Muslim to perform any of the five daily ritual prayers in time of security in any other direction. The Ka'ba will remain the only valid *ḳibla* for the Muslim until Judgment Day. Unfortunately, Shāfiʿī does not discuss whether this instance of *naskh* conforms to his special theory.[71] He concludes merely that the Jerusalem *ḳibla* had been of divine institution and that on it Muḥammad had based his *sunna*, as he was to base his *Sunna* on the Makkan *ḳibla* following its introduction. The obligation to face Makka has never been the subject of contention among the Muslims. It is unequivocally imposed in the Ḳur'ān. There was perhaps no necessity for any theorising until the academic discipline of the *uṣūl* had begun to develop in the post-Shāfiʿī period.

What is abundantly clear from the texts we have studied is that the Ḳur'ān maintains a doctrine of *naskh*: what had previously been declared lawful may be declared unlawful and the reverse; what had been earlier imposed may be alleviated. There being no Ḳur'ānic identification of the *ḳibla* that had been observed before the introduction of the Kaʿba *ḳibla*, it is nevertheless the case that the Ḳur'ān expends much space in rationalising a change of *ḳibla* of contemporary occurrence. The rationalisation and justification of that change is directed mainly at Jews. The references in Ḳ.2 do not cease here but continue to the discussion of the laws of this latest prophet in so far as they affect and modify the laws of the old dispensation. Thus, the *ṭawāf* between Ṣafā and Marwa is countenanced [Ḳ.2:158]. Simplified dietary laws, alluded to in Ḳ.2:166, are baldly stated in Ḳ.2:173. The immediately following verse which continues the denunciation of the Jews for having concealed the revelations foretelling Muḥammad's mission, – *kitmān*, not *tabdīl*/*taḥrīf* – contains an offensive reference to their being regarded by God as polluted. The *ḳibla* is once more mentioned at Ḳ.2:177, a celebrated statement of the Islamic credo. The next verse announces the Islamic modification of the ancient law of the talion, specifically and consciously characterised as *takhfīf*, alleviation. Ḳ.2:180–2 institute the bequests to parents and nearest kin; while K.2:183 opens the passage declaring the institution of the Islamic innovation of the Fast of Ramaḍān.

All three sections carry an expressed reference to the previous law, and, in addition to the *takhfīf* of Ḳ.2:178, Ḳ.2:185 proclaims in a celebrated phrase: 'God desires for you ease, not that you be burdened.' The reference in Ḳ.2:187 to a further alleviation of the Fast regulations, need not be treated, as the traditional Muslim interpretation has viewed it, as an instance of internal *naskh* affecting only Islamic regulations, the more so since it is now realised that the later concentration upon the 'purely Islamic' is a reflection of the later theories, fictitiously projected back for excellent methodological reasons upon the contemporary scene in Western Arabia at the time when the Ḳur'ān was being revealed. Indeed, that Ḳ.2:187 is not the discussion of the imagined 'purely Islamic' situation is betrayed by the wording, specifically by the expression 'until the white thread can be clearly distinguished from the black' which is strongly reminiscent of Mishna, Zer., Ber., I 2. The continued setting in the *sūra* identifies the contemporary situation. (– summarised as follows:) The Jews after Moses had demanded a king

> Presented with Saul, they rejected him, arguing that they had a greater right to authority than one who had not been given wealth. Their prophet had admonished them, stating that God grants authority to whom He chooses [Ḳ.2:147]. Abraham had been similarly resented. Indeed, rejection by the Jews is one of the marks of prophethood. The *sūra* closes with a re-affirmation that Muḥammad is indeed a prophet and with the repetition of the motif that the Muslims refuse to distinguish one prophet from another, together with a declaration before God that, having heard, they will obey, to which is added the prayer that God will not load upon their backs a burden such as that which He had laid upon their predecessors [Ḳ.2:286]. Part of that load had already been relieved, even before the coming of Muḥammad. Christ had come informing the Jews that he confirmed what had preceded him in the Tōra – yet declaring lawful part of what had been forbidden them [Ḳ.3:50]. Muḥammad likewise was instructed to declare that the food of the Muslims was lawful for the Jews, while marriage with their women was lawful for the Muslims [Ḳ.5:5] Muḥammad had been sent by God to make plain much that the Jews had hitherto concealed. He came also to relieve much that was in the Law [Ḳ.5:15]. This Ḳur'ān informs the Jews on most matters on which they were divided [Ḳ.27:76]. There had been a Jewish *ḳibla* instituted by Moses in Egypt before the Israelites had even reached the Holy Land, let alone established Jerusalem [Ḳ.10:87].

There was thus no lack of change throughout the history of the Law. The chief function of the practical law was to distinguish those who were genuine in their belief from those who were convinced only at a superficial level or from mere self-interest. A second function of the Law is to demonstrate divine displeasure:

> In requital of the evils committed by the Jews, We declared unlawful to them certain pure things which had previously been lawful. For continually preventing men from the path of God and for their accepting usury, although forbidden to do so, and for their usurpation of men's property without due legal claim. [Ḳ.4:160–1].

On account of Cain's homicide, God had imposed upon B. Isrā'īl the principle that he who kills, other than in the exercise of the talion, or for social retribution, is as if he had killed the entire race [Ḳ.5:32].

We declared lawful to the Jews all hooved animals, and of cattle

> and sheep, We forbade the fat, apart from the fat of the back or the entrails or fat attached to bone. We imposed this as punishment for their law-breaking [Ḳ.6:146]. In declaring unlawful to the Jews those things We have mentioned, We did them no wrong. They it was who wronged themselves. [Ḳ.16:118]

Over and above these divine declarations, parts of the Jewish dietary law had been self-imposed. 'All foods were lawful to B. Isrā'īl apart from those things which Isrā'īl had denied himself before the Tōra was even revealed.' [Ḳ.3:93] These and other regulations, divinely enacted or self-imposed, can be set aside by God as a mercy to those who believe in and support his latest prophet.

> Those who obey the gentile prophet and law-giver whom they find mentioned in their Tōra and Gospel, who commands generosity, forbids meanness, declares lawful to them all pure things and unlawful to them all things polluted, who relieves them of their burden and of the shackles that had been laid upon them. [Ḳ.7:157]

There is no room for doubt that the Ḳur'ān and therefore Muḥammad held a doctrine of external *naskh*. Islam, the latest revelation, sets aside certain of the social and ritual laws of the earlier systems. The very logic of the claim to prophethood requires that this must be so.

The post-Muḥammadan science of *al-nāsikh wa-'l-mansūkh* is primarily concerned, however, not with external, but with internal *naskh* – the allegation that within the body of documents that had come down to the Muslims from the age of the revelation to Muḥammad are occasionally to be found conflicting statements either within the Ḳur'ān alone, or within the *Sunna* alone, or within the Tradition in its widest sense, comprising both Ḳur'ān and *Sunna*. Those statements are incapable of reconciliation and hence of simultaneous implementation. In the light of the general theory of *naskh*, internal *naskh* was justified on the analogy of external *naskh*.[72] The scholars would maintain that one of the Islamic statements, the later of the two, had superseded the other. We have also seen that, in such discussions, statements on dating tend to be mere assertion. Where both statements were Ḳur'ānic, the theory alleged the *naskh* of the Ḳur'ān by the Ḳur'ān, appealing for 'proof' to certain verses of the Ḳur'ān itself, Ḳ.2:106, Ḳ.16:101, Ḳ.13:39. If both were statements of the *Sunna*, the *naskh* of the *Sunna* by the *Sunna* was alleged. Apart from Shāfi'ī and some of his followers, the scholars also alleged the *naskh* of the *Sunna* by the Ḳur'ān or the *naskh* of the Ḳur'ān by the *Sunna*. Not a few of the Muslim exegetes were conscious of the link between their 'proof'-verses and the phenomenon of external *naskh* and the Ḳur'ān's efforts to rationalise changes in the previous laws introduced in the legislation announced by Muḥammad.[73]

> The Jews resented the introduction of the Kaʿba *ḳibla* and used this to attack Islam. They said, 'Muḥammad commands his followers to do one thing, then later forbids them. This Ḳur'ān is something of his own creation which is why one finds contradictions in it.' In reply, God revealed Ḳ.2:106: *mā nansakh min āya aw nunsi-hā na'ti bi-khair min-hā aw mithli-hā*, and Ḳ.16:101: *wa idhā baddalnā āya makāna āya.*

Abū Muslim, the inveterate foe of the *uṣūlī* notion that the Ḳur'ān contains both *nāsikh* and *mansūkh* verses, interpreted the same verses as referring to the abandonment of Jewish and the substitution of Islamic rulings such as, for example, the abolition of the Sabbath and the alteration of the *ḳibla*.[74]

We have seen that Ḳ.2:106 occurred in the very midst of the address to the Jews and before a series of modifications in both ritual and legal spheres. It precedes the change of *ḳibla*: vv.115; 124–51; 177; change in the pilgrimage rites, v.158; in the dietary laws, vv.168–74; in the law relating to the talion, vv.178–9; in bequests, vv. 180–2; in the fast, vv.183–7; and once more in the pilgrimage rites, vv.191–203. Similarly, Ḳ.16:101 is followed by allusions to modifications in the dietary laws, vv. 114–9 and in the laws relating to the Sabbath, v.124.

What Abū Muslim had challenged was the traditional explanation of the notoriously versatile term *āya*, used in both 'proof'-verses as 'a verse of the Ḳur'ān'. For him, it referred to the laws of the prophets before Muḥammad.

Nine

INTERNAL *NASKH* AFFECTING THE ḲUR'ĀN TEXTS

To test every single alleged instance of the classical theory's '*naskh* of the Ḳur'ān by the Ḳur'ān' would be an impossible task. The number of verses held to have been affected by the phenomenon runs into hundreds.[1] We saw in a previous chapter that the number of the verses alleged to have been omitted from the *muṣḥaf* soon mounted into the hundreds. The statistics compiled by a contemporary writer make the scale of alleged Ḳur'ān 'loss' strikingly clear:[2] including the stoning-'verse' and the *riḍā'*-'verse', the total of verses 'missing' from the *muṣḥaf* reaches 564 verses. Given that, in the reckoning of the Basrans, the total number of verses in the *muṣḥaf* is 6204, this means the 'loss' of about an eleventh of the entire revelation, or approximately nine per cent. That marks the proportion of *naskh al-ḥukm wa-'l-tilāwa*.

As to the mode *naskh al-ḥukm dūna al-tilāwa*, or the 'inoperative' revelations whose wordings survive in the *muṣḥaf* despite the suppression of the legal validity of their rulings, Hibatullāh will be found to deal with some 237 instances, of which no fewer than 124 verses had been *naskh*ed by a single Ḳur'ān statement, the so-called 'Sword-verse', or Ḳ.9:5:[3] 'Kill the *mushrik*s wherever you find them.' Naḥḥās disputed the claims for the *naskh* of a sizeable number of Ḳur'ān verses, and yet is seen to treat himself of some 130 cases.

Fortunately, reaction to the enthusiasm of the scholars and to their inclination to multiply the instances of the alleged *naskh* of Ḳur'ān verses set in. By a process of rejecting claims of the *naskh* of verses which contained only exceptives, or *bayān* (i.e. clarification) or which were affirmative, as opposed to imperative, and verses which referred to the replacement of non-Islamic regulations, and by the transfer of other verses from the *naskh* category to other interpretive categories: *muṭlaḳ/muḳayyad*; djumla/mufassar; *'āmm/khāṣṣ*; conditionals, qualificatives, etc., the *uṣūlī*s were enabled considerably to reduce the number of actual instances of *naskh*.

The full success of these processes may be seen in Suyūṭī's reduction of 'the attested instances' of *naskh* to a mere twenty cases:[4]

the *ḳibla*;
the *waṣiyya*;
the restrictions applicable to 'the first form of the Fast';

the *fidya* 'originally' available, in place of the Fast;
fearing God to the full extent that He ought to be feared;
the ban on fighting in the *Ḥaram*;
the widow's *'idda* of twelve months and the associated *waṣiyya*;
calling men to account for their innermost thoughts;
alliances;
the imprisonment of the fornicator;
the testimony of unbelievers;
patience in the face of the taunts and provocations of the unbelievers;
the general summons to fighting;
marriage with fornicators;
the regulations governing the Prophet's freedom to marry;
the repayment to Ḳuraish of the dowries of refugee wives;
the demand to forward a fee in advance of an interview with the Prophet;
the night vigils;
the need for slaves to ask permission to enter their masters' quarters;
the provision of those attending the division of estates.

The twenty have since been further thinned out and, in the latest specialist study of the *naskh* in the Ḳur'ān by a Muslim scholar who accepts the general principle that *naskh* has indeed affected the Ḳur'ān, the surviving attested instances of *naskh* have been brought down to only seven. They concern:

i. the *ḳibla*;
ii. speaking during the ritual prayers;
iii. the regulations governing the Fast.

These three are still approved of as instances in which the Ḳur'ān has superseded the *Sunna* of the Prophet.

iv. the night prayers;
v. forwarding a fee in advance of an interview with the Prophet;
vi. the number of unbelievers against whom the Muslim is required to stand his ground; and,
vii. the penalties for fornication/adultery.

These four are approved of as instances of the *naskh* of the Ḳur'ān by the Ḳur'ān.[5]

Of the four, we have already examined two and found, in each case, reason to doubt the traditional scholastic arguments. For completeness' sake, it might be profitable to study briefly the remaining two instances of the alleged *naskh* of the Ḳur'ān, for, if only one were thought to be substantiated, we should be obliged to concede that *naskh* has, indeed, occurred within Islam and within the lifetime of the Prophet. There would then be grounds for accepting the arguments of the *uṣūlī*s that the Ḳur'ān and Muḥammad had also inculcated a doctrine of internal *naskh*, as unquestionably they had both inculcated a doctrine of external *naskh*.

1. The night prayers

Ḳ.73 opens:

> Oh you wearing the mantle, watch the night all but a little – half the night, or lessen the vigil somewhat, or increase it beyond the half and intone the Ḳur'ān.

Ḳ.73:20 reads:

> Your Lord knows that you watch almost[6] two-thirds of the night and five-sixths of the night, in company with a group of those who follow you. God measures the night and the day and knows that you will never reckon it, and thus is merciful to you. So recite what will not be burdensome . . .

Ḳ.73:1–4 are cast in the singular throughout. The verses are thus addressed to Muḥammad alone. The duration of his vigil is to be just less or just more than half the night. Ḳ.73:20 is cast in the plural. Hence it is addressed to the body of Muḥammad's followers. The length of their vigil varies between four-sixths and five-sixths of the night. That is somewhat above the length recommended in the opening verses, which are imperative; v.20 is indicative, and would thus appear to refer to the present practice. The future practice would appear to be the subject of vv.1–4 and the suggested period of prayer is somewhat shorter than the current practice, but would appear to be imposed upon Muḥammad alone. His followers, some of whom might be engaged in arduous activities during daytime, 'God knows that some of you will be ailing, others travelling and yet others engaging in the struggle,' are excused the major vigil and required to recite only a moderate portion of the Ḳur'ān.

The three classes: the ailing, the traveller and the warrior represent the usual beneficiaries of the Ḳur'ānic *rukhṣa*.

The post-Muḥammadan assertion that there is in this *sūra* an instance of the *naskh* of the Ḳur'ān by the Ḳur'ān, rests solely upon a statement of ʿĀ'isha's, one of the frequent cases in which ibn ʿAbbās is said to have deferred to the greater intimate knowledge of the Prophet's practice possessed by the Prophet's widow. Saʿd b. Hishām asked the Mother of the Faithful about the Prophet's conduct. 'Don't you read the Ḳur'ān?' she asks, 'the Prophet's conduct was the Ḳur'ān.'

From this point of departure, it is easy to see how it becomes possible to argue, as ʿĀ'isha is alleged to have done, that, in the opening verses of the *sūra*, God had imposed the night watch upon the Muslims generally. It was the *Sunna* of the Prophet, and as such, must have been the *sunna* of the Muslims. The obligation had been observed by Muḥammad and his followers for twelve months, during which God kept back[7] the final verse of the *sūra* until He revealed it the following year as an alleviation [*takhfīf*]. Thereupon, the vigil ceased to be obligatory, and became voluntary.[8] Bukhārī has a *tardjama*: 'The

Prophet's watching and sleeping by night and the *naskh* of the vigil,' but the heading is accompanied by no *ḥadīth*.[9] Uncharacteristically, Hibatullāh offers no extended *tafsīr*, and no *ḥadīth*s, restricting his comment to one laconic sentence: 'The majority of the exegetes regard the close of Ḳ.73 as the *nāsikh* of the opening of the *sūra*.'[10]

Part of the traditional lore imparted to Shāfiʿī by one scholar he attended was 'that God had imposed upon the Muslims a prayer obligation before the imposition of the five daily ritual prayers, as can be seen from the opening of Ḳ.73. That obligation was suppressed on the revelation of the final verse of the same *sūra*.'[11]

> The final verse represents a *takhfīf* clearly expressed in the text: 'Recite what will not be burdensome.' This text is, however, 'ambiguous'. It could be that this recital remains obligatory since, on its revelation, an earlier command was rescinded. Or it could well have been destined to be, in its turn, suppressed by a later statement. We find in Ḳ.17:79 the further command, 'Give over part of the night to devotions – a blessing specially vouchsaved to you,' [Muḥammad]. This could conceivably impose a fresh obligation upon the Prophet additional to that imposed upon the community by Ḳ.73:20.

Searching the *Sunna* for an indication as to which of the possible interpretations is historically correct, Shāfiʿī concludes that the Muslim has no obligation beyond the five daily ritual prayers. Any obligation imposed before their institution is therefore no longer valid. Both the vigil and reciting of what will not be burdensome are no longer required.

Two different scholars have thus attained the same objective by different paths. In searching the *Sunna*, Shāfiʿī appears not to have encountered the ʿĀ'isha *ḥadīth* which, with its assertion that the night watch had, indeed, been imposed and had been observed for a year, during which its *nāsikh* had been retained in Heaven and that, upon its eventual revelation the night watch had been suppressed, being replaced by an alleviation, so neatly coincides with his *uṣūl* theories that it would have made his task easier and his conclusion less speculative. He had located the Prophetic statement that there is no formal obligation beyond the five daily ritual prayers, and, on the grounds that the number is five, Shāfiʿī could conclude that the vigil had been suppressed. Muslim, who is somewhat more positive than Shāfiʿī as to the suppression of the vigil, could indicate that the number of the daily prayers must be five.

In a discussion of *naskh*, the night prayers had been mentioned. It had been objected that there is no record of the night prayer's having been *Sunna*. The reply was that the night prayer is mentioned in the Ḳur'ān. As Muḥammad's practice would not have differed from the Ḳur'ān, the night prayer must have been practised. The claim that *naskh* had then occurred requires evidence that the *mansūkh* had been observed for some time. Without data indicating disparity of date, there could be no assumption of *naskh*, since it might be alleged that the *sūra* had been revealed as a single unit of revelation. The 'Ā'isha *ḥadīth* both provided this evidence for the dating and incidentally established that *aw nansa'-hā* refers to the *ta'khir*, or retention of revelation until the time is propitious. Shāfi'ī's analysis so far contradicts the 'Ā'isha *ḥadīth*, or is contradicted by it in that, whereas 'she' had argued that Ḳ.73:1–4 had been superseded by Ḳ.73:20, he, while apparently arguing that both verses had been superseded by Ḳ.17:79, is advancing the view that all three passages are superseded by the *fact* of the five daily ritual prayers, as endorsed by the *Sunna*. The claim that Ḳ.73:20 had been superseded by Ḳ.17:79 fails on the consideration that, in the former, the imperative is plural, while, in the latter, and as we have seen, in Ḳ.73:1–4 also, it is singular. The passages are not directed to the same addressees. Ḳ.73:20 has not, therefore, been satisfactorily disposed of and, there being no conflict between it and Ḳ.17:79 which, in turn, endorses Ḳ.73:1–4, Ḳ.73:20 ought to be regarded as remaining valid. By setting out from the *fact* of the five daily prayers, Shāfi'ī shows that there had been dispute about the number of prayers imposed upon the Muslims, and that he was not himself disposed to be over-categorical is shown by his adding, 'but we should not like any Muslim to neglect the *tahadjdjud*, reciting what God renders easy for him of the Ḳur'ān in his prayer, and the more prolonged the *tahadjdjud*, the more I prefer it.'

In the course of the dispute, *tafsīr* has played its part, especially the argument that the root *ḳ r '* in Ḳ.73:20 can be shown from other verses to have the force of the root *ṣallā* – as in, for example, Ḳ.17:78: *inna Ḳur'ān al-fadjr kān mashhūdan*, thought by some to refer to *ṣalāt al-fadjr*, the dawn prayer. Those who argue that the root means *prayer* in Ḳ.73:20, allege that the number of prayers imposed upon the Muslims is greater than five, since the night prayer, given this interpretation, was and remains valid. The *imām* Bukhārī's materials on the question are somewhat equivocal, suggesting that the question itself was not positively decided in his own mind.[12] What we find here is not conflicting Ḳur'ān statements, but conflicting exegeses seeking reinforcement from the Ḳur'ān wording. Appreciating this, we have no further need to retain this as an historical instance of the *naskh* of the Ḳur'ān by the Ḳur'ān . Taking 'Recite what will not be burdensome' as an exhortation to recite the Ḳur'ān rather than a solemn formal imposition of an additional night-prayer, one disposes of any supposed Ḳur'ān -Ḳur'ān conflict. That was in fact, the approach reported as having been taken by Ka'b al-Aḥbār, Ḥasan Baṣrī and al-Suddī.[13]

2. THE OFFERING PAYABLE IN ADVANCE OF A PRIVATE AUDIENCE

> Oh ye who believe! Before a private audience with the Prophet, forward an offering. That will be better and purer for you. If you find nothing, God is forgiving, merciful.
>
> Have you hesitated to forward an offering before your private audiences? Since you have not done so and since God has relented towards you, then keep up the prayer and pay the *zakāt* and obey God and His Prophet. God knows well what you do.' [Ḳ.58:12–3]

As one of the least disputable instances of *naskh*, this passage figures prominently among the list of 'proofs' of *naskh* in the Ḳur'ān adduced in the forefront of the works on *naskh* 'to establish the facts.' It will be found in the company of Ḳ.2:234/240, Ḳ.8:65–6, Ḳ.73:1–4/20, Ḳ.2:142 and other verses used to still any remaining doubts that *naskh* has historically occurred, and especially between the texts of the Ḳur'ān.[14] These are regarded as among the 'classic evidences', not least on account of the appearance in these contexts of terms such as: *tāba allāh* [Ḳ.58:13] *'afā allāh* [Ḳ.2:187] and *khaffaf allāh* [Ḳ.8] which were alleged to indicate change. As usual, the 'fact' of this instance of *naskh* is supposedly to be settled by appeal to a narrative drawn from the Muslims' vast store of exegetical *haggada*.

> Ḳ.58:12–13 records a virtue peculiar to 'Alī b. abī Ṭālib. 'Alī is himself reported as saying, 'There is in the Book of God a verse which none put into practice before I did and which none will put into practice, since I did, until the Day of Judgment. The people were crowding upon the Prophet plying him with questions or clamouring with requests and he became anxious lest some of their questions when answered would lead to the imposition of fresh impositions binding upon them. So God revealed Ḳ.58:12. The people ceased crowding on Muḥammad. The only property I possessed at that time was a single *dīnār*. Exchanging it for ten *dirhams*, I would give one *dirham* in alms whenever I wished to consult him about anything. When I was down to my last *dirham*, I consulted him on some matter, after giving the usual alms. The verse was then superseded by Ḳ.58:13.[15]

The Ḳ.58 context would have had no interest for the *fiḳh* scholars and appealed, as we have seen, to the *uṣūlīs* and others interested in *naskh* as quite simply a 'proof-text'. The 'Alī *ḥadīth* shows unmistakable signs of originating in a simplistic exegesis, being grounded in the exegete's penchant for assigning a *sabab* to and identifying an *'illa* for the revelation of the individual verse. It also served to provide 'evidence' for disparity of date.[16] The 'earlier' v.12 was then seen to embody a command withdrawn in the 'later' v.13. Disparity of revelation date is, however, by no means clear from the context alone. It could equally well be argued, as ibn Ḥazm had argued in the case of Ḳ.8:65–6, that Ḳ.58:13 was the earlier of the two verses admonishing the Muslims for their failure hitherto to observe an element of court protocol now firmly and unambiguously instituted by v.12, with the promise that their earlier failure to comply was forgiven, together with the assurance that inability to comply relieved the individual Muslim of any obligation. Ḳ.58:12 may not even be as definite as the commentators make out. There is no difficulty in reading the passage in the sense that whereas the Muslims do not appear hitherto to have volunteered an offering before consulting the Prophet, they are hereby gently reproved for the fact that the thought had not occurred to them and overlooking their thoughtlessness, God now urges them to consider this offering on future occasions when they may seek a consultation. But inability to comply will involve no penalty as long as they continue to observe the *ṣalāt* and *zakāt* obligations. Desirable as the forwarding of the offering may be, it does not seem to be insisted upon. That in this matter, which for post-Muḥammadan society involved no practical considerations, since the receipt of fees in advance of private audiences with the Prophet being, apparently, a special prerogative and perquisite of the Prophetic office, would presumably have ceased on his death – if not sooner, supposing it to have been *naskh*ed – confirms that our discussion was purely academic. The exegesis was directed solely at establishing the fact of *naskh* as a phenomenon that affected the Ḳur'ān. Here, it was being argued, are two Ḳur'ān verses which are incontrovertibly in conflict with another, and we have seen that this is adduced as an instance that would discomfit those disposed to argue that there is no trace in the Ḳur'ān of a single attested instance of the *naskh* of one verse by another. It is, as we have seen, one of the 'classic' instances of the *naskh* of the Ḳur'ān by the Ḳur'ān. We have also seen that the 'classic' Ḳur'ānic 'proof-verses' for the reality of the phenomena of *naskh* were Ḳ.2:106; Ḳ.16:101, Ḳ.13:39 and Ḳ.87:6–7.

The Ḳur'ānic 'proof'-texts

We noted that Rāzī expressed serious reservations on the expediency of using Ḳ.2:106 as 'proof'-text owing to its conditional structure. In his view, it was more satisfactory to rely on Ḳ.16:101. There is, however, we also noted, a major difficulty attaching to use of this verse also which escaped the *imām*'s attention. No Muslim scholar has alleged that any instance of *naskh* affecting Islamic enactments occurred during the Makkan period of the Prophet's ministry. Yet, by common consent, the revelation of Ḳ.16 is placed in that period. If *naskh*, as commonly defined, did not occur at Makka, was a verse revealed at Makka likely to refer to the phenomenon? The difficulty posed no insuperable problem to the scholar persuaded of the fact of *naskh*. The verse in question occurs in a Makkan revelation. The statement, however, refers to the Madīnan period, since the particle *idhā*, having a proleptic function, projects its reference into the future.[17] Conversely, Ḳ.5:6, which imposes the *wuḍū'*, occurs in a Madīnan revelation but refers to a ritual obligation which Muḥammad ['must have'] introduced at Makka, as soon as the first ritual prayers in Islam were instituted. The practice is dated to Makka; the verse imposing it to Madīna.[17]

It has also been argued that the term *idhā*, being a *ẓarf*, that is, a 'container', logically implies the existence and hence the occurrence of what is contained – in this instance, the phenomenon of *tabdīl*, of substitution [of *āya* for *āya*].

Ḳ.13:39 may be used to document the occurrence within Islam of *naskh*, as commonly defined, but only by studiously ignoring the context in which the verse occurs. The verse is preceded by a *wa'd* and *wa'īd* passage. The argument can be paraphrased thus:

> some believe in Muḥammad, some do not. The believers will be rewarded, the unbelievers will be punished. A prophet cannot bring an intellectually compelling sign, save with God's permission. Every dispensation has its pre-ordained duration. When that moment comes, one nation must give way to another. All has been fore-determined in the eternal divine will. Should, however, a prophet come with a sign, that sign is truly from God. The alteration of the Jerusalem *ḳibla* dislodged by the Ka'ba *ḳibla* was just such a sign, and the Jews knew perfectly well that it had been brought by a prophet from God as clearly as they recognise their own sons.
>
> The dietary laws of Islam were just such a sign brought from God, and the Jews recognised that this was so as clearly as they recognise their own sons.
>
> The modification of the ancient *lex talionis* was just such a sign from God; the alterations in the Fast were such a sign; the setting aside of the Sabbath was a sign.
>
> Whenever a sign came from God setting aside some sign that had previously come to them, the Jews alleged that it was a fraud. Not all Jews, however, rejected all signs: 'Some of the sectaries repudiate part of what has come to Muḥammad.'[19] 'Some who hear it say that it is a parcel of hallucinations which he has lyingly imputed to God.'[20]
>
> Those who allege of the Ḳur'ān that it is Muḥammad's 'own creation' he is bidden to answer by saying, 'The Spirit of the Holy One brought it in truth to confirm those who have believed.'[21]
>
> 'This Ḳur'ān could not have been lyingly imputed to God. On the contrary, it is a confirmation of what preceded it and an

exposition of the Law, proceeding without any doubt from the Lord Sovereign of the generations.'[22]

It is not generally appreciated that, in those verses which appear to insist at the most elementary level upon the reality of the phenomenon of divine revelation, the address is directed not primarily at heathen Arabs, but at the Jews of Arabia who had

> not formed a satisfactory concept of God, since they say that God has not revealed anything to a mere human. Ask them, 'Who then sent down the Book with which Moses appeared, to be a guide and a light to men, which you record on vellum, publicly reciting, although much you conceal. You have been taught much that neither you nor your fathers knew.' Say, 'God sent it down,' then leave them to their sport.[23]
>
> This present is likewise a book which We have sent down, a blessed book which confirms what preceded it, that you might warn the chief city and its dependencies. Those who believe in the Hereafter believe in it, and keep watch over their prayers. Who might more heinously act than he who lyingly imputed his own creations to God? Or who said, 'Inspiration has come upon me,' when in fact, it had not. Or who said, 'I shall bring down the like of what God has revealed.'[24]

The two statements have naïvely been attributed to some rival of Muḥammad's, allegedly a defector from Islam. They were, in fact, uttered by Muḥammad as solemn oaths to reinforce the seriousness of his claims. Blasphemy of the kind alluded to in the verses is so 'inconceivable' that the mere assertion by the Prophet that his teachings are sent down from Heaven by God is, in his view, sufficient guarantee to attract belief in him, in his mission and in his God-given authority to rule.

> Oh my people! If there were to come to me a blindingly clear evidence from my Lord, and He were to grant me mercy from His presence which was, however, indiscernible to your eyes, could we force you to believe against your will?[25]
>
> They will insist that Muḥammad forged it and lyingly attributed it to God. Well, upon his head be it![26]
>
> If it were true that Muḥammad were lyingly imputing his own fabrications to God, God would, if He so wished, stop up his heart, erase the groundless and declare the Truth with His own words.[27]
>
> We should indeed be inventing lying fabrications and attributing them to God, if we were to return to your religion after God has delivered us from it.[28]

The main features in the polemic directed by Muḥammad against his contemporaries were, according to the Ḳur'ān (paraphrase):

> his claim to prophethood; his insistence that the Ḳur'ān was the

work of God Himself; the demand, flowing from these two assertions, for total obedience to his will.

Implicit in their rejection of this unambiguous demand and, although not expressed in the Ḳur'ān, nonetheless inspiring their entire opposition to him in his pretensions to authority to rule over them, was the Jewish view that the prophethood had 'been sealed' in the mission of Moses and that their Law, derived in the name of Moses, was accomplished, eternal and immutable. This provoked from Muḥammad two fresh assertions (paraphrased thus):

> that the Law is partially abrogated in his coming, as it had before him been abrogated in certain details in the coming of Christ;[29] and that the attitude of the Jews to himself was explicable only on the assumption that they were deliberately concealing that part of their revelation that spoke of the coming of Muḥammad. The assertion is frequent in the Ḳur'ān, being represented by functions of the root *k t m* whose use in Ḳur'ānic verses averring the truth of Muḥammad's claims is a Ḳur'ānic cliché:

'Who is more heinous in guilt than he who would conceal a testimony in his keeping from God?'[30] which refers to the concealment by the Jews of the revealed statement of God that Muḥammad is His Prophet 'who will come in the latter days'.

Assertions of this kind constantly occur alongside references in the Ḳur'ān to changes introduced by Muḥammad in various aspects of the revealed Law.[31] The import of the accusation is unmistakably evident in:

> children of Isrā'īl, be mindful of My favour wherewith I have favoured you. Render in full My covenant and I shall render in full your covenant. Fear Me and believe what I now reveal in confirmation of what is already in your hands. Be not the first to reject it. Do not barter My signs for a paltry price. Me alone fear. Do not obscure the Truth with what is groundless, wittingly concealing the Truth.[32]

When God entered into the covenant with those who were given the Book, He declared, 'You shall proclaim it before men. You shall not conceal it. But, for the sake of a paltry profit, they cast it behind their backs. Evil the bargain!'[33]

Of yet another doctrine which was to become a commonplace of Islamic anti-Jewish propaganda – the allegation that the Jews had even dared to tamper with the actual wording of the Tōra[34] – the *taḥrīf/tabdīl* charge, the Ḳur'ān texts afford not a trace. What the Ḳur'ān does charge the Jews, especially the Jewish scholars with, is deliberate concealment of their knowledge that the Prophet spoken of in the divine promise contained in their scriptures was indeed this prophet who has now appeared in their midst, in the person of Muḥammad.

The allusion in the later polemic (one childlike instance of which we looked at, in the story of the rabbi who placed his hand over the stoning-'verse' of the Tōra, reading what precedes and what follows it, until his ruse was detected) is to certain verses in the Ḳur'ān:

> Do you then entertain hopes that they will keep faith with you, when a party of them were in the habit of hearing the word of God and then, having understood its meaning, of distorting it deliberately and with full knowledge?[35]
>
> Among the Jews are some who distort the words, saying: 'We have heard and shall disobey,' and 'Listen, not to be listened to,' and, 'Herd us' – twisting their tongues and making attacks upon the religion.[36]
>
> By virtue of their having broken the Grand Covenant, We have cursed them and hardened their hearts. They distort the words and have ignored part of that wherewith they were addressed. You will constantly find treacherous conduct from all but a few of them.[37]
>
> Messenger, be not aggrieved by those who hasten into disbelief from among those who utter acceptance with their mouths alone, their hearts the while rejecting. Some Jews give ears to lies, eagerly hanging upon the words of another group who, not having come to you, distort the words, saying: 'If you are given this ruling, accept it; otherwise, beware!'

This passage [Ḳ.5:41] we have seen linked to the Muslim exegetes' allegation that the Jews had been so impudent as to abandon God's stoning penalty which 'is in the Tōra', replacing it with a man-made flogging penalty!

But nothing in these passages, nor in their Ḳur'ānic contexts remotely suggests that Muḥammad, in the course of his own polemic with his Jewish compatriots, ever accused them of tampering with the written texts of the scriptures. Only one passage uses the term: the Word of God, a form of words which in another Ḳur'ānic context[38] refers, not to the Tōra, but to the Word of God as mediated through the administrative instructions and regulations promulgated by Muḥammad himself.

It was a reasonable polemic device for Muḥammad to accuse his opponents of seeking to discredit him in the eyes of his public: by misrepresenting his statements; or by attributing to him assertions which he claims never to have made; or by satirically distorting the responses made by the enthusiastic Faithful at his public meetings; or by challenging the details of his various pronouncements on the Law by quoting the opinions of the Jewish learned. Their 'ignoring part of what wherewith they had been addressed' is a back-reference to *kitmān*: 'Those who distort and those who conceal' were, according to Mudjāhid,[39] the Jewish learned. Ṭabarī has reported, but perhaps not quite appreciated the spirit of a dictum of Rabī': 'They heard the Word of God as the contemporaries of the prophets hear it, then deliberately distorted it,' for he connects this statement with a lengthy story about a party of Jews said to have accompanied Moses up the mountain. Having heard the very voice of Jehovah, they disputed with God's prophet what had there been uttered. 'If their ancients were capable of such distortion, what more likely than that their descendants, the contemporaries of Muḥammad should also distort the mention and description of Muḥammad which they found in their books, thus denying and repudiating him?'

Ṭabarī is at pains to emphasise that the verses refer to only some Jews,[40] while, on the second of the above passages, he states that the *tabdīl/taghyīr/taḥrīf* affected only the exegeses of the passages of the revelation, not their actual texts.[41] Even this concession, arising perhaps from the reflection that the Ḳur'ān claims to confirm what preceded it, is inadequate, having regard to the specific examples of the Jewish 'tampering' which the Ḳur'ān itself actually quotes. For they carry the discussion away from the Tōra texts to the contemporary quarrels between Muḥammad and the Jewish doctors of Madīna. The appalling atomism of the Muslim exegesis is here heavily underlined, for the main authorities appealed to to establish that the reference at Ḳ.4:46a is to the Tōra, are again referred to in order to establish that Ḳ.4:46b refers to the words uttered by Muḥammad himself. I discussed the circumstantial background of Ḳ.5:45 earlier, outlining the charge that the Jews had tampered with their *Fiḳh* by altering the regulation revealed in the Tōra to govern the treatment of *muḥṣan* fornicators. The reference is thus, once again, not to the distortion of the actual words of scripture, but to certain modifications said to have been illegitimately made by the Jewish *fuḳahā'* to the rulings in the revealed texts.[42]

The Ḳur'ān and external *naskh*

We have now seen that the Ḳur'ān expounds a doctrine of external *naskh*. Within the historical series of the prophets, the later have been granted the prerogative both to introduce new elements into the Law and to modify, or even set aside, elements introduced by their predecessors. Muḥammad did so in the case of the *ḳibla*; the Ḥadjdj rites; the talion; the bequest and inheritance rules; the revenue system; the diet and the dietary laws; marriage and divorce; the Fast; and the laws of war. On all, or on most of these matters, the Ḳur'ān records resistance and dissension, none of which need have been expressed if the governed had submitted to Muḥammad's claim to the right to direct them.[43] Authority had been been bestowed upon him by virtue of his selection to play a part in the divine plan for self-revelation, and had long been announced in the earlier revelations entrusted to the

Jews and the Christians. That some of these now questioned Muḥammad's assumption of his God-given authority meant that they were prepared deliberately and wittingly to challenge the divine nomination from mere self-interest and to express their challenge by ignoring the divine command in the covenant. They had given their assent to proclaim it in full; but when the publication of the older statements became unavoidable, they deliberately and calculatingly concealed part of the contents, publishing only what was not felt to be obnoxious to themselves. According to the Ḳur'ān, this always means their concealing the divinely-foretold appointment of Muḥammad as the post-Mosaic, post-Christian Prophet of God.

For certain of the post-Muḥammadan Ḳur'ānic scholars, engaged in the task of 'defining Islam', it meant something wider. It was now envisaged as referring to the concealment by the Jews of, among other things, the stoning-'verse' which the rabbis, adjured by Muḥammad to unroll the scrolls of the Law, had sought to keep hidden. Being, however, a prophet of God, Muḥammad was notified by divine inspiration of their attempted ploy.[44] In the view of others, Muḥammad had been alerted to the ruse by the intervention of a Jewish convert to Islam. In the view of yet other scholars, the stoning penalty had been an Islamic revelation, specifically and directly made to Muḥammad, without intermediacy of Jewish renegades, Jewish doctors, or Jewish scrolls.[45] For some, this revelation had been part of the Ḳur'ān communicated to the Prophet by the archangel Gabriel. Such differences of opinion supplied us with indispensable clues to the movement of Islamic opinion on the questions of the historical source of the stoning penalty, the precise relation of *Fiḳh* to Ḳur'ān, and of both to the Law of previous dispensations. Clues were found also in this post-Muḥammadan literature, in the widening of anti-Jewish invective. Very harsh language had, of course, been used by the Ḳur'ān against the Jews, yet it is important to appreciate that there is in the Ḳur'ān no generalised, sustained attack on the Jews, but only occasional expressions of bitterness localised in the struggle waged by Muḥammad to secure recognition of his claim to prophethood, and focused on actual issues where he sought to introduce a fresh regulation, or to modify an already existing practice.

The Ḳur'ān and internal *naskh*

That the Ḳur'ān expounds a doctrine of internal *naskh* is doubtful in the extreme. Of only two instances of alleged *naskh* of Ḳur'ān by Ḳur'ān which have survived our analysis, out of the hundreds which swell the native literature on the topic, little more remains to be said. The concession held to have been made in the matter of the fee to be forwarded on seeking a private audience with the prophet was shown to be, at best, based on an ambiguity. Both in this, and in the case of the night prayer, it proved impossible, in the absence of any convincing evidence of disparity of revelation date to treat the relevant Ḳur'ān contexts as other than single statements revealed perhaps as a unit. The sole basis on which any conclusion may be drawn is thus that of the context alone. The regulation laid down in Ḳ.58:12, although not absolute, certainly seemed to express the hope that where the means are available, a suitable offering will be made. No penalty was laid down for non-fulfilment of the regulation and the practice seems to have failed to become general. As elsewhere in the Ḳur'ān,[46] when convinced of the futility of pressing a policy in the face of determined opposition, Muḥammad withdraws as gracefully as circumstances will permit. God has relented, and the measure is withdrawn.

Ḳ.73:20 represents a somewhat different position. Muḥammad and a party of the Muslims appear to have been observing a fairly arduous night vigil of prayer. God had relented, knowing that there will be among the worshippers who accompany the Prophet in his nightly devotions some who are unwell, some who travel in pursuit of commerce, and others engaged in the Holy War. Practical considerations must prevail. All three groups are excused the night watch, the maintenance of which will devolve upon their leader. This is consistent with the level-headed recognition of practical reality which led Muḥammad to excuse the same groups from the rigours of the Ramaḍān Fast.[47] The Ḳur'ānic legislation is not that of the impractical visionary. It is always tempered by common-sense.

There would have been nothing to deter Muḥammad, who asserted his right to set aside centuries-old practices derived from the legislation of Moses, from making concessions and granting exemptions from, or even withdrawing his own regulations, which, on their first introduction, he claimed to base upon a divine communication, in favour of a modified regulation which, on its introduction, was likewise alleged to have been divinely advised. In such an event, the Prophet must merely satisfy himself that he had succeeded in constructing a sufficiently solid foundation of authority among his following to enable him, for example, to command them to face south, after having earlier commanded them to face north. So acute a student of psychology as Muḥammad could not have been unaware that the alteration of the *ḳibla* would only serve to strengthen his hold on a now isolated party. By boldly and publicly issuing a challenge to the Jews on a fundamental detail of the cult, Muḥammad enhanced the aura of authority he had adopted in his claim to be a legislating prophet. His boldness would simultaneously depress the authority of the Jewish scholar class. At the same time, the severe test of personal obedience imposed on individual believers would, by exposing the lukewarm and weeding out the faint-hearted necessarily result in an actual strengthening of the resolve of his hard-core following. Most important of all, Muḥammad would benefit from the added impulse given to his own self-confidence, enabling him in future to prosecute his mission with refreshed vigour following the personal triumph in the test to which he had submitted his own will and nerve.

We ought here to repeat that the earlier *ḳibla*, now apparently abandoned, is nowhere referred to in the Ḳur'ān. As it was not imposed by the Ḳur'ān, that is not an instance of the *naskh* of the Ḳur'ān by the Ḳur'ān.

On such occasions where the Ḳur'ān appears to indicate Muḥammad's exercise of the right to modify or even withdraw regulations he himself had introduced, no general principle is stated. Instances such as the night prayer, or the fee for a private audience, must, therefore be treated strictly as *ad hoc* decisions, with no implication whatever for any other statement in any other Ḳur'ān context. Thus, even if we conceded that, in these two instances, the Prophet seems to have modified or withdrawn a ruling previously made, we do so solely on the reading of the relevant Ḳur'ān texts. This is to concede that in these instances there may appear to have occurred what the post-Muḥammadan scholars were to call *naskh*. That is not, however, to concede that the Ḳur'ān contains or that it endorses any justification of the wholesale generalisation of the 'modify/withdraw' concept which the Islamic scholars' use of the term *naskh* represents.

The Ḳur'ān may contain instances of *naskh*, but the Ḳur'ān does not expound a theory of *naskh*. That was the creation of those who assumed the task of reconciling the Islamic *Fiḳh* with its putative sources.

3. The three 'modes' of *naskh*

We have just seen that a case for the occurrence in the Ḳur'ān of one of the three modes of *naskh*, the alteration of the ruling of one verse and the substitution for it of the ruling of a second verse revealed to supersede the ruling of the first verse – *naskh al-ḥukm dūna 'l-tilāwa* – may possibly be conceded.

The case of Ḳ.58:12–3 seems to be clearer than that of Ḳ.73. The argument that Ḳ.73:20 replaced Ḳ73:1–4 rests solely upon a readiness to acquiesce in an extra-Ḳur'ānic *ḥadīth* assertion that v.20 was revealed later than the opening of the *sūra*; and in the exegetical view that both verses deal with the same topic, the night prayer, and are addressed to the same audience, the Muslim community. There being, however, no verse in the Ḳur'ān which specifically imposes upon every believer an obligatory night prayer, now to be withdrawn, it is equally possible that, as in the case of the Jerusalem *ḳibla*, what is here being solemnly relaxed is some imposition originally laid down outside the Ḳur'ān. If this were the conclusion that careful consideration of this context were to lead to, then the argument that this represents an instance of the *naskh* of the Ḳur'ān by the Ḳur'ān could not be sustained. The first verse commands the Prophet to observe the vigil; v.20 speaks of those who accompany the Prophet, imitating his vigil. It then exempts the ordinary Muslims. Distinguishing between the ritual prayers and the recital of a moderate portion of the Ḳur'ān, v.20 commends the ordinary believers, but, in view of their day-time preoccupations, it exempts them from having to imitate the prophet's night-time devotions. This does not read like the alteration of an earlier imposition. Rather, it corrects a false impression the ordinary believer had formed that it behoves him to imitate the Prophet's practice in watching by night.

The thoughtful reader must satisfy himself whether the case has been made for any other alleged instance of *naskh* in the Ḳur'ān. Were he, for example, to conclude that Ḳ.58:12 and Ḳ.58:13 are in undeniable conflict and that, of the two, v.13 supersedes v.12, this would represent the quite unique situation in which two immediately consecutive verses in such conflict remain as part of the Ḳur'ān text. One might thus feel justified in concluding that the Prophet's decision to leave in the Ḳur'ān an unmistakable sign of the alteration of a revealed provision was the strongest possible evidence of his desire to draw attention to the alteration. It might then appear the more perplexing that he had not been equally explicit in all instances of alleged *naskh*.

A second instance of alleged Ḳur'ānic *naskh* involving two consecutive verses was that of Ḳ.8:65–6. But we have seen that the case involved rather, a disputed exegesis of the two verses and the relation thought to subsist between them.

The determined analysis of the alleged *naskh* of Ḳ.2:240 by Ḳ.2:234, or by Ḳ.65:4, or by Ḳ.4:11–2, has, we trust, shown that the nature of the evidence adduced in support of what is regarded as one of the least doubted 'classic' instances of *naskh*, regularly adduced in the *tafsīr*s and the technical *uṣūl* works to still any doubts that *naskh* had, indeed, occurred in the Ḳur'ān, and hence to establish the 'fact of *naskh*', has demonstrated the complexities attending the *uṣūl* arguments and exposed the serious tensions between the *Fiḳh* and the contents of the *muṣḥaf*.

The *madhhab*s were unanimous in acknowledging the stoning penalty, despite the fact that it is nowhere directly referred to in the *muṣḥaf*. It can be assigned to the *Sunna*, but only at the expense of accepting that the *Sunna* has superseded the Ḳur'ān. Those who could not reconcile themselves to the acceptance of this *uṣūl* doctrine, must necessarily assign the stoning penalty to an omitted stoning-'verse'. Failing to locate stoning in the *muṣḥaf*, these scholars were forced by their own logic to assume a distinction between '*muṣḥaf*' and Ḳur'ān.

That led directly to: *naskh al-tilāwa dūna 'l-ḥukm*. Here, the 'classic' instances, the stoning-'verse' and the *riḍa*ʿ-'verse[s]' could again be sustained only on the basis of uncontrollable extra-Ḳur'ānic *ḥadīth* evidence. This is certainly the least established of all the three modes of *naskh*. It is also the most transparent, having its origin merely in an over-rigid *uṣūl* principle. The principle, having been called for in specific circumstances could be abandoned when those circumstances had altered.[48] The older *madhhab*s argued that the stoning penalty was an ascertained instance of the *naskh* of the Ḳur'ān by the *Sunna*, but what argues that the entire apparatus of *naskh* was mere theorising, is that we also note that adherents of these older *madhhab*s accepted, in addition, although they had no theoretical requirement to do so, in terms of their own *uṣūl* theories, the rubric of *naskh al-tilāwa dūna 'l-ḥukm*.[49] This shows clearly that the theorising on *naskh* had developed its own tradition.

Equally uncontrollable is *naskh al-tilāwa wa-'l-ḥukm*. That formula referred, we have seen, to the alleged withdrawal, or suppression of both ruling and wording of a revealed verse. This mode of *naskh* had, however, no relevance for the *Fiḳh*, being the product of purely exegetical discussions.

The three *naskh* formulae

That each of the three modes of *naskh* had sprung from different origins, and were originally quite unrelated, and only later brought together under the *naskh* rubric, is clear from a comparison of their wording. *naskh al-ḥukm wa-'l-tilāwa*: the suppression of both wording and ruling of a 'verse'. The 'replacement' of both wording and ruling of a 'verse' could never be demonstrated, while their suppression can be ascertained solely on the basis of *ḥadīth*-reports analysis of which shows them to be in part general, unspecific assertions that omission from the *muṣḥaf* had occurred. Reports of the kind were circulated owing to the need for 'evidence', in the course of the disputed exegesis of Ḳ.87:6–7, that Muḥammad had been capable of forgetting unspecified portions of the divine revelations. The view that was eventually to prevail was that a prophet may not be admitted to have ever just forgotten any part of revelation. He might, however, be miraculously deprived by God of once-revealed matter, in strict accordance with the divine plan for the ultimate contents of the *muṣḥaf*. This modification in the exegesis of Ḳ.87 was required in the light of the exegesis of Ḳ.2:106. Discomfort at the notion of the Prophet's forgetting was relieved by Ḳ.87's reference to the will of God and by Ḳ.2's use of the two roots: *n s kh* and *n s y*, the preferred reading of the latter being 'We cause the forgetting'. Here, then, was documentary evidence provided by God for two phenomena: a. replacement or supersession; b. withdrawal or suppression.

The replacement might refer to the ruling alone, both wording and ruling of the original verse surviving in the texts of the *muṣḥaf*. Having lost its legal force, the original ruling had been ignored by the *fuḳahā'* when they selected the ruling of the later, replacement verse. The earlier wording retained its sacred character and might be recited in the prayers.

In two instances of replacement, some, however, alleged the replacement of the ruling alone of the original verse. The wording of the earlier verse alone had survived in the *muṣḥaf* and it alone might be recited in the prayers. The wording of the later, the replacement verse, had not been established as part of the text which might be used in the prayers. Here, the stoning-'verse' was cited as replacement of Ḳ.24:2; the five sucklings 'verse' as replacement of Ḳ.4:23.

The replacement might refer to both ruling and wording of the earlier verse. Ḳ.24:2, for example, had allegedly replaced Ḳ.4:15–6; Ḳ.2:234 had allegedly replaced Ḳ.2:240. The earlier ruling had been in each case replaced, yet the wording of both earlier and later verses might be recited in the prayers, the wording of both appearing in the *muṣḥaf*.

There are thus varying applications of the concept of 'replacement', indicating the range of the scholars' understanding of the term and the modalities of its operation. For example, *naskh al-ḥukm wa-'l-tilāwa* may indifferently be interpreted: the replacement of both wording and ruling, or the suppression of both.

naskh al-ḥukm dūna 'l-tilāwa may similarly be interpreted indifferently as the suppression of the original ruling alone, the original wording surviving; or the replacement of the original ruling effected by replacing the original verse, both wording and ruling.

naskh al-tilāwa dūna 'l-ḥukm may, however, be interpreted only as the suppression of the later wording only, that is, the omission – rather, the non-adoption into the *muṣḥaf* of the wording of the later 'verse'. The wording of the earlier verse remains in the texts of the *muṣḥaf* and it alone may be recited in the prayers. Its ruling has, however, become a dead letter.

These confused formulations, especially the last, bring out clearly the inadequacy of the exegetical 'evidence'. For, in the first, what is alleged to have been either suppressed or replaced is material that had once appeared in the Ḳur'ān document and source. In the second, something that allegedly had once figured in the Ḳur'ān source had been either replaced or suppressed, although it continues to appear in the Ḳur'ān document. In the third, something is alleged to remain in the Ḳur'ān source, although it is admitted from the outset that it never had appeared in the Ḳur'ān document. By the *naskh* of the stoning-'verse' is meant quite simply that it is not now and never has been a verse in the *muṣḥaf*. Some Muslims had insisted on documenting the *Fiḳh's* stoning penalty on the basis of an alleged stoning-'verse' which they admit had never formed part of the Ḳur'ān text. The Muslims all agreed that certain of the rulings of the Islamic *Fiḳh* had replaced certain of the rulings of the Ḳur'ān. Having selected the Ḳur'ān's term *naskh* to express the technical concept of the replacement of a legal provision, they then fell into disagreement, some holding that this was the word's sole meaning, while others argued that it carried the additional connotation of suppression. We saw that the 'replacement' definition of *naskh* could never be fitted to the allegation that the wording of the stoning-'verse' had merely been omitted from the *muṣḥaf*. Failing to seize this point, both Nöldeke and Schwally, in exploiting a *tafsīr-ḥadīth* which had been deliberately designed to make the exegetical point that *naskh* means 'suppression', i.e. removal from the *muṣḥaf*, have set the standard for the continuing Western acquiescence in the essentially Islamic view that both Ḳur'ān and *Ḥadīth* indicate the incompleteness of the *muṣḥaf*.[50]

4. Definitions of *naskh*

We have argued in passing that if 'replacement' derives from Ḳ.2:106, it can derive neither from *nansakh* nor from *nunsi*, but only from: *na'ti bi-khair min-hā aw mithli-hā*. But we saw that this clause had given rise to its own peculiar brand of difficulty for the commentators. Development of the *i'djāz* doctrine suggested that, as nothing can be thought to be similar to a verse of the inimitable Book composed by God, save perhaps another verse of the Book, a revelation could be replaced only by another revelation. The argument was enlarged by Shāfi'ī into the principle that only Ḳur'ān may abrogate Ḳur'ān, but exploited by the non-Shāfi'ite scholars to show that *waḥy* may abrogate *waḥy*. It must also be true that not even a verse of the Ḳur'ān might be thought of as 'superior' to another verse. Such disputes emphasise that difficulties arise when the word *naskh* is taken, as here, to mean 'replacement'. But the concept of 'replacement' was the starting-point of the *naskh* theorising. That being the case, the indications, said to be provided in the revelation itself, for the interpolation of the word *ḥukm* into the text of Ḳ.2:106 were thought to be unavoidable. The *ḥukm*, ruling of a *sunna* might be similar, or even superior to the ruling of a Ḳur'ān verse, in being easier to perform, or, if more difficult to perform, presumably productive of an even greater reward in the Hereafter. Rulings might be equivalent in both these respects. Interpolation of the term *ḥukm* thus renders the reinstatement of Ḳ.2:106 as one of one's 'proof'-texts a simple matter, where *naskh* is taken to mean 'replacement'. Rulings derived from the Ḳur'ān and rulings derived from the *Sunna* could, therefore be said to have replaced other rulings derived from the Ḳur'ān. Supplementary 'proof' for this 'replacement' definition of the term *naskh*, based alike on the interpolation of the term *ḥukm*, could be summoned from the text of Ḳ.16:101: *idhā baddalnā [ḥukm] āya makāna āya* . . . We noted that Rāzī preferred reference to this verse to the customary reference to Ḳ.2:106, not least since Ḳ.16:101 uses the term *baddala*, 'replacement', itself. Pazdawī's discussion on *naskh* even opens with the statement: *bāb al-tabdīl wa huwa al-naskh*.[51] Sarakhsī also, however, made it clear that, as certain of the elders of the Ḥanafī *madhhab* shrank from the misunderstanding inevitable in the use of the term '*tabdīl*', it was probably preferable to employ the more neutral '*naskh*'.[52]

We noted that the two verses, Ḳ.16:101 and Ḳ.2:106 were interpreted each in the light of the other, but it was Shāfi'ī who least ambiguously certified the meaning of *naskh*: 'No imposition is ever suppressed without another being revealed in its place.'[53] Shāfi'ī's primary concern was to reconcile the contents of the *Fiḳh* with those of both *muṣḥaf* and *Sunna*, and for him, *naskh* meant: suppression, abandoning, withdrawal. So far as the phenomenon of withdrawal referred to wording alone, with no implication for rulings, as is the case in: *naskh al-ḥukm wa-'l-tilāwa*, the alleged omission of revealed matter from the *muṣḥaf*, with consequent disappearance of the ruling as well, it failed to arouse his interest. Only the alleged abandonment of the ruling of a verse which still remained in the *muṣḥaf* stimulated his demonstration that the suppression of the Ḳur'ān's regulation was followed by its replacement by a second regulation acknowledged by the *Fiḳh*. The several steps in the process can be traced in the *Sunna* with the aid of the relevant *ḥadīth*s. The bulk of the instances he analyses in his writings were of the type: *naskh al-ḥukm dūna 'l-tilāwa* – the replacement of the Ḳur'ān rulings, or the *Sunna* rulings, in cases in which the original wording remained as part of the texts alongside the wording of the replacement rulings, i.e. conflict of sources.

In one unique instance, that of the *riḍā'*, Shāfi'ī, faced with an apparent Ḳur'ān–*Sunna* conflict, seized with relief at a *ḥadīth* congenial to his views on the relations between the Book of God and the *Sunna* of the Prophet. Discovering amid the welter of *ḥadīth*s shoring up the various exegeses of Ḳ.4:23 aimed at determining the minimum number of breast-feedings that would constitute a life-long marriage ban for the various charges of a wet-nurse, the 'Ā'isha report that two further Ḳur'ān verses had been revealed during the lifetime of the Prophet, one of which, setting the limit at ten, had been replaced by the other which set the limit at five, and that this latter verse was still being recited as part of the Ḳur'ān when the Prophet died, Shāfi'ī introduced into his apparatus the sole instance of the type *naskh al-tilāwa dūna 'l-ḥukm*. For him, the minimum limit remains five breast-feeds, notwithstanding the absence of the wording of the 'verse' in our *muṣḥaf*.[54] He thus recognised two modes of *naskh*: 1. *naskh al-ḥukm dūna 'l-tilāwa*, and one instance only of 2. *naskh al-tilāwa dūna 'l-ḥukm*. Of the third mode of *nasth*, *naskh al-ḥukm wa-'l-tilāwa*, his writings afford no mention. That was the concern of exegetes alone, its wording indicating how the old 'forgetting' exegesis of Ḳ.87:6–7 had been accommodated, under the aegis of the discussion of *naskh*, under the rubric of *naskh*, allegedly based chiefly on Ḳ.2:106 which mentioned 'forgetting' in addition to 'replacing'. Ṭabarī's opponents had insisted that 'no part of the Ḳur'ān is forgotten – unless it is *mansūkh*.'[55] Ṭabarī himself accepted two modes of *naskh*: *naskh al-ḥukm dūna 'l-tilāwa*, and *raf'*, or *naskh al-ḥukm wa-'l-tilāwa*, which is properly an exegete's business.[56]

Other scholars with an equal dislike of 'forgetting' had formalised it in another way. Glossing the Ḳ.2:106 term *nansa* as '*taraka*', i.e. to abandon, they argued that Muḥammad had abandoned the Ḳur'ān regulation conveyed in certain verses to base his practice on the regulation conveyed in a second verse, or upon some other basis, such as the *Sunna*. Their rationalisation of the observable conflicts between the *Fiḳh* and the *muṣḥaf* had the merit that it could appeal to the usage of Ḳ.9:67.

Whether alleging that the wording or the ruling of a verse in the divine revelation had been 'set aside', one might continue to draw support from Ḳ.2:106, reading it, however, because of an ingrained dislike of the 'forgetting' interpretation, *aw nansa'-hā*. The multiplicity of 'escape-routes' from the 'forgetting' interpretation of *n s y* shows the wide unpopularity of the old 'forgetting' *tafsīr*.

Ṭabarī too, in his commentary on Ḳ.2:106 and emphatically elsewhere throughout his *Tafsīr*, like Shāfi'ī, regularly insists upon the *uṣūlī* definition of the term *naskh*: it is the negation of a ruling which had been established by an earlier statement by a second statement conveying a different ruling.[57]

In his comment, however, on Ḳ.22:52, the second Ḳur'ānic occurrence of the Arabic root *n s kh*, he equally emphatically insisted that the word means 'suppression' [*ibṭāl*].

The debates between the supporters of the two rival definitions of *naskh*, *ibdāl*, supersession, or replacement, and *ibṭāl*, suppression, or withdrawal, were long drawn-out and exhibited much ingenuity, best illustrated in the expositions of Ghazāli,[58] Rāzī,[59] and Āmidī,[60] all of whom freely admitted that the technical *uṣūlī* use of the term *naskh* to mean 'replace' has no linguistic warrant, but is defensible on the basis of the usage of the *uṣūlī*s. Concern about the precise definition and linguistic history of the term is mere arid pedantry. When scholars discuss *naskh*, it is clear what they are talking about. There is no need to go into the linguistic connotations of the term. We have our use of the word, not the same, perhaps, as that which it denotes in Arabic, yet similar.[61]

5. Conclusion

We earlier observed that the scholars had sought their 'proof' of *naskh* in an inappropriate Ḳur'ānic reference. Obviously they craved a Ḳur'ānic reference and we have learned that the choice fell upon Ḳ.2:106 rather than upon Ḳ.16:101. In their determination to appropriate a Ḳur'ānic term in the interests of providing themselves with the appearance of Ḳur'ānic sanction for their theories, the earliest scholars had chosen unwisely. As skills developed, the weakness of the choice became apparent, but later scholars, under obligation to the work of their predecessors in the exegetical, *ḥadīth* and *uṣūl* spheres, had now no licence to innovate. Nor did they wish to depart radically from the older definitions and exegeses which they had inherited and which were now long hallowed by the tradition of the *madhhab*. Rather, they felt called to defend the traditional statements, patching and mending at every fresh objection as the refutation of each new difficulty only raised further difficulties in an endless scholarly dialectic. A few brief examples will demonstrate the opportunism and subtlety of the scholars and the degree to which their interventions have made the literature on the *naskh* intolerably confusing.

The appropriateness both of the term *naskh* itself, and of the appeal to Ḳ.2:106 had been questioned. We have noted that those who interpreted *naskh* as 'replacement' had next had to interpolate the word *ḥukm* into Ḳ.2:106. The effort could rebound. Persuaded that *naskh* means 'to suppress', others argued that what Ḳ.2:106 promised was the suppression, not of the ruling, but of the *āya*. They further insisted that the same verse emphasised that what is suppressed would be replaced. This exegesis threatened not only two of the three modes of *naskh*, but certain of the classic instances of the classical mode of *naskh*: *naskh al-ḥukm dūna 'l-tilāwa*.

> The *naskh* spoken of by the *uṣūlīs* is indeed the *naskh* of the ruling. It is preferable to interpret technical terms in the sense which technical convention has imparted to them, rather than in their strict Arabic sense. The appropriateness of this term *naskh* has been questioned, and we concede that, since we are concerned with the withdrawal [*raf'*] of the earlier regulation, the objection has some merit. We cannot, however, admit that there could have been any difficulty about its meaning when the verse was first revealed. For our generation, however, the application of *ta'wīl* [that is, of re-interpretation] where necessary is essential, although reading Ḳ.2:106 literally and interpreting the root *n s kh* in accordance with its actual meaning in Arabic is certainly to be preferred to assuming ellipsis of the term *ḥukm*, or to interpreting the verse's term *āya* to include a reference to the ruling of the *āya* by a species of synecdoche.[62]

It was further objected that the verse speaks not of the withdrawal of the ruling, but of its replacement. There can be no *naskh* without replacement.

> Ḳ.2:106, is the reply, does not necessarily imply replacement, when it is only the ruling that is withdrawn. Replacement is implied only when it is the wording that is withdrawn. In the event of the withdrawal of the ruling, replacement is usual. But it is not what invariably occurs. This is proven by the fact that in certain actual cases of *naskh*, no replacement occurred. Thus, the requirement to offer a fee for a private audience with the Prophet is just one instance of withdrawal of a ruling without its being replaced. Besides, what it to prevent us from regarding the withdrawal of the ruling as being in itself the substitute for its enforcement and describing the absence of regulation, in terms of Ḳ.2:106, as being better than the imposition of a ruling?[63]

In reference to *naskh al-tilāwa dūna 'l-ḥukm*, another scholar was inclined to argue:

> If it be objected that no *naskh* can occur without a replacement ruling being promulgated in its place, since God says in Ḳ.2:106: *na'ti bi-khair minhā aw mithli-hā*, which is an affirmative statement of divine intent from which God cannot deviate, we reply that all that is now in the *muṣḥaf*, not having been withdrawn, replaces what has been withdrawn, and all that God has withdrawn from the revelation of which we have no knowledge has been replaced by this text whose wordings and rulings have been handed down to us.[64]

Anyone seeking to insist that *naskh* means merely the withdrawal of the ruling is, in Bayḍāwī's view, refuted by the fact that the *nāsikh* ruling is the contrary of the *mansūkh* ruling. Whence, the definition of *naskh* as *raf'* is in no way preferable to defining it as *daf'*.[65]

> It is not a condition of *naskh* that a replacement be promulgated. Some say that is essential, and we challenge them to declare whether that is intellectually or historically indicated. Logically, the absence of a replacement ruling involves no absurdity. One might say, 'God announced: "I have imposed warfare upon you, but I now relieve you of that imposition so that your obligation reverts to what it was before warfare was added to it."
>
> Replacement cannot be said to be indispensable on historical grounds, since there are actual instances of *naskh* in which no replacement has been recorded, for example, the fee for a private audience.[66]
>
> In *naskh*, the original ruling ceases to be valid. We therefore understand that it has no application for the future. If, however, there chances to be a replacement ruling, what makes the original ruling *mansūkh* is its ceasing to be valid, not the revelation of the replacement ruling. Of course, in cases where there is no

replacement ruling, our knowledge that *naskh* has occurred does not derive from the *Fiḳh*.[67]

These reflections illustrate the persistence of the realisation that 'replacement' derived from: *idhā baddalnā* and from *na'ti bi khair minhā aw mithli-hā*. They also show a realisation that the term *naskh*, both in Ḳ.22:52 and Ḳ.2:106 meant simply 'suppression'.

In the Hebrew of the Old Testament, the root *n s kh* is found four times: Deut. 28:63; Ps. 52:5; Prov. 2:22 and 15:25. In each case, it has the meaning: 'remove, eradicate'.

This agrees with Jeffrey's findings, based on comparison with the cognate languages:

> 'In Akkadian [nasāḫu] Hebrew, Old Aramaic and the Targumic, the original sense is clearly 'remove', 'tear away' (evellere), which original meaning is found in Ḳ.2:100; 22:51, where the word is used as Hirschfeld (Beiträge, 36) points out, precisely as in Deut., 28, 63 and Ezr. 6, 11.'[68]

The most obvious link between Ḳ.16:101, Ḳ.22:52 and Ḳ.2:106 is that all three verses carry the term *āya*. The majority of the Muslims, in line with their practice of placing upon words the interpretation indicated by scholars' conventions, assumed that this notoriously ambiguous term in all three contexts bore the meaning: verse of the Ḳur'ān. This exegesis was vigorously contested by Abū Muslim who was appalled at the suggestion that there could be contradictions or 'second thoughts' in a book sent down by God.[69] Throughout his monumental Ḳur'ān commentary, the *Mu'tazilī* scholar is said to have propounded exegeses designed to make the appeal to the theories of *naskh*, at least in respect of the Ḳur'ān, wholly unnecessary. It must be admitted, however, that his scholarship fell somewhat short of the piety of his motives.

Similarly, embarrassed like so many Muslim writers by criticism, actual or anticipated, from Christian commentators, the *imām* Muḥammad 'Abduh, expressing regret at the easy means the theories of *naskh* provided the enemies of Islam to make attacks on the faith and thus to undermine the confidence of unlearned Muslims, produced the same implausible definitions that Abū Muslim had advanced.[70]

We have already insisted that Ḳ.2:106 must be read against the entire Ḳ.2 context. That we summarised above, but it is probably worth rehearsing the matter once more. The verse immediately precedes a series of sweeping alterations and modifications introduced in both the ritual and legal spheres. The verse addresses changes in: the *ḳibla*, v.115; v.177 and vv.124–51; the Ḥadjdj rites, v.158; the dietary laws, vv.168–74; the talion, vv.178–9; the law on bequests, vv.180–2; the Fast, vv.183–7; once more the Ḥadjdj, vv.191–203.

Similarly, Ḳ.16:101 is followed by allusions to change or modification in the dietary laws, vv.114–19; the Sabbath, v.124.

We have also seen above the extent to which Muḥammad felt and responded to the need to offer a prolonged rationalisation of the change in *ḳibla*, and we stressed that his justification of the change was directed mainly at the Jews. It therefore seems more likely, given the total contexts in which both key verses occur, that in each case, the versatile term *āya* refers not to a verse in his own Ḳur'ān, but rather to the individual ritual or legal regulations which he is engaged in altering or modifying, replacing or suppressing. Muḥammad naturally justifies each such change with reference to God. If there were thought to be any merit in this idea, Ḳ.2:106 would read: 'Whatever existing ritual or legal regulation We suppress or cause you to abandon, We shall bring in its place another superior to it, or at least similar to it,' while Ḳ.16:101 would now read: 'Whenever We alter some existing legal or ritual regulation and replace it with another, they say of you, Muḥammad, "You are a fraud."'

The suggestion does, at least have the merit of considering the meaning of: *na'ti bi khair minhā aw mithli-hā* all too often left out of account in the Muslim exegeses.

The possibility of such an interpretation of the verses must work against the dogmatic certainty with which Nöldeke and his imitators confidently pronounce on the incompleteness of the Ḳur'ān on the one hand; and on the other hand, the legitimacy of the appeal by the Muslims to the Ḳur'ān texts for confirmation of the validity of their theories of *naskh*, not least when it is demonstrated that their procedures involve calling upon the Ḳur'ān to aid and abet the preservation of both *Fiḳh* and *Sunna* at the expense of the Ḳur'ān, whenever those two sources either contradict the Ḳur'ān, or seem to allege the divine revelation of matters nowhere referred to directly in the *muṣḥaf*.

That Muḥammad accepted a doctrine of external *naskh* cannot be doubted.

That Muḥammad indulged in instances of internal *naskh* is possible. But, apart from Ḳ.58:12–3, it is very doubtful that the allegation that traces remain in our *muṣḥaf* of verses revealed to repeal other verses still in the *muṣḥaf* can be traced to the texts of the *muṣḥaf*. One or two instances do not, however, amount to an entire theory. The Prophet may have modified elements of his own court protocol. But that provides no warrant for post-Muḥammadan scholars to relax a single regulation found to be represented by a verse in the *muṣḥaf*.

That Muḥammad accepted, or had even heard of the theories of *naskh* in all their three-fold modality is certainly untrue, for we have exposed the origins of the theories in gradual developments arising from the attempts of exegetes and *uṣūlīs* to resolve the painful problems posed by the conflicts they themselves noted between the contents of the *Fiḳh* and those of the *muṣḥaf*. But the 'conflict' we have seen was actually between different exegeses of the Ḳur'ānic passages.

If the *Fiḳh* had been from the first based directly upon the texts of the Ḳur'ān, as the classical statement of *uṣūl al-fiḳh* alleges, rather than indirectly and at one remove – that of *tafsīr*; and if the *uṣūlīs* had always understood the true import of such expressions as 'the Book of God', for example, and if they had appreciated the exegetical origin of much that passes for the *Sunna*, such conflicts need never have arisen, and, in consequence, the ingenious theories of *al-nāsikh wa-'l-mansūkh* would never have needed to be constructed.

POSTSCRIPT

The work presented here, while designed to investigate a specific topic, aims also to inculcate a method. My intention has been twofold: to show the results that can be achieved by the *simultaneous* study of the standard works in the fields of Islamic Law, legal theory, Ḳur'ān (both text and exegeses) and the Classical *Ḥadīth* collections with their chief commentaries. Attention has, I hope, been drawn to the interdependence of these studies and to the importance of recognising that it was not from any one of those fields primarily, but rather from their interplay and mutual effects that the thinking of the Muslims slowly evolved and gradually led to later, agreed positions after the earlier separate views of the original *madhhab*s perceptibly began to converge. The approach to the study of the development of ideas and methods in the realm of the Islamic sciences is thus best made on the basis of a broad programme of reading, if the essential mental connections made by the Muslims themselves are not to be missed by the modern, especially the Western student.

The young medieval Muslim was trained in just such a wide syllabus. He would not only know the Ḳur'ān by heart. He had also memorised great stretches of exegetical, legal and *ḥadīth* materials. Once matured and writing on his own account, he could take for granted in his readers the same broad grounding. Much did not, therefore, need to be spelled out directly, or in detail. Much would be assumed and compressed into a few signal words. Often only one single word would suffice to set up reverberations in the minds of the readers to create the desired response. One such word would have been *naskh*, but there was a host of others, both technical and common. Among those we have seen: *'āmm*; *khāṣṣ*; *ra'y*; *riwāya*; *sunna*, Djāhiliyya, even Muslim itself. The modern, non-Muslim reader must, therefore, school himself to recognise such 'trigger-words' if he is to penetrate beneath the surface of the medieval Islamic technical writings, more particularly, if he hopes to learn to make the vital mental connections he is invited to pursue by the Muslim authors.

The perils of singling out only one element in the wide medieval syllabus of studies to be considered in isolation from the horizontally associated subjects may be illustrated by what resulted from one scholar's opting to confine himself to only one branch of Islamic learning, in this particular case, to the essentially 'legal' traditions. Schacht's work, *The Origins of Muhammadan Jurisprudence*, has deservedly attracted a high degree of international respect. Yet the brief study he offers of the opposing views expressed on the institution of *mut'a*, or 'temporary marriage' highlights the inadequacies of the methods he adopted. Schacht, it will be remembered, took the view that Muhammadan Law

> did not derive directly from the Koran but developed, as we saw, out of popular and administrative practice under the Umaiyads, and this practice often diverged from the intentions and even the explicit wording of the Koran,[1]

although he modified this generalisation by stating that a number of legal rules

> particularly in family law and law of inheritance, not to mention cult and ritual, were based on the Koran from the beginning.[2]

But, apart from the most elementary rules, norms derived from the Ḳur'ān were, in Schacht's view, introduced into Muhammadan law almost invariably at a secondary stage.[3]

> This applies not only to those branches of law which are not covered in detail by the Koranic legislation . . . but to family law, the law of inheritance and even cult and ritual.

Marriage, the very core of family law, is regulated in considerable detail in the Ḳur'ān and the question of the *donatio propter nuptias* is addressed at Ḳ.4:24: *fa-mā stamta'tum bihi minhunna fa-ātū-hunna udjūra-hunna*. [In consideration of the sexual enjoyment you derive from them, give them their financial due]. On account of this revealed passage, the *mahr*, or dowry was quite properly seen to be a central and indispensable element in the construction of an Islamic marriage. Even more emphasised in this Ḳur'ān passage is the intention with which the dowry is offered: understood by the Muslims to be the intention to enter into a permanent arrangement. Thus, dowry and intent determine the validity of Islamic marriage. Ḳ.4:24 was preceded by a careful listing of the 'forbidden degrees of relationship' both biological and legal, and v.24 quite carefully states that outside these forbidden degrees men and women may validly aspire to matrimony. The 'permitted degrees of relationship' are thus stated negatively as other than those listed in v.23 and v.24[a]. The Ḳur'ān expresses this 'other than these' as *mā warā' dhālikum*. The phrase could be, and has been interpreted as meaning: 'for purposes other than marriage as hereby defined'. That is, it has been taken by some to mean temporary, as opposed to permanent marriage. But, that we are here dealing merely with one exegesis of the verses is betrayed by the choice of name adopted for such temporary marriages – *mut'a*, for the word is clearly extracted directly from the vocabularly of the Ḳur'ān verse itself. Schacht comments:[4]

> The *mut'a* is a marriage concluded for a fixed term,[5] at the end of which it is dissolved automatically. This was *presumably an*

ancient Arab institution, and seems to have been sanctioned and regulated in Koran iv. 24. It was certainly *a widespread practice in early* Islam which found expression in a *fuller* and unequivocal version of the Koranic passage in copies attributed to Ibn Mas'ūd, Ubai and Ibn 'Abbās, in *a tradition* attributed to Ibn Mas'ūd for Kufa, and in a doctrine attributed to Ibn 'Abbās and his Companions for Mecca. Its existence is also attested by the traditions directed against it.

The opposition to *mut'a* prevailed among the Iraqians and the Medinese.[6] In Iraq, the Ibn Mas'ūd tradition was turned into its contrary by *the assumption of a repeal* of *mut'a in the Koran*,[7] and to this was prefixed the standard *isnād* of the school of Kufa; and a more recent tradition with a Nāfi'-Ibn 'Umar *isnād* affirmed the prohibition of *mut'a* by the Prophet . . .

In the generation preceding Mālik, both doctrines [pro- and anti- *mut'a* views] were outwardly harmonised and the prohibition of *mut'a* maintained by making the Prophet allow and subsequently forbid it . . .

Schacht's exclusive concentration on the *Ḥadīth* and his general indifference to Ḳur'ān studies here prevented him from seeing beyond his hypothesis as to 'practice'. The matter is clear. This is a case of the *naskh* of the *Sunna* by the *Sunna*. But the *mansūkh Sunna* rested neither upon 'the practice in early Islam' – here, note the reference to the Djāhiliyya – nor upon the universally agreed texts of the Ḳur'ān. *Mut'a* derived from an exegesis and could claim a relation with the Ḳur'ān only by unsuccessfully appealing to the so-called texts of the usual Companion-figureheads. That is, *mut'a* could be 'sanctioned' only by an [unsuccessful] attempt to interpolate the necessary phrase into Ḳ.4:24: 'for a stipulated period', *ilā adjalin musamman*. This 'fuller and unequivocal version' of Ḳ.4:24 is not even relied upon by those who do advocate *mut'a*, the *Ithnā-'asharī* Shī'a, who prefer to adduce in its favour the *ḥadīth*s attributing the doctrine to 'Alī, ibn 'Abbās and 'Imrān. For the Shī'a share a common Ḳur'ān text with the *Sunnī*s and always have done. Schacht, mentioning that the Zaydī Shī'a, 'the first Shiite sect to secede from the Sunni community, rejected *mut'a*,' does not enquire whether the date of their secession might have some bearing on the dating of these disputes. As the *isnād*s of the Medinese traditions directed at their rejection of *mut'a* converge upon the name of Zuhrī, Schacht dates their explicit rejection of *mut'a* to the time of Zuhrī himself, [d. AH 124]. These traditions consist of 'Alī's supposed rejection of ibn 'Abbās' pro-*mut'a* stance, on the ground of the Prophet's prohibition and of 'Umar's vehement denunciation of *mut'a*. Traditions showing the Prophet at first permitting but later forbidding the practice of *mut'a* were incorporated in the biography of the Prophet where it proved difficult to reconcile them, one with another.

For Schacht, 'nothing of this is authentic historical information'. Very much less of it than even Schacht himself supposed, is authentic historical information. Indeed, nothing at all. Had Schacht looked further afield to discover the full extent of these ancient disputes, the *Tafsīr* works and the medieval commentaries on the *ḥadīth*s to which he alludes (especially those featuring ʿAlī, ibn ʿAbbās, ʿImrān and especially the Djābir report on ʿUmar's supposed prohibition and above all, ʿImrān's reports on precisely what the Prophet is supposed to have declared lawful) would have made it clear that the matter is considerably more complicated than he imagined. For the debates concerned not one *mutʿa*, but two! The exegeses of two circumstantially unrelated Ḳur'ān rulings, that of Ḳ.4:24 and that of Ḳ.2:196 had become hopelessly entangled one in the other, so that what the Prophet is envisaged as having allowed is wholly unconnected with what he is supposed to have declared quite forbidden. Nor have the Shīʿa fared any better, for that which ʿAlī is supposed to have regarded as quite unexceptionable (since the Prophet had done it!) is quite different from that which ʿAlī denounced in ibn ʿAbbās' supposed legal doctrine. The details of the relevant arguments on one side and the other will become intelligible only if it is fully appreciated that one regulation affecting the Ḥadjdj was confounded with a second regulation affecting marriage law at a very early stage in the Islamic working out of the implications of the Ḳur'ān verses.[8] Nothing in all the discussions is 'historical', for the very good reason that we are here in the realm of literary interpretation, i.e. pure exegesis. The discussions were thus entirely academic and therefore quite without connection with what Muslims outside the schoolroom were doing in their ordinary routine daily lives. As Shāfiʿī insisted, (although not quite in the sense I now mean here) the 'practice' is meaningless. Schacht perceived that the discussions of the *fuḳahā'* involved an ideal, as well as an actual element. Mālik's standard *al-ʿamal ʿindanā* is as likely to mean 'what we think', as it is to mean 'what we do.' For that, he could have said *ʿamalunā*.

NOTES AND REFERENCES

Foreword

[1] 1, 275.
[2] 2, 232 (Ḳ.4:11; Ḳ.2:180).
[3] 2, 118 (see below, Ḳ.4:23).
[4] G.E. von Grünebaum, *Islam*, London, 1955, 85.
[5] al-Shāfi'ī vigorously denied the very possibility; see further p. 000.
[6] R.Bell, *Introduction to the Qur'ān*, Edinburgh, 1954, 99–100.

Introduction

[1] Ḳ.42:5.
[2] Ḳ.40:7.
[3] Ḳ.2:62.
[4] Ḳ.3:85; see Hibatullāh, 32.
[5] Ḳ.2, 159–60; see Hibatullāh, 37.
[6] Hibatullāh, 46.
[7] ibid. 26–7.
[8] Hibatullāh, 27–8.
[9] Hibatullāh, 26–7.
[10] See v.2 of *Muslim Studies, passim.*
[11] Here cited from Sarakhsī, *Uṣūl*, 2, 77.
[12] Hibatullāh, 33.
[13] Sarakhsī, *Uṣūl*, 2, 68.
[14] ibn Ḳutayba, *Ta'wīl Mukhtalif al-Ḥadīth*, 195.
[15] Ḳ.2:106.
[16] ibn Ḳutayba, 196.
[17] Rāzī, *Tafsīr*, ad. Ḳ.2:106.
[18] *Pace* Richard Bell.
[19] *Risāla*, 17.
[20] Ḳ.4:23, cf. my 'Interpretation of Q.4:23 . . .' *Occasional Papers*, School of 'Abbāsid Studies 1, 1986, 40–54.
[21] See Muw. 2, 118 for Mālik's curt dismissal of this 'Ā'isha ḥadīth; (cf. *supra*, p. 3).
[22] Hibatullāh, 21–2, *āyat al-radjm*, the so-called 'stoning-verse'.

Chapter One

[1] *Risāla*, 3.
[2] *Umm*, 7, 246.
[3] Ḳ.2:189; 215; 219; 220; 222. Ḳ.4:127; 176. Ḳ.5:101. Ḳ.7:187. Ḳ.8:1.
[4] *Risāla*, 57.
[5] *Risāla*, 4. Shāfi'ī insists that the Ḳur'ān imposes the religious duty of adherence to the *Sunna*.
[6] Ḳ.48:10, note the use of the term *bay'a*.
[7] *Umm*, 7, 246.
[8] *Mustaṣfā*, 1, 100.
[9] Abū Zahra, *Uṣūl*, 70.
[10] *Umm*, 7, 240.
[11] *Origins*, 62–3 and *passim.*
[12] ibid. 79.
[13] *Umm*, 7, 246.
[14] *Ikhtilāf*, 19.
[15] *Umm*, 1, 110.
[16] Abū Zahra, op. cit. 13–14.
[17] *Origins*, 68.
[18] ibid. 80.
[19] *Risāla*, 50.

Chapter Two

[1] cf. *Hebrews* 8:13; 10:9.
[2] *Muḥallā*, 11, 230.
[3] *Risāla*, 19.
[4] *Ikhtilāf*, 253.
[5] Sarakhsī, *Uṣūl*, 2, 12.
[6] *Ma'rifat al-nāsikh wa-'l-mansūkh*, 2, 149 (cf. *I'tibār*, 4).
[7] *Rusūkh al-ikhbār*, f.4. cf. *BSOAS*, XLVII, pt.1, 1984, 22–43.
[8] *Ṣafwat al-Rāsikh, shurūṭ.*

[9]GdQ 1, 234–56; Bell, *Introduction*, 99–100; Blachère, *Introduction*, 17.
[10]*Risāla*, 16.
[11]ibn Mādja, 1, 10.
[12]*I'tibār*, 24.
[13]*Origins*, 80.
[14]Abū 'Abdullāh, 151.
[15]ibn Mādja, 1, 9.
[16]ibid. 13.
[17]*I'tibār*, 24.
[18]Ṭayālisī, *Musnad*, no. 618.
[19]cf. *Risāla*, 37.
[20]cf. *Risāla*, 5; *Umm*, 7, 271.
[21]Makkī, *Īḍāḥ*, f.10a.
[22]Baghdādī, ff.1–2.
[23]Sarakhsī, *Uṣūl*, 2, 20. (cf. *al-Manār*, 1912, 172.)
[24]*Itḳān*, 2, 24.
[25]*I'tibār*, 7; Dja'barī, f.5.
[26]*Umm*, 1, 108 ff.
[27]*Itḳān*, 1, 8.
[28]Sarakhsī, *Uṣūl*, 2, 20.
[29]*Risāla*, 20. The *ḥadīth*'s 'subsequently' refers to nothing more substantial than the fact that v.66 occurs *later* on the page than v.65.
[30]*Iḥkām*, 4, 462.
[31]*Risāla*, 36.
[32]*Muwaṭṭa'*, 1, 115.
[33]*Umm*, 7, 185.
[34]*Risāla*, 17.
[35]*Umm*, 1, 109.
[36]*Mustaṣfā*, 1, 110.
[37]*Risāla*, 13.
[38]*al-Manār*, 1912, 150ff.

Chapter Three

[1]*Risāla*, 16–8.
[2]*Risāla*, 20.
[3]His *nāsikh wa – 'l-mansūkh*, p. 6–7.
[4]*Risāla*, 17.
[5]ibid. 16.
[6]*Risāla*, 36–7 which shows, however, one case that has not been satisfactorily cleared up.
[7]*Mafātīḥ al-wuṣūl*, MS. Alex., B 1031, *bāb al-naskh*.
[8]op. cit. 151.
[9]His *nāsikh wa mansūkh*, pp. 4–5.
[10]ibidem.
[11]op. cit. 5ff.
[12]cf. Naḥḥās, op. cit. 6 with Hibatullāh, op. cit. 7.
[13]Bukhārī, *Ṣaḥīḥ*, 6, 19.
[14]*Fatḥ*, 10, 429. Cf. al-Dānī, *Muḳni'*, 128.
[15]*Collection*, 80–1.
[16]op. cit. 6.
[17]Abū 'Abdullāh, 150.
[18]P. 6.
[19]P. 7.
[20]P. 8.
[21]Baghdādī, f.1.
[22]*I'tibār*, 23.
[23]op. cit. f.4.
[24]*Risāla*, 17.
[25]cf. ibn Ḳutayba, *Ta'wīl mukhtalif al-Ḥadīth*, *passim*.
[26]Hibatullāh, 9; Abū 'Abdullāh, 155.
[27]*al-Manār*, loc. cit. 151.
[28]Naḥḥās, 9; Muṣṭafā Zayd, *al-Naskh fī 'l-Ḳur'ān al-Karīm*, 1, 284–5.

Chapter Four

[1]Naḥḥās, 9; *Umm*, 7, 251.
[2]cf. my 'The Interpretation of Q.87, 6–7', *Der Islam*, 62, 1, 1985, 5–19.
[3]See previous note.
[4]Hibatullāh, 11.
[5]Bukhārī, 6, 193.
[6]Ḳ.42:30.
[7]*Risāla*, 15.
[8]F.B. 10, 461. ibn Ḥadjar here is already engaging in re-interpretation of the *ḥadīth* in which the Prophet said, 'It is wrong to say that I have forgotten verse so-and-so.' Bukhārī, loc. cit. 194.
[9]*Ma'ānī*, 3, 256; *Irshād*, 9, 289.
[10]*Muwaṭṭa'*, 1, 121.
[11]See in the *Fiḳh* and *Ḥadīth* works under the heading: *sahū*.
[12]*Irshād*, 9, 289.
[13]*Ṣaḥīḥ*, loc. cit.
[14]F.B. 10, 462.
[15]*Mudawwana*, 1, 107, using for 'omitted' the root *asḳaṭ*.

[16] *al-Djawāhir al-Ḥisān*, ad. Ḳ.2:106.
[17] *Irshād*, loc. cit.
[18] *Ma'ānī*, 1, 64–5.
[19] *Itḳān*, 2, 26.
[20] Hibatullāh, 10–11.
[21] *Itḳān*, 2, 26.
[22] ibid. 25.
[23] ibid. 25.
[24] ibid. 25.
[25] ibid. 25.
[26] ibid. 25.
[27] ibid. 25.
[28] MS Dār al-Kutub, Taymūr, *Madjāmī'* 207. cf. *Muḳni'*, 128.
[29] GdQ³, 92 (on *Kanz* 4827).
[30] 8, 93.
[31] *Itḳān*, 2, 25.
[32] ibid. 25.
[33] ibid. 25.
[34] ibid. 25–6.
[35] ibid. 26.
[36] ibid. 26.
[37] *Collection*, 221.
[38] op. cit. f.2.
[39] *Itḳān*, 2, 25.
[40] Jeffery, (*MW*. 28, 1938, 64) read: *ḳīla* – 'it is said that . . .'
[41] *Itḳān*, loc. cit.
[42] *Collection*, 97.
[43] *Ta'wīl Mukhtalif al-Ḥadīth*, 310.
[44] FB. 10, 441.
[45] *Itḳān*, 161.
[46] FB. 10, 386.

Chapter Five

[1] *I'tibār*, 5–6.
[2] Naḥḥās, op. cit. 74.
[3] ibid. 75.
[4] *Itḳān*, 1, 60.
[5] Naḥḥās, op. cit. 74–5.
[6] ibn al-'Arabī, *Aḥkām*, 1, 207.
[7] *Tafsīr*, 5, 261.
[8] op. cit. 76.
[9] op. cit. 1, 208.
[10] loc. cit.
[11] op. cit. 77.
[12] *Umm*, 1, 212.
[13] op. cit. ff.87bff.
[14] loc. cit. 81ff.
[15] loc. cit. 213.
[16] ibid. 214.
[17] Naḥḥās, 77.
[18] loc. cit. 207.
[19] Naḥḥās, 75.
[20] ibn al-'Arabī, loc. cit. 208.
[21] *Mabsūṭ*, 6, 31.
[22] Naḥḥās, 75 [*lā'antu*]. (*Mabsūṭ*, 6, 31 [*bāhaltu*].)
[23] cf. Ḳ.2:235.
[24] *Tafsīr ibn Kathīr*, 1, 284.
[25] loc. cit. 208.
[26] *Mabsūṭ*, 6, 31ff. [cf. Ḳ.33:49; Ḳ.65:4.]
[27] loc. cit. 30.
[28] loc. cit. 78.
[29] loc. cit. 32.
[30] Ḳ.65:1 – but see my 'The Vowelling of Q.65:1', *JSS* XXIX, 2, 267–83.
[31] loc. cit. 209.
[32] loc. cit. 36.
[33] Naḥḥās, op. cit. 78.
[34] loc. cit. 36.
[35] Ṭabarī, loc. cit. 86.
[36] Naḥḥās, 78.
[37] *Mukhtaṣar*, 220.
[38] Loc. cit. 32.
[39] *Umm*, 5, 217.
[40] Loc. cit.
[41] Loc. cit.
[42] loc. cit. 79.
[43] *Umm*, 5, 209.
[44] 76, 78.
[45] 32.
[46] Ṭabarī, 5, 255.
[47] Naḥḥās, 75.
[48] f.87a.
[49] Ṭab. 5, 254.
[50] 74.
[51] *Umm*, 4, 28.
[52] Ṭab. loc. cit. 254.
[53] ibid. 256.
[54] Ṭab. 5, 261.
[55] Djaṣṣāṣ, *Aḥkām*, 1, 498.
[56] *Umm*, 4, 28.
[57] supra, p. 26.
[58] 2, 232
[59] *Risāla*, 21–2; *Umm*, 4, 27ff.
[60] *Uṣūl*, 2, 70ff.

[61] *Sīra*, 2, 661.
[62] *Umm*, 5, 205.
[63] *Umm*, 5, 205.
[64] *Mukhtaṣar al-Muzanī*, 5, 31.
[65] Naḥḥās, 79.
[66] Ṭab. 5, 251–2.
[67] The *tafsīr*, it should be noted, not of the Ḳur'ān verses, but of the *ḥadīth*: *lā waṣiyya li-wārith*.
[68] *Ṭabarī*, 2, 535.
[69] Ḳ.4:11–12.
[70] op. cit. *bāb al-waṣiyya*.
[71] *Uṣūl*, 2, 70. But it also occurs in the *Sīra*, cf. note 61.

Chapter Six

[1] cf. Sarakhsī, *Uṣūl*, 2, 54.
[2] cf. Ḳ.2:106; Ḳ.22:52, and *Itḳān*, 2, 20.
[3] Jeffery, *Materials*, 233.
[4] Ibid. 27.
[5] Below, p. 109.
[6] Below, p. 109.
[7] Jeffery, 246; below, p. 109.
[8] ibid. 276; 285; 119.
[9] Ṭabarī, 2, 487.
[10] ibn Khālawaih, *Mukhtaṣar*, 9.
[11] Jeffery, 185; (cf. 119).
[12] *Baḥr*, 1, 343.
[13] Abū ʿUbaida, *Madjāz*, 1, 49.
[14] Ubayy is said to have read: *mā nansakh min āya aw nunsi-ka*, Ṭabarsī, *Madjmaʿ al-Bayān*, 1, 181. The Abū Ḥudhayfa 'reading' is attributed to his *mawlā*, Sālim, ibid.
[15] Fazlur Rahman, *Islam*, 41.
[16] cf. Ḳ.16:101: *idhā baddalnā āya makāna āya . . .*
[17] 2, 478.
[18] i.e. *naskh al-ḥukm dūna 'l-tilāwa*.
[19] cf. Ḳ.13:39.
[20] cf. Ḳ.87:6–7.
[21] a paraphrase of the exegesis of Ḳ.87.
[22] Thaʿlabī, *al-Djawāhir*, 1, 95.
[23] Baghdādī, op. cit. Intro.
[24] Makkī, op. cit. f.1.
[25] loc. cit.
[26] Ṭūsī, *Tibyān*, 1, 393. cf. Farrā' *Maʿānī*, 1, 64.
[27] M. Zayd, op. cit. 1, 55.
[28] *Risāla*, 16–7 [cf. Ḳ.13:39].
[29] ibid. 17. [cf. Ḳ.13:39].
[30] ibid. 18.
[31] Sarakhsī, *Uṣūl*, 2, 69.
[32] *Itḳān*, 2, 23.
[33] *Risāla*, 20.
[34] op. cit. 151–2; cf. *Iʿtibār*, 5–6.
[35] *Tafsīr*, 8, 80.
[36] *Tafsīr*, 1, 63–4.
[37] *Umm*, 5, 23ff.
[38] e.g. Djaṣṣāṣ, op. cit. 1, 67.
[39] *Tafsīr*, ad. Ḳ.2:106.
[40] GdQ, 1, 60–1, *Itḳān*, 1, 9–11; 15, 26.
[41] M. Zayd, op. cit. 1, 242.
[42] loc. cit. 479; cf. *Collection*, 46–9; 64–5.
[43] loc. cit.
[44] Makkī, op. cit. *bāb*: 'Textual evidence' for *naskh* of the Ḳur'ān. (f.6a.)
[45] *Tafsīr*, Būlāḳ, 1954, 17, 185ff.
[46] *Risāla*, 20.
[47] al-Nīsāpūrī, pr. on margin of Ṭabarī, Būlāḳ 1954, ad. loc.
[48] loc. cit. 474.
[49] loc. cit.
[50] cf. Ṭab. 2, 477.
[51] 478.
[52] *Risāla*, 17.
[53] Ṭab. 2, 479.
[54] 478.
[55] 480.
[56] *Mustaṣfā*, 1, 123–4.
[57] Ṭab. 2, 482–3.
[58] *Mustaṣfā*, 1, 125.
[59] ibidem.
[60] *Kashshāf*, 1, 232.
[61] *Tafsīr*, Būlāḳ ed. 17–21, p. 131.
[62] *Tafsīr al-Ḳāḍī*, Cairo, 1305/1887, 1, 22.
[63] ibidem.
[64] Ḳurṭubī, *Djāmiʿ*, 2, 67.
[65] ibid. 62.
[66] 2, 62.
[67] 2, 479.

[68] This expression seems to be tautological, but see further p. 117.
[69] 2, 482–3.
[70] 3, 417.
[71] loc. cit.
[72] loc. cit. 396–7.
[73] e.g. 2, 216.
[74] Bu. 6, 193, cf. supra, p. 46–47.
[75] loc. cit. 68.
[76] Ḳurṭubī, loc. cit. 68.
[77] *Richtungen*, 24–5.
[78] *Itḳān*, 2, 188. cf. Naḥḥās, op. cit. 15.
[79] 2, 68.
[80] 3, 227.
[81] *Aḥkām*, 1, 67. cf. supra, p. 115, top.
[82] *Madjma'*, 1, 181.

Chapter Seven

[1] 8, 73ff.
[2] Ṭab. 8, 74.
[3] See further, p. 136.
[4] Ṭab. 8, 74; cf. p. 82: *al-radjulāni al-fā'ilāni*.
[5] 76, but cf. note 4.
[6] 83.
[7] loc. cit. 106.
[8] *Multaḳat Djāmi' al-Ta'wīl*, Calcutta, 1340/1921, 44.
[9] 84.
[10] 86.
[11] 80.
[12] Muw. 3, 41; *Risāla*, 20–1.
[13] Here, 'in the matter of stoning.' cf. Ṭabarī, 10, 328: 'in the matter of fornicators.'
[14] A very primitive *tafsīr* of *kitmān*, the standard Ḳur'ānic charge against the Jews.
[15] Ṭabarī, 10, 329–30.
[16] ibid.
[17] 330 ft.
[18] 332.
[19] 334.
[20] 328.
[21] 336.
[22] 337.
[23] 337.
[24] 319.
[25] 351.
[26] 338.
[27] 303.
[28] 304.
[29] *Sīra*, 2, 393ff.
[30] 306; 340
[31] 345–6; 341; 342; 343: *kitāb allāh alladhī huwa 'l-Tōra*.
[32] 312.
[33] 312; 306.
[34] 352.
[35] 327–8.
[36] 329.
[37] 330; 335.
[38] 329.
[39] 340.
[40] 303; 305; 338–9.
[41] 325.
[42] 310.
[43] 328.
[44] 3, 42.
[45] Baiyhaḳī, *al-Sunan al-Kubrā*, 8, 212ff.
[46] Tirmidhī, *Sunan*, 6, 204. cf. *Mabsūṭ*, 9, 36: part of the Ḳur'ān.
[47] loc. cit.
[48] ibidem.
[49] F.B. 15, 160.
[50] ibid. 130.
[51] Muslim, *Ṣaḥīḥ*, 2, 55.
[52] F.B. 15, 181.
[53] ibid. 150.
[54] *Minhādj al-wuṣūl, naskh.*
[55] This suggests that the wording attributed to the Prophet may have been extended. cf. p. 128.
[56] *Ikhtilāf al-Ḥadīth*, 251; cf. F.B. 15, 150–2.
[57] *Risāla*, 20–21.
[58] cf. *supra*, p. 127, middle.
[59] Nor, as the Mālikīs point out, did he say, 'Banish her.' ibn al-'Arabī, *Aḥkām*, 1, 359.
[60] *Risāla*, 17, 32 and *passim.*
[61] *Risāla*, 10.
[62] *Risāla*, 10.
[63] i.e. Shāfi'ī insisted on reading 'feet' in Ḳ.5:6 in the Accusative, cf. *Ikhtilāf*, p. 204. Others read the word in the genitive, indicating

that it is co-ordinate with 'heads' which the verse requires to be wiped.

[64] *Risāla*, 13.
[65] Ḳ.4:171.
[66] Ḳ.24:62.
[67] Ḳ.2:129; Ḳ.3:164; Ḳ.2:151; Ḳ.2:231; Ḳ.4:113; Ḳ.33:34.
[68] *Risāla*, 13–14.
[69] *Risāla*, 15.
[70] Ḳ.42:52–3.
[71] *Risāla*, 15.
[72] *Risāla*, 16.
[73] *Origins*, 16.
[74] *Risāla*, 17.
[75] *Risāla*, 21: *nusikha*.
[76] *nusikha*, *Risāla*, 36.
[77] *Umm*, 7, 76.
[78] *Risāla*, 36.
[79] *Risāla*, 21.
[80] ibid. cf. *Umm*, 6, 119.
[81] *Umm*, 7, 167.
[82] cf. *Ikhtilāf*, 251.
[83] loc. cit. 43.
[84] *Origins*, 15.
[85] Muslim, 2, 48.
[86] *Umm*, 7, 271.
[87] F.B. 15, 190.
[88] *Umm*, 6, 124ff.
[89] Ṭabari, 8, 73, arrived at by making *minkum* mean 'of the Muslims'.
[90] *Ta'wīl Mukhtalif al-Ḥadīth*, *passim*.
[91] *Umm*, 7, 251.
[92] Makkī, op. cit. *bāb*: What can be *nāsikh*.
[93] *Mabsūṭ*, 9, 36.
[94] *Risāla*, 36.
[95] ibn al-ʿArabī, op. cit. 1, 359: *taraka [turika] al-djild fi'lan fī kulli man radjam [rudjim] wa ḳawlan fī ḥadīth al – ʿasīf*.
[96] *Ikhtilāf*, 251.
[97] Except on the one question of the battle prayer. *Risāla*, 36.
[98] *Umm*, 6, 124; cf. *Umm*, 4, 130; cf. Ṭabarī, 10, 333–4.
[99] i.e. Ḳ.5:49 did not *naskh* Ḳ.5:42, as is commonly alleged by the exegetes.
[100] i.e. the *Fiḳh* is, indeed, a primary source.
[101] *Umm*, 4, 129.
[102] *Umm*, 4, 129.
[103] cf. my: 'The meaning of *iḥṣān*', *J.S.S.* 19, no. 1, 1974.
[104] Ṭabarī, 10, 303.
[105] *Mabsūṭ*, 9, 39 – because they were *dhimmīs*!
[106] Ṭabarī, loc. cit. 304.
[107] Ṭabarī, 10, 306.
[108] F.B. 15, 185–6.
[109] G. Vajda, *Journal Asiatique*, 229, (1937) 58ff.
[110] F.B. 15, 187.
[111] ibn al-ʿArabī, op. cit. 1, 361.
[112] *Umm*, 5, 23ff.
[113] Mālik rejected the implications of this report, Muw. 2, 118.
[114] *Umm*, 5, 24.
[115] *Umm*, 7, 208.
[116] *Collection*, 88–9. cf. Muw. 2, 118.
[117] Baghdādī, op. cit. Intro.
[118] ibn al-Djawzī, *Nawāsikh al-Ḳur'ān*, MS. Ahmet III, 192, f67. cf. Naḥḥās, pp. 11–12.
[119] *K. al-Tawḍīḥ*, Kazan, 1884, 416ff.
[120] *Risāla*, 32.
[121] op. cit. 313ff.
[122] Muw. 2, 118.
[123] i.e. than Muḥammad b. Isḥāḳ.
[124] op. cit. 4.
[125] ibid. p. 9.
[126] ibid. 11–12.

Chapter Eight

[1] Ḳ.2:124.
[2] Ḳ.3:50.
[3] Ḳ.5:48.
[4] Ḳ.3:93.
[5] Ḳ.3:65.
[6] Ḳ.42:13.
[7] Ḳ.3:67.
[8] Ḳ.28:43.
[9] Ḳ.3:23.
[10] Ḳ.7:34.
[11] Ḳ.13:38.
[12] Ḳ.45:16.
[13] Ḳ.2:105.
[14] Ḳ.47:29.
[15] Ḳ.59:6.
[16] Ḳ.3:26.
[17] Ḳ.3:23.

[18] Ḳ.2:40.
[19] Ḳ.2:42; Ḳ.3:71.
[20] Ḳ.3:187.
[21] Ḳ.3:81.
[22] Ḳ.5:15.
[23] Ḳ.2:134.
[24] Ḳ.2:141.
[25] Ḳ.48:29.
[26] Ḳ.7:157.
[27] Ḳ.2:91.
[28] Ḳ.61:6.
[29] Ḳ.62:5.
[30] Ḳ.4:153.
[31] Ḳ.2:91.
[32] Ḳ.2:136.
[33] Ḳ.3:19.
[34] Ḳ.3:85.
[35] Ḳ.4:163.
[36] Ḳ.4:166.
[37] Ḳ.6:124.
[38] Ḳ.63:1.
[39] Ḳ.48:8–10.
[40] Ḳ.24:62–3.
[41] Ḳ.33:36.
[42] N.J. Coulson, *A History of Islamic Law*, 12.
[43] Ḳ.2:142.
[44] Ṭabarī, 3, 172.
[45] ibid. 2, 527.
[46] ibid. 529.
[47] ibid. 530.
[48] ibid. 531.
[49] ibid. 532.
[50] Ḳurṭ, 2, 80.
[51] Ṭab. 2, 532.
[52] Naḥḥās, 15.
[53] Ṭab. 2, 534.
[54] Naḥḥās, 15.
[55] Ḳurṭ, 2, 79–83.
[56] op. cit. f.22a.
[57] Makkī, f.22a.
[58] Ḳurṭ. 80.
[59] Rāzī, 4, 18.
[60] ibid. 20.
[61] ibid. 21.
[62] Ḳurṭ. 2, 83.
[63] Ṭab. 2, 533–5.
[64] Rāzī, 4, 19.
[65] Ṭab. loc. cit. 529.
[66] Naḥḥās, 14.
[67] Ḳurṭ. 1, 66; Makkī, f.22a; Naḥḥās, 14–15.
[68] Naḥḥās, 15; Makkī, 21b.
[69] Naḥḥās, 15; Makkī, 22a.
[70] Makkī, 21b.
[71] *Risāla*, 31.
[72] Rāzī, 4, 227; Ḳurṭ. 2, 63. Instances of *naskh* within the OT were also listed here.
[73] Ḳurṭ. 2, 61.
[74] Rāzī, 4, 229.

Chapter Nine

[1] *Itḳān*, 2, 22–3.
[2] al-Djabrī, *al-Naskh*, 71.
[3] 46.
[4] *Itḳān*, 2, 23.
[5] Mus. Zayd, op. cit. 2, 805–38.
[6] or less than? *adnā* – cf. Bayḍāwī, ad. loc.
[7] *amsaka* – cf. *ta'khīr al-inzāl*. The *ḥadīth* has been affected by *naskh* theorising.
[8] Mus. 1, 299. cf. Naḥḥās, 250–1.
[9] 2, 52.
[10] 96.
[11] *Risāla*, 18–9.
[12] *Ṣaḥīḥ*, loc. cit. and ibn al-ʿArabi, *Aḥkām*, 4, 1869–70.
[13] Ṭabarī, *Tafsīr*, 29, 88–9.
[14] Rāzī, *Tafsīr*, 3, 229–30.
[15] Hibatullāh, 90; Naḥḥās, 231.
[16] ibn al-ʿArabī, loc. cit. 1750.
[17] M. Zayd, op. cit. 1, 242.
[18] cf. *Itḳān*, 1, 36.
[19] Ḳ.13:36.
[20] Ḳ.21:5; Ḳ.23:38; Ḳ.25:4.
[21] Ḳ.16:102.
[22] Ḳ.10:37.
[23] Ḳ.6:91.
[24] Ḳ.6:92–3.
[25] Ḳ.11:28.
[26] Ḳ.11:35.
[27] Ḳ.42:24; cf. Ḳ.22:52.
[28] Ḳ.7:89.
[29] Ḳ.5:15.
[30] Ḳ.2:140.
[31] Ḳ.2:146; 159; 174.
[32] Ḳ.2:40–2; Ḳ.3:71.

33 Ḳ.3:187.
34 *Umm*, 6, 128.
35 Ḳ.2:75.
36 Ḳ.4:46.
37 Ḳ.5:13.
38 Ḳ.48:15.
39 Ṭabarī, op. cit. 2, 246.
40 ibid. 247.
41 loc. cit. 8, 432.
42 ibid. 10, 313.
43 Fazlur Rahman, *Islam*, 50.
44 Ṭabarī, 10, 336.
45 cf. ibn al-ʿArabī, op. cit. 1, 24.
46 Ḳ.3:158.
47 Ḳ.2:185.
48 *Mustaṣfā*, loc. cit. 124; *Collection*, 58–9.
49 Kurṭubī, 2, 66.
50 cf. GdQ^1 1, 43; GdQ^2 1, 54.
51 Taftazānī, loc. cit.; cf. *Itḳān*, *nawʿ* 47, (2, 20ff.).
52 *Uṣūl*, 2, 54.
53 *Risāla*, 17.
54 *Umm*, 5, 23; 7, 208.
55 *Tafsīr*, 2, 479.
56 ibid. 472.
57 14, 140.
58 *Mustaṣfā*, 1, 107ff.
59 *Tafsīr*, ad Ḳ 2, 106; *al-Maḥṣūl*, *bāb: al-kalām fi-l-naskh.*
60 *Iḥkām*, 2, 236ff.
61 *Mafātīḥ al-wuṣūl*, ḥadd al-naskh.

60 *Iḥkām*, 2, 236ff.
61 *Mafātīḥ al-wuṣūl*, ḥadd al-naskh.
62 ibid.
63 Āmidī, loc. cit. 260–1.
64 *Itḳān*, 2, 27.
65 *Minhādj al-wuṣūl*, f.48.
66 *Mustaṣfā*, loc. cit. 119.
67 *Mafātīḥ al-wuṣūl*, loc. cit.
68 *The Foreign Vocabulary of the Qur'ān*, 279.
69 Rāzī, ad. Ḳ.2:106 and *passim*.
70 *Tafsīr al-Manār*, ad. Ḳ.2:106.

Postscript

1 Origins, 224.
2 ibid.
3 loc. cit.
4 *Origins*, 226–7.
5 Derived by *tafsīr* from: *mā tarāḍay-tum bihi*, isolated from its context which concerns the *mahr*.
6 Prohibition of *mutʿah* is *universal* among *Sunnīs*.
7 This Ḳur'ānic *nāsikh* is never specified.
8 See my '*Mutʿa*, *tamattuʿ* and *istimtāʿ* – a confusion of *tafsīrs*', *Proceedings*, *Union Européenne des Arabisants et Islamisants*, 10th Congress, Edinburgh, 1980, 1–11.

BIBLIOGRAPHY

ʿAbduh, Muḥammad, *Tafsīr al-manār*, 12 vols., Cairo, 1912–48.

Abū ʿAbdullāh, Muḥammad, *K. fī maʿrifat al-nāsikh wa-'l-mansūkh*, pr. on margin of *Tafsīr al-Djalālayn*, Cairo, 1342/1924.

al-Āmidī, abū 'l-Ḥasan, Sayf al-Dīn, *K. al-Iḥkām fī uṣūl al-Aḥkām*, 4 vols., Cairo, 1331/1913.

al-Anṣārī, Saʿīd *Multaḳat Djāmiʿ al-Ta'wīl*, Calcutta, 1340/1921.

ibn al-ʿArabī, Abū Bakr, Muḥammad b. ʿAbdullāh, *Aḥkām al-Ḳur'ān*, 4 vols., Cairo, 1376/1957.

al-ʿAsḳalānī, ibn Ḥadjar, Aḥmad b. ʿAlī, *Fatḥ al-Bārī*, 16 vols., Cairo, 1378/1959.

al-Baghdādī, Abū Manṣūr, 'Abd al-Ḳāhir b. Ṭāhir, *al-Nāsikh wa-'l-mansūkh*, MS., Berlin, Pet. 555.

al-Bayḍāwī, ʿAbdullāh b. ʿUmar, *Anwār al-Tanzīl*, Cairo, 1305/1887.

Minhādj al-wuṣūl ilā ʿilm al-uṣūl, MS., Istanbul, Bayazit, 1019.

al-Bayhaḳī, Aḥmad b. al-Ḥusain, *al-Sunan al-Kubrā*, 10 vols., Haiderabad, 1344–57/1925–38.

al-Bādjī, Burhān al-Dīn, *Djawāb*, MS, Dār al-Kutub, Taymūr, 207.

Bell, Richard, *Introduction to the Qur'ān*, Edinburgh, 1954.

Blachère, Régis, *Introduction au Coran*, Paris, 1947.

al-Bukhārī, Muḥammad b. Ismāʿīl, *al-Ṣaḥīḥ*, 9 pts., in 3, Cairo, 1314/1896.

Burton, John, 'Those are the high-flying cranes', *Journal of Semitic Studies*, XV, 1970, pp. 246–65.

'The meaning of *iḥṣān*', *JSS.*, XIX, 1974, pp. 47–75.

The Collection of the Qur'ān, Cambridge University Press, 1977.

'The origin of the Islamic penalty for adultery', *Trans. Glasgow University Oriental Society*, 26, 1978, pp. 16–26.

'The vowelling of Q. 65,1' *JSS.*, XXIX, 1984, pp. 267–83.

'The interpretation of Q 87, 6–7', *Der Islam*, 62, 1, 1985, pp. 5–19.

'The exegesis of Q 2,106', *Bulletin, S.O.A.S.*, XLVIII, 3, 1985, pp. 452–69.

Coulson, N. J., *A History of Islamic Law*, Edinburgh, 1964.

al-Dānī, Abū ʿAmr, ʿUthmān b. Saʿīd, *al-Muḳniʿ fī rasm maṣāḥif al-amṣār*, ed. O. Pretzl, Istanbul, 1932.

al-Dāraḳuṭnī, ʿAlī b. ʿUmar, *Sunan*, 4 vols., in 2, Madīna, 1386/1966.

al-Dārimī, Abū Muḥammad, ʿAbdullāh b. ʿAbdul Raḥmān, *Sunan*, Cairo, 1386/1966.

ibn Abī Da'ūd, Abū Bakr, ʿAbdullāh, *K. al-Maṣāḥif*, ed. A. Jeffery, Cairo, 1355/1936.

al-Farrā', Abū Zakariyā, Yaḥyā b. Ziyād, *Maʿānī al-Ḳur'ān*, 3 vols., Beirut, 1955, 1980.

Al-Ghazālī, Abū Ḥāmid, Muḥammad b. Muḥammad, *al-Mustaṣfā*, 2 vols., Cairo, 1322/1904.

Goldziher, I, *Die Richtungen der Islamischen Koranauslegung*, Leiden, 1952.

Muslim Studies, 2 vols., London, 1967–71.

von Grünebaum, G. E., *Islam*, London, 1955.

al-Hamadhānī, Abū Bakr, Muḥammad b. Mūsā, al-Ḥāzimī, *K. al-I'tibār fī 'l-nāsikh wa-'l-mansūkh min al-āthār*, Haiderabad, 1319/1901.

ibn Ḥaiyān, Abū 'Abdullāh, Muḥammad b. Yūsuf, *al-Baḥr al-muḥīṭ*, 8 vols., Riyāḍ, 1969.

ibn Ḥazm, Abū Muḥammad, 'Alī b. Sa'īd, *al-Iḥkām fī uṣūl al-Aḥkām*, 8 vols., in 4, Cairo, 1345/1926.

al-Muḥallā, 12 vols., Cairo, 1352/1933.

Hibatullāh, Abū *'l-Ḳāsim, ibn Sallāma, al-Nāsikh wa-'l-mansūkh*, Cairo, 1379/1960; Beirut, 1404/1984.

ibn Hishām, Abū Muḥammad, 'Abdul Malik, *al-Sīra*, 2 vols., Cairo, 1375/1955.

al-Djabrī, 'Abdul Muta'āl, Muḥammad, *al-Naskh fī-'l-sharī'a 'l-islāmiyya*, Cairo, n.d.

al-Djaṣṣāṣ, Abū Bakr, Aḥmad b. 'Alī, *Aḥkām al-Ḳur'ān*, 4 vols., Cairo, 1938.

al-Dja'barī, Burhān al-Dīn, Ibrāhīm b. 'Umar, *Rusūkh al-aḥbār fī-'l-nāsikh wa-'l-mansūkh min al-akhbār*, MS., Taymūr, *Ḥadīth* 153.

ibn al-Djawzī. Abū 'l-Faradj, 'Abdul Raḥmān b. 'Alī, *Nawāsikh al-Ḳur'ān*, MS., Istanbul, Ahmet III, 192, see now, Beirut, n.d.

Jeffery, A., *The Foreign Vocabulary of the Qur'ān*, Baroda, 1938.

'Abū 'Ubaid on the verses missing from the Qur'ān', *Muslim World*, 28, 1938, pp. 61–5.

Materials for the History of the Text of the Qur'ān, see above, ibn Abī Da'ūd, *K. al-Maṣāḥif*.

ibn Kathīr, Abū 'l-Fidā', Ismā'īl al-Ḳurashī, *Tafsīr al-Ḳur'ān*, 4 vols., Cairo, n.d.

ibn Khālawaih, *Mukhtaṣar fī shawwādh al-Ḳur'ān*, Cairo, 1934.

Ma'mar b. al-Muthannā, Abū Ubayda, *Madjāz al-Ḳur'ān*, 2 vols., Cairo, 1954.

ibn Mādja, Abū 'Abdullāh, Muḥammad b. Yazīd, *Sunan*, 2 vols., Cairo, 1372/1952.

Makkī, Abū Muḥammad b. Abī Ṭālib, *al-Nāsikh wa-'l-mansūkh*, MS., Istanbul, Shahīd 'Alī, 305; see now, *Ḳ al- īḍāḥ*, ed. Aḥmad Ḥasan Farḥat, Riyāḍ, 1976.

Mālik b. Anas, *al-Muwaṭṭa'*, 3 vols., in 1, Cairo, 1303/1885.

al-Mudawwana, 16 vols., in 6, Baghdād, 1970.

The Mishnah, tr. Herbert Danby, Oxford, 1933.

Muslim, Abū 'l-Ḥusain, ibn-Ḥadjdjādj, *Ṣaḥīḥ*, 2 vols., Cairo, n.d.

al-Muzanī, Abū Ibrāhīm, Ismā'īl b. Yaḥyā, *al-Mukhtaṣar*, pr. on margin *K. al-Umm*, 1–4.

ibn al-Nadīm, *al-Fihrist*, Cairo, n.d.

al-Naḥḥās, Abū Dja'far, Muḥammad b. Aḥmad, *K. al-nāsikh wa-'l-mansūkh fī 'l-Ḳur'ān al-Karīm*, Cairo, n.d.

al-Nawawī, Yaḥyā b. Sharaf, *al-Minhādj fī Sharḥ Ṣaḥīḥ Muslim*, pr. on margin of *Irshād al-Sārī*, see al-Ḳasṭallānī, below.

al-Nīsābūrī, Niẓām al-Dīn, al-Ḥasan b. Muḥammad, *Gharā'ib al-Ḳur'ān wa Raghā'ib al-Furḳān*, pr. on margin of *Tafsīr* al-Ṭabarī, 1328/1910; 1954.

Nöldeke, T., *Geschichte des Qorāns*, Göttingen, 1860; 2nd. ed., Leipzig, 2 vols., 1909–19; vol. III, G. Bergsträsser and O. Pretzl, Hildesheim, 1961.

al-Ḳāsim, Abū 'Ubayd, ibn Sallām, *K. al-nāsikh wa-'l-mansūkh, MS.*, Istanbul, Ahmet III, 143; see now, Gibb Memorial Trust, Cambridge, 1987.

Faḍā'il al-Ḳur'ān, MS., Berlin, CDXLIX, 160; Tübingen, Ma VI 96.

al-Ḳasṭallānī, Aḥmad b.

Muḥammad, *Irshād al-Sārī*, 12 vols., Cairo, 1326/1908.
al-Ḳurṭubī, Abū ʿAbdullāh, Muḥammad b. Aḥmad, *al-Djāmiʿ li-Aḥkām al-Ḳur'ān*, 20 pts., in 10, Cairo, 1369/1950.
ibn Ḳutayba, Abū Muḥammad, ʿAbdullāh b. Muslim, *K. ta'wīl mukhtalif al-ḥadīth*, Cairo, 1386/1966.
Rahman, Fazlur, *Islam*, London, 1967.
Al-Rāzī, al-Fakhr, Muḥammad b. ʿUmar, *al-Tafsīr al-Kabīr*, 32 pts., in 16, Tehran, n.d.
Rippin, A., 'al-Zuhrī, Naskh al-Qur'ān', *B.S.O.A.S.*, XLVII, 1, 1984, pp. 22–43.
al-Sarakhsī, Abū Bakr, Muḥammad b. Aḥmad, *Uṣūl*, 2 vols., Haiderabad, 1372/1952.
al-Mabsūṭ, 30 vols., Cairo, 1324/1906.
Schacht, J., *The Origins of Muhammadan Jurisprudence*, Oxford, 1950.
Sezgin, F., *Geschichte des Arabischen Schrifttums*, Leiden, 1967.
al-Shāfiʿī, Abū ʿAbdullāh, Muḥammad b. Idrīs, *al-Risāla, al-Umm, Ikhtilāf al-Ḥadīth*, 7 vols., Būlāḳ, 1321/1903.
Shams al-Dīn, Abū Muḥammad b. Aḥmad al-Mawṣilī, *Ṣafwat al-Rāsikh fī ʿilm al-mansūkh wa-'l-nāsikh*, MS., Taymūr, Tafsīr, 225.
al-Suyūṭī, Djalāl al-Dīn, ʿAbdul Raḥmạn, *al-Itḳān fī ʿulūm al-Ḳur'ān*, 2 vols., in 1, Cairo, 1354/1935.
al-Durr al-manthūr fī tafsīr al-ma'thūr, 6 vols., Cairo, 1314/1896.
Tafsīr al-Djalālayn, Cairo, 1342/1924.
al-Ṭabarī, Abū Djaʿfar Muḥammad b. Djarīr, *Djāmiʿ al-bayān ʿan ta'wīl āy al-Ḳur'ān*, 30 pts., in 12, Cairo, 1373/1954; 30 pts., in 10, Cairo, 1903; 15 vols., Cairo, ed. Shākir, 1374/1955.
al-Ṭabarsī, Abū ʿAlī, al-Faḍl b. al-Ḥasan, *Madjmaʿ al-bayān*, 5 vols., Damascus, 1355/1927.
al-Ṭabāṭabā'ī, Muḥammad b. ʿAlī, *Mafātīḥ al-wuṣūl fī uṣūl fiḳh al-Shīʿa*, MS., Alexandria, Baladiyya, B. 1031.
al-Taftazānī, Saʿd al-Dīn, Masʿūd b. ʿUmar, *K. al-Tawḍīḥ*, Kazan, 1884.
al-Ṭaḥāwī, Abū Djaʿfar, Aḥmad b. Muḥammad, *Mukhtaṣar*, Cairo, 1370/1951.
al-Ṭayālisī, Abū Da'ūd, Sulaymān b. Da'ūd, *Sunan*, Haiderabad, 1321/1904, also called *al-Musnad*.
al-Tirmidhī, Abū ʿIsā, Muḥammad b. ʿIsā, *Sunan*, 10 vols., Cairo, 1350–3/1931–4.
al-Ṭuṣī, Abū Djaʿfar, Muḥammad b. al-Ḥasan, *al-Tibyān fī tafsīr* al-*Ḳur'ān*, 10 vols., Nadjaf, 1376/1957.
al-Thaʿlabī, ʿAbdul Raḥmān, *al-Djawāhir al-Ḥisān fī tafsīr al-Ḳur'ān*, Algiers, 1905.
Vajda, G., 'Juifs et Musulmans selon le Hadith' *Journal Asiatique*, 229, 1937, pp. 57–127.
Abū Yūsuf, Yaʿḳūb b. Ibrāhīm, *K. al-Kharādj*, Cairo, 1352/1933.
Abū Zahra, M., *Uṣūl al-Fiḳh*, Cairo, 1377/1957.
Zayd, M. *al-Naskh fī 'l-Ḳur'ān al-Karīm*, 2 vols., Cairo, 1383/1963.
Al-Zamakhsharī, Maḥmūd b. ʿUmar, *al-Kashshāf, 4 vols., Cairo, 1368/1948.*
al-Zurḳānī, ʿAbdul ʿAẓīm, Manāhil al-ʿirfān fī ʿUlūm al-Ḳur'ān, 2 vols., Cairo, 1954.

GLOSSARY

asbāb al-nuzūl the historical circumstances leading to a revelation
āya a sign of divine action; a unit of revelation, a verse
badal a substitute
bayān clarification, elucidation
bikr unmarried, virgin (opposite: *thayyib*, non-virgin)
dirham a silver coin; cf. drachm
dīnār a gold coin; cf. denarius
djizya poll-tax levied on scriptuaries in Islamic lands
djumla general, unspecific
du'ā' invocation, private prayer
fatwā an authorative statement on a point of law
fiḳh comprehension (especially of divine teaching)
faḳīh possessed of comprehension (especially of the Law)
fuḳahā' pl. of *faḳīh*, the masters of Islamic Law
ghusl complete self-purification by water in the event of major pollution
ḥadīth report, item of information, individual tradition
ḥadjdj annual pilgrimage to the Ka'ba at Makka
'idda a number (of days), hence the period that must elapse between the dissolution of one marriage and eligibility to contract a second marriage
idjmā' consensus, agreement of the expert
idjtihād the exercise of expert judgment by those qualified
i'djāz inimitability (of the Ḳur'ān's literary excellence)
'illa underlying reason
'ilm knowledge of sources, especially in religious matters
īlā' the foreswearing by the husband of conjugal relations
imām leader; also founder of a school or sect
insā' causing another to forget
isnād support, used of list of guarantors, transmitters
istikhrādj extraction of rulings from the sources
istinbāṭ do
khabar report.*khabar wāḥid* a report coming down by a single *isnād* or from a single source
Khawāridj Khārijites, adherents of an ancient, fundamentalist sect in Islam
kitmān concealment of information
ḳibla direction faced during prayer
ḳiyās analogy
Ḳur'ān the book revealed by God to Muḥammad
lugha language
matā' *donatio propter separationem*
maḳṭū' not contemporary with the event reported, literally cut off
mīrāth inheritance

mubāḥ permissible, permitted
muḥṣan eligible for the penalty of stoning
muḳayyad restricted, conditional (opposite: *muṭlaḳ*)
mursal indirectly reported, hearsay
musnad supported, showing an unbroken *isnād*
muṣḥaf a written copy of the Ḳur'ān
Mu'tazila scholars inclined to the appeal to reason in addition to reference to Tradition
mutawātir supported by multiple *isnāds*
nabiyy continuator of a revealed Tradition, (see *rasūl*)
nāfila a voluntary act of devotion, pl. *nawāfil*
nasā' postponement, deferment
rak'a a cycle of the actions constituting ritual prayer. cf. *rukū'*, literally bowing
rasūl initiator of a fresh revelation, literally one sent
ra'y view, opinion, frequently opposed to *'ilm*
rāwiyy rāwī, transmitter
riwāya transmission of texts
riḍā' breast-feeding
rukhṣa concession
ṣalāt ritual prayer performed five times each day
sudjūd one element of the action constituting the *ṣalāt*, literally bowing in submission, prostration
sunna precedent, established custom. Adjective *sunnī*
sūra one of the one hundred and fourteen main sections of the Ḳur'ān, cf. chapter
sharī'a the sacred Law of Islam. Adjective *shar'ī*
Shī'a those Muslims who proclaim that leadership in Islam was vested in Muḥammad's cousin and son-in-law, 'Alī and his descendants on the Prophet's nomination rather than in the historical caliphs acknowledged by the *Sunnī* Muslims. Adjective *Shī'ī*
tabdīl substitution (see *badal*)
tafsīr exegesis, commentary
tahadjdjud prayer by night
taḥrīf distortion of wording or pronunciation
tarabbuṣ waiting, observing
takhfīf relaxation, alleviation
takhṣīṣ specifying, declaring a thing to be specific
taḳdīr restoring the full meaning of a text by holding certain words to be 'understood'
tilāwa reciting aloud, recitation
ta'yīn specifying, naming, identifying
ṭawāf formal procession around or between
tawsi'a as *takhfīf*
'ulamā' scholars, sing. *'ālim*, see *'ilm*
uṣūl basic principles or sources of any science
uṣūlī student of *uṣūl*
waḥy divine inspiration. May be of two forms, *matlū*, intended to be recited; *ghayr matlū*, not so intended

waʿd promise
waʿīd threat
wuḍūʾ self-purification by water in the event of minor pollution
zakāt annual impost on property above set limits to be put by the state to specified charitable uses
zinā sexual impropriety

INDEX OF SUBJECTS

Alleviation, 29, 32, 57, 91–7, 113, 149, 166, 178–80, 185, 191
(also: *taisīr, takhfif*), iii
attribution (*isnād*), 13, 17, 20, 22, 25, 38, 40, 43, 68, 93, 109–10, 118, 132, 147–8, 154, 159, 210
āya, 205–6

Book of God, 9, 11, 12–16, 28, 34, 37, 86, 90–7, 100–2, 107, 127–36, 140, 144–53, 159, 187, 200–1, 207
exegesis(es) (*tafsīr*), ii, 6–11, 19, 26–30, 44–6, 49–51, 62–4, 70, 73–80, 81–8, 90–4, 105, 112, 121, 138, 148–50, 153, 171–6, 186–8, 193–8, 201–6, 208–9
atomism of, 79, 116, 193
conflict of, 30
tafsīr-ḥadīth(s), 22, 37, 55, 67, 71, 78, 92, 98, 102, 106, 128, 141, 150, 155, 200

Fiḳh, 12–14
conflict of, 20, 23, 37
documentation of, 16–18, 36, 40, 72, 84–6, 147–50
sources of,
1. Ḳur'ān, iii, 9–10, 93, 96, 100–2;
2. *sunna*, 10ff., 136, 140–4, 160, 168–9, 177–8, 184–6, 201–2.
3. *sunna* and Ḳur'ān, i, iii.
4. *sunna* of Muslims, i, 10–14.
5. *Sunna* of Prophet, 7, 14–15, 33–4, 37, 40, 46, 63, 66, 79.
6. *sunna* revealed, 4, 16, 19, 32, 35, 71, 141–5, 149–51, 159–60
aya replaces *āya*, ii, iv
conflict of sources, 2, 19, 22, 25, 30, 36–7, 41, 84, 89, 93–8, 102, 139–41, 150, 180, 186, 188, 197, 201–2, 206.
in Ḳur'ān, iv, 1, 2, 16, 25, 57ff., 180, 201
in *Sunna*, ii, 3–4, 14, 16, 40, 180
between Ḳur'ān and *sunna*, 4, 15, 22–5, 30, 34, 36, 100, 180
between *Fiḳh* and Ḳur'ān, 30, 57ff
dating of, ii, iv, 17, 19–29, 31, 36, 57–62, 67, 71–2, 74–6, 83, 98, 104, 126, 132–6, 143–4, 149–53, 172–6, 180, 185–9, 195–6
djam', (reconciliation harmonisation), 26, 35–40, 44–5, 60, 63, 79, 88–90, 94, 99, 103, 111, 117, 138–9, 146–9, 180, 196, 201
harmonising techniques
1. *'āmm*, (general), 2, 62, 100, 140–2, 175–82, 208
2. *khāṣṣ* (specific), 2, 62, 100, 137, 140–1, 175, 182, 208
3. *takhṣıṣ*, 2, 23, 32–5, 37, 137–9, 144–8, 156, 159
4. *bayān*, 2, 100, 137–41, 145–8, 151, 159, 182
5. exclusion, 136–8, 142–8
6. Ḳur'ān 'ambiguous', 71, 74, 95, 100, 138–40, 185
7. Ḳur'ān 'incomplete', 44, 49ff., 96–7
8. Ḳur'ān's *i'djāz*, 5, 93, 100–2, 113, 200

Ḳur'ān source, iii, 9–10, 93, 96, 100–2, 199
Ḳur'ān document, 93, 96, 100
forgetting of, 198, 202
1. divinely cause, iv
2. in Prophet, 44–55, 89, 92–6, 105–10, 112–16, 121–2
3. in Companion(s), 45
4. Ḳur'ānic loss(es), 43–53, 49–55, 95–6, 101, 105, 112, 116, 182
variant reading of, 66, 70, 74–8, 85–8, 94, 108–11, 114–19, 121, 139
later replaces earlier, 2, 3, 5, 20, 26, 29, 58–9
uṣūl al-Fiḳh, 12–14

Ḥadīth, Tradition, 13–15, 21–5, 37, 41, 161
ahl al-ḥadīth, 23–4, 36, 148–9, 161
conflict of, 40, 60

'idda, 56–80, 98–9, 183
'illa, (*ratio*), 187
'iṣma, 45, 48

ḳibla, 33, 81, 83, 116, 169, 171–82, 189, 193–6, 205–6
kitmān, 192
Ḳur'ān, (*muṣḥaf*), 10–11, 37–41, 43–9, 51–9, 78, 86–101, 105, 111, 115, 119, 122–3, 127, 133–4, 146–50, 155–9, 162, 197–9, 201, 204–6
ahl al-Ḳur'ān, 23–4

mahr, 209
matā', 56ff
maxim, 78
mīrāth, 57, 70–80
Mishna, 179
mithl, 24, 33
mut'a, 209

Naskh
conditions of, 19, 22
definitions of,
1. suppression, (*ibṭāl, izāla*), 41–3, 49, 57, 89, 91–101, 108, 114–16, 121, 198–200, 201–5
of wording, 88–92, 103–6, 115–6
of ruling, 94–8, 106, 112–16, 163, 185
2. abandon (*taraka*), 33, 39, 92, 98–9, 108–11, 115–19, 121, 133, 136, 150, 201–2
3. replacement (*ibdāl*), 5, 18, 27, 32ff., 40–1, 57, 87, 90–9, 102, 108–14, 117–21, 187, 198, 200–4
of ruling, 88–101, 103–9, 112–15, 121, 143, 163, 172, 176, 180, 200–3
tabdīl, 82–91, 101, 104, 110, 115–17, 120, 189, 201
4. repeal, 18
5. reveal, 109–11, 115–19
6. withdrawal, 7, 18, 90–9, 103–6, 110–17, 121, 143, 158, 198, 201–4
external *naskh*, 163, 176, 180, 193, 205–6
general theory of, 18–22, 25–36
affects Ḳur'ān, 22, 27–8
affects *Sunna*, 28, 39ff
importance of, 37–9
internal *naskh*, 163, 177–80, 183, 189, 194–7, 206
modes of, 41–2, 47, 56, 84–5, 121, 157, 196

naskh al-ḥukm wa-'l-tilāwa, 41–54, 89, 93–9, 106, 112, 117, 157, 182, 198–202
naskh al-ḥukm dūna 'l-tilāwa, iv, 41, 47–9, 54, 58, 80, 89–90, 94–9, 106, 110–12, 117, 159–60, 182, 196, 199–203
naskh al-tilāwa dūna 'l-ḥukm, 7, 41, 54, 96–9, 102, 106, 117, 122, 135, 146, 155–60, 161–2, 198–201, 204
occurrence of during Muḥammad's lifetime, 81–2
special theories of, 85
Ḳur'ān *naskhs* Ḳur'ān, ii, 4–6, 32–4, 40–1, 57, 73, 78, 80–1, 89, 100–2, 141, 145, 152, 158–60, 162, 183–7, 194, 200
Ḳur'ān *naskhs* Sunna, 4–5, 158, 176–80, 183
Sunna naskhs Ḳur'ān, iii, 4–7, 26, 35, 46, 71–2, 78, 93–4, 100–6, 112–15, 136, 141, 144, 149, 153–60, 161, 180, 197–8
Sunna naskhs Sunna, 3–4, 5–7, 33–5, 40, 98, 100, 142, 146, 158–60, 180
variability
of divine Law, 163–5, 179, 191–3
of dietary law, 165, 178–81, 189, 193, 205

'proof'-verses, 35, 187, 200

rak'a, 59–60
Ramaḍān, ii, 116, 195
ra'y (*opinio*), 23, 25, 63, 83, 156–7, 208
riḍā', 7, 102, 155–60, 182
riḍā'-'verse(s)', 161–2, 198–201

sabab, asbāb al-nuzūl, 20, 26, 131, 172–5, 187
sharī'a, 12, 15, 25, 83
shar'iyy, 102

taḥrīf, 191–3
ta'yīn, 172
talion, 132, 178–81, 189, 193, 205
tarabbuṣ, 64–6
Tōra, 128–35, 147, 150–4, 165–7, 180, 191–3

al-waḥy al-matlū, 10, 40, 113, 146, 200
al-waḥy ghayr al-matlū, 11, 40, 146, 161
waṣiyya, 57, 68, 71–80, 159, 181–2, 205
wuḍū', 138, 189

zinā, 123, 138
adultery, 124–8, 136, 142–8
[non-] *muḥṣan*, 123–31, 135–6, 143–6, 150, 153, 193
[non-] *thayyib*, 126, 136, 143–9, 152
fornication, 124–8, 136, 142–8
penalties for
adultery: stoning, 4, 7, 54, 106, 123–36, 142–55, 160, 162, 192–7, 200
stoning-'verse', 50, 54, 128–33, 145–8, 150, 155–60, 161, 182, 194–200
fornication:
flogging, 4, 7, 123–8, 131–9, 142–50, 154, 192
banishment, 124–8, 135–6, 143–50

INDEX OF PROPER NAMES

'Abdullāh b. 'Abbās, 27, 30–1, 38, 46, 51, 53, 63–8, 75–9, 87, 90–2, 99, 109, 118, 123, 128–30, 158, 172, 176, 184, 210–11
'Abdullāh b. Mas'ūd, 45, 48, 62–6, 74–9, 87, 90–2, 210
'Abdullāh b. 'Umar, 38, 40, 49–50, 62, 65, 74–9, 128–30, 150, 173–4, 210
'Abdullāh b. al-Zubayr, 58, 156–7
Abū 'Abdullāh, 21, 37, 83–4, 97
'Abdul Raḥmān, b. 'Awf, 52
Abū 'Abdul Raḥmān al-Sulamī, 38
Abū Bakr, 127, 133
Abū Bakr b. al-'Arabī, 61–7
Abū Ḥanīfa, i, 65, 75, 158
Abū Hudhayfa, 87
Abū Hurayra, 63
Abū Mūsā, 51
Abū Muslim, 125, 181, 205
Abū 'Ubayd, 61, 68, 76, 118
Aḥmad b. Ḥanbal, 39, 51, 153, 158
'Ā'isha, 7, 45–8, 53, 60–1, 66, 156–60, 162, 184–6, 201
'Alī b. abī Ṭālib, 37–9, 53, 62–6, 75, 79, 87, 94–5, 99, 127, 144, 187, 210–11
Anas b. Mālik, 50–4
al-Bayḍāwī, 115–7, 121, 125, 135, 204
al-Bukhārī, 45–6, 51
al-Farrā', 46, 49

Furay'a, 67, 75, 79

Goldziher, I, 3, 118

ibn Ḥadjar, 46–7, 54
Ḥafṣa, 61, 156
Ḥanafī(s), 35, 72, 153, 162, 201
al-Ḥasan al-Baṣrī, 46, 61, 75, 89, 92–6, 129–31, 176, 187
al-Ḥāzimī, 56, 80
ibn Ḥazm al-Ẓāhirī, 27, 29, 188
Hibatullāh b. Sallāma, 37, 39, 182, 185
Ḥudhayfa, 39, 50, 54

'Imrān b. Ḥuṣain, 23, 210–11
Isḥāḳ, 39

al-Ḳasṭallānī, 48
Ḳatāda b. Di'āma, 46, 68, 76, 104, 108, 123–4, 129–31, 172–6
al-Ḳurṭubī, 118–9, 174

Mālik b. Anas, i, ii, 13, 15, 28, 63–5, 71, 75, 126–35, 145, 150–3, 155–60, 162, 174, 210–11
al-Muwaṭṭa', i, 13, 71, 126–30
Mālikī(s), 13, 26, 29, 72, 162
Muḥammad 'Abduh, 205
Mu'tazila, 9, 41, 112, 147, 151, 160, 205

al-Naḥḥās, 35–9, 59–61, 63–8, 83, 90, 161, 174, 182
Nöldeke, T., 200, 206

al-Rāzī, 104, 108, 119, 188, 201–2
al-Risāla, 15, 22, 25, 35, 83, 137, 141, 159

al-Sarakhsī, 64–7, 72, 79, 201
Schacht, J., 13, 141, 145, 208ff
Schwally, F., 200
al-Shāfi'ī, ii–iii, 6–8, 12–15, 22–8, 32–40, 45, 60–9, 73–8, 91–9, 100–2, 108–13, 117, 121, 128, 135ff., 161–2, 168, 174–80, 185, 200–2, 211
  defines naskh, 6, 33–4, 201
Shāfi'ites, 95–6, 114, 157
al-Shaybānī, i, 65, 75
Shīa, 210
Subay'a bt. al-Ḥārith, 63, 74, 79
al-Suyūṭī, iv 119, 182
al-Ṭabarī, 59, 61, 67–70, 76, 80, 82ff 121ff., 159, 172, 192–3, 202
  defines naskh, 88, 175
al-Ṭabarsī, 120
al-Tha'labī, 91

'Ubāda b. al-Ṣāmit, 136, 143–50, 158–9
Ubayy b. Ka'b, 31, 38–9, 47–54, 101, 118, 133, 210
'Umar b. al-Khaṭṭāb, 38–9, 51–4, 62, 65, 74, 79, 101, 118, 126–8, 132–4, 145, 148–50, 157–9, 161, 210

ʿUrwa b. al-Zubayr, 40, 156
ʿUthmān b. ʿAffān, 51–4, 58, 65, 78, 87, 92, 95, 101, 127
Umm Ḥabība, 60
Umm Salama, 60–5, 79

Yaʿḳūb b. Ibrāhīm, i, 75

Zaid b. Thābit, 52, 1334
Zainab bt. Djaḥsh, 60
Zainab bt. abī Salama, 60
al-Zamakhsharī, 114ff., 121–2
al-Zuhrī, ii, 22, 63, 127–9, 132, 210

INDEX OF ḲUR'ĀN VERSES

Ḳ2: 23, 100
40, 165, 169, 191
42, 165
62, 1
75, 192
91, 166
97, 9
105, 165
106, iii, iv, 5, 6, 24, 32, 38, 40, 47–9, 55, 82, 85, 89ff., 159–60, 180, 188, 198–206
109, 1
114, 175
114–9, 181
115, 172–7, 181, 205
122, 170
124, 164, 181, 205
125, 174
129, 140
134, 166
136, 167
140, 191
141, 166
142, 171–2, 176, 187
143, 176–7
144, 172–7
146, 191
147, 179
148, 177
151, 140
158, 178, 181, 205
159–60, 1–2, 191
166, 178
168–74, 181, 205
173, 178
174, 191
177, 178, 181, 205
178, 178, 181, 205
180, ii, 57, 71, 159, 178, 181, 205
183, 178, 181, 205
185, 178, 195, 205
187, 178, 187, 205
188, 135
189, 10
191–203, 181, 205
196, 211
215, 10
219, 10
220, 10
222–42, 10, 58
233, 127, 155
234, 56–80, 92, 98, 187, 197–9
235, 63
240, 56–80, 92, 98, 187, 197–9
256, 2
286, 179

Ḳ3: 19, 167
23, 165
26, 165
50, 165, 179
65, 165
67, 165
71, 165, 191
81, 166
85, 1, 167
93, 165, 180
110, 177
158, 195
164, 140
187, 166, 191
199, 173

Ḳ4: 11, ii
12, 67–80, 138, 159, 197
15–16, 4, 122, 127, 135–59, 199
23, ii, 7, 102, 155ff., 199, 201
24, 209ff.
25, 136, 139, 142–8
46, 192–3
59, 140
65, 140
80, 140
82, 93
101, 59
113, 140
127, 10
153, 166
160–1, 179

163, 167
166, 167
171, 140

Ḳ5: 3, 9
5, 179
6, 138–9, 189
13, 192
15, 166, 179, 191
32, 179
38, 139
41, 192
42–9, 128–9, 147, 151–5
45, 193
48, 165
101, 10

Ḳ6: 91, 190
92–3, 190
102, 137
106, 1
124, 167
146, 180

Ḳ7: 34, 165
89, 190
157, 166, 180
187, 10

Ḳ8: 1, 10
65–6, 27–9, 91, 97, 187–8, 197

Ḳ9: 5, 1–2, 182
29, 1, 2
31, 2
67, 49, 97, 109, 202
120, 137

Ḳ10: 15, 5, 32, 159
37, 190
38, 100
87, 179
109, 1

Ḳ11: 6, 137
13, 100
28, 190
35, 190

Ḳ12: 47, 2

Ḳ13: 36, 189
38, 165
39, 32, 88, 92, 97, 104, 108–10, 188–9

Ḳ14: 10, 137

Ḳ15: 9, 44–7, 93
85, 1

Ḳ16: 101, iii, 5–6, 33, 81–9, 94–9, 1–4–10, 180–1, 188, 200–6
102, 189
114–9, 181, 205
118, 180
124, 181, 205

Ḳ17: 78, 186
79, 185–6
86, 44, 52, 93, 105

Ḳ18: 24, 49, 109

Ḳ21: 5, 189

Ḳ22: 51–2, iii, iv, 82, 97, 99, 101, 107–10, 190, 202, 205

Ḳ23: 38, 189

Ḳ24: 2, 4, 7, 123, 126, 134–5, 139, 142–50, 155, 158, 162, 199
3, 2
4, 127
62, 140, 168

Ḳ25: 4, 189

Ḳ26: 108,
126,
144,
163,
179,
215–6, 163

Ḳ27: 76, 179

Ḳ28: 43, 165

Ḳ29: 46, 1
Ḳ33 50, 53, 134

Ḳ33: 34,140
36, 168
49, 64

Ḳ40: 7, 1–2
60, 173

Ḳ42: 5, 1–2
13, 165
24, 190
30, 45
52–3, 170

Ḳ45: 16, 165
28, 98, 115

Ḳ46: 15, 127

Ḳ47: 29, 165

Ḳ48: 10, 11, 168
15, 192
29, 166

Ḳ49: 13, 137

Ḳ53: 2–3, 5, 149

Ḳ55: 33, 175

Ḳ58: 7, 172
12–13, 117, 187ff., 195–7, 204–6

Ḳ59: 6, 165
7, 6, 148, 160, 161

Ḳ60: 11, 4

Ḳ61: 6, 166

Ḳ62: 5, 166

Ḳ63: 1, 167

Ḳ65: 1–4, 58ff., 64–5, 80, 197
6, 74

Ḳ73: 1–4, 116, 184–7
20, 184–7, 195–6

Ḳ87: 6–7, 44–9, 55, 88–9, 92–9, 1–5–12, 121, 198, 202

Ḳ102: 51